"John Lennox has done it again. Combining deep thought, pervasive research, and a keen eye on contemporary Western culture, Lennox has managed to draw tight, informative parallels between Daniel's life and circumstances and the contemporary believer's life and circumstances. In my view, the most interesting point in Against the Flow is Lennox's observation that while embedded in the top echelons of a pluralistic culture growingly hostile to biblical religion, Daniel did not rest content to shrink his witness to one of personal piety. Instead, Daniel maintained public engagement with the ideas and practices extant in his day. Finally, Lennox offers wise advice and practical application for how we can become modern-day Daniels. I highly recommend this book."
J. P. Moreland, Distinguished Professor of Philosophy, Biola University, La Mirada California, and author of *The Soul: How We Know It's Real and Why It Matters*

"Few parts of Scripture are more conscious of the clash between the wisdom of God and the wisdom of the world than the Old Testament book of Daniel. Few authors today are more expert at analysing and articulating both than John Lennox. It is a masterful combination, and the result is extraordinary."
Revd Dr John Dickson, Founding Director, Centre for Public Christianity, Jean Kvamme Distinguished Chair, and Distinguised Scholar in Public Christianity at Wheaton College, Illinois

"I read everything John Lennox writes because of his amazing blend of rigorous scholarship with practical insights and applications for all of us. You cannot afford to miss this important book! Read it, then pass it on to a friend."
Dr Rick Warren, *The Purpose Driven Life*

"This book is an outstanding example of our responsibility both to understand God's Word and the culture in which we live, and then to make the connections between the two. John Lennox is uniquely gifted to help us do this, as he addresses the big themes of God's work in history, the place of morality, the nature of humankind, the challenges to faith, the trustworthiness of scripture, and the call to proclaim the truth whatever the cost. As a Bible teacher, a scientist, and a courageous disciple of Christ, John Lennox has provided us with an extraordinary resource – I wholeheartedly recommend this remarkable book."
Jonathan Lamb, former CEO and current minister-at-large, Keswick Ministries

"I cannot think of a more important book for a secular, pluralist age. John Lennox challenges Christians to dare to be like Daniel, who witnessed boldly at the highest levels in a nation that did not share his faith. This book is a huge encouragement to all Christians who long to live faithfully and usefully for God in a hostile world."
Dr Amy Orr-Ewing, speaker, theologian and apologist

"John Lennox has a unique gift as a Bible teacher. He applies text to today's world and its prevailing philosophies in penetrating ways. This learned exposition of Daniel shows how the book offers powerful critiques of the modern idolatries, whether atheist or secularist. Every reader of this volume will see the depth and coherence of the book of Daniel in a new way."
Dr Peter J. Williams, Principal and CEO, Tyndale House, Cambridge

"John Lennox has achieved a rare thing – excellent scholarship, biblical faithfulness, and cultural application par excellence. His examination of the story of Daniel exposes the deep tensions that were faced by Israel and reminds us that many of those challenges still exist. Just as Daniel maintained integrity and faithfulness to God, so can we. This is a book of applied theological reflection that overflows with hope. The challenges it addresses are very real but the answers it gives are breathtakingly simple and profoundly challenging."
Malcolm Duncan, Lead Pastor, Dundonald Elim Church, Belfast

The Author

John C. Lennox MA MMath, MA (Bioethics) PhD DPhil DSc is Emeritus Professor of Mathematics at the University of Oxford and Emeritus Fellow in Mathematics and Philosophy of Science at Green Templeton College, Oxford. He has lectured on religion and science at many prestigious institutions around the world, and has publicly debated Richard Dawkins and Christopher Hitchens, among others. He is also the author of many books including, *Friend of God: The inspiration of Abraham in an age of doubt*; *Joseph: A story of love, hate, slavery, power and forgiveness*; *Gunning for God: Why the new atheists are missing the target*; *God and Stephen Hawking: Whose design is it anyway?*; *Can Science Explain Everything?*; *Cosmic Chemistry: Do God and science mix?*; *2084: Artificial intelligence and the future of humanity*. John is married to Sally and they have three children and ten grandchildren.

AGAINST THE FLOW

The Inspiration of Daniel
in an Age of Relativism

JOHN C. LENNOX

First published in 2015
by Monarch Books, an imprint of Lion Hudson Limited

SPCK
SPCK Group
Studio 101
The Record Hall
16 -16A Baldwin's Gardens
London EC1N 7RJ
www.spck.org.uk

This edition published 2024

Acknowledgments
Scripture quotations are from The Holy Bible, English Standard Version® (ESV®) copyright © 2001 by Crossway, a publishing ministry of Good News Publishers. All rights reserved.

Scripture quotations marked NIV taken from the Holy Bible, New International Version, copyright © 1973, 1978, 1984 International Bible Society. Used by permission of Hodder & Stoughton, a member of the Hodder Headline Group. All rights reserved. "NIV" is a trademark of Biblica™. UK trademark number 1448790.

Scripture quotations marked NRSV are from The New Revised Standard Version of the Bible copyright © 1989 by the Division of Christian Education of the National Council of Churches in the USA. Used by permission. All Rights Reserved.

British Library Cataloguing-in-Publication Data
A catalogue record for this book is available from the British Library

ISBN 978-0-281-08922-2
eBook ISBN 978-0-281-08923-9

3 5 7 9 10 8 6 4 2

Typeset by Fakenham Prepress Solutions, Fakenham, Norfolk NR21 8NL
Printed and bound in the UK by Clays Ltd

eBook by Fakenham Prepress Solutions, Fakenham, Norfolk NR21 8NL

Produced on paper from sustainable sources.

This book is dedicated to my grandchildren, Janie Grace, Freddie, Herbie, Sally, Lizzie, Jessica, Robin, Rowan, Jesse and Jonah in the hope that they will be part of a new generation that will take its inspiration from Daniel and live against the flow.

Contents

Acknowledgments

This book would never have been written were it not for the inspiration supplied over many years by my friend and mentor Professor David Gooding. It was he who first opened my eyes to the richness of Scripture and taught me to think biblically. His seminal work on Daniel as reflected in the Tyndale Lecture of 1981 was the stimulus to begin thinking about the value of this ancient book as a means of communicating the biblical worldview to the contemporary world.

I remain, as always, immensely grateful to Mrs Barbara Hamilton for her invaluable secretarial help not least in saving me from infelicities of grammar and style.

I would also like to thank my wife Sally for her constant encouragement to keep writing and for the many friends around the world, too numerous to mention individually, who told me that such an endeavour would prove to be worthwhile. I trust that they will not be disappointed.

Why We Should Read Daniel

Daniel's story is one of extraordinary faith in God lived out at the pinnacle of executive power in the full glare of public life. It relates pivotal events in the lives of four friends – Daniel, Hananiah, Mishael, and Azariah – who were born in the tiny state of Judah in the Middle East around two-and-a-half thousand years ago. As young members of the nobility, probably still teenagers, they were taken captive by the emperor Nebuchadnezzar and transported to his capital city Babylon in order to be trained in Babylonian administration. Daniel tells us how they eventually rose to the top echelons of power not only in the world empire of Babylon but also in the Medo-Persian empire that succeeded it. (I am well aware that this traditional dating of the book of Daniel has been challenged, and that many believe it is a work of the second and not the sixth century BC. This issue will be addressed at several points throughout the book, and a summary of the arguments can be found in Appendix E.)

What makes the story of their faith remarkable is that they did not simply continue the private devotion to God that they had developed in their homeland; they maintained a high-profile public witness in a pluralistic society that became increasingly antagonistic to their faith. That is why their story has such a powerful message for us today. Strong currents of pluralism and secularism in contemporary Western society, reinforced by a paralysing political correctness, increasingly push expression of faith in God to the margins, confining it if possible to the private sphere. It is becoming less and less the done thing to mention God in public, let alone to confess to believing in anything exclusive and absolute, such as the uniqueness of Jesus Christ as Son of God and Saviour. Society

1

tolerates the practice of the Christian faith in private devotions and in church services, but it increasingly deprecates public witness. To the relativist and secularist, public witness to faith in God smacks too much of proselytizing and fundamentalist extremism. They therefore regard it more and more as a threat to social stability and human freedom.

The story of Daniel and his friends is a clarion call to our generation to be courageous; not to lose our nerve and allow the expression of our faith to be diluted and squeezed out of the public space and thus rendered spineless and ineffective. Their story will also tell us that this objective is not likely to be achieved without cost.

As political correctness stifles Christian witness, atheism seems to become more and more vocal in the public arena. Richard Dawkins in *The God Delusion*, Sam Harris in his *Letter to a Christian Nation*, Christopher Hitchens in *God is Not Great*, and Michel Onfray in *Atheist Manifesto* have been rallying the troops behind them by heralding the dangers of religion and the desirability of eliminating it. In order to do this, these so-called New Atheists harness the immense cultural power of science. At a conference at the Salk Institute of Biological Sciences in La Jolla, California, in November 1994, Nobel Laureate Steven Weinberg suggested ominously that the best contribution that scientists could make in this generation was the complete elimination of religion.

Weinberg and others portray atheism as the only intellectually respectable worldview. Intolerance of religion and growing disrespect of those with religious convictions are central features of their increasingly shrill onslaught. Indeed, their constant repetition of ragged and philosophically superficial arguments leads one to suspect that their great emperor of atheism is beginning to shiver through lack of clothes.

If Daniel and his three friends were with us today I have no doubt that they would be in the vanguard of the public debate, leading the counter-charge against the self-styled "four horsemen of the New Atheism", as Dawkins and his allies Dennett, Harris, and Hitchens call themselves. In this book we shall try to learn something about what it was that gave that ancient foursome the strength and conviction to be prepared, often at great risk, to swim against the flow in their society and give unequivocal, courageous public expression to what they believed. This will surely strengthen our resolve, not only to put our heads above the parapet, but also to make sure in advance that our minds and hearts are prepared – that our helmets are securely on – so that we do not get blown away in the first salvo.

CHAPTER 1

A MATTER OF HISTORY
Daniel 1

We need some background that will help us to get into the atmosphere of Daniel's story.[1] (For additional background, I recommend relevant articles in *The New Bible Dictionary* published by IVP.) The diminutive state of Judah was located at a geographical nexus in the ancient Middle East, where the interests of the great powers frequently clashed, and so it lived under constant threat of invasion by the neighbouring superpowers of that age. About half a century before Daniel was born, the world (at least, the relevant part of it for us) was dominated by the superpower Assyria. In the days of Hezekiah, one of the better kings of Judah, the Assyrian emperor Sennacherib marched on Judah in 701 BC. As Byron put it (in "The Destruction of Sennacherib"): "The Assyrian came down like the wolf on the fold." The sheep prepared themselves for a holocaust. Suddenly and unexpectedly Sennacherib withdrew (but that is another story), and Jerusalem was temporarily spared.

Eventually the great Assyrian capital city of Nineveh fell in 612 BC to the Babylonian and Mede armies, who subsequently continued the tradition of threatening to snuff Judah out completely. As if that were not enough, there was always Egypt in the south – no longer a superpower, its ancient glory already fading, but nevertheless a constant irritant. Earlier one of the reformist kings of Judah, Josiah, had lost his sense of perspective and embarked on a foolhardy mission to assist the Babylonians in their attempt to take on the might of the Egyptian army. His attempt backfired and he was killed. Pharaoh quickly deposed Josiah's son, Jehoahaz, and deported him to Egypt, installing as a puppet ruler Jehoahaz's brother Eliakim, now called Jehoiakim. Adding insult to injury, Pharaoh imposed a swingeing fine on Judah of a hundred talents of silver and one of gold – a princely sum in those impoverished times.

Jehoiakim proved ineffective, and it was not long before he too was removed: not by the Egyptians but by the emperor of Babylon, Nabu-kudurri-usur II (Nebuchadnezzar II as he is more commonly known, or Nebuchadrezzar – there is evidence of shifting from r to n in transcriptions of Babylonian names). Earlier, in the summer of 605 BC, Nebuchadnezzar had defeated the Egyptians at the decisive battle at Carchemish on the Euphrates far to the north-east of Jerusalem. Not long after that signal military triumph, Nebuchadnezzar's father Nabopolassar died and Nebuchadnezzar returned to Babylon as king. Thereafter he made regular visits to his conquered territories in the west, in order to take tribute and personnel from them and to dispense justice (see Wiseman 1991, page 22). It was one of those visits that permanently changed the trajectory of the lives of Daniel and his friends.[2]

It happened like this. As part of his policy for dealing with conquered nations, Nebuchadnezzar took the best of their young men to Babylon in order to have them trained to serve in his administration. Daniel and his friends were judged to be suitable material for that training, and so they were taken from their families, society, and culture, and transported to a strange and unfamiliar land many miles away. They had to cope not only with the emotional trauma of forcible removal from their parents, but also with the sheer strangeness of their new surroundings – new language, new customs, new political system, new laws, new education system, new beliefs. It must have been overwhelming. How did they come to terms with it?

God and history

Daniel's explanation of how they did finally adjust is the fruit of a lifetime's reflection on the key events that shaped his life and made him what he was. He starts his book with a terse description of what was for him the momentous siege of Jerusalem by Nebuchadnezzar and his subsequent deportation to that most illustrious of ancient capital cities, Babylon on the Euphrates.

> *In the third year of the reign of Jehoiakim king of Judah,*
> *Nebuchadnezzar king of Babylon came to Jerusalem and*
> *besieged it. And the Lord gave Jehoiakim king of Judah into*
> *his hand, with some of the vessels of the house of God. And*
> *he brought them to the land of Shinar, to the house of his god,*
> *and placed the vessels in the treasury of his god. Then the king*
> *commanded Ashpenaz, his chief eunuch, to bring some of the*
> *people of Israel, both of the royal family and of the nobility,*
> *youths without blemish, of good appearance and skilful in all*
> *wisdom, endowed with knowledge, understanding learning,*
> *and competent to stand in the king's palace, and to teach*
> *them the literature and language of the Chaldeans. The king*
> *assigned them a daily portion of the food that the king ate,*
> *and of the wine that he drank. They were to be educated*
> *for three years, and at the end of that time they were to*
> *stand before the king. Among these were Daniel, Hananiah,*
> *Mishael, and Azariah of the tribe of Judah.* (Daniel 1:1–6.)

Many things that Daniel could have mentioned, which we would have liked to read about, are tantalizingly omitted. For instance, there is nothing at all about his childhood in Judah, and nothing of the sorry political intrigue and turmoil in the years leading up to his deportation. Daniel chooses to start with the events of the year 605 BC, when Nebuchadnezzar turned his military attention to Jerusalem at the edge of his empire. Its rebelliousness chafed the emperor and so he set siege to it. Given the sheer military power involved, the outcome was a foregone conclusion. The city was taken, the king of Judah became a vassal, and the first wave of deportations to Babylon began. Jerusalem city itself survived at that time, until Nebuchadnezzar eventually destroyed it in 586 BC.

These events are documented in more detail in the ancient Babylonian Chronicles, like the one below. Such stone cuneiform tablets confirm that Daniel is telling us actual history and not figments of his own imagination. We shall have more to say about the historicity of his account later, since it has often been called into question.

Babylonian Chronicle mentioning the capture of Jerusalem in 597 BC

The big question for someone with Daniel's background was: why had God allowed such a thing to happen? After all, was not his nation a special nation? Was it not the nation of Moses, who had been given the law directly by God? Was it not the nation that that same Moses had led out of the slave labour camps of Egypt and brought to the land that God had promised them as an inheritance? Was it not also the nation of David, the great consolidating king, who had made Jerusalem his capital, and whose son Solomon had built a unique temple to the living God? Had not God spoken to the patriarchs, priests, prophets, and kings of that nation, with ever increasing clarity, of a coming King, the Messiah (Anointed One), who would be a descendant of King David and preside in the future over an unparalleled period of peace and prosperity on earth? Indeed, this messianic vision finds an echo in the hearts of human beings from every culture, and it has captured the minds of contemporary nations to such an extent that it is recorded on the wall of the United Nations building in New York for the whole world to read:

> ... and they shall beat their swords into ploughshares, and
> their spears into pruning-hooks; nation shall not lift up sword
> against nation, neither shall they learn war any more.
> (Isaiah 2:4.)

What would become of that vision if Jerusalem were to be sacked and the lineage of David eliminated? Would the promise of Messiah have to be relegated to the bulging dustbin of failed utopian ideas? What about God himself? Could he, so to speak, survive such a failure? How could Daniel and his friends any longer believe that there was a God who had revealed himself to their nation in a special way? If God is real, how could a pagan emperor like Nebuchadnezzar violate the sanctity of God's unique temple and get away with it? *Why did God do nothing?* This is in essence the hard question that is still very much with us today in a thousand different specific forms. Why does history so often take a turn that shakes confidence in the existence of a God who cares?

For the secular historian, of course, there is nothing strange about what happened in far-off 605 BC. The conquest of Judah was simply one more instance of the power law of the jungle – a huge heavily militarized nation smashes a tiny state. Judah just did not have the firepower to make any real impression on the highly trained and heavily armed troops of Nebuchadnezzar's forces. There is no contest between peashooters and tanks. Surely there was nothing more to it than that....

Indeed the secularist might well add that if the victory had gone the other way and Judah had put Babylon to flight, one could perhaps begin to talk about God being involved. But it did not go that way; it went the way anyone would have predicted. So they say that we must simply face the fact that the idea of the descendants of David being special is no more than a tribal myth, invented to support a rather unstable royal house in a tiny Middle-Eastern state. The temple in Jerusalem was nothing but a building, its vessels nothing but human artefacts, however beautiful and valuable. The idea that God, if there were a God, would be interested in such an insignificant matter is patently absurd. Is not the easiest explanation, and by far the most likely one, that there is no God for the temple in any sense to be his? Why would you expect anything to happen? Don't people steal valuable items from churches these days? Does God stop them with a bolt of lightning from the sky?

This view seems very plausible to many people, if for no other reason than it is the only logical view open to the secularist. However, it was certainly not the view held by Daniel – and at least we can say that he was personally caught up with the events in question. He also knew what was at stake in terms of his credibility when he boldly stated that God was behind Nebuchadnezzar's victory: *And the Lord gave Jehoiakim king of Judah into his hand...* (Daniel 1:2).

Thus, the first thing that Daniel says about God in his book is that he is involved in human history: a statement of immense import, if it is true. Daniel is not content to inform us of what happened; he is much more interested in why it happened. He is interpreting history, and interpreting it in a way that is very provocative for the contemporary mind, to say the least. To assert that there is a God behind history is to fly in the face of the prevailing wind of secularism, and therefore to invite pity, if not ridicule – certainly in a university history department. Yet, as Lesslie Newbigin says: "From Augustine till the eighteenth century, history in Europe was written in the belief that divine providence was the key to understanding events" (1989, page 71). However, the days are long gone when a leading historian, such as Herbert Butterfield, could readily write of God's providence as "a living and active agency both in ourselves and in its movement over the length and breadth of history" (1957, page 147).

It is an illusion to think that the interpretation of history that rejects any possibility of divine action is the objective way, while Daniel's way is subjective. All history is interpreted history. The real question is: is there evidence that Daniel's interpretation is true?

Belief and evidence

Next time that somebody tells you that something is true, why not say to them: "What kind of evidence is there for that?" And if they can't give you a good answer, I hope you'll think very carefully before you believe a word they say. (Dawkins, 2003, page 248.)

I agree wholeheartedly with Richard Dawkins on this point. Indeed, as David Hume pointed out long ago, it is of the very essence of science to proportion belief to evidence. So far so good. But then Dawkins makes a distinction between the legitimate evidence-based thinking that is the stock-in-trade of the scientist and what he calls religious faith, which belongs to a very different category.

I think that a case can be made that faith is one of the world's great evils, comparable to the smallpox virus but harder to eradicate. Faith, being belief that isn't based on evidence, is the principal vice of any religion.[3]

It would be a mistake to think that this extreme view is typical. Many atheists are far from happy with its militancy, not to mention its repressive, even totalitarian, overtones. However, it is these excessive statements that receive media exposure, with the result that many people are aware of those views and have been affected by them. It would, therefore, be folly to ignore them. We must take them seriously.

From what he says, it is clear that one of the things that (sadly) has generated Dawkins' hostility to faith in God is his impression that whereas "scientific belief is based upon publicly checkable evidence, religious faith not only lacks evidence; its independence from evidence is its joy, shouted from the rooftops".[4] In other words, he takes all religious faith to be blind faith. However, taking Dawkins' own advice, headlined above, we must ask: what is the evidence that religious faith is not based on evidence? Unfortunately there are people who, while professing faith in God, take an overtly anti-scientific and obscurantist viewpoint. Their attitude brings faith in God into disrepute and is to be deplored. Perhaps Richard Dawkins has had the misfortune to meet disproportionately many of them.

But that does not alter the fact that mainstream Christianity will insist that faith and evidence are inseparable. Indeed, faith is a response to evidence, not a rejoicing in the absence of evidence. The Christian apostle John gives the following explanation for his account of Jesus: *these are written so that you may believe...* (John 20:31). That is, he understands that what he is writing is to be regarded as part of the evidence on which faith is based. The apostle Paul says what many pioneers of modern science believed, that nature itself is part of the evidence for the existence of God:

> For his invisible attributes, namely, his eternal power and divine nature, have been clearly perceived, ever since the creation of the world, in the things that have been made. So they are without excuse. (Romans 1:20.)

It is no part of the biblical view that things should be believed where there is no evidence. Just as in science faith, reason, and evidence belong together. Dawkins' definition of faith as "blind faith" turns out, therefore, to be the exact opposite of the biblical one. It is curious that he does not seem to be aware of the discrepancy.

Dawkins' idiosyncratic definition of faith provides a striking example of the very kind of thinking he claims to abhor – thinking that is not based on evidence. In an exhibition of breathtaking inconsistency, evidence is the very thing he fails to supply for his claim that faith rejoices in the independence of evidence. And the reason he fails to supply such evidence is not hard to find, for there is none. It does not take any great research effort to ascertain that no serious biblical scholar or thinker would support Dawkins' definition of faith. One might well be forgiven for yielding to the temptation to apply Dawkins' maxim to himself – and not believe a word he says about the Christian faith.

History and morality

So, what evidence did Daniel possess as the basis for his interpretation of history? The evidence is cumulative, and there is a sense in which it consists of his whole book. For instance, he later informs us (Daniel 9) that it was his belief in God that led him to expect a Babylonian invasion and conquest. We might reasonably say that he was so convinced of this that if Nebuchadnezzar had been stopped by an unexpectedly spirited defence by Judah, or even by some direct divine intervention, it would have created problems for his faith in God. We shall leave the details for their proper context, pausing only to focus on the central issue: the relation of history to morality.

From his parents and teachers in Jerusalem Daniel would have learned of the Genesis account that human beings are moral beings, made in the image of God. It formed the foundation of his understanding of the universe and life. The universe was a moral universe. The Creator was not some kind of cosmic magician, living in a box-like temple and performing magic to protect his possessions or his group of favourites. The moral character of God demanded that he was not neutral towards human behaviour. This message formed a central part of the writings of the Hebrew prophets. In the years before Jerusalem was attacked Jeremiah had repeatedly warned the nation of the serious consequences of their increasing compromise with immoral pagan practices and the idolatry of the nations around them. They did not listen to Jeremiah, and it was not long before Babylon overran the nation and exiled most of the population, as he had explicitly predicted.

Judah had failed to grasp that God's loyalty to his own character, and therefore to his own creatures, has serious implications. Some of Judah's leaders had fallen into thinking that, because their nation had been chosen to play a special role for God in history, it did not really matter how the leaders or the nation behaved. This was dangerously irresponsible and undermined the moral fibre of the people, because it led to the rationalization of corrupt and immoral behaviour that was incompatible with the law of God, albeit widely practised in the surrounding nations. Such behaviour had the knock-on effect of making the nation's claim to have a special role look absurd.

In our world today inconsistent moral behaviour on the part of those who claim to follow Christ devalues the Christian faith and causes people to mock it. What the leaders and many of the people in Judah had failed to see was that God does not have any favourites whose sins he simply disregards. God is no respecter of persons, no matter from which nation or level of society they come.

The point had been made many times before Daniel's day. The eminent Cambridge historian Herbert Butterfield (1957, page 92) writes:

> The ancient Hebrews are remarkable for the way in which they carried to its logical conclusion the belief that there is morality in the processes and the course of history. They recognised that if morality existed at all it was there all the time and was the most important element in human conduct; also that life, experience and history were to be interpreted in terms of it.

Moses and the prophets had constantly stressed that God would discipline the people if they ignored the moral demands of the law. What is more, the nation of Judah ought to have known this best of all. About a century earlier it was exactly for this reason that the Assyrians had invaded Israel and deported most of them. God had warned them through Isaiah, and the nation had ignored it. History was now repeating itself. Judah, the only part still left, was driving at full speed past all the warning lights, and heading for the same disaster that had already befallen her sister, Israel.

Not long before Nebuchadnezzar besieged Jerusalem, Jeremiah gave a direct warning of precisely what would happen, and why:

> *Thus says the Lord: Do justice and righteousness, and deliver from the hand of the oppressor him who has been robbed. And do no wrong or violence to the resident alien, the fatherless, and the widow, nor shed innocent blood in this place. For if you will indeed obey this word, then there shall enter the gates of this house kings who sit on the throne of David, riding in chariots and on horses, they and their servants and their people. But if you will not obey these words, I swear by myself, declares the Lord, that this house shall become a desolation. For thus says the Lord concerning the house of the king of Judah: "' You are like Gilead to me, like the summit of Lebanon, yet surely I will make you a desert, an uninhabited city. I will prepare destroyers against you, each with his weapons, and they shall cut down your choicest cedars and cast them into the fire. And many nations will pass by this city, and every man will say to his neighbour, "Why has the Lord dealt thus with this great city?" And they will answer, "Because they have forsaken the covenant of the Lord their God and worshipped other gods and served them."'"* (Jeremiah 22:3–9.)

Judah did not listen, and the morally inevitable happened. Daniel draws attention to it in the opening statement of his book, where he records that Nebuchadnezzar besieged the city, *and the Lord gave Jehoiakim king of Judah into his hand.* That bit of history made sense when analysed from a moral perspective in the light of God's warnings. The punishment fitted the crime. The nation had compromised with immorality, injustice and idolatry, and so it would be taken into captivity by the most idolatrous nation on earth.

Yes, the conquest of Judah by Nebuchadnezzar made moral sense in the divine scheme of things, but that does not mean that Daniel and his friends came to terms with it either immediately or easily. It is one thing to come to a sober estimate of turbulent and traumatic events after many years of reflection; it is quite another to have to live through them, which is what Daniel and the others had to do. At one level they could see the events as representing the judgment of God on the behaviour of the nation, and especially that of its leaders. But as thinking, feeling human beings, surely they would have had questions, just as we would.

Why, for example, should they (or we) have to suffer for other people's actions? After all, they were normal young people, full of energy and ambition; yet already in their hearts they were determined to try to follow God. So why should they have to go through the pain of separation from their families? There were (and are) no immediate easy answers to these questions. Indeed, such answers as there were may well have taken a long time in coming. But in the end Daniel and his friends came to understand that God is interested not only in global history but also in the personal history of those who are often innocently caught up in its tragic aftermath.

I am aware, of course, that some will wish to question the fact that there is any overarching meaning in history. They regard the whole idea as an outmoded legacy of what they dub the "Judaeo-Christian way of thinking". John Gray, Professor of the History of European Thought at the London School of Economics, puts it this way (2003, page 48):

> If you believe that humans are animals, there can be no such thing as the history of humanity, only the lives of particular humans. If we speak of the history of the species at all, it is only to signify the unknowable sum of these lives. As with

other animals, some lives are happy, some are wretched.
None has a meaning that lies beyond itself. Looking for
meaning in history is like looking for patterns in clouds.
Nietzsche knew this, but he could not accept it. He was
trapped in the chalk circle of Christian hopes.

I wonder how Gray knows this. I presume he would accept that his
book, from which I have just quoted, is part of his life and history.
If he is right in what he asserts, then his book can have no meaning
beyond himself – and hence, surely, none for you or me. His theory
of the meaninglessness of history fails to be valid for us, so he cannot
know that your history or mine has no meaning. The circle in which
he is trapped by his logical incoherence is made of sterner stuff
than chalk. Like all who espouse such relativism, he falls into the
error of making himself and his ideas an exception to the logical
consequences of those ideas. His epistemology is incoherent.

Herbert Butterfield takes a very different view (1957, pages 10–
11):

> The significance of the connection between religion and
> history became momentous in the days when the ancient
> Hebrews, though so small a people, found themselves
> between the competing empires of Egypt, then Assyria or
> Babylon, so that they became actors, and in a particularly
> tragic sense proved to be victims in the kind of history
> making that involves colossal struggles for power...
> Altogether we have here the greatest and most deliberate
> attempts ever made to wrestle with destiny and interpret
> history and discover meaning in the human drama; above
> all to grapple with the moral difficulties that history
> presents to the religious mind.

What this amounts to is the importance of realizing that the meaning
of history lies outside history. This is a particular instance of the
principle that the meaning of a system is outside the system. Ludwig
Wittgenstein expressed this well (1922, 6.41):

> The sense of the world must lie outside the world. In the
> world everything is as it is and happens as it does happen.
> In it there is no value – and if there were it would be of no
> value. If there is a value, which is of value, it must lie outside
> all happening and being-so. For all happening and being-so
> is accidental. What makes it non-accidental cannot lie in
> the world, for otherwise this would again be accidental. It
> must be outside the world.

The heart of monotheism is that God, who is outside history, is the guarantor of meaning. As One who stands outside of the unfolding cosmos he is uniquely qualified to give it meaning. Grappling with the moral difficulties that history presents is one of the main foci of Daniel's work. But Daniel, in common with the other biblical writers, does not mean thereby to imply a fatalism or determinism that reduces human beings to helpless pawns whose individual lives, with their loves and choices, their successes and failures, have no ultimate meaning whatsoever. It is surely self-evident that in an utterly deterministic universe love and genuine choice would be impossible.

When the Christian apostle Paul addressed the august Athenian philosophical court, the Areopagus, he pointed out that neither the Stoic explanation of the universe (featuring deterministic processes) nor the Epicurean explanation (featuring chance processes) was adequate to grasp the subtlety of things as they are.

> And he made from one man every nation of mankind to
> live on all the face of the earth, having determined allotted
> periods and the boundaries of their dwelling place, that they
> should seek God, in the hope that they might feel their way
> towards him and find him. Yet he is actually not far from
> each one of us. (Acts 17:26–27.)

According to Paul, God is in ultimate control of history; but this does not eliminate, bypass, or otherwise invalidate human responsibility to seek and reach out for God.

This topic has been the food of philosophical debate for centuries. However, the Bible does not discuss the matter so much by giving us a philosophical treatise on it, as by focusing attention on the way it works out in down-to-earth history. This is a method of communicating ideas we encounter in the great literature of Russia. There is a real sense in which their philosophers are their novelists. If Russians wish to explore deep and complex ideas, like the problem of evil and suffering, they write novels about them, Tolstoy's *War and Peace* or Dostoyevsky's *The Brothers Karamazov* being cases in point.

So too in the Bible. The apostle Paul indicates elsewhere (in Romans 9–11) that we can gain insight into the relationship between God's involvement in history and human responsibility by having a look at the (complex) story of Jacob, whose parents were told even before his birth that he would have a special role. As the Genesis account shows, this sovereign choice certainly did not imply a divine determinism that robbed Jacob of his freedom to choose. Indeed, the narrative shows in detail how God held Jacob both responsible and accountable for the methods he adopted in securing that role, and God disciplined him accordingly – particularly through his relationships with his own children. For instance Jacob deceived his own father Isaac, who was almost blind, by wearing the rough skin of a goat in order to pretend to be his older brother Esau. Many years later Jacob was himself deceived into thinking that his favourite son Joseph was dead, when his other sons brought Joseph's coat to him drenched in the blood of a goat. This story on its own is enough to show just how complex the outworking of God's overall control of history is, in making allowance for a degree of real human freedom and responsibility.

Such stories also show that we, with all the limitations of our humanity, can never have full understanding of the relationship between God's rule in history and human freedom and responsibility. That does not mean, however, that we should not believe in them. After all, most of us believe in energy, even though none of us knows what it is. The belief that both God's rule and human freedom are real is warranted primarily because this view has considerable explanatory power. (In a similar way, the tension of seeing light simultaneously as particles and as a wave is tolerated in physical explanations of light.) The biblical narrative, and indeed history itself, makes more sense in light of this complex view, rather than if we deny either God's rule or a degree of human freedom. A great deal of humility is also called for, in view of what is ultimately (and probably necessarily) characterized by a certain degree of mystery.

Explanatory power

On one occasion, after giving a lecture on the relationship of science to theology in a major scientific institution in England, a physicist asked me how I could possibly be a mathematical scientist in the twenty-first century and hold the central belief of the Christian faith, that Jesus Christ was simultaneously human and God. I replied that I would be delighted to face his question if he could answer me a much easier scientific question first. He agreed.

"What is consciousness?" I asked.

"I don't know," he replied, after a little hesitation.

"Never mind," I said. "Let's think of something easier. What is energy?"

"Well," he said, "we can measure it and write down the equations governing its conservation."

"Yes, I know, but that was not my question. My question was: what is it?"

"We don't know," he said with a grin, "and I think you were aware of that."

"Yes, like you I have read Feynman and he says that no one knows what energy is. That brings me to my main point. Would I be right in thinking that you were about to dismiss me (and my belief in God) if I failed to explain the divine and human nature of Christ?"

He grinned again, and said nothing. I went on: "Well, by the same token, would you be happy if I now dismiss you and all your knowledge of physics because you cannot explain to me the nature of energy? After all, energy is surely by definition much less complex than the God who created it?"

"Please don't!" he said.

"No, I am not going to do that, but I am going to put another question to you: why do you believe in the concepts of consciousness and energy, even though you do not understand them fully? Is it not because of the explanatory power of those concepts?"

"I see what you are driving at," he replied. "You believe that Jesus Christ is both God and man because that is the only explanation that has the power to make sense of what we know of him?"

"Exactly."

If we are not to be unnecessarily cowed by this kind of argument, we need to grasp that it is not only believers in God who believe in concepts they do not fully understand. Scientists do as well. It would be just as foolish and arbitrary to dismiss believers in God as having nothing to say, because they cannot ultimately explain the nature of God, as it would be to dismiss physicists because they do not know what energy is. And yet that is exactly what often happens.

This argument, useful at the level of academic discussion, can also help calm the stormy waters of practical experience. Daniel does not give a detailed philosophical explanation, resolving the tension between God's sovereignty and human responsibility – although, with his knowledge of Scripture, I suspect he would have been well able to do so. Whatever the answer to that question is, it is not hard to imagine that Jeremiah's predictions were an immense help in preparing him and his friends for the dark and turbulent days surrounding their deportation:

> For thus says the Lord: When seventy years are completed for Babylon, I will visit you, and I will fulfil to you my promise and bring you back to this place. For I know the plans I have for you, declares the Lord, plans for wholeness and not for evil, to give you a future and a hope. Then you will call upon me and come and pray to me, and I will hear you. You will seek me and find me. When you seek me with all your heart, I will be found by you.... (Jeremiah 29:10–14.)

It is clear from Daniel's analysis of history that he took to heart what Jeremiah said – and so should we. In times of stress and upheaval it is profoundly reassuring to know that the God who is ultimately sovereign over global history is not aloof or remote from the ups and downs of our personal trajectory. God has plans, individual plans, for those who trust him. It certainly did not look like that as the four teenagers stumbled out of Jerusalem, watching (as we may imagine them) through tear-dimmed eyes as the anxious faces of their distraught parents receded into the distance. In those poignant moments they may not have felt that God was going to give them *a future and a hope*. But eventually he did.

That should encourage us when our faith in God is being put through severe testing, when our prayers seem to bounce off an apparently impenetrable heaven and doubts are mounting in the face of adverse circumstances and mounting public attack on the Christian faith. When Daniel and his friends' emotions were torn they took real comfort from the knowledge that, although deeply traumatic, what was happening to them had been predicted by the prophets. And we can do the same. After all, the Lord Jesus himself made it plain that those who followed him would eventually be treated as he was:

> *I have said all these things to you to keep you from falling*
> *away. They will put you out of the synagogues. Indeed,*
> *the hour is coming when whoever kills you will think he is*
> *offering service to God. (John 16:1–2.)*

Jesus said this to his disciples in advance so that when they were eventually harassed and persecuted, they would know they had not fallen out of God's hands. Perhaps an analogy can help us. Think of a road map. You scarcely ever need it when the road is broad and the signs are well illuminated. However, when the road gets narrow and rough and appears to be leading nowhere, it is very reassuring to have a map that shows you that this difficult terrain is precisely what you should expect at this stage in the journey, if you are on course. And it is that kind of "map" that can help us when the "road" of life

21

is rough. For Daniel it was very rough, but it was plainly marked on the map Jeremiah had provided.

Of course, realism tells us that there are many disturbing questions still to be faced. What does Jeremiah mean when he says that God has plans not to harm us? Were Daniel and his friends not harmed by being wrenched from the stability of their homes and taken to Babylon? Is a person not harmed by injury or disease, persecution or famine? Does a cancer that takes a wife from her husband, or a mother from her children, not harm that husband and family? What then can it mean, that God has plans not to harm us? The answer may be in considering what harm is from God's perspective. Jesus said:

> *And do not fear those who kill the body but cannot kill the soul.*
> *Rather fear him who can destroy both soul and body in hell.*
> *Are not two sparrows sold for a penny? And not one of them*
> *will fall to the ground apart from your Father. But even the*
> *hairs of your head are all numbered. Fear not, therefore; you*
> *are of more value than many sparrows. (Matthew 10:28–31.)*

Jesus makes it clear that the kind of harm that kills the body is not harm as God counts harm. The apostle Peter said something similar, to buttress the faith of Christians who were about to go through a rough time of persecution:

> *Now who is there to harm you if you are zealous for what is*
> *good? But even if you should suffer for righteousness' sake,*
> *you will be blessed. Have no fear of them, nor be troubled....*
> *(1 Peter 3:13–14.)*

It is a sad fact that sometimes professing Christians bring trouble and suffering upon themselves because they have not been righteous. Peter is here writing to those who are suffering because they have been righteous, and he tells them not to be afraid.

What is it that makes the difference? Could it be that what we think is harm looks different from God's eternal perspective? If physical death is the end of existence, as atheists assert, then Peter's words are utterly empty. Worse than that, they are positively deceitful. If death is not the end, but a doorway that marks a transition into something much bigger, everything looks different.

Daniel had that perspective. He ends his book by confidently asserting the hope of the resurrection. The very last words he records are those that were said to him by a messenger from another world:

> But go your way till the end. And you shall rest and shall
> stand in your allotted place at the end of the days. (Daniel
> 12:13.)

To talk of another world beyond this one, and a resurrection in this world, is like waving red rags to the New Atheists. Well, perhaps not quite. They would be happy with other worlds on the basis of their conviction of a universal evolution that must have spawned life aplenty. But they are certainly not happy to envisage resurrection. By definition, a supernatural hole in history cannot be seen through the lens of a materialistic (or naturalistic) world-view. But that does not prove it isn't there. A physical apparatus that is designed only to detect light in the visible spectrum will never detect X-rays, but it doesn't prove that X-rays don't exist.

And there is such a well-attested hole in history, a singular point that does not fit into a reductionist theory of either history or science. As Cambridge theologian C. F. D. Moule has written (1967, pages 3, 13):

> If the coming into existence of the Nazarenes, a
> phenomenon undeniably attested by the New Testament,
> rips a great hole in history, a hole the size and shape of the
> Resurrection, what does the secular historian propose to
> stop it up with? ... The birth and rapid rise of the Christian
> Church... remain an unsolved enigma for any historian
> who refuses to take seriously the only explanation offered
> by the Church itself.

History already bears witness to the bodily resurrection of Jesus, around 600 years after Daniel's time. The resurrection constitutes powerful evidence establishing that he was the Messiah, the Son of God. It also shows, of course, that physical death is not the end.

But we are moving too rapidly. We must leave discussion of the end of Daniel's book to the appropriate place. I mention the resurrection here simply to point out that we shall never understand the stability and purposefulness of Daniel's life until we grasp the attitude of mind that characterized it. Although he lived *in* this world, he did not live *for* it. It was in another world that he invested his life, and it is there that he now enjoys his inheritance.

It goes without saying that one would be a fool to live for another world if that world did not exist. That really would be seriously delusional. On the other hand, if it does exist, not to invest one's life in it would be equally delusional, would it not?

CHAPTER 2

CITY OF IDOLS
Daniel 1

Even the trauma and pain of the preceding months were probably unable to prevent Daniel and his friends reacting with open-mouthed wonder at their first glimpse of Babylon. It will help us to understand him better, and the implications of his choices, if we pause here to take a look at it.

Near-Eastern expert Alan Millard writes (in Hoffmeier and Magary 2012, page 279):

> The book of Daniel correctly reflects the building works of Nebuchadnezzar, in common with Herodotus and other Greek writers, and the use of Aramaic in the Babylonian court, also, no doubt, a widely known fact.

Babylon was a spectacular city, in a completely different category from anything a young man from Judah could ever have seen or even imagined. It was in fact the largest city in the world at the time, covering over 1,000 hectares (2,500 acres). Compared with this vast metropolis on the eastern bank of the great river Euphrates, Daniel's capital city Jerusalem must have seemed very small indeed.

Clay brick inscribed with the name of King Nebuchadnezzar II,
King of Babylon dating c. 604-561 BC

The Assyrian emperor Sennacherib had destroyed Babylon about
a century earlier, and the Babylonian emperors, particularly
Nebuchadnezzar, had embarked on a massive programme of
reconstruction that was fairly well completed by the time Daniel
arrived. Indeed, Nebuchadnezzar's name is found inscribed on
nine-tenths of the bricks unearthed from the city – a practice that
Saddam Hussein was to follow many centuries later with lesser
success. Nebuchadnezzar made Babylon a unique city. When the
Greek historian Herodotus saw it much later, in 450 BC, he said that
it surpassed in splendour any city in the known world.

Babylon in the time of Nebuchadnezzar

The city was roughly rectangular in outline and straddled the Euphrates, which cut through the city from north to south. Coming in from the north with the Euphrates on the right, one would enter the city through a spectacularly beautiful gate named after one or other of the Babylonian gods, as were the other major city gates. This was the Ishtar gate. Ishtar (the Lightbringer) was the goddess of fertility, love and war, and as such she was the high mother-goddess of the Babylonian pantheon. There was also a magnificent temple dedicated to her worship inside the city, not far from the gate.

The Ishtar gate was one of eight fortified gates set in an invincible-looking broad wall that surrounded the city. (According to Herodotus the walls were 80 feet thick, 320 feet high and 56 miles long, though this is disputed by archaeologists, who reckon that the walls were only 11 miles long and not nearly as high.) The vast tower in which the gate was set was covered with brilliantly sparkling ceramic tiles of deep blue, adorned with the alternating motif of white and yellow lions, dragons and yellow bulls. It was very striking: built with a view to impressing all who entered with the power, wealth, architectural brilliance and permanence of the

Babylonian empire and, above all, the glorious majesty of Emperor Nebuchadnezzar himself.

Reconstruction of the Ishtar gate in the Pergamon Museum, Berlin

NEBUCHADNEZZAR'S DEDICATORY INSCRIPTION ON THE ISHTAR GATE

Nebuchadnezzar, King of Babylon, the faithful prince appointed by the will of Marduk, the highest of princely princes, beloved of Nabu, of prudent counsel, who has learned to embrace wisdom, who fathomed their divine being and reveres their majesty, the untiring governor, who always takes to heart the care of the cult of Esagila and Ezida and is constantly concerned with the well-being of Babylon and Borsippa, the wise, the humble, the caretaker of Esagila and Ezida, the firstborn son of Nabopolassar, the King of Babylon.

Both gate entrances of Imgur-Ellil and Nemetti-Ellil following the filling of the street from Babylon had become increasingly lower. Therefore, I pulled down these gates and laid their foundations at the water-table with asphalt and bricks and had them made of bricks with blue stone on which wonderful bulls and dragons were depicted. I covered their roofs by laying majestic cedars length-wise over them. I hung doors of cedar adorned with bronze at all the gate openings. I placed wild bulls and ferocious dragons in the gateways and thus adorned them with luxurious splendour so that people might gaze on them in wonder.

I let the temple of Esiskursiskur (the highest festival house of Marduk, the Lord of the Gods – a place of joy and celebration for the major and minor gods) be built firm like a mountain in the precinct of Babylon of asphalt and fired bricks.

Just outside the Ishtar gate was the temple of Akitu, which played a key role in the Babylonian celebration of their interpretation of history. Once a year there was a great spring festival to involve human beings in the renewal of nature. The Babylonians believed that past history was abolished at the end of winter when cosmos reverted to chaos. The whole fate of the country then depended on the judgment of the gods, and the spring festival was held in order to placate them and avert the crisis. At that time the priests brought the idol of the god Nabu from its temple in Borsippa to the temple of Akitu. Nabu was the patron god of wisdom and writing, and son of Marduk, the chief of all the gods. There followed a spectacular and colourful series of ceremonies that centred on the reading of one of Babylon's most famous pieces of literature, the *Enuma Elish* ("When on high"), which describes war among the gods and the creation of the universe.

The temple-priests wielded enormous power. They controlled a great deal of the land and therefore were in receipt of immense revenues. Even the emperor had to publicly acknowledge that reality. At the climax of the spring festival Nebuchadnezzar had to submit to a public ritual humiliation by the priests, during which the custom was to slap him hard until his tears flowed.[5] This was to remind everyone that the priests were the power behind the throne, and it was only after this ceremony had been performed that the great banquet to herald the advent of spring could begin.

The Ishtar gate was positioned at one end of the great Processional Way that traversed the full length of the city. Its scale – nearly twenty metres wide – and the sheer size and grandeur of the buildings on either side of it, left visiting travellers lost in wonder and admiration. The Babylonians were brilliant architects and engineers. Dominating the city skyline was a spectacular tower or ziggurat (*Akkadian zaqqaru* means "to rise high") called Etemenanki. This name in Sumerian means the House of the Foundations of Heaven and Earth, which immediately reminds us of Babel, the original city that stood on the same site, with its famous attempt to construct a tower that reached heaven (Genesis 11:4).

Of course that ancient tower had long since crumbled to dust and been replaced with something that had taken a hundred years to build. Its seven lofty storeys towered nearly 100 metres above street level, and it was probably the nearest the ancient world got to building a skyscraper. On the top were several rooms dedicated to the chief deities of the Babylonians. Marduk, the chief god, shared his room with his wife Sarpanitum; the scribe-god Nabu and his wife Tashmetu were in a second room; and in yet further rooms were the water god, Ea; the god of light, Nusku; and the god of heaven, Anu. Finally, there was a place for Marduk's predecessor, the Sumerian God Enlil (Lord of the Air). A seventh room was called "The House of the Bed". It contained a throne as well as a bed. Another bed was to be found in the inner court of the temple, on the very highest platform of the ziggurat. No one seems quite sure what the beds were for. Some even thought that Bel would come and sleep there, others that a Babylonian woman slept there alone. It is probable that the roof was used as an observatory, a field that was highly developed in Babylon because of the place they gave to astrology.

Many other magnificent buildings lined the Processional Way. Notable among them was Nebuchadnezzar's palace just west of the Ishtar gate, whose Sumerian name meant "The House the Marvel of Mankind". Its throne room was spectacular and designed to inspire any visitor with awe, indeed fear, of the emperor. Its roof gardens were one of the seven so-called wonders of the ancient world. They had been designed, so the story goes, to make Nebuchadnezzar's country-born wife feel more at home, by dint of landscaping part of the city to look like her birthplace. Their actual appearance remains a matter of imaginative speculation that forms the subject of many paintings.

Just past Etemenanki and on the same side of the Processional Way was Esagila (The House that Raises its Head), the vast temple complex dedicated to the supreme god Marduk. He was regarded as being so holy that his name was never pronounced, and he was referred to as Bel – "the Lord". But Babylon was far more than a religious centre. It was a commercial and intellectual hub as well. Many of its temples had substantial libraries; and there were centres devoted to the study of law, astronomy and astrology, architecture, engineering, medicine, and art. In modern terms, it was a thriving university city.

Two things must simultaneously have struck Daniel and his friends about Babylon. The first was the sheer elegance of the architecture and the advanced state to which learning had been brought; the second was the fact that idolatry permeated the whole society to an almost unbelievable degree. There were gods all over the place: the main gates were named after them, and there were temples galore – over a thousand at that time.

This juxtaposition must have posed a hard question for Daniel and his friends. Their Hebrew prophets would have told them that the gods of the Babylonians were idolatrous deifications of the basic powers of nature – sex, aggression, greed, power, wealth, and so on. But if that were so, how could such a high culture (far superior in many ways to the culture Daniel had left behind) have emerged from such inadequate, unsophisticated and, in their opinion, completely false religious and philosophical ideas? Was it really possible for such commerce, culture, and education to be built on a false philosophy? Or was this yet more evidence that their God was a delusion?

There was much to be pondered in their first days in Babylon.

CHAPTER 3

A QUESTION OF VALUES
Daniel 1

And the Lord gave Jehoiakim king of Judah into his hand,
with some of the vessels of the house of God. And he brought
them to the land of Shinar, to the house of his god, and placed
the vessels in the treasury of his god. (Daniel 1:2.)

The mention of Nebuchadnezzar's taking of the vessels from the temple at Jerusalem to Babylon may initially strike us as odd, since we might at first think that it is a detail of very little significance compared with the overthrow of Judah's king and the deportation of Daniel and many others. Yet Daniel chooses to mention these vessels here because of what was to follow.

It may well have been in the Esagila temple complex that Nebuchadnezzar had his treasure house. It was presumably much like a museum, with suites of rooms containing innumerable beautiful and valuable artefacts – the very best of the "tribute" (booty, really!). This Nebuchadnezzar collected on a regular basis from the vassal states in his vast empire in the course of his conquests. Many of these artefacts are still to be seen today in the major museums of the world.

An inventory of the treasure taken from Jerusalem is given to us in the book of Ezra – at least this is an inventory of what Cyrus, king of Persia, eventually gave the Jews to take back to Jerusalem from Babylonia at the end of their exile. It amounted to 5,400 vessels of gold and silver (Ezra 1:11).

A question of values

One can imagine that Daniel and his friends went from time to time to the museum in order to admire the vessels that Nebuchadnezzar had taken from Jerusalem, and to reflect on their meaning. To them, those golden vessels that glittered on the display tables were holy, in the original sense of that word: they were vessels set apart for the glory of God. The gold from which they had been made was the most precious metal known at the time. In addition, gold was very hard to come by in Israel, so it was particularly suitable for expressing the glory of God and the fact that he was "the supreme value" (as we might say) of the nation. The temple vessels from Jerusalem had been made by craftsmen who loved God, as Daniel and his friends did.

Christians should also be familiar with this concept of sacredness. When the Lord Jesus taught his disciples to pray he said that they should start with the words *Our Father in heaven, hallowed be your name* (Matthew 6:9). The word "hallowed" is an older variant of the word "holy". The first and most important thing that believers are to do is deliberately to set apart the name of God as special. God is to be their supreme value, and they are to remind themselves of this fact when they address him. (All the more sad, then, when this concept, fundamental to the expression of Christian life, gets lost in a formal prayer muttered unthinkingly by a church congregation.)

Those beautifully crafted golden vessels represented all that was central to the lives of the four young men. To them the vessels were a very tangible link with the temple of God in Jerusalem and all that it stood for. The fact that the vessels were no longer in that temple was a poignant reminder of the moral and spiritual catastrophe that had engulfed their homeland. It reminded them that their nation had lost a sense of the glory and the holiness of God.

Something similar can still happen today. We do not have to think very hard to realize that, in the eyes of many people, God has lost his glory and value; holiness has degenerated into an exclusively negative concept. Far from thinking of God's holiness as glorious, they associate holiness with drabness and the absence of life and colour – the very opposite of glory.

When we see images from the Hubble telescope of the breath-taking beauty of the star clusters in the night sky, whose scintillating light is the product of billions of stars; or even when we look through an earth-based telescope; how could we ever begin to think that the Creator is dull?

And yet, just as dark clouds or light pollution from the glare of earth's artificial lamps sometimes make it impossible for us to see the night sky in all its glory, maybe there is moral and spiritual pollution that hides the glory of God. Could it also be that we have lost some of that sensitivity to our own inadequacy and failure that Isaiah the prophet pointed out when, long before the time of Daniel, he saw the glory of God in the temple?

> *In the year that King Uzziah died I saw the Lord sitting upon*
> *a throne, high and lifted up; and the train of his robe filled the*
> *temple. Above him stood the seraphim. Each had six wings:*
> *with two he covered his face, and with two he covered his feet,*
> *and with two he flew. And one called to another and said:*
> *"Holy, holy, holy is the Lord of hosts; the whole earth is full of his*
> *glory!" And the foundations of the thresholds shook at the voice*
> *of him who called, and the house was filled with smoke. And I*
> *said: "Woe is me! For I am lost; for I am a man of unclean lips,*
> *and I dwell in the midst of a people of unclean lips; for my eyes*
> *have seen the King, the Lord of hosts!" (Isaiah 6:1–5.)*

The awe of the holiness of God, which the glory of Jerusalem's temple was designed to convey, is easily lost. And when it is lost, the danger is that symbols that once pointed the way to deeper spiritual and moral realities tend to become ends in themselves. An admiration for church architecture, or an appreciation of religious art and ritual, is not the same as the worship of a glorious God. After all, one does not even have to believe in God to admire the towering spires and the lofty vaulted roof of a cathedral, or to enjoy the singing of a well-trained church choir.

For the exiled students those golden vessels were points of light in a dark world, reminders of the heart of the value-system that had shaped their lives. To them God, his name, and his reputation were sacred.

Am I in danger of making too much of these temple vessels from Jerusalem? Scarcely, for we meet them again in the middle of the book, where they will take centre-stage at King Belshazzar's feast, where they will be inextricably caught up in his dramatic downfall.

Relativizing the absolute

Daniel has one more important thing to say about the golden vessels. He emphasizes that not only were they taken from temple to temple, but they were placed in the treasure house of the temple of Nebuchadnezzar's god. The mention of a treasure house reinforces the fact that we are still thinking of values, but this time the values of Nebuchadnezzar. By placing the golden vessels here, Nebuchadnezzar doubtless intended to show that they had a certain value. They were, after all, artefacts gained in one of his conquests, so their value would have been simplistically imagined to demonstrate the superior glory of Nebuchadnezzar and his gods. However, these particular treasures from Jerusalem were no more special in the eyes of Nebuchadnezzar than any of the myriad other artefacts he had collected on his exploits. The vessels certainly did not convey any sense of absolute value to him, as they did to Daniel. For Nebuchadnezzar, they had only relative value.

Daniel may well have mentioned the vessels at this prominent position at the beginning of his book because what Nebuchadnezzar did with them was an example of a tendency that Daniel was to observe throughout his long life. Indeed, it is a trend found in cultures and societies throughout history; and that is to take something of absolute value and reduce it to something of relative value.

In this way Nebuchadnezzar's action can therefore be understood as relativizing the absolute. By taking symbols that were designed to point to the one true God, Creator of heaven and earth, and placing them at the same level as cultic symbols of other gods, Nebuchadnezzar, whether he realized it or not, was demoting God from his absoluteness and making him just one of any number of other possible deities.

Such relativization of the absolute is endemic in the "pick-and-mix" postmodern society of our own century, particularly in the West. Whether you believe in Jesus, Buddha, the Beatles, crystals, mother earth, or anything else that takes your interest, all are held to be on the same footing; all have equal validity for the relativist. Indeed, many people are convinced that this is by far the safest position to adopt. Absolutes are dangerous, they say, especially religious absolutes. Sam Harris writes (2005, page 15): "We have been slow to recognize the degree to which religious faith perpetuates man's inhumanity to man." His suggested solution is radical: "Words like 'God' and 'Allah' must go the way of 'Apollo' and 'Baal,' or they will unmake our world" (page 14). He does not only wish to relativize them, he wishes to relegate them to the museum of the history of outmoded and discarded ideas. He regards atheism as the only defensible option.

History has surely shown that it cannot be as simple as that – if for no other reason than the glaring but easily ignored fact that atheism-inspired communism has been responsible for more bloodshed than all religiously motivated conflicts put together, no matter how much Dawkins, Harris, Hitchens, and others try to water this down (see Lennox 2011, chapter 4). We need, however, to take their criticisms seriously, since Christendom has been tragically scarred by sad and inexcusable scandals, not least the Crusades of the Middle Ages and the violence in Northern Ireland. It is very important to see why they were inexcusable. The reason is that the very Person the Crusaders claimed to be representing explicitly forbade his followers to use the sword to defend him and his message. Far from being followers of Christ, they were disobeying him. (Note that the question of the defence of a particular country or nation is logically separate from the defence of Christ and his message.)

It needs to be made clear to our generation (many of whom are only vaguely aware of the facts, if at all) that when Jesus was tried before the Roman Procurator on the charge of anti-state political activism – that is, fomenting terrorism – Pilate publicly declared him not guilty of the charge. Under cross-examination Jesus carefully explained to Pilate the nature of his kingdom and rule: *My kingdom is not of this world. If my kingdom were of this world, my servants would have been fighting* (John 18:36). So it was abundantly clear to the Roman governor that Jesus posed no revolutionary threat whatsoever. Pilate would have known that Jesus meant what he said, because he would have been in receipt of the report of the circumstances surrounding his arrest. In particular he would have known that when one of Jesus' disciples, Peter, had taken a wild sweep with a sword and cut off the ear of the high priest's servant, Jesus had told Peter to put his sword away, and healed the ear. One might just be forgiven for observing that using swords, or any other physical force, to defend Jesus and his kingdom has the effect of cutting off ears, one way or another: violence remains one of the main reasons why many people will not listen to Christ's message.

The main implication of all this is obvious. Anyone who uses force of any kind to impose Christ's message on people is acting in defiance of Christ's explicit commands. In other words, they are engaging in anti-Christian activity. Their claim to be followers of Christ is, therefore, proved to be spurious. The existence of counterfeit money does not prove that the real and genuine thing does not exist, even though it may make it harder to find.

To dismiss Christ's claims on the basis that they are absolutist and inevitably lead to bloodshed would be a very superficial and unbalanced reaction. It would be much fairer to history to read his claims against the background that, from very early times, genuine Christianity has had a positive record for caring for the weak and defenceless members of society.

Relativizing truth

The trend to relativize does not end with religion. Indeed, once you think about it, you realize that any relativizing tendency inevitably affects values and ultimately even truth itself. This aspect of postmodernism is far from being new. About three centuries after Daniel's time the Greek sophist Protagoras dismissed the notion of absolute truth on the basis that people might well have different opinions on whether the wind felt cold or not. Socrates later exposed the flaw in Protagoras's logic, making the distinction between objective truth and our subjective response to it. One wonders what Protagoras would have made of a thermometer.

At the heart of postmodernism lies a patent self-contradiction. It expects us to accept, as absolute truth, that there are no absolute truths. We should note this common, fatally flawed characteristic of relativistic thinking: it tries to exclude itself from its own pronouncements. The fact is that no one can live without a concept of absolute truth. If you do not believe this, try convincing a bank manager that the red figures he sees on his computer under your account number are not absolute values.

Indeed, in the ordinary practical business of life, people tend to be relativists only in those areas that they consider to be matters of opinion rather than matters of fact. All of us act as if we believe that clocks and watches tell us the truth about the time. We are not pluralists about whether London is the capital of England, or whether 2+2=4. The New Atheists are not postmodern when it comes to proclaiming the truth of atheism, and denying the existence of God.

The point I am making deserves emphasis. It is far too glib to say that someone *is* a relativist, for the simple reason that no one is a relativist in all areas. Indeed, in most areas, everyone turns out to be an absolutist.

CHAPTER 4

A QUESTION OF IDENTITY
Daniel 1

Nebuchadnezzar, although undoubtedly a ruthless absolute monarch, was sufficiently intelligent and far-sighted not to adopt a policy of total oppression in governing the disparate peoples of his empire. He believed that he could change people, and hence he deliberately chose the most able of the captives from any nation he conquered, and trained them thoroughly. They had to be young – older people are often fixed in their ways and cannot be moulded so easily. They had to be physically fit and impressive-looking, with strong intellectual and administrative aptitude. They had to learn both the language and literature of the Babylonians. Nebuchadnezzar knew the importance of language and literature for the process of assimilation. He insisted on a three-year intensive cultural-immersion course for his future elite. It was clearly his intention that, by the time they had finished, they would be insiders and not foreigners. Some of the graduates would eventually be sent back to their own countries, to combine their training with local knowledge, and act as representatives of the government in Babylon. Daniel and his friends proved so outstanding, however, that they remained at the centre of power in Babylon.

Daniel is sparing with details, choosing to record only one incident, which happened early on, that gives a revealing insight into the kind of social engineering that was part of the nation's philosophy. It had to do with names. Ashpenaz, the official in charge of the new recruits to the elite course in the university, told the four men that they were to be assigned new names. Their Hebrew names were to be replaced by Babylonian names. This may sound quite innocuous to us, but it clearly represented a move to eradicate any outward distinctiveness that their foreign-sounding names might signify.

Such distinctiveness might well have proved unwelcome to the authorities because, in fact, their names did not merely indicate their Hebrew origin but bore witness to the God in whom they believed. And, judging by the subsequent account, they could easily have used their names in conversation to get across some of the attributes of God that would have been entirely new to their fellow students from Babylon.

What's in a name?

Let us imagine a conversation between Daniel, his friends, and three Babylonian students whom we shall call Adapa, Ninurta, and Nabu. We break into the conversation just after the friends have learned that Adapa was named after the first mortal, the son of the gods Enlil and Ninlil. Ninurta means "lord of the earth", the Sumerian god of war, fertility, rain, and the south wind. Nabu was the name of the son of the god Marduk.

"Do the Hebrews have the same kind of thing?" asks Nabu.

"Yes," replies Daniel. "My name means 'God is my Judge.'"

"That's a bit tough," says Adapa. "Sounds like a very depressing and narrow view of God. It's as if your God is a killjoy, always snooping around in the hope he will catch you out so that he can punish you."

"It's not that bad," says Daniel. "Our concept of a judge is not simply a person who presides over a court of law, although of course that is part of his function. There was a time earlier in our history, before we had kings like King David, when we were ruled by men called 'judges'. So the word 'judge' to me conveys much more the idea that God is my ruler and guide in life, which is something positive. It means that God is not distant from me. He is interested in my life and wants the best for me. That's why I follow his law."

"That still sounds pretty stifling and legalistic to me," says Ninurta.

"Really?" says Azariah. "But that doesn't necessarily follow logically, does it? You like playing the lyre, and we all enjoy listening to you. I have noticed that before you play (and even sometimes while you are playing) you look at a clay tablet with musical notes on it. Isn't that because your performance will not be a success if you don't follow the notes? It is only when you know the notes, and submit yourself to their discipline so to speak, that you are free to play top-quality music. It's exactly the same with us. We want to make music with our lives, and the quality of that music depends on our attention to the 'score' of our laws – the Torah."

"That analogy only holds up to a point," protests Mishael. "We mustn't give the impression that we're simply machines obeying some kind of mechanical devising. After all, our Torah tends to give us principles rather than detailed courses of action; and we have to think hard about how the principles apply in any given situation."

"Point taken," says Azariah. "Perhaps I could flesh out my musical metaphor even more then. The music shows what notes to play, but the actual emphasis, the timbre, and precise phrasing, are determined by Ninurta, so there is freedom for his personality to come through. No two performances by different musicians playing the same notes are the same. In fact, no two performances by the same musician playing the same notes are the same!"

"But you did hint that there was also a legal side to the concept of judge, Daniel. Are you going to say something about that?"

"Yes. To some people the idea of judgment is negative, especially a final judgment. But if there is no judgment it follows logically that there is no ultimate accountability, so that it doesn't really matter what I do, since I shall never be called to account for it. No society can operate like that without falling into anarchy. That's why you have the Code of Hammurabi and enforce it in the law courts. The Babylonian state holds that the law must be upheld with the sanction of punishment, otherwise it's pointless. If that makes sense at the level of society, surely it applies also to our relationship with God?

"The bottom line is that accountability confers dignity and value on human beings. In ordinary life none of us likes to be treated as if we are not accountable or responsible. God has created us with a certain degree of freedom. We are capable of making choices. Denying ultimate accountability devalues me as a human being, because if what I do doesn't really matter then I don't matter either.

"In addition, if there is no accountability, the sense of justice we all seem to possess is nothing but a hollow illusion. It corresponds to no objective moral reality. It mocks us with its false promise that things will be put right sometime.

"Against that background you can understand why our poets frequently expressed sheer delight at the thought of God one day intervening to judge the world. Here's an example:

> *Let the heavens be glad, and let the earth rejoice; let the sea roar, and all that fills it; let the field exult, and everything in it! Then shall all the trees of the forest sing for joy before the Lord, for he comes, for he comes to judge the earth. He will judge the world in righteousness, and the peoples in his faithfulness. (Psalm 96:11–13.)*

"The poet imagined the whole of creation rejoicing in anticipation that one day God will step into history and make his final assessment. Surely that is something to be welcomed?"

"But I don't like the idea of a judgment, especially if it's final," says Nabu. "I'm not sure that I want to be accountable to a god, and certainly not to your god. In any case, if there is only one God, and he is holy as you say he is, won't it be uncomfortable for you too? After all, you are not perfect – are you?"

(In his famous book *The Brothers Karamazov* the Russian novelist Fyodor Dostoyevsky wrote: "If God does not exist, then everything is permissible." Dostoyevsky is not suggesting, of course, that no atheist can be moral. Indeed, atheists can sometimes put professing Christians to shame. What he is suggesting is that if there is no God, there is no base for morality. Many contemporary thinkers disagree, and propose that an adequate morality can be found in aspects of biology or even that morality is genetically determined. My reasons for questioning this proposition are to be found elsewhere [2011, pages 97–114].)

"I think you will have to have a word with Hananiah here," says Daniel, "since my name doesn't tell you everything about God."

"That's right," says Hananiah. "My name means 'the Lord shows grace.'"

"What is grace?" Adapa asks.

"Grace means the sheer generosity of God, in giving to us what we do not deserve. For instance, do you think that I deserved to be spared by Nebuchadnezzar at the siege of Jerusalem, when many were not? Did I deserve to have the wonderful parents and family I had, while others have had such tragic experiences of home? Indeed, do I deserve to have good new friends like you here in Babylon? I see this, and many other things, as an expression of the grace of God."

"Hang on! Isn't that completely different from what Daniel was telling us? Does Daniel worship the judge-god, and you worship the grace-god? You have different gods, just like us."

"Not at all!" they chorus in unison. "There is only one God. Think about it this way. Our claim is that human beings are made in God's image, which implies that you can learn something about God from looking at humans. In particular, we are persons, and so is God. Now think of some person you respect. He is one person, yet his personality is not monolithic and undifferentiated. It has distinct characteristics: he can be gracious but firm, for example. What we are trying to say is that our names reflect the breadth of the character of the one true God. I hope that makes better sense to you."

"I think I should say something here," says Mishael, "because my name is associated with this very issue of the uniqueness of God. It means 'Who is like God?' It is of course a question that expects a negative answer: 'No one is like God. He is unique.' I think my parents got the name from reading Isaiah the prophet: *To whom then will you liken God, or what likeness compare with him?* (Isaiah 40:18). It was in these terms that Isaiah protested against polytheism in the name of the one true God."

"What about you, Azariah? We want to hear the meaning of your name too."

"It means 'the Lord helps,'" he replies. "My parents gave it to me as an expression of their gratitude to God for the help he had given them in life. But it is not only my parents who felt like this. We have experienced the help of God ourselves. His word has been a lifesaver to us. For instance, if we had not been told in advance through Jeremiah not only that Nebuchadnezzar would invade and deport many of us, but also why it had to happen, we would not have been able to cope with it. Indeed, as I look back over life, a lot of God's help comes in his dealings with us through Scripture, when we sense that we hear his voice."

"Forgive me," says Nabu. "But that sounds very thin. That's just your highly subjective interpretation of things. Perhaps I ought to emphasize that my name is that of the patron god of science – and, oddly enough, I am a scientist. You say that we human beings are made in God's image. Surely it could be the other way round. We have a professor of psychology in the university who has taught us that all gods are essentially projections of our own ideas, which is why they are all so horribly and predictably human – they have no separate existence. Incidentally, the priests don't like this sort of talk; so this professor has to be careful what he says in public. It's hard to go against the reigning paradigm here.

"What's more, when it comes to your claim that your God helps you, by the same token I could say that Nabu has helped me to become a scientist and get a distinction in my exams; or that Ishtar has helped me get a stunning girlfriend. How would that be any different from what you are saying? You cannot escape the epistemological question: how do you know that God helps you? How can you tell that you are not simply reading that interpretation into your experience because it suits you?"

"There is not much that escapes you!" Azariah replies. "I grant at once that your question is completely justified. However, your point cuts both ways. Suppose I were to ask you how you know that the stunning girlfriend you mentioned loves you? To any argument you raise like that, I can give a counter argument. Proof of love, in the strict sense of the term that Hananiah likes to see in his mathematics, is impossible. But perception is not impossible, is it? If I spent some time observing you and your girlfriend, I think I could tell whether she loved you or not. So why don't you watch us closely for the next months? If you cannot perceive that God is with us and helps us in our daily lives, then it would be idle for us to assert it. But I just hope you will come to see, maybe through us, that God is real."

Such opportunity to use their names as conversation starters would not have lasted long – if indeed they ever had the opportunity. Very early on Ashpenaz, the official in charge of the students, called the foreign student intake to a meeting at which he informed them that, in order to facilitate their assimilation into Babylonian society, they would be given Babylonian names. Foreign names were to be banned with immediate effect.

Their new names had already been chosen. Daniel was to be called Belteshazzar (*Balat su ussur*), which means "May Bel (Marduk) protect his life" (or possibly, and intriguingly, "treasurer of Bel"). Hananiah was assigned the name Shadrach, which means "command of Aku" (the moon-god); and Azariah the name Abednego, which means "servant of Nabu" (the son of Marduk). Nabu or Nebo is part of the name Nebuchadnezzar (*Nabu kudurri usur*), and so both Azariah and Daniel were given names after part of the emperor's name. But they were hardest on Mishael. His Babylonian name sounded like his Hebrew name, and was in fact a linguistic parody of it. He became Meshach, which means "Who is like Aku (the moon-god)?" No public trace was allowed to remain of Mishael's concept of the uniqueness of the one true God. It is hard to imagine that the young friends stopped using their proper names when speaking to one another, and they might also have been able to explain their Hebrew names to some people, but clearly they would have had to be very careful. Babylon wanted those names and their meanings to be forgotten. (It has been suggested that Daniel deliberately misspells some of these Babylonian names, as if to say, "It doesn't really matter what you call me; you cannot change my identity.")

This name-changing was no innocent action. It was an early attempt at social engineering, with the objective of obliterating inconvenient distinctions and homogenizing people, so that they would be easier to control. Throughout history such attempts have often been marked by the undermining of human dignity. A contemporary example of this phenomenon is political correctness which, though originally intended to avoid offence, has become an intolerant suppressor of open and honest public discussion.

It must have been a difficult moment for Daniel and his friends, and the idea of protest may well have crossed their minds. However, there is no mention of protest, and so we can only speculate. One thing is evident: Babylon could change their names but it could not change their identities. As a matter of historical fact Daniel's name survived the Babylonian empire, thanks to the book he has given us. He didn't lose his identity either. And one can well imagine that among themselves they used their proper names all the time.

Babylon and the search for meaning

There is more to be said about names and identities in this context, for it is the issue that lay at the very heart of the original foundation of the city of Babylon. The Genesis account says:

> Now the whole earth had one language and the same words. And as people migrated from the east, they found a plain in the land of Shinar and settled there. And they said to one another, "Come, let us make bricks, and burn them thoroughly." And they had brick for stone, and bitumen for mortar. Then they said, "Come, let us build ourselves a city and a tower with its top in the heavens, and let us make a **name** for ourselves, lest we be dispersed over the face of the whole earth." (Genesis 11:1–4, emphasis mine.)

Each great capital city of the world tends to stand as a symbol for the ideology that characterizes the nation. During the Cold War, for instance, it was commonplace to hear radio announcements along these lines: "Moscow says X, to which Washington has replied Y, but

London thinks Z." All listeners knew what Moscow, Washington, and London stood for. They represented contrasting ideologies. This passage from Genesis tells us what Babylon stood for. The defining slogan, *let us make a name for ourselves*, shows us the philosophy on which it was built and its driving ambition.

We need, however, to think this through rather carefully. After all, does this not simply mean that the Babylonian project was a genuine search for identity? What is wrong with that? Surely we all want to have an identity? Isn't meaning one of the fundamental things that make life what it is; so what could be so wrong with searching for it?

Nothing! The Genesis text is not telling us that we should not search for meaning; but it is saying that it matters how we search for it. From God's perspective there certainly seemed to be something wrong with the way these ancients went about the original project, because he intervened and put a summary stop to it.

Babel was searching for its identity, in the cutting edge of the scientific and technological achievement of the time. As we have seen, the ancient Babylonians were clever architects and skilled engineers, and their drive to build the most impressive buildings on earth found its outlet in a succession of emperors, notably Nebuchadnezzar.

And through the centuries it has been the same, with the drive to push buildings higher into the heavens as potent images of human achievement: the Pyramids, the lofty structures built by the Mayans, the Empire State Building, the Petronas Towers, the Shard, the Burj Khalifa; and even higher buildings are being planned. They are powerful symbols – so powerful, indeed, that when terrorists wanted to strike a blow against the USA they chose the Twin Towers as their target.

There is nothing wrong with striving for excellence in architecture and engineering, and we rightly admire the Babylonians and other nations for their magnificent achievements. So, what is the problem with the way they set about finding meaning? Genesis tells us in its very next chapter. There we have a record of God's command to Daniel's forefather Abraham, ordering him to leave the city of Haran, an ancient city in the same general area as Babylon.

*Now the Lord said to Abram, "Go from your country and
your kindred and your father's house to the land that I will
show you. And I will make of you a great nation, and I will
bless you and make your **name** great, so that you will be
a blessing. I will bless those who bless you, and him who
dishonours you I will curse, and in you all the families of the
earth shall be blessed." (Genesis 12:1–3, emphasis mine.)*

The call of God to Abraham must rank as one of the most important
events in world history. Lord Sacks, the Chief Rabbi of the United
Kingdom, writes (2011, page 8):

All other civilizations rise and fall. The faith of Abraham
survives... What made Abrahamic monotheism unique is
that it endowed life with meaning. That is a point rarely and
barely understood... We make a great mistake if we think of
monotheism as a linear development from polytheism, as if
people first worshipped many gods and then reduced them
to one. Monotheism is something else entirely. The meaning
of a system lies outside the system. Therefore the meaning
of the universe lies outside the universe. Monotheism, by
discovering the transcendental God, the God who stands
outside the universe and creates it, made it possible for
the first time to believe that life has a meaning, not just a
mythic or scientific explanation.

Babylon's philosophy resonates with the scientism of today that
encourages us to look for both meaning and salvation in science and
technology. But scientific analysis and explanation does not yield to
us the meaning for which we as persons long. Babylon will leave you
empty.

God will not leave you empty, as the philosopher Ludwig
Wittgenstein clearly saw (1979, page 74e):

*To believe in God means to understand the question about the
meaning of life. To believe in God means to see that the facts*

of the world are not the end of the matter. To believe in God
means to see that life has a meaning.

The transcendent Lord God reveals himself to Abraham and tells him where his life's meaning will be found: *I will make your name great.* This statement, coming hard on the heels of the description of the ideology of Babel, invites us to contrast the foundation philosophy of Babel with Abraham's faith in God. What is more, in the New Testament, Abraham's faith is said to be the foundation philosophy of another city that plays a polar-opposite role to Babylon in the Bible's storyline. It is a heavenly city that bears the name Jerusalem.

Here is the account given in the letter to the Hebrews of why Abraham left the city of Ur:

By faith Abraham obeyed when he was called to go out to a
place that he was to receive as an inheritance. And he went
out, not knowing where he was going. By faith he went to live
in the land of promise, as in a foreign land, living in tents
with Isaac and Jacob, heirs with him of the same promise.
For he was looking forward to the city that has foundations,
whose designer and builder is God. By faith Sarah herself
received power to conceive, even when she was past the
age, since she considered him faithful who had promised.
Therefore from one man, and him as good as dead, were born
descendants as many as the stars of heaven and as many as
the innumerable grains of sand by the seashore.

These all died in faith, not having received the things
promised, but having seen them and greeted them from afar,
and having acknowledged that they were strangers and exiles
on the earth. For people who speak thus make it clear that
they are seeking a homeland. If they had been thinking of that
land from which they had gone out, they would have had
opportunity to return. But as it is, they desire a better country,
that is, a heavenly one. Therefore God is not ashamed to
be called their God, for he has prepared for them a city.
(Hebrews 11:8–16.)

Abraham, like the rest of us, was naturally and rightly interested in his own identity. However, the difference between his attitude and that of the citizens of Babel was that they were confident in their own ability and effort to create a "name" or identity. They would do it, Sinatra-like, "my way" – whereas Abraham was prepared to accept the identity and significance that God gave to him. That marked him out as a man who had remarkable confidence and trust in God. And faith is the foundation principle of God's heavenly city. God is not against cities! It is a matter of what they stand for that is vital.

The question for Abraham, for Daniel, and for us, is not which city we live *in* so much as which city we live *for*. In this sense, the Bible is a tale of two cities. We shall return to this idea when we look at Daniel 9.

What Abraham did was much easier said than done. Many, if not all, of us struggle with this very same issue of identity. We find it difficult to find much meaning in our lives at times, and we gloomily ask, "What is it all about?" At the same time we are acutely aware of others who apparently lead lives filled with achievement, and we may even begin to wish we were one of them. They may be more talented than we are, they may possess what we conceive to be more depth of personality. To us they often appear to have relatively few problems – personally, in their families, or at work. Their "name" seems to be easy to recognize, whereas ours is not. They seem to have a clear "why" in their lives, and we do not.

If we are honest it is sometimes a battle, even for those of us who are believers in God, to come to accept the significance he has given us. It is so easy to try to find our significance in something other than God – and to tear ourselves apart in the process.

The question "Who am I really?" is one of the deepest questions we can ask. Nola Passmore, a psychologist, puts it well:

> The heart cry of the human race is for meaning and
> purpose, a sense of belonging when human relationships
> fail to satisfy, a need to know we are unconditionally
> loved in spite of our circumstances, a need to know that
> we are not an accident of chance but people of design, a

51

need to know that we have a future and a hope even when everything around us seems to be falling apart.

Viktor Frankl, the Viennese psychotherapist who survived the Holocaust, wrote a book entitled *Man's Search for Meaning*, in which he described a psychotherapeutic treatment that he named "logotherapy" (from the Greek word *logos* that denotes "word" or "meaning" and which had been used by the Stoic philosophers to denote the rational principle behind the universe, and then by Christians in the New Testament to denote Christ as the Word of God). He believed that the primary human motivational force is the search for meaning. The fact that millions of copies of his book have been sold in many languages demonstrates the aching void that exists in the human heart. Frankl believed that the most important thing we can do for our fellow human beings is to give them hope for the future. God gave Abraham hope by making a promise to him that was later fulfilled. He gave him a *logos*, or word of hope.

In this connection it is worth thinking not only of individual names but the generic name attached to human beings. Where did it come from? The biblical answer is that it came from God himself. According to Genesis:

> *This is the book of the generations of Adam. When God created man, he made him in the likeness of God. Male and female he created them, and he blessed them and named them Man [Hebrew: adam] when they were created. (Genesis 5:1–2.)*

The interesting thing here is that, according to Genesis, there are relatively few parts of creation to which God is recorded as having assigned a name (day, night, heaven, earth, and seas in Genesis 1:5, 8, 10), whereas Adam was given the task of naming the many animals.

By indicating that God personally gave humans their name, Genesis is surely emphasizing the fact that humans derive their ultimate significance from being made in the image of God. It follows that if we cut ourselves off from God, we lose that sense of ultimate meaning. (I am not implying that atheists cannot and do not create a sense of meaning and purpose for themselves. What I am suggesting is that their own world-view denies to them any ultimate meaning.)

The central claim of Christianity is that Jesus is the Word (*Logos*), identical to God and with God from the beginning (John 1:1–2). He is the Word that became human in order that we could hear from him words that give us meaning. Indeed, it is with that motivation that this book is being written: that, as we read what Daniel has to say, we shall hear the voice of God speaking to us. For that is what the book of Daniel is: it is the voice of God to Daniel and, through him, to us. This is a very provocative claim to make in a sceptical secular society. More on this later.

We finally highlight a major difference between Daniel and Abraham. Abraham was called out of Mesopotamia. He left it voluntarily at the command of God and became a nomad, travelling to the land that later bore the name of his grandson, Israel (Jacob). He learned what it means to trust God; and in the New Testament he is given as an example for us to emulate (Hebrews 11). By contrast Daniel was taken forcibly from the land of promise back to the very region that Abraham had left. Daniel, as a true son of Abraham, was called upon to live and witness publicly in Babylon to his faith in God. This is the other side of the lesson for us. Having learned like Abraham to trust God as a pilgrim on the journey of life, God will then send us back into society to function as "salt and light" (Matthew 5:13–14) – to stimulate thirst for God there and to illuminate the path to him through the Lord Jesus Christ his incarnate Son.

Matthew Arnold

> But often, in the world's most crowded streets,
> But often, in the din of strife,
> There rises an unspeakable desire
> After the knowledge of our buried life:
> A thirst to spend our fire and restless force
> In tracking out our true, original course;
> A longing to inquire

Into the mystery of this heart which beats
So wild, so deep in us – to know
Whence our lives come and where they go.

The Buried Life (1852)

Friedrich Nietzsche

He who has a why to live can bear almost any how.

Twilight of the Idols [Maxim 12] (1889)

The confusion of language

The passage in Genesis that records the origins of Babylon gives us the meaning of its name:

> *And the Lord came down to see the city and the tower, which the children of man had built. And the Lord said, "Behold, they are one people, and they have all one language, and this is only the beginning of what they will do. And nothing that they propose to do will now be impossible for them. Come, let us go down and there confuse their language, so that they may not understand one another's speech." So the Lord dispersed them from there over the face of all the earth, and they left off building the city. Therefore its name was called Babel, because there the Lord confused the language of all the earth. And from there the Lord dispersed them over the face of all the earth. (Genesis 11:5–9.)*

According to Scripture here is the origin of our multiplicity of languages which, in particular, ultimately led to Hebrew being different from Aramaic and Chaldean. As we have seen, Nebuchadnezzar was clearly determined to reverse the effects of linguistic and cultural differences in his educational policy, by insisting that young captives like Daniel and his friends should learn the language and literature of the Babylonian empire. By changing their names the emperor was going even further. It was almost as if he was attempting to take these names out of circulation.

I may be accused of reading too much into this, but even if I am it will not weaken the point I wish to make. The wave of relativism now swamping Western thinking has increased the pressure to drop certain words from our languages and replace them with others that drive forward the secularist agenda of deconstructing the very nature of human beings and the society we live in.

For instance, some words tend to fall foul of political correctness: truth, commandment, dogma, faith, conscience, morality, sin, chastity, charity, justice, authority, husband, wife; whereas a host of other words and concepts take centre-stage: rights, non-discrimination, choice, gender equality, plurality, cultural diversity.

These profound changes arise from a postmodern deconstruction of truth, which involves removing truth from the objective realm to the subjective, and thus effectively relativizing it. Cardinal Ratzinger, before he became Pope Benedict XVI, warned of a "dictatorship of relativism" in European society. He said:

> We are building a dictatorship of relativism that does not recognize anything as definitive and whose ultimate goal consists solely of one's own ego and desires.[6]

This sounds quite paradoxical, but it is not. The pressure to conform will be felt the moment one questions any aspect of this relativism – that all lifestyles must be approved, for instance. The right to choose trumps everything else, including tradition and divine revelation. It is the one absolute in a sea of relativism, however self-contradictory that may be.

We have noted that postmodernism contains within itself the blatant self-contradiction that "there is no absolute truth" is stated as an absolute truth; so it is not surprising that its language is very confused. Indeed, postmodernism thrives on linguistic ambivalence. Its agenda is to remove all objectivity from our apprehension of "reality" and reduce everything to a text that has to be interpreted, with each interpretation being equally valid, not least in the realm of values.

Jürgen Habermas (an atheist, be it noted) has given clear warning of the dangers of this shift from a Judaeo-Christian moral base to the postmodern (2006, pages 150–51):

> *Universalistic egalitarianism, from which sprang the ideals of freedom and a collective life in solidarity, the autonomous conduct of life and emancipation, the individual morality of conscience, human rights, and democracy, is the direct legacy of the Judaic ethic of justice and the Christian ethic of love. This legacy, substantially unchanged, has been the object of continual critical appropriation and reinterpretation. To this day, there is no alternative to it. And in light of the current challenges of a post-national constellation, we continue to draw on the substance of this heritage. Everything else is just idle postmodern talk.*

A postmodern "Babel" indeed!

CHAPTER 5

THE RESOLUTION AND THE PROTEST
Daniel 1

There may well have been no opportunity for Daniel and his friends to protest against being given pagan names. We do not know, as the matter is passed over in silence. But we watch with interest to find out at what point the three young men begin to plant their flag of witness to God in the University of Babylon. It is not long in coming.

A student of holiness

Daniel tells us that the elite students like himself and his friends were trained for three years in a broad curriculum, involving the languages and literature of the Babylonians. No expense was spared by the government and, since Babylonian culture put a high premium on physical image, the students were given the very best of food – in fact the same food that was served to the emperor himself. Students being students, such food was a great perk of being selected for the course. It is certain that these four captives from a city brought to its knees by an impoverishing siege had never seen anything like this quality of food before: it was beyond the dreams of those used to war rations.

> *But Daniel resolved that he would not defile himself with the king's food, or with the wine that he drank. (Daniel 1:8.)*

Dissatisfaction with college food is nothing new. Many generations of students have found much to be vocal about in the lack of quantity or quality of their refectory food. That was certainly not the case here. The food was Michelin Star quality, direct from the emperor's own kitchen. It was high table food. So why did Daniel decide not to eat it?

His own explanation is that he did not wish to "defile himself". So we are talking about an inward resolution of heart and mind that preceded his outward action. It arose in connection with Daniel's biblical convictions about holiness. This concept has both positive and negative aspects. Positively, holiness is dedication and commitment to God. As we know, Daniel was intending to live in light of all that the golden temple vessels stood for – the glory and the holiness of God.

In the second half of chapter 1 of his book we see how Daniel clearly understood that in order to witness to the glory and holiness of God, he needed to ensure that his character and personality were moulded by that holiness. That would mean avoiding defilement. Before we try to identify what precisely was involved we should pause to think about this decision, since it is crucial for an understanding of the quality and power of Daniel's subsequent witness. It was a decision taken in his heart *before* he did anything. In a famous statement the apostle Peter says that Christians are to be characterized by a willingness to engage in discussion: *always being prepared to make a defence to anyone who asks you for a reason for the hope that is in you* (1 Peter 3:15).

At least, that is the part which is usually cited. However, as it stands here, the quotation is incomplete as it has no direct verb. Here is the complete sentence (verses 14–16):

> *Have no fear of them, nor be troubled, but in your hearts regard Christ the Lord as holy, always being prepared to make a defence to anyone who asks you for a reason for the hope that is in you; yet do it with gentleness and respect, having a good conscience, so that, when you are slandered, those who revile your good behaviour in Christ may be put to shame.*

Peter's full statement can help us to analyse not only why Daniel made his resolution but also how he went about carrying it out. The first thing to be noted is that the context is fear. In Peter's time it was fear of a hostile and possibly violent reaction to the Christian message. Fear was surely not far from the minds of Daniel and his friends. As we have already seen, conformity was the name of the game in Babylon – nobody would want to draw attention to any religious distinctiveness they might have. Yet these students were thinking of making a move that, at the least, would immediately provoke questioning, and who knows what else. It must have been an anxious moment. Even if we have never experienced violent hostility, fear is something we can all easily identify with if we have made any attempt to give public expression to our faith.

What was it that strengthened the hearts and minds of Daniel and his friends, so that they had courage to overcome a natural fear of the unknown? It was surely the fact that they had set God apart as holy in their hearts. They had made God sole director of their lives. That is exactly what Peter says we are to do. In order to combat our anxieties and prepare ourselves to give an answer to those who will ask, we are first and foremost to set Christ apart in our hearts as Lord. Indeed, how can there be conviction and power in our evangelism if it is not so? Surely it is but elementary spiritual logic that if we wish to persuade others that God is real and that it is possible to have a vibrantly meaningful relationship with him, we shall have to be personally loyal to God and his Son and adjust our lives to be consistent with our fundamental Christian confession, "Jesus Christ is Lord." Daniel knew that defilement could spoil his relationship with God and undermine his personal testimony. And so do we.

Daniel also knew that God had frequently warned Israel through Moses and a succession of prophets of the danger of being defiled by the practices of certain neighbouring pagan cultures; particularly the Canaanites, who were well known for their immorality, infanticide (child sacrifice), and idolatry. In the New Testament, God warns us of similar dangers. None of us is exempt from the pressured temptations of a world that has no interest in God. If we are honest, we don't need to be told the things that defile; we know them too well, especially in this internet age when evil influence is only one click away. In order to serve God we shall have to fight against them. Nothing less than our loyalty to God is at stake.

The food laws

At an early stage in Israel's history God communicated this message by instituting certain ritual and ceremonial laws. For instance, the people were instructed that they should not eat certain designated "unclean" foods. Such regulations inevitably made social mixing with other cultures difficult. We can see an example of this in the New Testament account of the visit of the apostle Peter to the home of the Roman centurion Cornelius (see Acts 10). As a pious Jew with an adherence to the kosher food laws Peter would not have been able to accept Cornelius's invitation. God had to prepare Peter by giving him a vision to remind him of what Christ had taught, namely that the food laws had been annulled. Christ had pointed out the evident fact that physical food cannot of itself defile a person. His concern was with real moral and spiritual defilement.

> ... whatever goes into a person from outside cannot defile
> him, since it enters not his heart but his stomach ...
> What comes out of a person is what defiles him. For from
> within, out of the heart of man, come evil thoughts, sexual
> immorality, theft, murder, adultery, coveting, wickedness,
> deceit, sensuality, envy, slander, pride, foolishness. All these
> evil things come from within, and they defile a person.
> (Mark 7:18–23.)

It was, therefore, God's prohibition that made the food unclean, which raises the question as to why the food laws were instituted in the first place. Why not simply speak of the need to avoid defiling inner attitudes of mind? Paul gives us the answer in his letter to the Galatians. He tells us that, just as in ancient custom a child had a guardian to protect it until maturity, for Israel the law acted as a guardian until Christ came. There is a sense in which God treated the infant nation of Israel as a child, guarding it with rules and regulations for the early stages of its development.

Following that analogy we can see one possible reason for the imposition of regulations that provided a barrier against negative external influence. Think of it this way: only a minority of adults abuse children. Yet we regard it wise for parents to teach their children not to take anything from any adult they do not know. Similarly, not all Gentiles were morally corrupt at that time. But enough of them were for God to put up a barrier in order to instil into Israel the dangers of compromise with idolatry and its attendant practices.

Now the obvious drawback with this scheme is that those who are brought up under it could fall into the dangerous error of confusing the keeping of rules and regulations concerning outward ceremonial cleanness with real inner moral cleanness. In consequence, they may begin to think that they are better than others when, in fact, they are not. They may even wrongly think that they are acceptable to God no matter what evil they do (as some in Israel did, and sadly even some professing Christians do today); whereas Gentiles are unacceptable to God no matter what good they do. Of course, this is moral nonsense.

When Christ came he cancelled the system of food laws (Mark 7:19), and something completely new took its place. The Holy Spirit came to indwell believers and give them the inner power to resist corruption so that they could take their witness to the Gentiles, mix with them and yet resist the pressures of evil in both thought and behaviour.[7] However, the food laws were in force when Daniel lived, and would therefore have constituted a strong reason for him and his friends to reject the imperial food.

A second reason for their action has to do with the slaughtering and preparation of meat. The levitical laws prohibited eating blood or blood products, on the grounds that *the life of the flesh is in the blood* (Leviticus 17:11). This regulation was designed to remind Israel in a symbolic way of the sanctity of life, but those laws would scarcely have been operating in the Babylonian meat market.

A choice: God or idols?

The third possible reason for Daniel's refusal may have been that the food had been sacrificed to idols, or in some way ceremonially involved with the paganism that characterized the Babylonian world-view. The text itself does not actually mention idolatry at this precise juncture, so many think that it is an unwarranted speculation to introduce this as an explanation for Daniel's refusal. However, we do know that Babylonian culture was permeated with polytheistic worship in a way unique for the ancient world. In his authoritative work (1992, page 85) Georges Roux writes:

> For more than three thousand years the gods of Sumer were
> worshipped by Sumerians and Semites alike; and for more
> than three thousand years the religious ideas promoted by
> the Sumerians played an extraordinary part in the public
> and private life of the Mesopotamians, modelling their
> institutions, colouring their works of art and literature,
> pervading every form of activity from the highest functions
> of the kings to the day-to-day occupations of their subjects. In
> no other antique society did religion occupy such a prominent
> position, because in no other antique society did man feel
> himself so utterly dependent upon the will of the gods.

Libraries and educational institutions in particular were closely attached to temples in the major cities of the empire. According to the archaeologists, Babylon had temples galore at the time – over a thousand of them. In contemporary, secular England most colleges in the universities of Oxford and Cambridge still have a Latin grace said at meals by a scholar or fellow of the college. It would surely be almost incredible if the University of Babylon, permeated as it was with idolatry, did not have pagan rituals at meal times. There would have been constant offerings and toasts to the gods.

Daniel gives us an important bit of evidence that points strongly in this direction. He mentions his intention of refusing not only the food but also the wine. The biblical laws had nothing to say about wine (except for warning against the dangers of excess). So why mention it here? The answer is not hard to find, as there is one meal described later in Daniel's book where wine takes centre-stage – that famous feast where Belshazzar the king sent for the golden goblets that Nebuchadnezzar had taken from the temple at Jerusalem and forced his nobles to join him in a calculated insult to God by filling the goblets with wine and toasting the pagan gods of wood and stone. God did not remain silent and wrote his doom-laden verdict on the wall of the palace.

Thus the golden goblets mentioned in the first half of chapter 1, and the wine mentioned in the second half, come together in a spectacular and tragic way in the fateful banquet of pagan worship described in Daniel 5.

In light of this, it is surely not unreasonable to think that Daniel, even in his early days as a student, saw the danger of compromising his loyalty to God. He refused to become involved in the kind of pagan drinking ritual that, written large – metaphorically and literally – was ultimately to spell the downfall of both Belshazzar and the empire. Daniel rightly and courageously decided at the very beginning of his university career that a line had to be drawn; a compass bearing had to be set.

If this is the case, Daniel's protest was in essence a protest against the idolatrous world-view of the Babylonians: a world-view that formed the background paradigm for their educational system. He was determined not to defile himself with it. It is surely not hard for us to relate to that. In the West the academy is dominated by the idea that atheism is the only intellectually respectable world-view, which calls for protest on the part of those of us who believe that to be false.

But how is this to be done? Daniel tells us how he and his friends responded to their situation. He does not tell us, of course, how we should apply what they did to our day. At first sight their culture looks very different from ours, so we need to proceed carefully and try to think our way through the issues that were involved in Babylon, and then see if any parallels can be drawn for us today.

CHAPTER 6

THE WORLD-VIEW OF BABYLON
Daniel 1

Our first task at this stage, then, is to find out a bit more about the Babylonian world-view against which Daniel was protesting, in order to see how it contrasted with his.

God, the gods, and the universe

Take, for instance, the question of origins. Daniel believed that there was one true God, the Creator of heaven and earth. By contrast, the Babylonians believed in many gods; and we learn about them from the kind of literature to which Daniel would have been exposed – for instance, the famous Babylonian creation epic, the *Enuma Elish*. This is a myth about the origins of both the universe and the gods (cosmogony and theogony), detailing the war for supremacy among them that led to Marduk replacing Enlil as the highest god of the Mesopotamian pantheon.

Here we are told that the gods emerged out of some sort of primeval combination of the eternal freshwater Apsu and the saltwater Tiamat. Here are the first few lines:

When in the height heaven was not named,
And the earth beneath did not yet bear a name,
And the primeval Apsu, who begat them,
And chaos, Tiamat, the mother of them both

Their waters were mingled together,
And no field was formed, no marsh was to be seen;
When of the gods none had been called into being,
And none bore a name, and no destinies were ordained;
Then were created the gods in the midst of heaven,
Lahmu and Lahamu were called into being...
Ages increased...[8]

In this poetic description we see that the Babylonian gods were essentially part of the basic (material) stuff of the universe, although in Babylonian mythology the very beginning seems to be shrouded in the mists of distant time, going back even further to Nammu, who was called the Lady of the gods, the mother who gave birth to the universe.

The Greeks had very similar ideas. Hesiod's work *Theogony* was written around the seventh century BC, though it probably drew on more ancient sources. He writes:

The race of venerable Gods, who rose From the beginning, whom the spacious Heaven And Earth produced ... [lines 64–66].

Ye Muses! Dwellers of the heavenly mount

From the beginning; say, who first arose?

First Chaos was: next ample-bosomed Earth [lines 164–66].

Third, in hollow depth .... The gloomy Tartarus. Love (Eros) then arose, Most beauteous of immortals ....
[lines 169, 171–2].

Werner Jaeger (1967, pages 16–17) draws out the profound difference between the Greek and Hebrew world-views:

If we compare this Greek hypostasis of the world-creative Eros with that of the Logos in the Hebrew account of creation, we may observe a deep-lying difference in the outlook of the two peoples. The Logos is a substantialization of an intellectual property or power of God the creator, who is stationed outside the world and brings that world into existence by his own personal fiat. The Greek gods are stationed inside the world; they are descended from Heaven and Earth ... they are generated by the mighty power of Eros who likewise belongs within the world as an all-engendering primitive force. Thus they are already subject to what we should call natural law... When Hesiod's thought at last gives way to truly philosophical thinking, the Divine is sought inside the world – not outside it, as in the Jewish Christian theology that develops out of the book of Genesis.

The key statement here is: "The Greek gods are stationed inside the world." We should not think that the only difference between the Hebrew and Greek world-view is that the Hebrews reduced the number of gods to one. Hebrew monotheism is not a slimmed-down version of pagan polytheism. The God of the Hebrews is *outside the world*. This is an absolute difference in category – not a mere difference in degree. It is also why, as we have already noted, the God of the Hebrews gives meaning to the world, whereas the pagan gods do not. The meaning of the system will not be found in the system.

This shows the flaw in an increasingly popular atheist argument. Addressing believers in the God of the Bible it says: "You are atheists with respect to Artemis, Baal, Diana, Wotan, Zeus, and thousands of other gods just like we are. We just go one god more."

This argument appeals to some because of its apparent cleverness, but what it fails to appreciate is the point we have just been making. The God of the Bible is not "just one god more" in the pantheon of all the gods available. Those are products of heaven and earth, whereas the God revealed in the Bible created heaven and earth. This difference is profound and annihilates the atheist argument.

We might sum up these ancient philosophies as follows:

- Matter is eternal and existed *before* the gods.

- In its basic state, matter was a formless, unorganized and boundless chaos.
- Some god imposed order and form on the basic stuff of the universe (cosmos), and this process is what is meant by creation.
- Even this god, like all the others, arose out of original matter, and is part of the stuff, or one of the forces, of the universe.
- Everything in the universe emanates out of this god, like sunbeams out of the sun; and so, in some sense, everything *is* god.

According to this view, matter is the primitive stuff of the universe and everything else, including the gods, derives from it. Indeed the Lady of the gods, Nammu, mentioned above, was sometimes described as a primeval sea out of which the gods emerged. The notion of a primeval soup is clearly far from new! In that sense, their philosophy was essentially naturalistic – indeed, materialistic. Many of their gods were deifications of the basic forces and instincts they found in nature. Their world-view was therefore at the opposite pole from the biblical world-view, which holds that it is not matter that is eternal and self-existent but God, who is Spirit. God is not derived. He created matter; it did not create him. Matter and everything else derive from him.

Materialistic reductionism is alive and well

Our immediate interest is how closely the thinking of Babylon parallels that of the contemporary world. The idea that mass-energy is primitive, and all else derives from it, is the essence of the materialistic reductionism that tries to dominate Western society. On this view, mass-energy is subject to the laws of nature (wherever they came from – a question that is easily forgotten, and needs to be addressed by materialists) and must have the latent capacity to produce all we see around us, including life, the human brain, the human mind and the idea of God – since on such a hypothesis God himself does not exist.

Is it not ironic that those who abolish God ascribe creative powers to blind, unguided material processes? Of course, in the closed world of the materialistic reductionist no alternative explanation is possible. As Harvard geneticist Richard Lewontin says, no divine foot must be allowed through the door:

> It is not that the methods and institutions of science somehow compel us to accept a material explanation of the phenomenal world but, on the contrary, that we are forced by our *a priori* adherence to material causes to create an apparatus of investigation and a set of concepts that produce material explanations, no matter how counterintuitive, no matter how mystifying to the uninitiated ... Moreover that materialism is absolute, for we cannot allow a Divine foot in the door.[9]

We should notice Lewontin's honesty here. He claims that his materialism is *a priori* – that is, he is a convinced believer in materialism before he does any science at all. Far from claiming that his materialism is derived from his science, he is openly prepared to bring his materialism to his science and allow the former to influence the latter.

So strong is this materialistic conviction on the part of many scientists that, even if they were to find evidence of superior intelligence in the universe, many of them would turn round and say that such intelligence cannot of course be supernatural – it must be natural intelligence, produced by mindless unguided natural forces like everything else. For instance, Paul Davies holds that the fine-tuning of the universe is evidence of the activity of some kind of superior intelligence. Picking up on the fact that the fundamental physical constants of the cosmos have to be set within unbelievably fine tolerance ranges in order for life to be possible, he writes (1988, page 203):

> It seems as though someone has fine-tuned nature's numbers to make the universe.... The impression of design is overwhelming.

Yet, when asked about the nature of that intelligence Davies holds that it is ultimately part of the stuff of the universe – that is, although it may be a superhuman intelligence, it is not supernatural. In his thinking here Davies appears not very far removed from the ancient Babylonians.

Understanding the surrounding world-view

At first glance, then, the world of Babylon seems remote from ours, but on reflection we see that there is a real sense in which Daniel faced a world-view very similar to the naturalism we face today; and, out of his deep loyalty to God, he was determined to set his face against it. We should take careful note, however, that Daniel did not protest against the education in the University of Babylon as such. He clearly devoted himself to it, and we can well imagine that he enjoyed his university course. He and his friends put such energy into the learning of the languages, literature, philosophy, science, economics, history, and so on, that they were star pupils and ended up with the top distinctions, far ahead of the rest. Daniel did not protest as an observer outside the system: he protested as a participant.

It is important to bear this in mind, not least when we hear the term "apocalyptic literature" being used in connection with the book of Daniel. This description tends to conjure up the idea of some wild and irrational prophet of doom, warning people to flee society, barricade themselves like monks or hermits against the world and await the imminent, all-engulfing cataclysm that marks the end of history. Well, if that is what "apocalyptic" means, it clearly does not apply to Daniel or his friends. We do not deny that Daniel has much to say about the future in his book, some of it bleak in its implications. But, far from leading him to run away from society and responsibility, the revelation he had of the future led him to live a very full professional life at the highest levels of administration in the empire. Daniel's understanding of God did not lead to his developing a ghetto mentality but to taking a full and prominent part in the life of Babylon.

It is important to realize at this juncture that Daniel's understanding did not represent a compromise position; it was thoroughly biblical. He was well acquainted with the writings of Jeremiah, a prophet who had not only predicted the Babylonian exile but had also written a letter to the leaders of the group of Jews that had been deported:

These are the words of the letter that Jeremiah the prophet sent from Jerusalem to the surviving elders of the exiles, and to the priests, the prophets, and all the people, whom Nebuchadnezzar had taken into exile from Jerusalem to Babylon. This was after King Jeconiah and the queen mother, the eunuchs, the officials of Judah and Jerusalem, the craftsmen, and the metal workers had departed from Jerusalem. The letter was sent by the hand of Elasah the son of Shaphan and Gemariah the son of Hilkiah, whom Zedekiah king of Judah sent to Babylon to Nebuchadnezzar king of Babylon. It said: "Thus says the Lord of hosts, the God of Israel, to all the exiles whom I have sent into exile from Jerusalem to Babylon: Build houses and live in them; plant gardens and eat their produce. Take wives and have sons and daughters; take wives for your sons, and give your daughters in marriage, that they may bear sons and daughters; multiply there, and do not decrease. But seek the welfare of the city where I have sent you into exile, and pray to the Lord on its behalf, for in its welfare you will find your welfare. For thus says the Lord of hosts, the God of Israel: Do not let your prophets and your diviners who are among you deceive you, and do not listen to the dreams that they dream, for it is a lie that they are prophesying to you in my name; I did not send them, declares the Lord.

"For thus says the Lord: When seventy years are completed for Babylon, I will visit you, and I will fulfil to you my promise and bring you back to this place. For I know the plans I have for you, declares the Lord, plans for wholeness and not for evil, to give you a future and a hope. Then you

will call upon me and come and pray to me, and I will hear you. You will seek me and find me. When you seek me with all your heart, I will be found by you, declares the Lord, and I will restore your fortunes and gather you from all the nations and all the places where I have driven you, declares the Lord, and I will bring you back to the place from which I sent you into exile." (Jeremiah 29:1–14.)

I have quoted enough of the letter to make it clear that Daniel was aware of its contents, since he quotes the prediction about the duration of the exile in Daniel 9. We do not know how early on he was aware of the full details of this message, but what is evident is that he acted completely in its spirit. Jeremiah's message is still valid for us, as we face the encroaching Babylon of our day. Indeed these words can be an immense support to young people leaving a Christian home to go to university. As ambassadors of our heavenly King we are encouraged to seek the welfare of the "city" – first in the university and then in the wider world.

We need to pause for a moment, for there will be those who say that a very different reaction to Babylon is given to us in Psalm 137:

By the waters of Babylon, there we sat down and wept, when we remembered Zion. On the willows there we hung up our lyres. For there our captors required of us songs, and our tormentors, mirth, saying, "Sing us one of the songs of Zion!" How shall we sing the Lord's song in a foreign land? If I forget you, O Jerusalem, let my right hand forget its skill! Let my tongue stick to the roof of my mouth, if I do not remember you, if I do not set Jerusalem above my highest joy!" (Psalm 137:1–6.)

Yes, it is a different reaction, but not incompatible with the message of the Lord through Jeremiah. There may well have been times when Daniel and his friends wept, and found it difficult to sing their songs with any enthusiasm. It would have been very strange if they had not. Apart from anything else, homesickness was as real then as it is today. Obedience to the message of Jeremiah did not mean having to forget Jerusalem and all that it stood for. Inevitably, many from Judah ended up doing just that; but Daniel and his friends did not forget their national and spiritual identity. They sought the wellbeing of Babylon by living in that city as salt and light for God. That stance involved sticking their heads above the parapet and protesting against the world-view that underlay the Babylonian system – and taking the consequences of doing so. It did not mean forgetting Jerusalem or never weeping over its fate.

The language of protest

What about us today? If we are convinced of the biblical world-view, should we not protest against the secularism that threatens to engulf us in the West? Should we not take action against the notion that atheism is the only intellectually respectable position? Of course we may do this. But if we do, we must use the language of protest with great care, for our world is all too full of violent and cruel protest that blights and destroys the lives of millions. We need constantly to remind ourselves (as we did in Chapter 3) that Christ prohibited the use of violence to impose truth – which is something that violence cannot do anyway.

The battle in which the Christian is involved – and it is a battle – is the same non-violent conflict of which Daniel's protest formed a part. This battle takes place in the thought-world: in the realm of ideas and world-views, not in the realm of military weaponry. The apostle Paul describes it as follows:

> For though we walk in the flesh, we are not waging war according to the flesh. For the weapons of our warfare are not of the flesh but have divine power to destroy strongholds. We destroy arguments and every lofty opinion raised against the knowledge of God, and take every thought captive to obey Christ.... (2 Corinthians 10:3–5.)

We notice that the emphasis here is on reasoned argument. Everywhere the early Christian apostles went they reasoned with the people. In the synagogues, the market places and, if they got a chance, in the academic lecture rooms of the world, they entered into dialogue (see Acts 17:2,17; 18:4; 19:9–10). The Greek word *apologia*, from which we get the word "apologist", simply means "defender". It is important to realize this, since in the New Testament no distinction is made between evangelism and apologetics: all evangelism involved the defence of the gospel. The early Christians were constantly meeting objections to their message. They were often misunderstood and accused of preaching political revolution, antinomian behaviour, or introducing foreign gods. And so, in order to clear a path for the gospel message, they had to remove the barriers in people's minds. They did this by engaging with them, answering their questions, and defending the Christian message against misunderstanding, misrepresentation, and vilification. Indeed, it was (and is) part of the convincing power of the Christian message that it gave credible answers. What these men and women were engaging in was "persuasive evangelism".[10] It is the essence of Christian witness to which we are also called.

A call to commitment

But, precisely because the battle is of this nature, serious preparation is necessary to enter it. We have already discussed the fundamental prerequisite – our loyalty to Jesus Christ, demonstrated by our deliberate resolve to set him apart in our hearts as Lord. But there is more; for not only is moral loyalty required, we need to develop intellectual and spiritual loyalty also.

It is perhaps easier to understand what we mean by moral loyalty, as we are all very much aware of the things that threaten moral integrity. But what is meant by intellectual and spiritual loyalty? Paul explains it to the Christians at Corinth as follows:

> *I feel a divine jealousy for you, for I betrothed you to one husband, to present you as a pure virgin to Christ. But I am afraid that as the serpent deceived Eve by his cunning, your thoughts will be led astray from a sincere and pure devotion to Christ. For if someone comes and proclaims another Jesus than the one we proclaimed, or if you receive a different spirit from the one you received, or if you accept a different gospel from the one you accepted, you put up with it readily enough. (2 Corinthians 11:2–4.)*

Paul was concerned with their intellectual and spiritual commitment to Christ. The imagery that he uses is eloquent. He speaks of betrothal: a relationship between a man and a woman that preceded marriage in the ancient world. It was much stronger than the modern equivalent of engagement. Betrothal was like marriage in the sense that it could only be dissolved by divorce. Before a woman was betrothed she could consider all prospective suitors; but once she had committed herself in betrothal – once she had "given her troth" – to let her eyes or heart wander to someone else would have been regarded as immoral. It would represent nothing less than disloyalty to her future husband.

The analogy is powerfully apt. The Christians in pluralist and polytheistic Corinth had given their lives to Christ. They had set him apart in their hearts as Lord and pledged their loyalty to him alone. At least, that is what they claimed. Paul was disturbed, however, by growing rumours that this loyalty was being undermined. Their loyalty had once been pure – that is to say, single in its focus, with Christ as its unique object. However, other voices that were not content with historic Christianity had begun to clamour for the attention of the Corinthian Christians, and some of them were allowing themselves to be seduced by these new and heady ideas.

All through history it has been the same. Sooner or later the innovators will move in, bringing with them their "reinterpretations" of the gospel. Their message will involve another Jesus – one stripped of uniqueness and deity, cut down to the level of all other teachers, however great they may be. Or, perhaps, another spirit – trying to fuse the gospel with animism or spiritism. Or another gospel, confused about the true basis of relationship with God that is through faith in Christ alone, perverting the truth by elevating human merit, and cashing in on it. Or twisting the message in the other direction, as a licence for immorality under the guise of "love". The list is long.

Today, in the name of tolerance, the uniqueness of Christ and many defining doctrines of Christianity are being attacked as never before. Under such pressure it is easy to begin to flirt with theological ideas that are disloyal to Christ. Many in the pew, pulpit, and theological college have been so overwhelmed with pseudo-scientific Enlightenment thinking that they have abandoned belief in the pre-existence of Christ, his supernatural conception, his miracles, resurrection, and ascension, and have retreated into a vague agnosticism.

We all need to give our intellectual and theological loyalty to Christ a regular health-check, and we can only do this by constantly exposing ourselves to the Bible. It is so easy to forget how Scripture got into our hands in the first place. John Wycliffe and William Tyndale laboured hard in dangerous conditions to give us the Bible in English. Betrayed by an Englishman, Tyndale was burnt alive in Belgium. Cranmer, Ridley, and Latimer were burnt alive in Oxford. These courageous men were determined to get the Scriptures to the people. Their efforts lit a fire in the hearts of men and women throughout the world, encouraging and inspiring even the humblest of them to study the Bible on their own and listen for the voice of God, rather than bow to some oppressive external ecclesiastic authority. What would they think if they were to see Bibles, now freely available by dint of their sacrificial labours, sitting unread on so many shelves?

We all love to stay in touch. That's why mobile phones now outnumber Bibles in the hands and pockets of Christians up and down the land (even allowing for the fact that phones have Bibles in them!). But however important it may be to hear from others, surely hearing from God is our priority. At least, that is one of the challenges of the life of Daniel.

CHAPTER 7

THE MANNER OF THE PROTEST
Daniel 1

The way in which Daniel went about his protest is a model for us. We again use Peter's statement to illuminate it:

Have no fear of them, nor be troubled, but in your hearts regard Christ the Lord as holy [or: "sanctify Christ in your hearts"], always being prepared to make a defence to anyone who asks you for a reason for the hope that is in you; yet do it with gentleness and respect, having a good conscience, so that, when you are slandered, those who revile your good behaviour in Christ may be put to shame. (1 Peter 3:14–16.)

The need for sensitivity

We focus now on the last part of Peter's statement, where he concentrates on the way in which we defend the message. We are to do it, he says, "with gentleness and respect". Daniel models this attitude exactly. He first speaks to Ashpenaz, the chief of the eunuchs at the court, who seems to have been a kind of administrative officer responsible for the students' wellbeing. Daniel asks for Ashpenaz's permission not to take the food. He does not suddenly bang the table in the dining hall and demand alternative food as a right (in the name of his religion, human rights, or anything else). He politely asks Ashpenaz in private.

The man is scared *and admits his fear to Daniel*. This is remarkable. The explanation is: "God gave Daniel favour and compassion" in the eyes of the official. We are not told, but we can be sure that Daniel had prayed about the situation. We can also be sure from what follows that Daniel had behaved in a friendly and respectful way towards the official and earned the man's trust. If we are to cut any ice with people we must similarly learn to be gentle and respectful towards them. It is sad that there are some Christians who seem to find these two things very difficult. It is worth analysing why that should be.

For some, the conviction that they "know the truth" produces in them an aggressive attitude that reeks of superiority and is very off-putting. They forget that the One about whom they profess to be witnessing – he who was the truth (John 14:6) – was the most gentle of men. He was *gentle and lowly in heart* (Matthew 11:29). But this clearly does not mean that he was a soppy, insipid, and spineless pushover. Christ was full of moral courage and authority, and showed (righteous) anger when necessary. But he was always courteous and respectful. Those of us who find it very difficult to respect or be gentle with those who disagree with us need to put a lot of effort into *learning* how to be like that.

How readily we forget that the man or woman to whom we are speaking is a creature, like ourselves, infinitely precious because they were made in the image of God. Indeed, that is part of the glory of the message we wish to convey to our fellow human beings. They are not mere random excrescences on the face of the universe but have a dignity given to them by God as their Creator. We fall on our faces at the first hurdle, then, if we do not mirror that dignity in our attitudes. We also want them to know that God loved the world – loved it in such a way that he actually gave his Son to die for it. It will scarcely help us to communicate that message if we convey it with an air of superiority or disdain. Our objective should be to befriend people as Jesus did – not simply to target potential converts. If I am not interested in a person as a person, it is understandable that they are not going to be interested in me or in my faith.

How then shall we approach others with true motivation? C. S. Lewis, as in so many things, is helpful on this point. He once suggested that if we want to know what love for someone looks like, we should ask ourselves what we would do if we loved the person – and then go and do it! It is the same with respect. We need to take time to think what we would do if we respected the person we are speaking to, and then do it. Rather than wait for our motives to be perfect, we do the right thing and let the motives sort themselves out.

It scarcely needs to be added that respecting others does not mean acting in such a way as to appear to condone all that they do. The Lord Jesus never condoned sin. He exposed it and brought it to the light but (and this is central) he did it in such a way that people who were genuinely repentant could understand that he was offering to freely forgive them. Jesus did not approve of the adultery of the woman who was dragged into his presence (John 8:1–11). He told her to go and sin no more and simultaneously offered her forgiveness and a way back to decency on the basis of her repentance and trust in him. But at the same time he exposed the hypocrisy in the hearts of those who were condemning her.

Take another example. The two men who were crucified with Christ were insurgents. Christ did not approve of their violence, yet he was gentle with the repentant terrorist. In his dying moments Christ assured him that he would, that day, be with him in paradise (Luke 23:39–43).

The sensitive way in which the Lord dealt with such people is uniquely magnificent. But does not something tell us that he has left footsteps for us to follow, however inadequately we may do so?

A quiet confidence

Ashpenaz did not simply tell Daniel that he was afraid. He trusted him enough to reveal the reason for his anxiety:

> *I fear my lord the king, who assigned your food and your drink; for why should he see that you were in worse condition than the youths who are of your own age? So you would endanger my head with the king. (Daniel 1:10.)*

Ashpenaz had been responsible for changing the names of Daniel and his friends, in accordance with Nebuchadnezzar's policy of making everyone look the same. This time Ashpenaz was afraid that Daniel would look worse than his peers, and that he would be held responsible. It is not now so much a question of identity but of image. Like many ancient cultures Babylon placed a premium on physical appearance. People, especially those seeking high office, not only had to be good, they had to look good. (Seem familiar?) What people look like can count more than what they have to say, even in the realm of politics and administration. Have they got the right image? If not, then can we produce enough spin to create the right image?

Ashpenaz lived long before the days of sophisticated spin-doctors, but he had a similar and serious responsibility to see that his charges presented well. It was clearly more than his life was worth to have Daniel not looking as physically fit as the others. He could not risk it. It never occurred to him that if he agreed to what Daniel suggested, there could be any other possible outcome. He knew of no other source of looking good than the food supplied by the king.

The matter might have ended there, but Daniel was not inclined to give in so easily. He could clearly see that there was no point in pressing Ashpenaz too hard, so he had a word with the more junior official whom Ashpenaz had assigned to the four students. Presumably this official knew what his boss had said to Daniel, yet he was sufficiently impressed with Daniel to listen to his proposal. Daniel suggested that, quietly and without fuss, they should conduct a controlled trial – the first we read of in history. The test was that they should eat simple food consisting only of vegetables for a limited period of ten days. The steward should then act according to what he saw. The trial was successful, and there was evidence of a marked difference in the appearance of the four. They actually looked better now than the students who were eating the royal food, and they were allowed to continue with this basic diet.

Daniel's conviction that he must honour God irrespective of the consequences is impressive, but so also is the sensitive way in which he went about his protest. Daniel understood the responsibilities of the officials and what their fears were, and he was careful to respect their feelings. He gave the junior official space to collect evidence that there was truth in what he said. It took courage to do that, and God honoured him and his friends for it.

There is a simple but important lesson here for us. Daniel took time. He was not in a frantic hurry, and he was sensitive to others' need for space. We sometimes forget that the Christian message is very strange and new to many people. It contains ideas with which they are not familiar, and we need to give them space to assimilate them. It is so easy, by the sheer quantity of our arguments, to make interested people feel that they are being crowded out. We must give people space to breathe, or we shall only put them off – and the fault will be ours.

How good will we look? Isn't that one of the pressures that can affect our willingness to stand up for our faith and be counted? I can well remember when this was first brought home to me. There was one occasion while I was a student when I found myself at a dinner, seated beside a Nobel Laureate. I tried, as best I knew at the time, to engage him in a discussion about the reality of God. After dinner he invited me, together with some of his professorial colleagues, to his room for coffee. I was the only student present and the atmosphere was intimidating, to say the least. When we were more or less settled (less in my case) he asked me whether or not I should like to make a serious career in science. "Yes sir," I replied. "Then give up these childish ideas of God," he said. "They will only disadvantage you intellectually among your peers."

It was a defining moment. I asked him what he had to offer as a rational explanation for the universe and its laws, as an alternative to God. He surprised me then by trying to explain that some kind of "life force" was responsible. I had thought that such thinking was dead. I tried to gently point out that this appeared to me much less rational than what I already believed. I was summarily dismissed.

The pressure is mounting today. If you are going to look good, from the point of view of many scientists and those who follow them, then you had better be an atheist. A brilliant Oxford biology student told me that her teachers had said as much to her. They told her that any world-view convictions she had would only hinder her science.

As if their own atheism is not a world-view! The New Atheists call themselves the "Brights" (Dan Dennett's term) – the implication being that the rest of us are dull.

If you are going to look tolerant these days, you will be informed that you cannot afford to confess publicly that Jesus Christ is *the way, and the truth, and the life* (John 14:6). You must recognize that all religions are equally valid ways of searching for some kind of ultimate reality: God, gods, or whatever. A global village cannot afford to be divided by claims to absolute truth. And so on and so on…

It is, therefore, increasingly difficult to avoid the marginalization that results from stepping out of the politically correct line. It can be an expensive business. Daniel and his friends were prepared to pay whatever the cost in order to maintain God as their supreme value.

We read that God honoured them, and not only in their improved physical appearance: he gave them learning and skill in all wisdom and literature. In addition, Daniel turned out to be specially gifted in understanding visions and dreams – a gift that would soon be put to the test. When Nebuchadnezzar personally examined them at the end of the three-year intensive course, Ashpenaz must have been proud to see that his charges were at the very top of the class. In fact, the emperor found them ten times better than anyone else in all of the empire. They were clearly destined for prominence.

It would be a mistake, however (possibly a painful one), to think that this story somehow guarantees that if we honour God in our witness he will make us into intellectual and administrative geniuses like Daniel and his friends. It is perfectly true that God gave *them* their ability. That is what God did for four particular people at that time. It is no guarantee that he will do the same for us in our time. He had a very special role for them to fulfil, and he also has one for us. Just as God equipped them for their role, so he will equip us for ours; but those roles may be very different. In Christian terms: as it pleased him, God has set us in the great body of Christ, that organic unity that is the church. Each of us has a different function. All those functions are equally necessary and valuable, although not all are so obvious (see 1 Corinthians 12:1–26). We must learn to be content with the significance that God gives us, like Abraham did (as we saw in our study of the ideology of Babylon); and contentment comes when we understand that it has pleased God to make us just as we are.

The first stage of Daniel's account is now complete. He and his friends have set their compass bearing on God. The rest of the book will tell us how that initial resolve developed into the established habit of a lifetime.

CHAPTER 8

THE LOGICAL STRUCTURE OF DANIEL

Now that we have seen some of the themes that introduce Daniel's work, we should pause to survey the book as a whole in order to get some idea of how it is constructed. This will give us a sense of the thought flow and momentum of the book and therefore help get its living message into our minds and hearts.

When compared with the work of great prophets like Isaiah and Jeremiah, the book is relatively short. It is unique in biblical literature in that it was written in two languages. A short section in Hebrew is followed by a long section in Aramaic and finally another section in Hebrew. Aramaic was a *lingua franca* at that time, and would have been accessible therefore to many more people than Hebrew, which was much more localized in its use. Perhaps Daniel had different kinds of readers in mind. We can only speculate. At least we can see that the Aramaic section contains a remarkable statement written in the first person by the emperor Nebuchadnezzar. It tells how he came to acknowledge the existence and power of the one true God, and to worship him. The availability in writing of the emperor's testimony would have been very useful to the exiles in their witness to God among the nations.

In my comments on the structure of the book of Daniel a central role is played by the seminal article by Professor D. W. Gooding MRIA.[11] We can gain some idea of what is in the book as a whole by making a simple list of its contents.

TABLE OF CONTENTS OF THE BOOK OF DANIEL

1. Daniel refuses the king's food.
2. Nebuchadnezzar's dream image.

3. Nebuchadnezzar's golden image: three men in the fiery furnace.

4. Discipline and restoration of Nebuchadnezzar.

5. Judgment of Belshazzar: end of Babylon's imperial power.

6. Daniel refuses to pray to King Darius: Daniel in the den of lions.

7. Daniel's vision of four animals.

8. Daniel's vision of two animals.

9. Jeremiah's prophecy about Jerusalem: Daniel's prayer.

10. The writing of truth: the time of the end.

Thus there would appear to be ten main sections to Daniel's work. The first nine of them correspond to the chapter divisions that have been made (much later) in our translations, and the tenth comprises the rest of the book, as it is obvious that chapters 10–12 form one literary unit.

What sense do they make as a whole? The first six sections appear to be in chronological order, but the seventh and eighth go back again to the reign of Belshazzar, so the order of the material is not uniformly chronological. There are, of course, many different ways of ordering material: chronologically, geographically, thematically, and so on, and each of them is logical in its own way. So we need to ask what logical considerations might have been in Daniel's mind as he put his material together.

As we look at our table of contents, a pattern begins to emerge which functions as a kind of skeleton or scaffolding supporting the logic and thought flow of the argument. It shows the connections between the series of issues that Daniel had selected. The sections readily group themselves in the following way.

The book starts with a court scene in Babylon, the main incident being the account of Daniel and his friends' refusal to eat the royal food in King's College. The next two sections concern images of enormous proportions: the huge dream image that Nebuchadnezzar saw is followed by the colossal actual image that he built. The first image had a head of gold, which is interpreted to be Nebuchadnezzar himself; and the second image was made altogether of gold.

The next two sections concern God's discipline of two kings. First, Nebuchadnezzar is cut down because of his pride. Something touches his mind and for seven years he behaves in a deranged fashion, more like an animal than a human. Yet he is eventually restored to his power and glory. Second, God judges Belshazzar for using the golden vessels from the temple of God to drink to the gods of the Babylonians at his feast. The supernatural, terrifying writing on the wall condemns him. He is killed that very night by the invading Medo-Persian army. The imperial power of Babylon is brought to a dramatic end. There is no restoration.

The fall of Babylon is clearly a major climax in the thought flow of the book, marking the end of the first half. This is confirmed by two other considerations.

1. Nebuchadnezzar features in each of the first five chapters: in the first four directly, as one of the *dramatis personae*; in the fifth indirectly, as Daniel reminds Belshazzar that his judgment will be final because he knows that God has spoken to Nebuchadnezzar (as recorded in the preceding sections) and yet he has not repented. Nebuchadnezzar is a common theme therefore, uniting the first five chapters – suggesting, incidentally, that it might be useful to look through his eyes at what happened.

2. The golden vessels that Nebuchadnezzar took from the temple of God in Jerusalem are mentioned in chapter 1 and reappear centre-stage in chapter 5. We have seen how they have to do with questions of values, so values are clearly important in chapters 1 and 5. But values also form one of the main themes in the intervening chapters. The dream image in chapter 2 is made of metals of decreasing value, starting with gold. The image of chapter 3 is made entirely of gold. Chapter 4 has to do with Nebuchadnezzar's values, in particular his pride in the glory and magnificence of his great city of Babylon. Thus, the theme of values runs through the first five chapters, and

the two references to the golden vessels serve to bracket them all together. It would seem reasonable, therefore, to take them as a main theme to the first half of the book.

On looking at the contents of these chapters once more, we see that they follow a simple pattern:

Court scene: administration in Babylon;
Two images;
Two kings disciplined.

If we turn now to the second half of the book, we can discern a similar pattern.

1. There is another court scene. It is in the Medo-Persian court, after the transfer of power in Babylon. Like the first court scene in chapter 1, chapter 6 focuses on a refusal. This time it is Daniel's refusal to cease praying to God, and to pray instead to the emperor Darius.

2. That section is followed by two visions of strange animals that Daniel had seen earlier, during the reign of Belshazzar. And, finally, we have what we might describe as two writings explained to us. The first is the writing of the prophet Jeremiah, regarding the duration of the captivity in Babylon, which Daniel had been studying from the scrolls in his library. The second is what Daniel calls *the writing of truth*. This was something specially revealed to him by God about the unrolling of history, future to his time.

Thus the second half of the book looks like this:

Court scene: administration in Medo-Persia;
Two visions of animals;
Two writings explained.

Putting the two halves of the book side by side and adding a little more detail, we have this table of contents:

PART A	PART B
Chapter 1	Chapter 6
Babylonian Court.	**Medo-Persian Court.**
Daniel refuses to eat the king's food.	Daniel refuses to obey the king's command and refrain from praying to God.
He and his friends are vindicated.	He is vindicated.
TWO IMAGES	**TWO VISIONS OF BEASTS**
Chapter 2	Chapter 7
Nebuchadnezzar's dream image.	Four beasts.
Chapter 3	Chapter 8
Nebuchadnezzar's golden image.	Two beasts.
TWO KINGS DISCIPLINED	**TWO WRITINGS EXPLAINED**
Chapter 4	Chapter 9
The discipline and restoration of Nebuchadnezzar.	The prophecy in the book of Jeremiah about the destruction and restoration of Jerusalem.
Chapter 5	Chapters 10–13
The "writing on the wall" and the destruction of Belshazzar.	The "Writing of Truth" and the eventual destruction of "the king".
The end of Babylonian supremacy.	The end of world history.

On the surface there appears to be a symmetrical structure to the book; but pattern or structure on its own is not enough. Perceived structure has credibility only if there is evidence that it helps to carry the thought flow. The significance of the structure, therefore, will gradually emerge as we get down to the detail of the book. (A more detailed thought flow is given in Appendix C, while readers who are interested in the technical details and implications of structures of this kind may also refer to the article by D. W. Gooding.)

CHAPTER 9

DREAMS AND REVELATIONS
Daniel 2

We noted above that Nebuchadnezzar is explicitly mentioned in each of the first five chapters of the book of Daniel. Chapter 4 is actually written by him and describes how he came to faith in Daniel's God. In chapter 5 Belshazzar is disciplined by God because, in spite of knowing what had happened to Nebuchadnezzar, he had deliberately turned away from the true God.

Thus, part of the thought flow of chapters 1–4 is the dawning of the reality of God on the mind and heart of the emperor, leading to his "conversion". As we come to the end of the first chapter Nebuchadnezzar is simply aware that he has four remarkably able young graduates entering his service. He can see that they are streets ahead of the others intellectually, but he does not know yet why this is so.

That is all about to change, because Nebuchadnezzar is going to discover that a source of knowledge exists to which even his brightest and most experienced experts have no access. In short, he is about to find out that there is a God in heaven who can reveal the secrets of men and women, and what is to come. So, as its major theme, chapter 2 addresses the question: is there such a thing as revelation? It goes without saying that Daniel's affirmative answer to that question constitutes a major challenge to contemporary secularism, in its atheistic insistence that the universe is a closed system of cause and effect.

Revelation and the dating of the book of Daniel

The dating of the book of Daniel has been a matter of considerable controversy. One reason for that bears directly on this issue of revelation. Daniel made predictions about what would happen in subsequent centuries, and it turns out that he got it right.

That should not seem completely "off the wall", even to those who do not believe in God. After all, many of us have read George Orwell's *1984*, Aldous Huxley's *Brave New World*, and Alvin Toffler's *Future Shock*. We find these books interesting because the authors got some of the future right. So what is the problem with Daniel? Some people are of the opinion that he got too much of it right!

According to his book, Daniel lived to see that dramatic turning point in history, the end of the Babylonian empire and its replacement by the Medo-Persian empire. After Daniel's time that empire was in turn succeeded by the vast Greek empire of Alexander the Great. After Alexander's death his empire was split among four of his generals.

Daniel outlines this and the subsequent history of the Hellenistic period in the last section of his book, particularly in chapter 11. Although he does not name the characters, he gives a great number of accurate details of the complex relationships between the northern kingdom of the Seleucids and the southern kingdom of the Ptolemies. He then concentrates on the activities of one Seleucid emperor who is easily recognizable as Antiochus IV "Epiphanes". By comparing what Daniel said with later historical records of the Hellenistic period, it is not hard to see that Daniel got the details right.

But then comes the crunch. Some scholars argue that there was absolutely no way the author of the book of Daniel could have known such twists and turns of historical detail, unless he had lived after the events he records. Therefore the book must have been written – or completed – no earlier than the second century BC. The detail given in the text is just not the kind of information that he could have guessed, however brilliant he was. And, as these scholars deny revelation, there was no other possible source of information. They do not believe that any source of knowledge exists that could accurately supply details of the course of world events in advance. Jerome and Augustine tell us that this later dating of the book of Daniel was first advanced by a third-century opponent of Christianity, the writer Porphyry of Tyre, who was a disciple of the neo-Platonic philosopher Plotinus. The Christian response from Methodius (Jerome, translation 1958, pages 15–16) is interesting:

> And because Porphyry saw that all these things had been fulfilled and could not deny that they had taken place, he overcame this evidence of historical accuracy by taking refuge in this evasion, contending that whatever is foretold concerning Antichrist at the end of the world was actually fulfilled in the reign of Antiochus Epiphanes, because of certain similarities to things that took place at his time. But this very attack testifies to Daniel's accuracy. For so striking was the reliability of what the prophet foretold, that he could not appear to unbelievers as a predictor of the future, but rather a narrator of things already past.

The view that dates Daniel specifically to the time of the Maccabees gained ground with the rise of higher criticism and the anti-supernaturalism of the Enlightenment. (This view is also held by some scholars who do believe that God could have given Daniel prophetic information in the sixth century but who, for theological reasons, question whether God did do it. Of course it is obvious that the book itself claims that God did do it.)

One of the central areas of philosophy is epistemology: how do we know what we know, and what is our warrant for claiming to know it? Scholars who subscribe to a naturalistic epistemology are bound to come to the conclusion that Daniel wrote after the fact. However, we can – and must – question the validity of their naturalistic presuppositions – not least because the book of Daniel itself questions these presuppositions. Modern scholars in the rationalist tradition were not the first to think of the issue at stake here. No less than the emperor of Babylon thought of it long ago; and it is considered in the first part of Daniel 2. It is a delightful irony that Daniel himself discusses the very question that would eventually cause a storm regarding the dating of his book.

We shall return to the issue of the dating of the book of Daniel more than once before we are finished.

Revealing and interpreting the king's dream

The story goes like this. Daniel and his friends were not long into their careers in the Babylonian civil service when something very dramatic occurred. At first it looked as if it might lead to their execution, though it actually ended with them all being catapulted into the public eye and receiving unprecedented promotion to very high office. It started with a dream that Nebuchadnezzar had. Like any ancient oriental he took his dreams very seriously and he employed a special team of experts, mainly from the Imperial Institute of Futurology in the university, to interpret them for him. They were his think-tank: his political, economic, social, and religious forecasters. He was normally quite satisfied with their explanations. After all, it was not for nothing that they were trained in diplomacy, an essential discipline when you work in an absolute monarchy where your emperor does precisely what he wants. *Those the king wanted to put to death, he put to death ... those he wanted to promote, he promoted* (Daniel 5:19 NIV). These men were understandably skilled at giving him what he wanted.

This time it was very different. When the advisors entered the vast throne room in the palace, their immediate concern was that the imperial face looked grim. One can almost detect an unconscious reaching of hands to necks, as if to ensure that their heads were still firmly fixed in the right place. The emperor came straight to the point. "Gentlemen," he said, "I have had a dream. It troubles me deeply and I wish to know what it means."

"Of course, your Majesty," they replied. "Just tell us the dream, and we will interpret it."

These advisors passionately believed in the power of the human mind to study historical movements, economic developments, and cultural shifts in order to be able to give some sort of advice to the emperor regarding the future. Their ancestors who founded Babel also believed in it, and their counterparts are to be found in virtually every nation today. They were the brightest men that Nebuchadnezzar had; and of course they were prepared to have a go at interpreting the emperor's dream. All he had to do was to tell them what the dream was. After all, isn't the business of interpreting all about being supplied with data of whatever kind and giving your expert opinion on its significance?

"No," said the emperor, "I will not tell you the dream. I expect you to tell me the dream and to interpret it." They were stunned. He was not going to give them the data. Nothing like it had ever happened before. Nebuchadnezzar might have been an autocrat, and expected a lot from his advisors, but he paid them well, and he was not usually unreasonable. There was no time now to wonder why Nebuchadnezzar should suddenly depart from his usual form. He was waiting for their answer. With exaggerated politeness, driven by sickening fear, once more they asked him to tell them the dream. In a desperate attempt to get him to be reasonable, they pointed out that their records showed that no emperor had ever expected his advisors to tell him the contents of a dream as well as the interpretation. They finished their appeal by saying that this kind of information was possessed by the gods, whose dwelling place was not with human beings. They were forced into the embarrassing position of having to admit that they had no access to the world of the gods.

> The thing that the king asks is difficult, and no one can show
> it to the king except the gods, whose dwelling is not with flesh.
> (Daniel 2:11.)

It was a very telling admission. Many of these advisors would surely have been senior priests in the many temples scattered around Babylon. They were supposed to be in touch with the gods, and have access to information that was inaccessible to normal human minds. After all, that was what they were handsomely paid for. It would seem that Nebuchadnezzar had finally decided to test them.

He wanted to see for himself if there was anything in their claim to have contact with the divine and be able to get secret information from that source. He caught them out big time.

Now we should remember that Daniel and his friends were among this group of experts, though at what level we do not know at this stage. And we have just learned that they were ten times better than the others. "Better" is a relative term, so let's ask ourselves a question. As a tool for gaining knowledge, is relative brilliance all there is? Some people are brighter than others, and they will make a better guess than others. Is there nothing more? Clearly the Babylonian experts did not believe there was. As we shall see, Daniel and his friends did not agree with them.

Nebuchadnezzar's top Babylonian advisors did not believe there was such a thing as revelation. Their gods did not communicate with humans; their epistemology was naturalistic. Their views were no different in essence from the views of scholars who think that Daniel could not have written his book in the sixth century BC because he could not have had access then to information about events that had not yet occurred. Such scholars do not believe in the category of revelation either. Their universe is that of the naturalist, or possibly even the materialist: a closed system of cause and effect undisturbed by the supernatural. Their epistemology is that of the Enlightenment.

I can imagine that nothing concentrates the mind, or sets the adrenalin flowing, like suddenly being informed that you are going to be executed. It was Arioch, the captain of the Palace Guard, who came to execute Daniel and his friends. Daniel was able to control his reaction and calm Arioch sufficiently to discuss with him why the execution order had been issued. This is impressive. The very fact that Daniel caused Arioch to delay shows the tact with which he must have spoken. After all, Daniel was probably still on his way up in the civil-service ranking. He may have had a reputation for brilliant insight, but why should Arioch pause for a minute to listen to him? Yet he did.

It would seem that Daniel was one of those men that people listen to. One can guess that this was not the first time he and Arioch had met. The willingness of these senior men (Ashpenaz earlier, and now Arioch) to speak to Daniel is evidence that he was a good listener. Perhaps we need to take a leaf out of his book. In the business of communicating what we believe, we can be so full of what we want to say that we never listen to anyone else. Why then should we be surprised that they show no particular interest in listening to us?

Daniel was able to persuade Arioch to delay the killing of the Babylonian experts. He requested an audience with the emperor (possibly through Arioch, though we are not told). The striking thing is that Daniel initiated this appointment without yet having the information that the king requested. It would be revealed to Daniel later that same night, but he did not know that at the time. He committed himself to providing the answer. Where did he get the assurance from, to send such a confident message to the emperor? He does not tell us, but he must surely have had an inner conviction that one of his peculiar gifts, the ability to understand dreams, was about to be used at the highest level of state.

What we do know is that he immediately made the matter known to his friends and asked them to pray to God for mercy. There is something very moving about this. Here are four captive students, alone in ancient Iraq, daring to believe not only that there is a God in heaven but also that he is sufficiently interested in them to communicate with them and answer their prayer. It was the first student prayer meeting recorded in history.

It would not be the last. Around the world today in all kinds of educational establishments there are many such groups of friends, praying that they will be empowered to witness to their contemporaries about their faith in the living God who has revealed himself in Jesus Christ his Son. We thank God for them. Many who read these words will be deeply indebted spiritually to such groups. Who knows where some of us (myself included) would have ended up without their faithfulness? We need to pray for them, and to support and encourage such groups wherever they are to be found. They are God's outposts in the university. As we see from this story, they can be very effective.

The prayers of Daniel and his friends were far from pious play-actors. The emperor had to be faced. They would all die if they could not answer him convincingly. They would all die if there were no such thing as revelation. They would all die if there were no such thing as a wisdom that came from above. They would all die if God did not speak.

He is There and He is not Silent is the title of a book by Francis Schaeffer. It fits this situation exactly. In that night God spoke to Daniel. When morning came he knew exactly what Nebuchadnezzar had dreamed, and what it meant. He knew what he needed to say to the king.

Reason and revelation

The story of Nebuchadnezzar and his dream also raises the question of the relationship between reason and revelation. Atheist thinkers often pit these against each other, as if revelation was anti-reason. Our story here shows that this is false. Reason and revelation are not even in the same category. Think of it on the human level first of all. The Babylonian advisors were prepared to use their reason on any data presented to them. Their problem was that Nebuchadnezzar was not prepared to reveal to them what he had dreamed. If he had been prepared to reveal it to them they would not have abandoned their reason; but they would have used it on the new data (the content of the dream as *revealed* to them by Nebuchadnezzar) in order to try to interpret it. In the very nature of the situation, however, their unaided reason could not produce that data. Only revelation by the emperor could do that.

At this juncture Daniel stepped in. He knew that Nebuchadnezzar was not prepared to reveal the content of the dream. But Daniel believed that there was a God who knew not only the content of the dream but its meaning. He also believed that, if he so desired, God could reveal that information to him. So now the story advances the concept of revelation one level deeper. It is not human revelation now, but divine.

However, the same principle applies. When God revealed the matter to Daniel this did not suspend his use of reason. Daniel had to use his reason to understand the words God said to him, and to formulate his response to Nebuchadnezzar. In turn the emperor had to use his reason to grasp that Daniel not only knew the content of the dream, but that his interpretation made sense.

These distinctions are so important that it is worth illustrating them further. When a crime is committed Hercule Poirot investigates the crime scene and uses his "little grey cells" on what he sees. But an equally (if not more) important part of his enquiry consists in talking to people. There he is dependent on what they are prepared to reveal to him. If they do not speak, he will not know. If they speak, he will again use his little grey cells to process what they say. It is perfectly obvious that reason operates in both situations, even though in the second situation reason must be assisted by revelation; and revelation produces information that unaided reason cannot access. To say that reason and revelation are antithetic does not even rise to the dignity of being false. It simply doesn't make sense – it is a confusion of categories, as the philosophers say.

It is possible, however, that when the sceptics say that reason and revelation are antithetical, what they actually mean is that there is no reason to believe in revelation. Our story says otherwise. When Daniel related the content of the dream to Nebuchadnezzar in all of its detail, Nebuchadnezzar had all the evidence he needed to believe in revelation. That belief was warranted, since there was no way, apart from divine revelation, that Daniel could have known what thoughts had gone through the king's mind while he dreamed. Nebuchadnezzar now had strong reason to take seriously the claim that God had given Daniel the interpretation. But that did not mean that Nebuchadnezzar would be uncritical – he would also use his reason to see if the proffered interpretation made sense. And so can we, since the whole account lies before us.

Before we do that, let us notice that our story gets to the essence of one important aspect of biblical prophecy. The apostle Peter, writing to Christians towards the end of his life (2 Peter 1:14), is at pains to stress to them that there is another world apart from this one: there is a real eternal dimension. Peter recalls the momentous experience he had when, along with James and John, he witnessed the transfiguration of Jesus on a mountain in Galilee. On that occasion the three disciples had seen Jesus' face shine more powerfully than the eastern sun at midday. They had seen Moses and Elijah talking with Jesus, and heard a voice from God in heaven saying, *This is my beloved Son, with whom I am well pleased; listen to him* (Matthew 17:5). That experience convinced Peter of the fact that this is not the only world. There is a "higher" realm, just as real as this one, where Christ is not despised but he is the kingly source of light and power. The implications are clear: life invested for Christ is not a waste, as some may think.

Peter knew, of course, that he was uniquely privileged to have been with Christ on that occasion. What about the vast majority of Christ's disciples, who were not there? How could they – how can we – be convinced that Christ's eternal kingdom is no delusion? Peter's answer is framed in terms of the nature and purpose of prophecy:

> *And we have something more sure, the prophetic word, to which you will do well to pay attention as to a lamp shining in a dark place, until the day dawns and the morning star rises in your hearts, knowing this first of all, that no prophecy of Scripture comes from someone's own interpretation. For no prophecy was ever produced by the will of man, but men spoke from God as they were carried along by the Holy Spirit.* (2 Peter 1:19–21.)

Let us take the nature of prophecy first. Peter explains, *No prophecy of Scripture comes from someone's own interpretation.* That means that biblical prophecy is not a product of private analysis. It is not like the forecasts of the Babylonian, or any other, think tank, where clever people use their ability and expertise in analysing data of all kinds to give some idea of what to expect. Daniel was a very bright person, but his information about Nebuchadnezzar's dream (and many other things) came from God. It was Daniel who spoke to Nebuchadnezzar, of course: his personality was not overridden. But there was more to it. Daniel *spoke from God.* According to Peter, he was borne along by the Holy Spirit. As an inspired apostle of Christ, Peter authoritatively tells us that prophecy had a supernatural dimension, and that it is of major importance that we take this on board. Here is his critical emphasis: *knowing this first of all…*

Why is Peter so concerned that in our Christian knowing (our epistemology in that sense) we should prioritize the conviction that God actually spoke through the prophets? His answer has to do with the purpose of prophecy. He tells us that, as a source of light, the prophetic word (the book of Daniel included) is to be regarded as even *more sure* than the transfiguration experience. It was given to generate in us an awareness of the reality of Christ's eternal kingdom, so that we should invest our lives in it. Through the prophets we are meant to hear the voice of God, authenticating itself and leaving us in no doubt that the transcendent and eternal is no less substantial than the material.

Under the pressure of secular naturalism it is relatively easy for Christians to lose sight of the very meaning of their name – "those who believe in Christ". Indeed, such is the confusion that some people (in the UK) think that "Christian" simply means "decent". However, the word "Christ" is a Greek translation of "Messiah" (the Anointed One), and the fundamental Christian confession is that *Jesus is the Christ, the Son of God* (John 20:31). That is, a Christian believes that Jesus is the One whose coming was announced by the prophets and became the centre of Jewish hope for centuries. The prophets claimed supernatural inspiration for their predictions that the Messiah would come – they claimed to be speaking the word of God.

The supernatural origin of biblical prophecy

In other words, the fulfilment of (supernatural) prophecy lies at the heart of what Christianity is. To claim to be a Christian and not to take it seriously is a contradiction in terms. Yet, in my experience, many professing Christians seem somewhat embarrassed by this dimension to their faith. In part this is an understandable result of certain dogmatic interpretations of prophecy (not least the book of Daniel) that have subsequently proved embarrassingly erroneous. Clearly the interpretation of prophecy is an area fraught with potential difficulty, but we should not allow that to detract us from seeing that Christianity is thoroughly embedded in history and prophecy. Many of its central events, including the crucifixion and resurrection of Christ, were the subject of predictions made centuries earlier. In fact, Christ was crucified for claiming to be the Son of Man (Matthew 26:64), predicted by Daniel, who would one day come on the clouds of heaven (Daniel 7:13). He also told them frequently that he would be rejected by the religious leaders of his day, be crucified, and subsequently he would rise from the dead (see, for example, Matthew 16:21). These predictions and their fulfilment are part of the evidence that Jesus is the Son of God.

I am only too well aware that contemporary culture in the West is so dominated by the naturalistic world-view that anyone who claims there is a supernatural dimension to reality is looked at askance, even mocked. When I mentioned the resurrection at the culmination of my God Delusion debate with Richard Dawkins in Alabama, he responded in amazement at what he thought was my utter naivety. "So we come down to the resurrection of Jesus Christ. It's so petty; it's so trivial; it's so local; it's so earthbound; it's so unworthy of the universe."

Richard Dawkins' view is that we have a simple choice. Either we believe in miracles (and things like biblical prophecy), or we believe in the scientific understanding of the laws of nature, but not both. For him, of course, the latter is by definition the only option for the intelligent person. He writes (2006, page 187):

> The nineteenth century is the last time when it was possible
> for an educated person to admit to believing in miracles
> like the virgin birth without embarrassment. When pressed,
> many educated Christians today are too loyal to deny the
> virgin birth and the resurrection. But it embarrasses them
> because their rational minds know that it is absurd, so they
> would much rather not be asked.

He would feel the same about biblical prophecy.

However, his statement is false – patently and inexcusably so. There were many educated people in the twentieth century, and there are many in the twenty-first, who wholeheartedly believe in the resurrection of Jesus without embarrassment. I am happy to be one of them. Furthermore, my rational mind tells me that, for an educated person who values the scientific understanding of the universe, it is not belief in the virgin birth and the resurrection that is absurd. It is the atheistic world-view that is absurd, because it negates the validity of the very rationality we need in order to do science. Indeed, having debated with Richard Dawkins twice in public, discussed biblical miracles with him once on the air, and spent much time analysing his arguments, I find myself more than ever convinced of the truth of the resurrection of Jesus, and of the truth of biblical prophecy concerning him.[12]

The vociferousness of the New Atheists does not alter the fact, as Keith Ward points out (Ward, 2008), that their vaunted naturalism is still a minority world-view – even among philosophers.

Returning now to the issue that precipitated this discussion – the dating of Daniel – it is important to record that the challenge to the late dating of Daniel does not depend only on questioning the naturalistic presupposition that lies behind it. There is historical evidence arising from the discovery of the Dead Sea Scrolls at Qumran that supports the early date.

Gerhard Hasel, a leading authority on the Scrolls, writes:

> Inasmuch as Daniel was already canonical at Qumran
> at about 100 BC, how could it have become so quickly
> canonical if it had just been produced a mere half century
> before? While we do not know exactly how long it took for
> books to become canonical, it may be surmised that insofar
> as Daniel was reckoned to belong to the canonical books,
> it had a longer existence than a mere five decades, as the
> Maccabean dating hypothesis suggests. Both the canonical
> status and the fact that Daniel was considered a "prophet"
> speak for the antiquity of the book of Daniel. An existence
> of a mere five decades between the production of a Biblical

book in its final form and canonization does not seem reasonable.[13]

Thus the canonical acceptance of the book of Daniel at Qumran suggests an earlier origin of the book than the second century BC. In 1969, based on the evidence available at that time regarding the Qumran Daniel texts, Roland K. Harrison had already concluded (1969, page 1127) that the second-century dating of the book of Daniel was

> absolutely precluded by the evidence from Qumran, partly
> because there are no indications whatever that the sectaries
> compiled any of the Biblical manuscripts recovered from
> the site, and partly because there would, in the latter event,
> have been insufficient time for Maccabean compositions
> to be circulated, venerated, and accepted as canonical
> Scripture by a Maccabean sect.

Subsequent to this he stated that, based on the Qumran manuscripts, "there can no longer be any possible reason for considering the book as a Maccabean product".[14] The most recent publications of Daniel manuscripts confirm this conclusion.

We shall see in due course that Daniel's retelling and explanation of Nebuchadnezzar's dream will also have something to say even to a sceptical audience. But first let us pause to consider Daniel's response to the revelation of the dream. He was so deeply moved by the fact that God had deigned to speak to him that he records his prayer of joyful praise and thanksgiving:

> *Blessed be the name of God for ever and ever, to whom belong*
> *wisdom and might. He changes times and seasons; he removes*
> *kings and sets up kings; he gives wisdom to the wise and*
> *knowledge to those who have understanding; he reveals deep*
> *and hidden things; he knows what is in the darkness, and*
> *the light dwells with him. To you, O God of my fathers, I*
> *give thanks and praise, for you have given me wisdom and*

might, and have now made known to me what we asked of
you, for you have made known to us the king's matter. (Daniel
2:20–23.)

This is a prayer of gratitude to God, who is the source of wisdom, for the gift of wisdom. It is echoed in the New Testament, where the apostle James speaks of the same resource:

If any of you lacks wisdom, let him ask of God, who gives
generously to all without reproach, and it will be given him.
But let him ask in faith, with no doubting, for the one who
doubts is like a wave of the sea that is driven and tossed
by the wind. For that person must not suppose that he will
receive anything from the Lord; he is a double-minded man,
unstable in all his ways. (James 1:5–8.)

The content of the wisdom Daniel received is important. He learned that God *changes times and seasons*. At first sight this is a strange expression. However, earlier in the chapter we are told that Nebuchadnezzar's anger is aroused by his advisors' delaying tactics. As Nebuchadnezzar put it, they were waiting *till the times change* (Daniel 2:9). The meaning is clear: they were hoping that Nebuchadnezzar would eventually cool his anger and come to see that what he was asking was unreasonable. But Daniel and his friends sensed that Nebuchadnezzar would not relent until his question had been answered. All of their lives were on the line, and that was Daniel's express reason for getting them to pray. Now that God had answered that prayer, and Daniel knew both the content and meaning of the dream, he could see that the times would change as a result of God's intervention. The "season" of Nebuchadnezzar's anger would only cease when he got his answer in terms of God's revelation.

Of course this is but one example of an important principle. God can, and does, intervene in human affairs in response to believing prayer. On the other hand, Daniel perceived God's sovereign prerogative at the level of history, in setting up or removing kings.

We saw his first-hand experience of it in chapter 1, where God gave Jehoiakim King of Judah "into the hand" of Nebuchadnezzar. Although for Daniel this was a traumatic experience way beyond his control, it is clear that he did not understand it as evidence of a rigid determinism that vitiates the meaning of all human response and responsibility. Now Daniel had his data, he needed to use it wisely.

CHAPTER 10

A SUCCESSION OF EMPIRES
Daniel 2

Daniel now had the information that Nebuchadnezzar required, so he hastened to tell Arioch, the official who had been appointed to execute the terrified futurologists of Babylon, to stay the execution, and requested an audience with the emperor (Daniel 2:24).

It was a characteristically generous move on Daniel's part. He knew that these "wise men" were, at least in part, charlatans. Presumably, they were also senior to him in rank. A man of lesser character, especially in those days, might well have been tempted to let Arioch get on with the executions and get the old guard out of the way, leaving Daniel and his friends a clear field. Indeed, it was these very same men or their successors who, some years later under Medo-Persian rule, tried to get rid of Daniel by having him eaten by lions. Yet even if Daniel had known that, something tells us that he would still have protected them.

This is a very important principle. Daniel disagreed with these men; he was implacably opposed to their world-view. Yet even though it was a risky thing to do, he would still make it his business to intervene on their behalf in order to preserve their lives. This is a lesson in true tolerance. We do not tolerate people with whom we agree – the word itself indicates that it is people with whom we disagree. But we support their right to hold and express their world-view, provided it is without threat or incitement to violence. However, in many countries tolerance has degenerated into a simplistic, all-affirming political correctness: a debilitating and very dangerous attitude that prevents people saying what they believe in case anyone should take offence. It is the very antithesis of free speech, and it is having a paralysing effect on public discourse.

Arioch respected Daniel enough to take the risk and give him a chance to prove himself, so he redirected his energy to securing Daniel an audience with Nebuchadnezzar. And what about Daniel himself? From a sceptical perspective he was risking his life. How could he be sure that his vision in the night was really a revelation from God? Did he really know what Nebuchadnezzar's dream was, and its interpretation? Nebuchadnezzar was not exactly in a good mood, and everyone knew what that meant – a tetchy king was a sure recipe for heads rolling.

And yet, as he waited for the imperial summons, Daniel was confident. That actually makes sense in light of what Peter has to say about prophecy. If God designed the written prophetic word to convey his self-authenticating voice, so that when we read it we may know deep in our hearts that it is from God, then it would be very surprising if the original recipients like Daniel did not have a similar, if not an even more powerful, sense of its authenticity.

Daniel before the king

Arioch ushered Daniel into the presence of the emperor and announced that he had *found among the exiles from Judah a man who will make known to the king the interpretation* (2:25). One cannot help smiling at the way Arioch takes credit for the discovery; although, to be fair, he had been remarkably open in sharing the predicament with Daniel in the first place.

I would love to have been there to see what happened next. A young captive exile, perhaps now just into his twenties, stands before the most powerful man on earth who is sitting in his incredibly opulent throne room on an ornate throne. Some historical records suggest that live lions were chained at each side of the throne to add to the impression of supreme power. It is only because God, his matchless heavenly King, is real that this young man has the courage to stand there.

Nebuchadnezzar comes straight to the point. *Are you able to make known to me the dream that I have seen and its interpretation?* (2:26). The question was about Daniel's ability, and one can detect in it a touch of incredulity on the part of the emperor. How could such a young man have insights into something that all the senior advisors in the palace deemed utterly impossible? Daniel echoes the thought, as if to focus it clearly in Nebuchadnezzar's mind. *No wise men, enchanters, magicians, or astrologers can show to the king the mystery that the king has asked...* (2:27). The world-view of those futurologists excluded such knowledge *a priori*. In spite of their extreme embarrassment, they had been forced to admit as much to the king.

So far, so familiar. But Daniel had not finished speaking: *... but there is a God in heaven who reveals mysteries, and he has made known to King Nebuchadnezzar what will be in the latter days* (2:28).

But there is a God in heaven... Magnificent, isn't it? I am lost in admiration when I think of the courage of the man standing in that ancient throne room, unashamedly witnessing to his faith. God had called the Hebrew nation to witness to the Gentiles, but as a nation they had signally failed. Yet, at least there was one who knew about the light that Abraham's descendants were meant to bring to the world, and here he shone it brilliantly.

There is a God in heaven... Of course, Nebuchadnezzar believed in gods, almost without number. His capital city was crammed with temples dedicated to them. But there was none like this, "who reveals secrets". And none of them was a God who was prepared to speak to the king directly in a dream and then send someone to tell him what he had dreamed, and why.

Without hesitation Daniel proceeded to describe the dream; first, modestly making it clear that God had not revealed it to him because he was superior in intellect and wisdom to all the others. It was so that the king would know and understand that God was interested in him, and wanted him to know it.

Now, according to the world-views of Babylon's wise men and the naturalist thinkers of today, there is no God that can reveal the future course of history. By definition, therefore, Daniel could have no special knowledge. He could not know the contents of the dream: all he could do was to guess. The wise men had not dared to guess because they knew that the probability of them getting the answer right was vanishingly small. They would have stalled for ever, if possible, rather than risk getting it wrong. Chance was not on their side. On that view, Daniel was taking a colossal gamble with his life. If he guessed wrongly, the rage of the emperor would know no bounds, and death would be swift and terrible.

But Daniel was not guessing. He was not calculating probabilities. He knew what Nebuchadnezzar had dreamed, and within a few seconds Nebuchadnezzar knew that Daniel knew. He said nothing as he listened spellbound to the young man who stood before his throne, whose every word recalled the dream that had so troubled his mind and left him sleepless for the rest of the night.

Nebuchadnezzar had dreamed about a terrifying statue that was an image of a colossal man of almost unendurable brightness. It was a strange statue for, as Nebuchadnezzar's eye traversed it from head to foot, he could make out that it was composite in form, made from a sequence of different substances. Its head was gold, its chest and arms silver, its middle and thighs bronze, its legs iron. That was bizarre enough, but the feet of the image were the strangest of all. They seemed to be out of keeping with all the rest, made of an odd mixture of iron and clay, or ceramic. (This is the source of the common expression "feet of clay".) They gave an immediate ominous impression of instability, even though the appearance of the colossus as a whole was terrifying. The impression of instability was rapidly confirmed. In the background of his vision he saw a stone suddenly detach from a mountain and come crashing onto the fragile feet of the statue. They crumbled instantly, bringing the whole statue crashing to the ground. It rapidly disintegrated into tiny chaff-like particles that were swept away by a powerful wind.

The famous poem of Shelley, "Ozymandias", captures something of this:

I met a traveller from an antique land
Who said, "Two vast and trunkless legs of stone

Stand in the desert. Near them, on the sand,
Half sunk, a shattered visage lies…
Nothing beside remains. Round the decay
Of that colossal wreck, boundless and bare
The lone and level sands stretch far away…"

But in Nebuchadnezzar's dream soon nothing was left except the stone; and he watched with spine-chilling fascination as it gradually but inexorably swelled up into a colossal mountain that did not stop growing until it had filled the entire earth. Nebuchadnezzar felt crushed out of existence – suffocated by the stone. At that point he had awakened in terror.

No wonder the vision frightened him, and no wonder he was reluctant to relate it to his wise men. After all, was not he, Nebuchadnezzar, the biggest man in the empire in every sense? If the biggest man was going to be toppled it was not hard to see what the power brokers in Babylon might have done, if they were informed of the contents of the dream. In the manner of the East, they might well have been tempted to anticipate the interpretation by eliminating Nebuchadnezzar and seizing power for themselves.

There were other puzzles for Nebuchadnezzar in the dream. Why the different metals? And what was wrong with the feet of the dream-man? Was Nebuchadnezzar's kingdom suffering from an instability of which he was unaware? And the terrible stone: what threat did it represent? It was terrifying in the extreme to an oriental mind, steeped in the lore of dreams.

Nebuchadnezzar was appalled.

Yet standing now before him there was a young man who confidently related the dream. How could he know its contents, let alone its meaning? What else did this young man know? Nebuchadnezzar was way out of his depth. He waited with baited breath for the interpretation that he knew was coming.

The interpretation of the dream

The first words of the interpretation, *You, O king*, must have hit him like a hammer. The message was indeed for him. His worst fears were true after all. Or were they? For Daniel was still speaking:

> *You, O king, the king of kings, to whom the God of heaven has given the kingdom, the power, and the might, and the glory, and into whose hand he has given, wherever they dwell, the children of man, the beasts of the field, and the birds of the heavens, making you rule over them all – you are the head of gold. (Daniel 2:37–38.)*

What was this he was hearing? It sounded surprisingly positive. So, he was the head of gold! We should pause to take in one immediate implication of this. We are often told that the language of Daniel is "apocalyptic": a term that often conveys unrelieved doom and gloom. However, God's assessment of Nebuchadnezzar given in the dream was not entirely negative. There was something golden and glorious about his kingdom, which a visit to the British Museum will amply confirm. This does not mean that Nebuchadnezzar's rule was faultless – far from it, as we shall see when we come to consider Daniel's fourth chapter. Nonetheless, there was a glory about it that God recognized and affirmed.

The key statement here is that God had given Nebuchadnezzar his kingdom. This picks up Daniel's own comment with which he begins his book:

> *In the third year of the reign of Jehoiakim king of Judah, Nebuchadnezzar king of Babylon came to Jerusalem and besieged it. And the Lord gave Jehoiakim king of Judah into his hand, with some of the vessels of the house of God. (Daniel 1:1–2.)*

God gave the power to the king of Babylon, just as much as he took it away from the king of Judah. This was not an arbitrary decision. Daniel will later give us the deep moral reasons that lie behind this seismic movement away from the rule of the kings of Judah to begin what is aptly described by the Lord Jesus himself as *the times of the Gentiles*. But the first and foremost fact that God wished to communicate to Nebuchadnezzar was that his rule and authority were derivative: they came from God.

That is, of course, the Christian position, as explained in the New Testament. The governments and authorities in this world are *from God*, as Paul says (Romans 13:1); and it is the general Christian duty to honour them as such, support them, and indeed to publicly pray for them (1 Timothy 2:1–2). Christians are not subversives; although when we come to Daniel 6 we shall see that circumstances may arise in which believers should disobey those powers, even though God has instituted them.

The fact that Nebuchadnezzar was the head of gold, and not the whole image, told him that his rule was neither absolute nor permanent. He would have successors. What, then, did the rest of the image mean? His descendants? He did not have to wait long for the answer. Daniel continued:

> *Another kingdom inferior to you shall arise after you, and yet a third kingdom of bronze, which shall rule over all the earth. And there shall be a fourth kingdom, strong as iron... (Daniel 2:39–40.)*

So the succession of metals did not represent a dynasty founded by Nebuchadnezzar. It represented a series of world empires stretching into the future.

It is perhaps hard for us to grasp just how unsettling such ideas would have been for an ancient emperor like Nebuchadnezzar. There had not been that many world empires up to that time – Egypt and Assyria being the only two that figured prominently in that part of the world. Nebuchadnezzar had not much reason, therefore, to suspect that his empire would not last for ever. Yet this young captive foreigner, who had not long graduated, was predicting that the mighty empire of Babylon that bore the stamp of Nebuchadnezzar's genius would not only come to an end but be replaced by an inferior kingdom. That would normally have been enough for the king to have had Daniel summarily executed for treason; but not this time. The relationship between the emperor and Daniel had changed for ever. Daniel had authority that the king did not possess, and wisdom that he desperately needed.

What, then, were the empires represented in the image? Historically, we know that the empire of Babylon gave way successively to the empires of Medo-Persia, Greece, and Rome. Daniel himself experienced the first transition, from Babylon to Medo-Persia. He describes it in chapters 5 and 6. Some scholars who deny the element of predictive prophecy in the book of Daniel, and hold that it was written in the second century BC in the time of the Maccabees, think that the sequence of empires in the image is Babylon, Media, Persia, and Greece. However, Daniel himself points out explicitly that after the transition from Babylonian rule, the law that replaced Babylonian law was that of the Medes and the Persians, not the law of the Medes (Daniel 6:8,12). Not only that, but in Daniel's own vision of the ram and the male goat (Daniel 8), the ram is explicitly stated to be the kings of Media and Persia, and the goat Greece (Daniel 8:20–21).

The vision is concerned, among other things, with time. Nebuchadnezzar is informed that the vision is about that which is to be; and the sequence of empires in the image is explicitly said to be a time sequence (Daniel 2:29, 39). History informs us that the Babylonian empire lasted roughly seventy years. It was followed by the Medo-Persian empire that lasted roughly 200 years. Then the Greek empire took power for around another 130 years, before Rome took over. It is interesting to note in passing that the transition from the Greek to the Roman empire corresponds with the shift from the Bronze Age to the Iron Age, thus lending a certain appropriateness of the metals to the respective empires that they symbolize.[15]

The Roman empire lasted a long time in various forms. The western Roman empire lasted until AD 476, but the eastern empire (Byzantium, the inhabitants of which never ceased to refer to themselves as Romans – *Rhomaioi*) lasted another thousand years, formally ending with the fall of Constantinople in 1453. The empire then fragmented, but left a legacy that is still with us. Latin, the first language of modern science, continued for that purpose until the eighteenth century, when more modern languages supplanted it. Latin script is used for most European languages, many of which are derived from Latin itself, and Roman law has had a deep influence on contemporary jurisprudence.

The important thing in Nebuchadnezzar's image, however, is not so much the identification of the empires, but the character of their representation in the image itself. This point is worth emphasizing, since sometimes such symbolism has been interpreted superficially as code. That is, the metals form a simple code, identifying the empires; so that when we see gold we read Babylon, silver Medo-Persia, and so on. Any other code, like the numbers 1, 2, 3… would have done just as well.

But if that were the case, why not simply use the proper names of the empires, without any code? The metals are not simple code. They are symbols embodying metaphors that help us to understand some important aspect of the empire they represent. So in the book of Revelation in the New Testament, when John is told that *the Lion of the tribe of Judah … has conquered* (Revelation 5:5), and he turns and sees a lamb standing, the terms "lion" and "lamb" are not simply codes to identify the Lord Jesus. They are metaphors used to tell us something about the Lord: he is in certain ways like a lion, and in other ways like a lamb. That is, the symbols add meaning.

Returning to Daniel, the point here is that the vision given to Nebuchadnezzar and the subsequent visions in the book are not just concerned with the bare *prediction* of history but also with the *interpretation* of history.

The metals, with their different relative strengths and values, highlight the fact that empires differ in both relative value and relative strength. Babylon, the head of gold, had an aura of splendour, but it was not as strong and efficient as Rome would be, the kingdom of iron. Each system had its strengths and weaknesses, its advantages and disadvantages. Historians have spent much effort on the fascinating task of trying to ascertain why it is that civilizations rise, flourish, and then decay and die, like flowers in a field. One lesson of the image has been confirmed by subsequent history: no system of government has absolute value. All have strengths and weaknesses.

It could not have been easy to get that message across to an emperor like Nebuchadnezzar. Nor would it go on to prove straightforward to communicate it to any of the other rulers of Babylon, Medo-Persia, Greece, or Rome. One reason is that the vast majority, if not all, of these rulers regarded themselves as chosen by the gods (in extreme cases, they regarded themselves as gods), so that their rule was by definition the best there could be.

In more recent times many of the power brokers of this world, whether they claimed to believe in the divine or not, have been all too convinced of the absolute nature of their rule, often with horrific consequences for their citizens.

Again and again in the book of Daniel we shall be brought face to face with arrogant and proud leaders, and that arrogance will be seen to be one of the reasons why their kingdoms do not survive. Historian Herbert Butterfield wrote (1957, page 82):

> There seems to be one fundamental law of a very solemn
> kind which touches this question of judgment; and when
> I turn to the ancient prophets and recall the limited area
> of history they had at their disposal for making their
> inductions, I am always surprised at the curious aptness
> with which they seem to have found the formula in
> this connection – a formula which they put in a special
> position of priority. Judgment in history falls heaviest
> on those who come to think themselves gods, who fly in
> the face of Providence and history, who put their trust in
> man-made systems and worship the work of their own
> hands, and who say that the strength of their own right
> arm gave them the victory.

The fact that world empires are of relative value reminds us to be thankful for any progress that has been made. As we look back to the civilizations of the past, represented in the image – Babylonian, Medo-Persian, Greek and Roman – we can see that each of them contributed positively and not just negatively to human flourishing. We owe much to them: art and architecture, mathematics, medicine, music and literature, law and philosophy, engineering and road building.

If we live in a part of the world where there has been improvement in the way in which its citizens are treated, we should certainly be grateful. For instance, in England it wasn't all that long ago when you could be hanged for stealing a sheep, or deported to the other side of the world for stealing a shilling. Children are no longer forced to work in the mines, where they would be liable to get pneumoconiosis before they reached twenty years old. And slavery is no longer permitted, thanks to the courage and tireless campaigning of William Wilberforce and others. In some countries there has been real progress in human rights legislation.

But there is another side. No system of government has been without its flaws, many of them deep and serious. Many emperors have been despotic and cruel in their abuse of power. History is littered with accounts of the powerful who become wealthy by impoverishing their subjects. Still today child labour, child soldiers, and slavery of all kinds are blemishes on the face of civilization. Not only that, but the twentieth century, instead of ushering in a new world order of peace and prosperity as many had hoped, saw more bloodshed than all the centuries that preceded it.

Daniel's interpretation of the dream does not give equal prominence to each of the empires. The second and third empires are dismissed in a single verse. When we come to the fourth kingdom of iron, much more detail is given, which means that the fourth kingdom is of particular importance. Here is what Daniel says to Nebuchadnezzar:

> And there shall be a fourth kingdom, strong as iron, because
> iron breaks to pieces and shatters all things. And like iron that
> crushes, it shall break and crush all these. And as you saw
> the feet and toes, partly of potter's clay and partly of iron, it
> shall be a divided kingdom, but some of the firmness of iron

*shall be in it, just as you saw iron mixed with the soft clay.
And as the toes of the feet were partly iron and partly clay,
so the kingdom shall be partly strong and partly brittle. As
you saw the iron mixed with soft clay, so they will mix with
one another in marriage [Aramaic, by the seed of men], but
they will not hold together, just as iron does not mix with
clay. And in the days of those kings the God of heaven will
set up a kingdom that shall never be destroyed, nor shall the
kingdom be left to another people. It shall break in pieces all
these kingdoms and bring them to an end, and it shall stand
for ever, just as you saw that a stone was cut from a mountain
by no human hand, and that it broke in pieces the iron, the
bronze, the clay, the silver, and the gold. A great God has
made known to the king what shall be after this. The dream is
certain, and its interpretation sure. (Daniel 2:40–45.)*

By common scholarly consent certain elements of this text are
difficult to understand; notably, the strikingly odd mixture of iron
and clay that formed the feet and toes of the image. The fourth empire
is characterized (at least initially) by the great strength of iron that
breaks to pieces and shatters all things (verse 40). Yet in the end that
strength appears to be diluted in some strange way, by being mixed
with ceramic clay, so that the image is dangerously unstable on its
feet and toes. Mysterious!

The stone and the kingdom

Before looking at the detail, we should notice something very
obvious: the stone is not part of the statue. The metals succeed each
other as parts of the same man; the stone comes from elsewhere.

If the imagery is saying anything, it is surely that we are not
to think of the kingdom of God either as one of the empires in the
image or as a new member of the sequence to be added on at the
end. In particular it is not a final stage of world government, reached
by advancing human experience and wisdom. It is not part of the

political process at all. As the phrase used of the stone indicates – *cut out by no human hand* – the kingdom of God is a supernatural kingdom (see Hebrews 9:11) that replaces all world empires and is brought into existence from outside by the power of God.

Yet throughout history it has been all too common for people professing Christianity to think that the system of government that happened to be in power in their nation in their era was nothing less than the kingdom of God on earth. Indeed, the very concepts of Christendom and the Holy Roman Empire embodied that notion. A core belief was the so-called "divine right of kings": the monarch is subject to no earthly authority, having derived his or her right to rule directly from God.

Even today it is sometimes difficult to persuade Christians that their own particular form of government (say, Western liberal democracy) is not the kingdom of God on earth. It is so easy to think that at last we have got it right. Furthermore, it is possible to lose sight of the supernatural dimension altogether. One of the consequences of the Enlightenment's rejection of the supernatural was:

> Little room was left for the great eschatological event
> Christians had long awaited, namely the Second Coming.
> Belief in Christ's return on the clouds was superseded
> by the idea of God's kingdom in the world which would
> be introduced step by step through successful labours in
> missionary endeavour abroad and in creating an egalitarian
> society at home. Along with the prominent nineteenth
> century German theologian, Albrecht Ritschl, the
> proponents of the American Social Gospel perceived God's
> kingdom as a present ethical reality rather than a dominion
> to be introduced in the future. ... The coming kingdom was
> not regarded as involving both death and resurrection, both
> crisis and promise, but only as the completion of tendencies
> now established. (Bosch, 2011, page 328.)

Behind this kind of thinking lies the notion of progress that marked the Enlightenment, and the great strides that were made in science, technology, and industry that brought so much wealth to Europe. Unbridled optimism in human potential reigned and Utopia was just around the corner. But the imagined Marxist Utopia that was to arise out of the workings of the inexorable laws of history turned into a nightmare of human carnage and cost the lives of millions. Not only Marxism, of course. Extreme nationalism of different kinds has produced similar results. History has taught the hard lesson: there is no pathway to paradise that bypasses the problem of the dark side of human nature.

Well-known Harvard psychologist Stephen Pinker thinks that violence is decreasing specifically as a result of Enlightenment thinking (Pinker, 2012) – a view which John Gray, a British professor of the history of European thought, is swift to rebut in his review of Pinker's book. The review is entitled "Stephen Pinker's Delusions of Peace". Gray writes:

> Like other latter-day partisans of "Enlightenment values"
> Pinker prefers to ignore the fact that many Enlightenment
> thinkers have been doctrinally anti-liberal, while quite a few
> have favoured the large-scale use of political violence, from
> the Jacobins who insisted on the necessity of terror during
> the French revolution, to Engels who welcomed a world war
> in which the Slavs – "aborigines in the heart of Europe" –
> would be wiped out.
>
> The idea that a new world can be constructed through
> the rational application of force is peculiarly modern,
> animating ideas of revolutionary war and pedagogic terror
> that feature in an influential tradition of radical Enlightenment
> thinking. Downplaying this tradition is extremely important
> for Pinker. Along with liberal humanists everywhere, he
> regards the core of the Enlightenment as a commitment
> to rationality. The fact that prominent Enlightenment
> figures have favoured violence as an instrument of social
> transformation is – to put it mildly – inconvenient.
>
> There is a deeper difficulty. Like so many contemporary
> evangelists for humanism, Pinker takes for granted that

science endorses an Enlightenment account of human reason. Since science is a human creation, how could humans not be rational? Surely science and humanism are one and the same. Actually it's extremely curious – though entirely typical of current thinking – that science should be linked with humanism in this way. A method of inquiry rather than a settled view of the world, there can be no guarantee that science will vindicate Enlightenment ideals of human rationality. Science could just as well end up showing them to be unrealisable...

Pinker's attempt to ground the hope of peace in science is profoundly instructive, for it testifies to our enduring need for faith. We don't need science to tell us that humans are violent animals. History and contemporary experience provide more than sufficient evidence. For liberal humanists, the role of science is, in effect, to explain away this evidence. They look to science to show that, over the long run, violence will decline – hence the panoply of statistics and graphs and the resolute avoidance of inconvenient facts.

The result is no more credible than the efforts of Marxists to show the scientific necessity of socialism, or free-market economists to demonstrate the permanence of what was until quite recently hailed as the Long Boom. The Long Peace is another such delusion, and just as ephemeral.[16]

Daniel's interpretation of Nebuchadnezzar's image challenges Pinker's perspective head on. The kingdom rule of God should certainly be an ethical reality in the hearts and lives of those who believe in him; but his kingdom in its fullest sense will not come as the result of present tendencies. History will not reach its promised goal by means of the processes that are within it. It will reach its goal by supernatural action from outside earth altogether. The Stone will fall.

The imagery of a stone would have been peculiarly apt for Nebuchadnezzar. Firstly, there was little natural stone to be found around Babylon, which is why its buildings were mainly of clay bricks. The area was also under constant threat from flooding. Stone suggests something solid and endurable.

Secondly, we are told that the stone was cut out from a mountain; and after destroying the image it became a "great mountain that filled the earth". The term "Great Mountain" would have been very familiar to Nebuchadnezzar. It was a term used to describe the Sumerian god Enlil, who had been usurped by Nebuchadnezzar's god Marduk. Here is an excerpt from the famous Hymn to Enlil:

Without Enlil, the Great Mountain,
No city would be built, no settlement founded,
No stalls would be built, no sheepfolds established,
No king would be raised, no high priest born…
The rivers – their floodwaters would not bring overflow,
The fish in the sea would not lay eggs in the canebrake,
The birds of heaven would not build nests on the wild earth,
In heaven the drifting clouds would not yield their moisture,
Plants and herbs, the glory of the plain, would fail to grow,
In fields and meadows the rich grain would fail to flower,
The trees planted in the mountain-forest would not yield
their fruit….[17]

Furthermore, the name Enlil means "Lord of the Air". He was in charge of the sky and the winds, among other things. In his dream Nebuchadnezzar watched as the wind swept away all traces of the pulverized statue, and the combination of wind and a great mountain may well have reinforced the impression that here was some kind of reference to a deity.

If this is what the imagery suggested to Nebuchadnezzar, then what should we make of it? Was God speaking to him in language that he could understand, but putting it in an entirely new context through the interpretation given by Daniel? For the dream was not about Enlil, one god among many; but about the sole Creator, the God of heaven.

Understood this way, it could be seen as a parallel to Paul's speech at Athens. He reminded the philosophers of what one of their Greek poets had said: *In him we live and move and have our being...* (Acts 17:28). The poem in question referred to a Greek god, but Paul regarded it as a helpful insight worth citing. Paul was not compromising with pagan thought. He was pointing out that, in some of their ideas, they were on the right track. Their concept of god needed adjusting. So did Nebuchadnezzar's. Paul and Daniel pointed them in the right direction.

What, then, is this "stone kingdom"?

We shall try to answer this question by looking first of all at the way in which the metaphor of a stone is used in Scripture, particularly in connection with the kingdom of God.

In the New Testament we first meet the stone metaphor in connection with the renaming of Simon, one of the original disciples. Jesus called him Cephas, which is the Aramaic word for stone, and this gets translated into Peter, derived from the Greek equivalent. Subsequently, this same Peter cites several Old Testament sources that refer to Jesus as a stone:

> As you come to him, a living stone rejected by men but in
> the sight of God chosen and precious, you yourselves like
> living stones are being built up as a spiritual house, to be a
> holy priesthood, to offer spiritual sacrifices acceptable to God
> through Jesus Christ. For it stands in Scripture: "Behold, I am
> laying in Zion a stone, a cornerstone chosen and precious,
> and whoever believes in him will not be put to shame." So
> the honour is for you who believe, but for those who do not
> believe, "The stone that the builders rejected has become the
> cornerstone," and "A stone of stumbling, and a rock of offence."
> (1 Peter 2:4–8, quoting from Isaiah 8:14; 28:16.)

Peter understands Jesus to be the stone that is to be laid in Jerusalem (Zion) – a stone that would be rejected by the builders: those leaders who claimed to be the architects of the nation of Israel. Yet he would turn out to be the chief cornerstone.

Some people suggest, therefore, that the falling of the stone in Daniel 2 refers to the first coming of Christ into the world, when he announced his (spiritual) kingdom – a kingdom that gradually grows as more and more people enter into it by the new birth. However, the crushing of a statue by a falling stone does not immediately strike one as a natural way to convey the idea of preaching the gospel.

There is one occasion where Jesus refers to himself as a stone that crushes when it falls. It occurs in a parable recorded by Luke:

> And he began to tell the people this parable: "A man planted a vineyard and let it out to tenants and went into another country for a long while. When the time came, he sent a servant to the tenants, so that they would give him some of the fruit of the vineyard. But the tenants beat him and sent him away empty-handed. And he sent another servant. But they also beat and treated him shamefully, and sent him away empty-handed. And he sent yet a third. This one also they wounded and cast out. Then the owner of the vineyard said, 'What shall I do? I will send my beloved son; perhaps they will respect him.' But when the tenants saw him, they said to themselves, 'This is the heir. Let us kill him, so that the inheritance may be ours.' And they threw him out of the vineyard and killed him. What then will the owner of the vineyard do to them? He will come and destroy those tenants and give the vineyard to others." When they heard this, they said, "Surely not!" But he looked directly at them and said, "What then is this that is written: 'The stone that the builders rejected has become the cornerstone'? Everyone who falls on that stone will be broken to pieces, and when it falls on anyone, it will crush him." (Luke 20:9–18.)

Here Jesus is thinking of the fact that, as the Son of the Owner of the vineyard (Israel), he would be rejected and murdered by those religious leaders in Jerusalem who claimed to be the tenants of the vineyard. The result would be that the Owner would eventually come and destroy them. It is in the context of that coming that Jesus speaks of the Stone falling and crushing his enemies.

In his Olivet discourse Jesus subsequently explains in detail the implications of this parable. He taught his disciples that Jerusalem would be destroyed – an event that occurred in AD 70 when the Romans sacked Jerusalem with massive violence. He further predicted of the nation of Israel: *They will fall by the edge of the sword and be led captive among all nations, and Jerusalem will be trampled underfoot by the Gentiles, until the times of the Gentiles are fulfilled* (Luke 21:24).

It is clear from this that *the times of the Gentiles* (the time of Gentile world domination) would come to an end. Its end would be connected with the return of Christ:

> *And there will be signs in sun and moon and stars, and on the earth distress of nations in perplexity because of the roaring of the sea and the waves, people fainting with fear and with foreboding of what is coming on the world. For the powers of the heavens will be shaken. And then they will see the Son of Man coming in a cloud with power and great glory. Now when these things begin to take place, straighten up and raise your heads, because your redemption is drawing near. (Luke 21:25–28.)*

Imagine the colossal statue laid on its side, with head to the left and feet to the right. Putting all of the above information together it seems reasonable to conclude that it gives us a visual time-line of "the times of the Gentiles" right up to the moment when Christ, the Stone, returns to set up his kingdom. Daniel and the Lord Jesus are surely referring to something still future to our time that will occur at Christ's second coming.

Other details that support this interpretation:

First, the stone does not hit the image at the top of the legs. On the corresponding time-line, that would represent the early stages of the Roman empire when Jesus lived and taught. No, the stone hits the image on the feet and toes; that is, the very final stages of that empire among whose fragments we in Europe still live.

Secondly, Daniel speaks of certain kings (plural) in whose days

God will set up his kingdom. The book of Revelation similarly talks about a group of kings – oddly enough the same number as the toes on the feet of the image, ten of whom appear to cede their power to a central government that is destroyed by the coming of Christ.

I am aware that some readers will already be uncomfortable with the idea that there is yet to be an outward, visible manifestation of God's kingdom on earth. For such readers, and all who are interested in the matter, I discuss the nature of the kingdom of God in more detail in Appendix A.

The instability of human governments

We need now to pay more attention to that other major feature of the colossal image in Nebuchadnezzar's dream – its instability. If its feet had been of iron, presumably it would have had the strength to stand. But the strange mixture of iron and ceramics in the feet makes it vulnerable. As we have seen, the stone fell on those feet and toppled the image. Let us look again at the relevant verses:

> And there shall be a fourth kingdom, strong as iron, because iron breaks to pieces and shatters all things. And like iron that crushes, it shall break and crush all these. And as you saw the feet and toes, partly of potter's clay and partly of iron, it shall be a divided kingdom, but some of the firmness of iron shall be in it, just as you saw iron mixed with the soft clay. And as the toes of the feet were partly iron and partly clay, so the kingdom shall be partly strong and partly brittle. As you saw the iron mixed with soft clay, so they will mix with one another in marriage [Aramaic, by the seed of men], but they will not hold together, just as iron does not mix with clay. (Daniel 2:40–43.)

Several points are made here: 1) iron is strong; 2) clay is brittle; 3) iron and clay do not mix. So far so good! The intriguing question is: what does the text mean about the lack of cohesion of iron and clay, particularly by the reference to mixing with one another in marriage?

As indicated, the Aramaic text does not use the word "marriage", but says rather "they will mix with one another by the seed of men". The statement is obscure and so has lent itself to a wide spectrum of interpretation. Could it be a reference to the way in which the Roman empire began to weaken as a result of the invasion of the Goths, who eventually mingled with the Romans? Or could it be focusing on the mingling of different types of government, whereby the iron symbolizes a more autocratic or even absolutist rule, vying with the clay that symbolizes the mass of humanity engaged in rule by the people – democracy?

Certainly, whatever the correct interpretation may be, it is true that the invasion of foreign troops contributed to the weakening and eventual downfall of Rome. It is also true that one of the instabilities of government lies in the whole area of leadership. Some (even today) favour the powerful leader who takes the decisions as an autocrat and expects everyone else to obey. Others prefer the democratic system that gives the voice to the people (more precisely, to their elected representatives). Due to the complexity of human behaviour, it is not hard to see that these systems are not necessarily mutually exclusive. Not only do they generate their own particular problems, but in any given society there may be sizeable factions, each advocating a different system. A glance at any serious newspaper will show that the potential for tension is limitless.

The claim of the book of Daniel is that there are absolute values and they stem from God himself. Could it be that an acid test for leadership is its commitment to God's values? We shall see within the book itself that this issue is raised more than once when Daniel and his friends confront absolutist rulers. But similar problems are raised by democratic majority decisions to alter biblical values. In the Western world today we are faced regularly with the aggressive secularist marginalization of religion in general and specific Christian values in particular. If there are absolutes and the majority decides against them, where does that leave the minority that holds to them?

However, perhaps the most important way of understanding this aspect of the image is to be found in the well-known phrase "feet of clay". That phrase is used of individuals, particularly those of high status, to describe character flaws – particularly hidden faults that could eventually bring about their downfall. The French call it *la condition humaine*. The writer Anthony Trollope used it in a memorable allusion to the dream image (*Fortnightly Review*, 1865): "The woman … finds that her golden-headed god has got an iron body and feet of clay."

The colossal man that Nebuchadnezzar saw had feet of clay, which alerts us at once to the problem that all systems of government have. To varying degrees, all their citizens have feet of clay. That is to say, the fundamental weakness indicated by the image is a weakness in humanity that makes people difficult to govern. It is a weakness to which much thought has been given in politics, and much has been written about in literature. We are all aware of it. The novelist G. K. Chesterton got it exactly right when he reportedly responded to a request in *The Times* newspaper for answers to the question "What is wrong with the world?" Chesterton is believed to have written:

Dear Sir,

I am.

Yours faithfully,

G. K. Chesterton[18]

The problem with humanity is humanity itself. History teaches a consistent lesson: there is something obviously wrong with human nature. In one of the clearest analyses of this fact Herbert Butterfield, writing in the aftermath of the Second World War (1949, page 30), says:

> It seems to me… that in regard to the relations between
> human nature and the external conditions of the world,
> the study of history does open one's eyes to a significant
> fact… if you were to remove certain subtle safeguards

in society many men who had been respectable all their lives would be transformed by the discovery of the things which it was now possible to do with impunity; weak men would apparently take to crime who had been previously kept on the rails by a certain balance existing in society; and you can produce a certain condition of affairs in which people go plundering and stealing, though hitherto throughout their lives it had never occurred to them even to want to steal. A great and prolonged police strike, the existence of a revolutionary situation in a capital city, and the exhilaration of conquest in an enemy country are likely to show up a seamy side of human nature amongst people who, cushioned and guided by the influences of normal social life, have hitherto presented a respectable figure to the world.

Butterfield concludes from this:

The difference between civilisation and barbarism is a revelation of what is essentially the same human nature when it works under different conditions. (Page 31.)

One point is fundamental, however. Nobody may pretend that there has been an elimination of the selfishness, and self-centredness of man. (Page 35.)

If in a well-run city crime has significantly reduced, because the police have successfully restrained it, no one would argue that there is no longer any need for the police. Without them basic human nature would resume its criminal activity. (Page 33.)

Butterfield goes on to say that unrecognized flaws in human nature such as pride, cupidity, and self-centredness can produce a dangerous self-righteousness that convinces people they are one hundred per cent right, and others similarly wrong. He writes:

… it seems to me that Christianity alone attacks the seat
of evil in the kind of world we have been considering … It
addresses itself precisely to that crust of self-righteousness
which, by the nature of its teaching, it has to dissolve before
it can do anything else with man. The more human beings
are … incapable … of any profound self-analysis, the
more we shall find that their self-righteousness hardens,
so that it is just the thick-skinned who are more sure of
being right than anybody else … At its worst it brings us to
that mythical messianism – that messianic hoax – of the
twentieth century which comes perilously near to the thesis:
"Just one little war more against the last remaining enemies
of righteousness, and then the world will be cleansed, and
we can start building Paradise." (Page 41.)

We have to admit at once that Christendom itself has been guilty
at times of such self-righteousness, when it tortured and burned
heretics in a supposed effort to "save" their souls. But that attitude
has also characterized great political movements, such as Nazism
and Marxism, with their vast toll on human life.

Butterfield's critique applies not only to global politics but also
to private citizens:

That same human nature, which in happy conditions is
frail, seems to me in other conditions capable of becoming
hideous, unless it has found a way of putting itself above the
effects of wind and weather. I have seen little people so wilful
in their little kingdoms that it seems to me merely their good
fortune that they were not crowned heads or prime ministers,
with peace and war depending on their coolness of mind.
(Page 44.)

To me, therefore, it seems that nothing could be more exact
perhaps for any man than the statement that "all men are
sinners and I the chief of them"; or the thesis "There but for
the grace of God go I". (Page 45.)

Butterfield finally recalls the words of a bishop who said that if we totally disarmed, he had too high an opinion of human nature to think that anybody would attack us. Butterfield disagrees:

> There might be great virtue in disarming and consenting to be made martyrs for the sake of the good cause; but to promise that we should not have to endure martyrdom in that situation, or to rely on such a supposition, is against both theology and history. It is essential not to have faith in human nature. Such faith is a recent heresy and a very disastrous one. (Page 47.)

In these last sentences Butterfield has put his finger on the central message of Nebuchadnezzar's image. There is a deep flaw in human nature, but humans still perversely insist on placing their faith in it.

One such was Ludwig Feuerbach (1804–72), whose philosophy had considerable influence on Marx:

> We have reduced the supermundane, supernatural, and superhuman nature of God to the elements of human nature as its fundamental elements. Our process of analysis has brought us again to the position with which we set out. The beginning, middle and end of religion is MAN. (1957, page 184.)

> My fellow-man is per se the mediator between me and the sacred reality of the species. *Homo homini Deus est* [Latin for "Man is man's God"]. (Page 159.)

In the Foreword to his doctoral thesis Karl Marx wrote (1955, page 15):

> Philosophy makes no secret of it. Prometheus' admission "I hate all gods" is its own admission, its own motto against all gods, heavenly and earthly, who do not acknowledge the consciousness of man as the supreme divinity.[19]

Marx was not prepared to acknowledge God as mankind's source, creator and sustainer, for to acknowledge any such Being superior to man himself would be to compromise humanity's absolute autonomy:

> Religion is only the illusory sun about which man revolves so long as he does not revolve about himself ... To put it succinctly: man is the highest being for man. (Pages 15, 19.)

This view, the rejection of the supernatural, lies at the heart of secular humanism. In one of the earliest meetings of the Annual Humanist Convention in 1945, Arthur Briggs said: "A humanist is one who believes in man as centre of the universe."[20] J.A.C.F. Auer of Harvard amplified this definition a little later:

> Man would worship God if man felt that he could admire God. But if not, if God fell below the level of moral excellence which he, man, set up, he would refuse his worship. That is Humanism – Man the measure of all things, including religion.[21]

Much more recently we have the definition of humanism as advanced by the British Humanist Society. At the time of writing this is what they said (at www.humanism.org.uk):

> Humanism, in the sense that we are interested in, is a view of the world which rejects religious beliefs ... we shall simply say that humanists do not believe in the existence of a god or gods. By "gods" we mean beings who, like human beings, possess the attributes of intellect and will, have beliefs and knowledge and can make choices and decisions to act, but who are immensely more knowledgeable and more powerful than human beings, and whose supernatural power lies behind some or all of the natural forces we see at work in the universe.

There is an older usage of the word "humanism" dating from the Renaissance and exemplified by men like Erasmus and Leonardo da Vinci. It is still sometimes used to describe the subjects taught by those who profess "the humanities" – the study of literature, philosophy, the arts, ancient Greek and Latin languages, and philosophical anthropology. And in a still more general sense nowadays a sympathetic practical concern for the welfare of others is referred to as humanism. However, this is not the meaning implied today by most of those who describe themselves as humanists.

In his book on Feuerbach, Oxford philosopher M. J. Inwood writes:

> God is in fact the essence of man himself, abstracted from individual, embodied men, and objectified and worshipped as a distinct entity ... We need to heal the fissure between heaven and earth, to replace love of God by love of man, and faith in God by faith in man, to recognise that man's fate depends on man alone and not on supernatural sources ...[22]

An idol is something or someone in whom humans put their ultimate trust, instead of putting it in God. It follows that Feuerbach's dictum, "MAN is man's god", is straight idolatry. (They are his capital letters.) And with that we are right back in Babylon, the city *par excellence* that symbolizes the limitless secular faith of human beings in themselves and their own achievements. Nebuchadnezzar's vast image of a man encapsulates exactly the essence of that idolatrous philosophy. As we shall see in subsequent chapters of Daniel's record, it will be that philosophy with which he has to wrestle.

Contemporary humanists may feel that Feuerbach's dictum is somewhat crude. Nevertheless, when it comes to identifying the source of values, the Humanist Society is explicit:

> Consider the claim that human beings are the source of all value. There's a sense in which this is a claim which humanists ought to accept, but the sense needs to be properly defined. Most obviously, it stands in contrast to the counter-claim made by many religious believers, that only

if we have a set of moral rules revealed to us by a divine authority can we know how we ought to live.

Putting faith in human beings, while at the same time recognizing that they are flawed, has in the past led to grandiose "scientific" schemes for their radical improvement. For instance, the following statement was made at the 1961 Communist Party Congress:

> The Party regards the education of the new man as the most difficult task in the communist reshaping of society. Until we remove bourgeois moral principles, roots and all, train men in the spirit of communist morality and renew them spiritually and morally, it will not be possible to build a communist society.

This statement shows the Party's awareness, learned perhaps by experience, that it is not enough to educate the people systematically in the principles of Marxist ethics and to exhort them to conform their outward behaviour to the strict letter of Marxist theory. What was necessary was nothing less than the creation and education of a "new man" by means of spiritual and moral renewal.

The language of this confession is striking. It is almost religious and remarkably parallels that of the New Testament which (in older English translations) also talks of putting on "the new man" (Ephesians 4:24).

As Marxism speaks of the necessity of renewing people spiritually and morally, if ever an acceptable society is to be achieved, so does the New Testament: *Do not be conformed to this world, but be transformed by the renewal of your mind...* (Romans 12:2).

These resemblances highlight the profound differences between Marxism and Christianity, both in the diagnosis of the root cause of man's defective behaviour and in the formulation of its cure. For Marx, God and religion were part of the apparatus that had connived at and helped to perpetuate man's alienation from the means of production. Therefore, the cure for man's alienation, and the way to spiritual and moral renewal and to the proper education of the "new man", was to set mankind free from "the tyranny of God", among other things, and from the very concept of God.

It is a simple fact of history that, in the place of what they held to be the tyranny of God, communist regimes substituted totalitarian control of every department of life, as though sheer force could change people's hearts and produce this "new man". But many of those who reject such totalitarianism nevertheless follow Marxism inasmuch as they also reject God both as the authority behind morality and as the source of mankind's possible moral regeneration. They fear that the introduction of God into ethics simply imposes another form of totalitarian authority that diminishes human dignity and freedom. They claim that it treats human beings morally as children rather than as adults who are quite capable of setting and obeying their own ethical rules.

In the light of these fears, it surely makes sense to investigate exactly what Christianity actually says about the cause of the admittedly universal moral weakness of mankind; and what strategy it proposes for producing its version of what the Communist Party called "the new man".

Nebuchadnezzar's vision can help point us in the right direction. By contrast with a fatally flawed man, the stable stone had supernatural origin. This apposition is important since it suggests that the only satisfactory answer to man's fatal flaw is God's supernatural power coming in from outside our world.

We saw that Christ changed the name of one of his apostles from Simon to Peter, "the rock", to indicate the fundamental change that had taken place in his life when, in his own words, he was *born again … of a seed* that is *imperishable* (1 Peter 1:23) by coming to trust in Christ, the Rock. Peter is referring of course to the "new birth" of Christian conversion. Jesus himself discussed the topic with Nicodemus, a leading theologian in Jerusalem, in connection with the kingdom of God: *Truly, truly, I say to you, unless one is born again he cannot see the kingdom of God* (John 3:3).

It is crucially important to see that the Christian solution to the problem is not what many people think. It is often claimed that religion sets impossibly high standards, and this inevitably leads to a psychologically unhealthy obsession with guilt and failure that undermines confidence in the possibility of human development. Whatever may or may not be true of other religions, this is certainly not the case with Christianity. For it starts with the offer of a new life; new powers that enable people to battle against weakness and sin.

The Christian diagnosis of humanity's fatal flaw is radical. Sin has alienated us from God and we cannot put it right ourselves. But the solution is equally radical. God in Christ has taken the burden of sin upon himself on the cross, so that through repentance and faith in Christ we can receive a new, supernatural life as an unmerited gift.

Nebuchadnezzar's response

We have seen that Nebuchadnezzar was deeply impressed by Daniel's knowledge of his dream and its interpretation. It is difficult for us to imagine just how much of a shock the whole experience must have been to his system. He thought that he understood and controlled the world around him. Now he was beginning to see that he neither understood nor controlled that world. There was another realm that he had been unaware of until now: a realm on which he was unconsciously dependent for all that he counted as his own. It is a humbling and sobering experience for anyone who has long been unaware of God, and even denied his very existence, to wake up to the fact that God is real. C. S. Lewis records his experience:

> An "impersonal God" – well and good. A subjective God of beauty, truth and goodness, inside our own heads – better still. A formless life-force surging through us, a vast power which we can tap – best of all. But God Himself, alive, pulling at the other end of the cord, perhaps approaching an infinite speed, the hunter, king, husband – that is quite another matter. There comes a moment when the children who have been playing at burglars hush suddenly: was that a real footstep in the hall? There comes a moment when people who have been dabbling in religion ("Man's

search for God"!) suddenly draw back. Supposing we really found Him? We never meant it to come to that! Worse still, supposing He had found us? (Lewis, 1960, page 98.)

Nebuchadnezzar was facing precisely that: God had found him. Of that there was no doubt. It also dawned on him that there were people in his realm like Daniel, people he had thought were way below him in status and power, who nevertheless knew about this other world. They had contact with it and enjoyed a wisdom and authority beyond anything that Nebuchadnezzar or his highly paid advisors knew. His spontaneous reaction was to fall down and worship Daniel – to Daniel's amazement and embarrassed protest, I'm sure:

> *Then King Nebuchadnezzar fell upon his face and paid homage to Daniel, and commanded that an offering and incense be offered up to him. The king answered and said to Daniel, "Truly, your God is God of gods and Lord of kings, and a revealer of mysteries, for you have been able to reveal this mystery." (Daniel 2:46–47.)*

Nebuchadnezzar had learned something vital about the true God: he is unique, the supreme authority over all kings, and he can speak and reveal mysteries.

Those lessons are just as important for us today. The New Atheists are loud in their demand for evidence that a supernatural God exists; yet the genuineness of their demand is questionable since they seem reluctant to pay serious attention to evidence that is offered to them. What Daniel has written is part of that evidence, but it offers such a direct threat to naturalism that it is scarcely likely even to be taken into consideration. When I reflect on the atheists' false definition of faith, "believing where there is no evidence", I am tempted to say that "atheistic faith" might well be defined as a studied refusal to consider evidence that does not lead to atheistic conclusions.

This section of Daniel has punctured the view that this world is all there is. Daniel (and now Nebuchadnezzar) claimed that there is a God who reveals secrets, and the secret that was revealed can be checked from our vantage point in history. That is, we now have more evidence than Nebuchadnezzar did that Daniel was right. Daniel predicted that there would be a succession of four empires, three of which are explicitly named in his book. And there *has* been a succession of four empires, all bearing the characteristics that Daniel ascribed to them.

Oddly enough, the very fact that atheistic thinkers try so hard to discredit Daniel, by claiming (against strong evidence to the contrary) that he must have been writing in the second century BC, shows that they are troubled, deeply troubled, that he got his facts right. That "divine foot" must not be allowed in the door.

This was heady stuff (as it still is). Nebuchadnezzar had more to learn about God, and God would teach him in due time. Meanwhile he promoted Daniel to very high office over the province of Babylon, to be his supreme advisor in the empire. Daniel put in a word for his friends and secured better positions for them, which one must infer were very well merited.

CHAPTER 11

WHEN THE STATE BECOMES GOD
Daniel 3

The account of Daniel's three friends, Shadrach, Meshach, and Abednego, and their ordeal in Nebuchadnezzar's fiery furnace is justifiably one of the most famous stories in biblical, perhaps in all, literature – a story much loved by the children who are still fortunate enough to be taught it. It records how Nebuchadnezzar decided to construct a vast golden statue towering above the plain of Dura. Perhaps one of the motives behind the project was an obsession with the fact that he had been told he was the head of gold in the dream image. We cannot say for certain that this was the case; if it was, it is clear that Nebuchadnezzar had seriously misunderstood the message of the dream.

Nebuchadnezzar didn't intend his image simply to be an impressive reminder of the fact that he was very much in charge of his empire. It was more than that. By assembling the top officials in his kingdom at the base of the statue, and calling upon them to bow down to it, he intended it to play a role in consolidating his power. Perhaps a further consequence of the dream image was a growing fear in Nebuchadnezzar's heart that he himself would inevitably be toppled sooner or later.

Religion and the state

It is an all too familiar scenario, as history repeatedly testifies – the attempt to harness religion in the interests of the totalitarian state, by making the state an object of worship. Its appearance at this juncture in Daniel's book gives it a particular emphasis. We have been introduced to the question of values in Daniel 1, where we observed that Nebuchadnezzar's treatment of the temple vessels from Jerusalem represents a ubiquitous tendency to relativize the absolute. In Daniel 2, Nebuchadnezzar is shown that no state or political system has absolute value in the eyes of God. Yet now, in Daniel 3, Nebuchadnezzar defies that notion by making his empire and rule an absolute, to the extent that he insists on it being treated as a god and worshipped. And so Nebuchadnezzar absolutizes the relative.

In chapters 1 and 3 Daniel draws our attention to two parallel yet opposite trends that he had come to observe during his long life at the pinnacle of power. Even though there is a drive to relativize absolutes, men and women cannot live without them. So they eventually take something of relative value and absolutize it. That is, they regard it as the core value that determines their attitude to everything else. From time immemorial the obvious candidates have been the state, power, wealth, and sex. Daniel chooses here to record an incident regarding the first two of these issues that involves not himself but his three friends.

Daniel is careful to list the main groups of officials who were commanded to attend the dedication of the idol. The main political leaders are at the top of the list, but we note in particular that the magistrates were there. One of the important safeguards of a society is to have a degree of independence between the political system and the judiciary, so that there can be checks and balances to avoid corruption and extremism. Nebuchadnezzar had no time for such niceties. He insisted on having the bench bow in front of his statue. His authority was to hold sway even over the judges.

When an absolute monarch like Nebuchadnezzar gets it into his head that he must prove his invincibility, it is inevitable that others will suffer. Those of us who live in Western democracies may respond by saying, "But that was a totalitarian extreme – it could never happen to us!" Well, perhaps we should remind ourselves of the situation in just the past century when, in Albania, Russia,

China, and Cambodia, acknowledgment of the leaders' effectively divine status was mandatory.

As far as Christianity is concerned, it is easy for some of us to forget that, at the moment, persecution is raging in many parts of the world.

> For 27 years, the *International Bulletin of Missionary Research* has published an annual Status of Global Mission report, which attempts to quantify the world Christian reality, comparing Christianity's circumstances to those of other faiths, and assaying how Christianity's various expressions are faring when measured against the recent (and not-so-recent) past. The report is unfailingly interesting, sometimes jarring, and occasionally provocative. The provocation in the 2011 report involves martyrdom. For purposes of research the report defines "martyrs" as "believers in Christ who have lost their lives, prematurely, in situations of witness, as a result of human hostility." The report estimates that there were, on average, 270 new Christian martyrs every 24 hours over the past decade, such that "the number of martyrs [in the period 2000–2010] was approximately 1 million."[23]

Of course, martyrdom represents the ultimate in a spectrum that includes discrimination, harassment, and many other lesser expressions of antagonism to Christianity. One example in the West is the increasing secularist chorus that clamours for the removal of God from public discourse. Such demands are already leading to discrimination. Threat of the return of intolerance from totalitarian regimes of relatively recent times looms ever larger.

Daniel records an extreme situation. Even though many of us may never have to face the ultimate penalty for public witness to our faith (although the likelihood of having to do so is increasing), the principles involved in the stand made by Daniel's three friends apply to all of us at different levels. By studying the ultimate case, we can learn much that will be of relevance to our everyday witness.

Sometimes, when the story of Daniel's three friends' deliverance from the furnace is explained, the impression is given that because God eventually rescued them and they were found to be unhurt they did not suffer. A moment's thought, however, will show us that this is far from the case. They suffered – not in the furnace, but before they were thrown into it. They were human beings like the rest of us, presumably with families; and so, from the moment the edict was announced by the emperor, these men inevitably went through mental agony.

It would have been immediately obvious to them that this was the hardest test of loyalty to God they had ever faced. Indeed, it was the hardest test anyone could face. It was the ultimate value decision. On one side of the equation was position, family, wealth, security, life itself; and on the other side there was God. Their lives had been on the line before. In chapter 2 Nebuchadnezzar made the decision to kill all the wise men, including Daniel and his friends, if they could not tell him what his dream was. Whether they lived or died depended entirely on God revealing the dream to them. This time it was different. They could save themselves simply by bowing down to the image.

But was it worth it? Is there really something more valuable than human life? Especially when that life is *my* life?

Imagine being one of these men and having to explain the situation to your family and friends. It is easy to see how they might try to talk you out of opposing Nebuchadnezzar.

> "We all know that this idolatry is bogus – there is nothing
> real in it except the emperor wishing us to acknowledge his
> authority. What does it matter if we outwardly bow down
> to him? It doesn't mean that he controls our heads and our
> hearts. And if good men like you three – men of proven
> ability and integrity – refuse to bow down and get killed,
> that will make the situation even worse. You are top people;
> if you are not there to continue your powerful influence
> for good at the very highest levels of the state, what hope
> is there for the rest of us? And think of your wife and your

children. What are they going to do if you throw your life away like this – needlessly? No, you must take part in the ceremony like everyone else for our sakes. We need you there in the corridors of power."

Yet they were not prepared to compromise. Yes, bowing was an outward gesture; but it was calculated by Nebuchadnezzar to express acceptance of his idolatrous regime. The three friends were not prepared to do that – at any cost.

Their mental agony must have been intense as they wrestled with these issues in their own minds, and as they met incomprehension on the part of their friends and possibly even their own families. We have no details of how their friends and families reacted, but we don't need to have exact information in order to know that it was a horrifying situation for all of them, and that it intensified as the time for the ceremony drew nearer.

Let Daniel describe it to us:

> King Nebuchadnezzar made an image of gold, whose height was sixty cubits and its breadth six cubits [about 27 x 2.7 metres, or 90 x 9 feet]. He set it up on the plain of Dura, in the province of Babylon. Then King Nebuchadnezzar sent to gather the satraps, the prefects, and the governors, the counsellors, the treasurers, the justices, the magistrates, and all the officials of the provinces to come to the dedication of the image that King Nebuchadnezzar had set up. Then the satraps, the prefects, and the governors, the counsellors, the treasurers, the justices, the magistrates, and all the officials of the provinces gathered for the dedication of the image that King Nebuchadnezzar had set up. And they stood before the image that Nebuchadnezzar had set up. (Daniel 3:1–3.)

The scene was suitably impressive – dominated by the vast golden statue that the emperor had built. One cannot help thinking that it somehow reflected the colossal man that he had seen in his dream. Certainly the message it was meant to radiate to the host of dignitaries assembled at its feet was of MAN writ large in the person of Nebuchadnezzar. It was an expression of idolatry – the ultimate consequence of rejecting the true God.

The top orchestra in the land was at hand ready to play. A herald stepped forward:

> *You are commanded, O peoples, nations, and languages, that when you hear the sound of the horn, pipe, lyre, trigon, harp, bagpipe, and every kind of music, you are to fall down and worship the golden image that King Nebuchadnezzar has set up. And whoever does not fall down and worship shall immediately be cast into a burning fiery furnace. (Daniel 3:4–6.)*

Silence fell as the king and his nobles waited for the music to begin. It was no accident that music was involved as well as a furnace. The furnace was an ugly, crude threat of instant cremation for defectors. (Burning was a punishment prescribed by the ancient law code of Hammurabi for various crimes.) The music was to perform an opposite role – seduction. Music has a power to influence the mind and reduce inhibitions. The 1960s generation was not the first to discover that; it has been well known for centuries. In the contemporary world music can play a similar role – its throbbing beat can anaesthetize one's mind to the lyrics. Nebuchadnezzar knew this well: he would dispel any lingering doubts by making it easy for his nobles to bow. Listening to the strains of magnificent music would overcome any lingering moral or intellectual resistance. (It is worth asking the question: do I really approve of the words that accompany the music that I buy?)

At one time it was thought that the words for musical instruments used here demanded a second-century date for Daniel. However, more recent scholarship has changed that verdict. Alan Millard writes:

> The Greek words in Chapter 3, which are all names of musical instruments, became more acceptable in a sixth-century setting with the publication of lists of rations issued

to people kept in the palace of Nebuchadnezzar. Beside Jehoiachin, king of Judah, there were other people from the Levant and Anatolia, including Greeks. A few further attestations of Greeks living, even owning property, in Babylonia have been traced in legal texts.

Millard goes on to make a general comment on the language of Daniel that is worth recording:

> The history of biblical Hebrew has come under renewed study, especially in the light of the Dead Sea Scrolls, and the differences appearing between the books are no longer viewed as so clearly marking distinct periods. While the Hebrew of Daniel might support a second-century date, it could equally support an earlier date. The presence of Persian words in a Hebrew (and Aramaic) book written in the Persian period is unexceptionable. (Hoffmeier and Magary 2012, page 278.)

The price of spiritual integrity

The event appeared at first to be an unqualified success:

> *Therefore, as soon as all the peoples heard the sound of the horn, pipe, lyre, trigon, harp, bagpipe, and every kind of music, all the peoples, nations, and languages fell down and worshipped the golden image that King Nebuchadnezzar had set up. (Daniel 3:7.)*

Maybe, due to the sheer size of the crowd, the king had not noticed the three men who alone remained erect when all the others fell to the ground in front of the golden image. But that would not last long:

> *Therefore at that time certain Chaldeans came forward and maliciously accused the Jews. They declared to King*

Nebuchadnezzar, "O king, live for ever! You, O king, have
made a decree, that every man who hears the sound of the
horn, pipe, lyre, trigon, harp, bagpipe, and every kind of
music, shall fall down and worship the golden image. And
whoever does not fall down and worship shall be cast into
a burning fiery furnace. There are certain Jews whom you
have appointed over the affairs of the province of Babylon:
Shadrach, Meshach, and Abednego. These men, O king, pay
no attention to you; they do not serve your gods or worship
the golden image that you have set up." (Daniel 3:8–12.)

Were these accusers the same men that Daniel's intervention had
saved? If so, their gratitude was short-lived. They quickly played
the anti-Semitic card: *there are certain Jews…* Then they told a lie,
followed by a truth: *These men, O king, pay no attention to you.* That
was an absurd charge. Nebuchadnezzar himself had appointed them
to their positions in recognition of their ability. But it was completely
true that they did not serve the emperor's gods, nor had they bowed
before the golden image.

It stung the king into enraged reaction:

Then Nebuchadnezzar in furious rage commanded that
Shadrach, Meshach, and Abednego be brought. So they
brought these men before the king. Nebuchadnezzar answered
and said to them, "Is it true, O Shadrach, Meshach, and
Abednego, that you do not serve my gods or worship the
golden image that I have set up? Now if you are ready when
you hear the sound of the horn, pipe, lyre, trigon, harp,
bagpipe, and every kind of music, to fall down and worship
the image that I have made, well and good. But if you do not
worship, you shall immediately be cast into a burning fiery
furnace. And who is the god who will deliver you out of my
hands?" (Daniel 3:13–15.)

The gloves were off. In his intemperate rage, the emperor let slip what
really lay behind the whole ceremony. He did not say: "Who is the

god who will deliver you out of the hands of my god?" He said: "Who is the god who will deliver you out of *my* hands?" The golden image was but a representation of Nebuchadnezzar himself – after all, as the text repeatedly points out, Nebuchadnezzar had himself set it up! It was Nebuchadnezzar's *power* that the three men had challenged, and he was giving them another chance to acknowledge that his power had no limit. How things had changed. In the previous chapter we saw how Nebuchadnezzar himself fell down before Daniel and paid homage to him. All that was forgotten as he raged at the young men.

He was in for a shock. They refused.

> *Shadrach, Meshach, and Abednego answered and said to the king: "O Nebuchadnezzar, we have no need to answer you in this matter. If this be so, our God whom we serve is able to deliver us from the burning fiery furnace, and he will deliver us out of your hand, O king. But if not, be it known to you, O king, that we will not serve your gods or worship the golden image that you have set up." (Daniel 3:16–18.)*

They totally rejected Nebuchadnezzar's claim that their God could not deliver them. They were convinced that God was well able to set them free, and they said so to Nebuchadnezzar. However, in a statement of breathtaking courage and confidence in God, they told the emperor that they had taken into consideration the possibility that God might not deliver them. They were not prepared to prescribe what God would do. That was for God to decide. But, no matter whether God delivered them or not, they were not going to bow to the statue. The issue was one of principled morality.

Nebuchadnezzar had never in his life before encountered such studied defiance. As it began to dawn upon him that there was a very real sense in which he was powerless against these men, his anger knew no bounds. Of course he could kill them, but that was not the point. What he could not do was to force them to bow. Up to now he had thought that human beings would do anything to save their lives. His whole scheme of getting his nobles to bow depended on the assumption that, for each person, life was of absolute value.

To his utter amazement he discovered that this was not always the case. Even in his own very administration there were men, men of proven ability and high office, who regarded their lives as of relative value compared with the absolute value of God. Nebuchadnezzar's reaction was a fury of impotent frustration.

One of the major lessons that God had earlier attempted to teach Nebuchadnezzar through his dream (Daniel 2) was that his tenure of power was limited: there would be empires after his. That knowledge had disturbed him profoundly. Perhaps it had subconsciously led him to build the golden image, in order to stave off the inevitable. But what he was now facing seemed even worse. Not only was his tenure of power limited, his exercise of that power was limited as well, even as he held it. He had no authority over the three men who were prepared to sacrifice their lives for what they believed. It was just too much to take.

The ordinary heat of the furnace was not enough for the emperor, so he had the fire heated up to such a degree that it instantly cremated the men who manhandled the three friends into it. Not that Nebuchadnezzar cared about their lives – he had got rid of the three rebellious men.

Or so he thought.

Saved in the fire

Then King Nebuchadnezzar was astonished and rose up in haste. He declared to his counsellors, "Did we not cast three men bound into the fire?" They answered and said to the king, "True, O king." He answered and said, "But I see four men unbound, walking in the midst of the fire, and they are not hurt; and the appearance of the fourth is like a son of the gods." Then Nebuchadnezzar came near to the door of the burning fiery furnace; he declared, "Shadrach, Meshach, and Abednego, servants of the Most High God, come out, and come here!" Then Shadrach, Meshach, and Abednego came out from the fire. (Daniel 3:24–26.)

It was a moment of high drama. It went way beyond anything Nebuchadnezzar could have conceived even in his wildest dreams. The men had not died – indeed the fire that had consumed others seemed to have had no effect on them whatsoever:

> And the satraps, the prefects, the governors, and the king's counsellors gathered together and saw that the fire had not had any power over the bodies of those men. The hair of their heads was not singed, their cloaks were not harmed, and no smell of fire had come upon them. (Daniel 3:27.)

The whole experience was utterly unnerving, particularly the presence of the mysterious fourth figure that had been seen in the fire – a figure that seemed to Nebuchadnezzar to resemble *a son of the gods*. Nebuchadnezzar had issued what he thought was a rhetorical challenge to the heavens: *What god shall deliver you out of my hands?* To his utter horror he discovered there was a God in the heavens who could do precisely that – a God to whom Nebuchadnezzar's threats meant nothing. That God had identified himself with the men in the fire, loosed them, and delivered them. Once again God had invaded Nebuchadnezzar's world, and he was demanding the emperor's attention.

> Nebuchadnezzar answered and said, "Blessed be the God of Shadrach, Meshach, and Abednego, who has sent his angel and delivered his servants, who trusted in him, and set aside the king's command, and yielded up their bodies rather than serve and worship any god except their own God. Therefore I make a decree: Any people, nation, or language that speaks anything against the God of Shadrach, Meshach, and Abednego shall be torn limb from limb, and their houses laid in ruins, for there is no other god who is able to rescue in this way." Then the king promoted Shadrach, Meshach, and Abednego in the province of Babylon. (Daniel 3:28–30.)

Not surprisingly, it was the manner of the rescue that impressed Nebuchadnezzar. God had not merely delivered the three friends *from* the fire – though he could have done so, as they had said earlier to Nebuchadnezzar. God had delivered them *in* the fire. Their suffering was real, but it all occurred before they got to the fire. The horrors that they had naturally anticipated and surely feared had not occurred.

There is an important matter of principle here. God is a great deliverer – but he will not deliver us from having to make our own decisions. This is not because he is impotent but because he wants us to be strong. The development of our character depends crucially on the fact that we make responsible decisions before God for ourselves. For God to "decide" for us would be to de-humanize us and essentially turn us into amoral robots.

When children are very small, parents often have to decide for them in order to teach them. But it is sad when we see a situation where parents have to decide for grown-up children, since that is often a sign that something has gone wrong in the development of their character.

So there is a sense in which God, precisely because he loves us, will not save us either from the need to make such decisions or from the decisions themselves. Shadrach, Meshach, and Abednego had to make up their own minds as to whether they were going to put God first. That does not mean they had no guidance. Their guidance was all the accumulated experience of God's trustworthiness up to that fateful moment. They therefore had decided to trust him once more, no matter what it cost. Then God convincingly vindicated them.

One cannot help wondering if there were some in the great crowd of Babylonian officials who, when they saw the three men coming unscathed from the fire, wished in their hearts that they had had the same courage. But it was too late.

Nebuchadnezzar was a man of impulsive and volatile extremes. One moment he was raging against God; the next he was threatening to kill and destroy not only individuals but entire nations if they said anything defamatory about the very same God.

He also promoted the three men.

This cross on Broad Street, Oxford, marks the place where the Oxford Martyrs
– Bishops Ridley and Latimer and Archbishop Thomas Cranmer – were
immolated for their faith: Ridley and Latimer on 16 October 1555, and Cranmer
on 21 March 1556

One can imagine that this incident, witnessed as it was by so many high-ranking officials, was talked about for years afterwards. No doubt it also gave Shadrach, Meshach, Abednego, and Daniel himself many opportunities to witness to God.

In the centuries following this incident many believers have faced the threat of being burned alive, in an attempt to get them to recant. I am reminded of this every time I walk along Broad Street in Oxford. Just opposite Balliol College, largely unnoticed by the passing pedestrians and cyclists, there is a stone cross surrounded by a small disc of cobblestones. This cross on Broad Street, Oxford, marks the place where the Oxford Martyrs – Bishops Ridley and Latimer and Archbishop Thomas Cranmer – were immolated for their faith: Ridley and Latimer on 16 October 1555, and Cranmer on 21 March 1556.

These burnings (and many others throughout the years) were not accompanied by a supernatural deliverance. God's promise through Isaiah is not to be understood as a guarantee to believers that no water will ever drown, or fire burn:

> When you pass through the waters, I will be with you; and through the rivers, they shall not overwhelm you; when you walk through fire you shall not be burned, and the flame shall not consume you. For I am the Lord your God, the Holy One of Israel, your Saviour. (Isaiah 43:2–3.)

God can deliver, but he does not always choose to do so. On those occasions when he does not, our hearts are rightly moved at the courage exemplified by believers. Latimer's last words at the stake were: "Be of good cheer, Master Ridley, and play the man, for we shall this day light such a candle in England as I trust by God's grace shall never be put out." That candle still burns today.

Earlier in this chapter I indicated that the story of Daniel's three friends is so remote from everyday experience that it would be easy to miss its general implication. But all of us who follow Jesus as Lord have to face decisions that put our values to the test. Indeed, the challenge lies at the heart of the gospel message itself. On one occasion Jesus himself described salvation as a banquet to which people are invited, without payment or merit. This illustrates the heart of the gospel: salvation cannot be earned or deserved – it is a gift of God's grace to be accepted by faith in Christ. However, as D. W. Gooding points out:

> But because it is free that does not mean it is cheap. Quite the reverse. This paragraph is about to tell us that salvation is so valuable that if receiving it as a gift involved the loss of everything else, we should be foolish indeed not to accept the loss.

Here are Jesus' words:

> *If anyone comes to me and does not hate his own father and mother and wife and children and brothers and sisters, yes, and even his own life, he cannot be my disciple. Whoever does not bear his own cross and come after me cannot be my disciple. (Luke 14:26–27.)*

Thousands have been and still are confronted with this choice right at the outset of their Christian lives. They see, as clearly as Saul of Tarsus saw, that salvation is a free gift. Equally clearly they see that confession of faith in Christ will cost them career, family, friends, perhaps life itself; and they have to decide between Christ and salvation on the one side and all else on the other. All disciples of Christ must be prepared for that choice at some time. They must be ready to "hate" – that is, give second place to and, if need be, let go – all else (see D. W. Gooding, 1987, page 268).

It is this that makes the story of Shadrach, Meshach, and Abednego relevant in every age. After all, the confession that lies at the heart of the Christian faith is *Jesus Christ is Lord*. This section of Daniel asks us how seriously we take it. His three friends did not shrink from presenting their bodies as a living sacrifice. Would I?

In my visits to Russia, particularly in the years immediately after the fall of the Berlin Wall, I came across people who had suffered detention in the Soviet Gulag. The first such man I met had spent several years detained in a Siberian labour camp for the crime of teaching children from the Bible. He described to me that he had seen things that no man should ever have to see. I listened, thinking how little I really knew about life, and wondering how I would have fared under his circumstances. As if he had read my thoughts, he suddenly said: "You couldn't cope with that, could you?" Embarrassed, I stumbled out something like: "No, I am sure you are right." He then grinned and said: "Nor could I! I was a man who fainted at the sight of his own blood, let alone that of others. But what I discovered in the camp was this: God does not help us to face theoretical situations but real ones. Like you, I couldn't imagine how one could cope in the Gulag. But once there I found that God met me, exactly as Jesus had promised his disciples when he was preparing them for victimization and persecution."

What Jesus said is of immense importance:

> *Beware of men, for they will deliver you over to courts and flog you in their synagogues, and you will be dragged before governors and kings for my sake, to bear witness before them and the Gentiles. When they deliver you over, do not be anxious how you are to speak or what you are to say, for what you are to say will be given to you in that hour. For it is not you who speak, but the Spirit of your Father speaking through you. (Matthew 10:17–20.)*

Of course, Jesus did not mean that his disciples were to face every situation unprepared. For instance, his statement is no excuse for us to insult an audience by failing to prepare for an invited talk. Jesus is speaking of situations where believers are threatened by court appearances, persecution, or worse, and have no opportunity to make special preparation. He promises to give them the courage and the wisdom to say the right thing. That promise means much to believers in many parts of the world today.

The cost of resisting idolatry is high. But it does not compare with the cost of rejecting God, as we shall see in the climax of the first half of the book when we come to Belshazzar's feast.

First, however, King Nebuchadnezzar has something to say.

CHAPTER 12

THE TESTIMONY OF NEBUCHADNEZZAR
Daniel 4

Nebuchadnezzar: William Blake, 1795, Tate Gallery, London

Chapters 2 and 3 of Daniel have taken us into the world of power politics. Chapters 4 and 5 will take us into the world of architecture, art, and beauty, which was also very much part of Babylonian culture.

Chapter 4 is cast in the shape of a statement by the emperor Nebuchadnezzar in which he testifies to his personal experience of God. As a powerful testimony of a world leader to his faith in God this section of Daniel is a remarkable piece of literature, and it must have attracted considerable interest in the ancient world – just as a similar statement by one of our present world leaders would today. World leaders (at least in the West) do not usually "do God", as the saying goes. Nebuchadnezzar did – and this is what he said:

> *King Nebuchadnezzar to all peoples, nations, and languages,*
> *that dwell in all the earth: Peace be multiplied to you! It has*
> *seemed good to me to show the signs and wonders that the*
> *Most High God has done for me. How great are his signs, how*
> *mighty his wonders! His kingdom is an everlasting kingdom,*
> *and his dominion endures from generation to generation.*
> *(Daniel 4:1–3.)*

Presumably Nebuchadnezzar gave Daniel permission to publish his statement. Indeed it is possible that the emperor may have involved Daniel in drafting it. This raises the interesting question of how much Nebuchadnezzar got to know about what Daniel himself wrote. We would love to know more, but we don't; and so we must be content to think our way through the text that we have.

At the outset Nebuchadnezzar states that his purpose is that the whole earth (or at least that part over which he had influence) should get to know the nature of the signs and wonders that God has shown him. Nebuchadnezzar had come to learn that God's kingdom existed and was everlasting – as distinct from every earthly empire, including Babylon.

The emperor now relates another of his dreams. He does not refer to the earlier dream which is the focus of Daniel 2. Maybe the king decided to concentrate on this particular dream because it had turned out to be the most decisive in his turning to God. Nebuchadnezzar confesses right away that his dream was so disturbing that it had prompted him once more to consult with his experts. Interestingly enough, this time he did not try to test them by withholding the content of the dream. He told them straight away what it was.

He may well have thought there was no point in testing them again, since he knew how hollow their claims were. As if to confirm this, they said that they were unable to interpret it. It was a shrewd move on their part. Daniel was now a very senior man in the administration (*chief of the magicians*, Nebuchadnezzar calls him) and had a proven track record of the successful interpretation of dreams. One can imagine therefore that the advisors preferred to confess their ignorance rather than risk their best guess being proved wrong by Daniel's superior wisdom and insight. Once again, their incapacity was evident.

Nebuchadnezzar goes on to describe how Daniel eventually appeared before him. We note in passing that Daniel's Hebrew name has not been forgotten. Nebuchadnezzar uses it here, but he also mentions Daniel's Babylonian name, Belteshazzar, pointing out that it derives from the name of the emperor's god (Bel, or Marduk), and that Daniel was a man *in whom is the spirit of the holy gods.* Nebuchadnezzar's polytheism is still not far from the surface. He is a man on a journey: still confused, but wishing nevertheless to testify to what Daniel's God has done for him.

Nebuchadnezzar addresses Daniel with great respect as he outlines his dream:

> "O Belteshazzar, chief of the magicians, because I know that the spirit of the holy gods is in you and that no mystery is too difficult for you, tell me the visions of my dream that I saw and their interpretation. The visions of my head as I lay in bed were these: I saw, and behold, a tree in the midst of the earth, and its height was great. The tree grew and became strong, and its top reached to heaven, and it was visible to the end of the whole earth. Its leaves were beautiful and its fruit abundant, and in it was food for all. The beasts of the field found shade under it, and the birds of the heavens lived in its branches, and all flesh was fed from it.
>
> "I saw in the visions of my head as I lay in bed, and behold, a watcher, a holy one, came down from heaven. He proclaimed aloud and said thus: 'Chop down the tree and lop off its branches, strip off its leaves and scatter its fruit. Let the beasts flee from under it and the birds from its branches. But leave the stump of its roots in the earth, bound with a band of iron and bronze, amid the tender grass of the field. Let him

be wet with the dew of heaven. Let his portion be with the beasts in the grass of the earth. Let his mind be changed from a man's, and let a beast's mind be given to him; and let seven periods of time pass over him. The sentence is by the decree of the watchers, the decision by the word of the holy ones, to the end that the living may know that the Most High rules the kingdom of men and gives it to whom he will and sets over it the lowliest of men.' This dream I, King Nebuchadnezzar, saw. And you, O Belteshazzar, tell me the interpretation, because all the wise men of my kingdom are not able to make known to me the interpretation, but you are able, for the spirit of the holy gods is in you."

Then Daniel, whose name was Belteshazzar, was dismayed for a while, and his thoughts alarmed him. The king answered and said, "Belteshazzar, let not the dream or the interpretation alarm you." Belteshazzar answered and said, "My lord, may the dream be for those who hate you and its interpretation for your enemies! The tree you saw, which grew and became strong, so that its top reached to heaven, and it was visible to the end of the whole earth, whose leaves were beautiful and its fruit abundant, and in which was food for all, under which beasts of the field found shade, and in whose branches the birds of the heavens lived – it is you, O king, who have grown and become strong. Your greatness has grown and reaches to heaven, and your dominion to the ends of the earth. And because the king saw a watcher, a holy one, coming down from heaven and saying, 'Chop down the tree and destroy it, but leave the stump of its roots in the earth, bound with a band of iron and bronze, in the tender grass of the field, and let him be wet with the dew of heaven, and let his portion be with the beasts of the field, till seven periods of time pass over him', this is the interpretation, O king: It is a decree of the Most High, which has come upon my lord the king, that you shall be driven from among men, and your dwelling shall be with the beasts of the field. You shall be made to eat grass like an ox, and you shall be wet with the

dew of heaven, and seven periods of time shall pass over you,
till you know that the Most High rules the kingdom of men
and gives it to whom he will. And as it was commanded to
leave the stump of the roots of the tree, your kingdom shall be
confirmed for you from the time that you know that Heaven
rules. Therefore, O king, let my counsel be acceptable to you:
break off your sins by practicing righteousness, and your
iniquities by showing mercy to the oppressed, that there may
perhaps be a lengthening of your prosperity."

All this came upon King Nebuchadnezzar. At the end of
twelve months he was walking on the roof of the royal palace
of Babylon, and the king answered and said, "Is not this great
Babylon, which I have built by my mighty power as a royal
residence and for the glory of my majesty?" While the words
were still in the king's mouth, there fell a voice from heaven,
"O King Nebuchadnezzar, to you it is spoken: The kingdom
has departed from you, and you shall be driven from among
men, and your dwelling shall be with the beasts of the field.
And you shall be made to eat grass like an ox, and seven
periods of time shall pass over you, until you know that the
Most High rules the kingdom of men and gives it to whom he
will."

Immediately the word was fulfilled against
Nebuchadnezzar. He was driven from among men and ate
grass like an ox, and his body was wet with the dew of heaven
till his hair grew as long as eagles' feathers, and his nails were
like birds' claws.

At the end of the days I, Nebuchadnezzar, lifted my eyes
to heaven, and my reason returned to me, and I blessed the
Most High, and praised and honoured him who lives for ever,

for his dominion is an everlasting dominion,
and his kingdom endures from generation to generation;
all the inhabitants of the earth are accounted as nothing,
and he does according to his will among the host of
heaven

> *and among the inhabitants of the earth;*
> *and none can stay his hand*
> *or say to him, "What have you done?"*
> *At the same time my reason returned to me, and for the*
> *glory of my kingdom, my majesty and splendour returned*
> *to me. My counsellors and my lords sought me, and I was*
> *established in my kingdom, and still more greatness was*
> *added to me. Now I, Nebuchadnezzar, praise and extol and*
> *honour the King of heaven, for all his works are right and*
> *his ways are just; and those who walk in pride he is able to*
> *humble. (Daniel 4:9–37.)*

The main contours are clear. In his dream Nebuchadnezzar sees a beautiful tree that is a source of food, protection and shade for the whole earth, such is its colossal size and luxuriant fruitfulness. It is aesthetically pleasing in every sense. Yet Nebuchadnezzar hears an order given "from above" to cut the tree down – not to destroy it completely but to leave its stump in the ground.

The majestic tree is symbolic of a man, which is made clear by the statement that its human mind is to be removed and an animal's mind given to it for a period of *seven times*, until it learns that *the Most High rules the kingdom of men*.

When Daniel hears the dream and he realizes what it signifies for the emperor, alarm and dismay register on his face. Nebuchadnezzar encourages Daniel not to be concerned, so he proceeds to tell the king what his dream means. It was, as Nebuchadnezzar must have realized, about none other than himself.

The nature of true greatness

It is striking that all three stages of God's self-disclosure to Nebuchadnezzar (in chapters 2, 3, and 4) focus on something of immense size: a colossal dream statue, a colossal actual golden statue, and a colossal dream tree. Each of them is saying something about Nebuchadnezzar: he is the imposing head of gold in the dream image, the *eminence grise* that lurks thinly disguised behind the golden image, and the great tree that looms over the land. One gets the impression that Nebuchadnezzar was a big man in every sense of the word. As Daniel says: *it is you, O king, who have grown and become strong. Your greatness has grown and reaches to heaven, and your dominion to the ends of the earth.*

Nebuchadnezzar was a big man in charge of a huge empire whose capital city was a wonder of the ancient world – a city originally engineered to reflect human achievement, symbolized in its famous ziggurat whose top pierced the heavens. Daniel makes sure that Nebuchadnezzar sees the connection – it is now the emperor whose *greatness has grown and reaches to heaven.*

As we saw earlier, Nebuchadnezzar was Man writ large. Like his ideological ancestors, the movers and shakers of ancient Babel, Nebuchadnezzar had succeeded in making a name for himself. And, just as in a much earlier time, when God had come down to see what was motivating Babel and had to judge it, so now God takes an interest in the motivations of Babylon's king – and, as a result, has to discipline him physically and mentally. The question is: what are the issues at stake?

The tree was extremely attractive. Its leaves were beautiful; it gave protection, shade, and food to a vast empire. Once more we notice that this is God's assessment of Nebuchadnezzar; and it is far from the gloom-and-doom negativism that is characteristic of some apocalyptic literature. There was something positively glorious about Nebuchadnezzar's achievements, and God approved of them.

The imagery of a beautiful tree is very suggestive, since the very first comment made about trees in the biblical creation narrative has to do with their aesthetic qualities:

> *And out of the ground the Lord God made to spring up every tree that is pleasant to the sight and good for food. The tree of life was in the midst of the garden, and the tree of the knowledge of good and evil. (Genesis 2:9.)*

Human beings have an aesthetic sense that responds to the natural beauty of trees. Part of the worldwide fame of Babylon had to do with its hanging gardens.[24] No doubt they contained a breathtaking collection of trees that were a sheer delight to walk among.

Beyond the gardens, Babylon was full of architectural and artistic expressions of Nebuchadnezzar's aesthetic imagination. He had made it a glorious city. He had also ensured that everyone was aware that he was responsible for its magnificence, by having his name stamped on the vast majority of the bricks that were used. "I have examined," says Sir Henry Rawlinson, "the bricks belonging perhaps to a hundred different towns and cities in the neighbourhood of Baghdad, and I never found any other legend than that of Nebuchadnezzar, son of Nabopolassar, king of Babylon."

Trees are not only aesthetically pleasing, but according to Genesis they are also *good for food*. And the great "tree" that was Nebuchadnezzar had provided food for his empire. Nebuchadnezzar had filled his empire with myriad things for his citizens that he imagined would contribute to a fulfilled life at all levels. His own description of his state of mind when he had the dream is revealing: *I, Nebuchadnezzar, was at ease in my house and prospering in my palace* (Daniel 4:4). The word here translated "prospering" is related to a Hebrew word that is used to denote the luxuriant foliage of a tree (see, for instance, Psalm 92:12–14).

Perhaps Nebuchadnezzar even imagined himself to be a veritable tree of life, in the middle of a garden in the middle of the earth. This imagery immediately and powerfully evokes memories of a more ancient garden – the Garden of Eden. According to the Genesis account, God planted that garden, and he put the first humans into it as his stewards to look after it.

That ought to be enough to show us that Nebuchadnezzar was not being disciplined by God because he was a brilliant architect and town planner who had built a magnificent city and festooned it with beautiful gardens. God is not against human cultural flourishing in terms of the creative use of aesthetics. On the contrary, he gave it to the first humans and encouraged them to use it. He did the same with Nebuchadnezzar.

No, the emperor was not being disciplined because he had used his aesthetic sense to create a marvellous city. Indeed, when the king had learned his lesson, God not only restored to him all the glory he had lost, he gave him even more.

To see what the real problem was, let's think of that other tree in the Garden of Eden – the tree of the knowledge of good and evil. Human beings not only possess an aesthetic sense but also a moral sense. We are moral beings. Nebuchadnezzar's fault lay in the realm of the moral. One might say that he had concentrated on the tree of life and neglected the significance of the tree of the knowledge of good and evil. Daniel says as much as he reaches the heart of his interpretation of the dream:

> *Therefore, O king, let my counsel be acceptable to you: break off your sins by practicing righteousness, and your iniquities by showing mercy to the oppressed, that there may perhaps be a lengthening of your prosperity. (Daniel 4:27.)*

According to God's analysis of his life, Nebuchadnezzar had three principal character faults. The first two were that he had neglected righteousness and had shown insufficient mercy to the oppressed. God regarded these failures as so serious that the emperor would have to endure a lengthy period of discipline that would involve him losing his reason and being excluded from human company to eat grass like an ox. He would eventually be restored, but not until he realized that God ruled in the kingdoms of men.

Thirdly, like many powerful men Nebuchadnezzar was guilty of an overweening pride. Coupled with his lack of moral integrity and humanitarian mercy, this trait fuelled a driving ambition to create an aesthetic legacy that bore the unmistakable stamp of his name. How many dictators, past and present, have robbed and oppressed the poor in order to build vast buildings to glorify their own names?

One leisure activity that my wife and I enjoy is visiting the stately homes of Britain. Their grand designs, spacious rooms filled with exquisite furniture, and walls lined with famous paintings, give great pleasure. Walking in their beautifully planned gardens in the spring is a sheer delight. But one cannot help recalling that many of these grand estates are the spoils of war, or the fruits of the labour of thousands of underpaid and overworked people.

However, let us emphasize it once more – since it runs contrary to the impression given down through the ages by some people – Christianity does not regard enjoying beautiful things as wrong in itself. After all, God created our aesthetic sense, and most of us love to have flowers and colour around us. We find drabness depressing.

The proper use of our aesthetic sense should lead us to God himself, who is the ultimate source of beauty. But if our aesthetic sense (or anything else) becomes our master, it can drive a wedge between us and God and lead us into much evil. Indeed, according to the Genesis account, that is precisely the way in which the poison of sin entered the world in the first place. The man and the woman were encouraged by the enemy to set themselves loose from God and follow their senses, with the false promise that they would be *like God, knowing good and evil* (Genesis 3:5). Nebuchadnezzar was now facing that very same issue.

We face it also. This is a hedonistic age, and we are encouraged on all sides to follow our desires, whatever they are – to "do our own thing". God is represented as the Great Inhibitor, and people are encouraged to rid themselves of these "non-existent gods" that stifle human flourishing. The only limit on behaviour is that which is set by the law of the land, in terms of causing harm to others – although how this might be measured is another matter.

Through Daniel God gave Nebuchadnezzar an opportunity to repent and mend his ways, but he failed to take it. A year after his dream the judgment of God was executed against him. It happened when the king was admiring the superb panoramic vista of his great city from the top of his world, the roof of the royal palace. His heart swelled with pride and he said to himself (or to those around him): *Is not this great Babylon, which I have built by my mighty power as a royal residence and for the glory of my majesty?* (Daniel 4:30). At that precise moment a voice from heaven announced his fate, and the hapless king descended into the darkness of a strange kind of insanity.

There has been much speculation about the nature of what afflicted Nebuchadnezzar's mind. Some have suggested *boanthropy*, a mental affliction where a person imagines himself to be an ox and behaves like it. Others have suggested a similar mental illness, *lycanthropy*, where the afflicted person believes that he or she is a wolf (a disease that has no doubt fuelled stories about werewolves). Whatever it was, the text of Daniel attributes its onset to the direct intervention of God, and emphasizes its behavioural aspect: Nebuchadnezzar began to live like an animal and was eventually driven out from human company.

In due course Daniel will relate two visions of his own, in which he sees strange composite animals that have certain human characteristics. There is a question raised by all of this that is very important and highly relevant to our discussion as we think about the source of morality: what is the nature of the relationship between humans and animals?

Human and animal - what's the difference?

The Bible insists that human beings are unique, since they are made in the image of God. To use biblical terminology, *God is spirit* (John 4:24); human beings are part spirit and part flesh; animals are flesh.

Princeton bio-ethicist Peter Singer vehemently disagrees, and he traces many of our contemporary problems in practical ethics to the biblical view that human beings are a special creation. Singer regards this view as an unwarranted "speciesism" that must be rejected. According to the *Oxford English Dictionary* speciesism is defined as "discrimination against or exploitation of certain animal species by human beings, based on the assumption of mankind's superiority". Oddly enough, at first sight, speciesism can look like the very reverse of Nebuchadnezzar's exaltation of himself above every other creature in his kingdom.

Singer writes:

Whatever the future holds, it is likely to prove impossible
to restore in full the sanctity-of-life view. The philosophical
foundations of this view have been knocked asunder. We can
no longer base our ethics on the idea that human beings are
a special form of creation made in the image of God, singled
out from all other animals, and alone possessing an immortal
soul. Our better understanding of our own nature has bridged
the gulf that was once thought to lie between ourselves and
other species, so why should we believe that the mere fact that
a being is a member of the species *Homo Sapiens* endows its
life with some unique, almost infinite value?[25]

John Gray (2003, page 37) thinks similarly:

Over the past two hundred years philosophy has shaken off
Christian faith. It has not shaken off Christianity's cardinal
error – the belief that humans are radically different from
all other animals.

Thus Singer and Gray query the distinction between humans and
animals, and regard any special status for human beings as an
example of speciesism, and therefore to be deprecated.[26]

Now it is only fair to point out that this does not mean that
such philosophers necessarily hold that human beings have no
value. In fact Singer has written a challenging book, *The Life You
Can Save*, and he is a leading spokesman for animal rights who has
been laudably successful in curbing some of the cruel excesses of
factory farming. What it does mean, however, is that they regard
human beings as part of nature and therefore to be respected as all
of nature is to be respected (with which, so far, most theists would
agree), but only to that extent. Human beings, accordingly, belong
to a (presumably temporary) stage in the continuum of the process
of animal evolution, and therefore should be respected only to the
extent that this status accords them moral value (with which theists
would disagree).

In an interview with an Australian newspaper, Singer stated that he belonged to the intellectual tradition of the utilitarian Jeremy Bentham, who once said:

> From an ethical perspective, we all stand on an equal footing
> – whether we stand on two feet, or four, or none at all.[27]

And, according to Singer, on this premiss of the continuity of animal species it is logical to think that, under certain circumstances, human beings may be less valuable than other animals. Here are two samples to give an idea of his view:

> There is no reason to think that a fish suffers less when dying in a net than a foetus suffers during an abortion, hence the argument for not eating fish is much stronger than the argument against abortion. (1995, page 209.)

> The life of a newborn baby is of less value than the life of a pig, a dog or a chimpanzee. (1979, pages 112–13.)

To get to such a radical view (a view, one might say, so utterly abhorrent to common moral intuition) Singer denies that there is a Creator. He denies that human beings are special creatures made in the image of God, and he denies the existence of a soul. As his main reason for doing so he offers "our better understanding of our own nature", claiming that science has bridged the gulf between ourselves and other species, so that membership of *homo sapiens* is reduced to "a mere fact".

On closer inspection Singer's view rests on a profound misunderstanding of biblical teaching. He imagines that God made humans to be arbiters of everything *so that they can do what they like*, including the exploitation of animals. However, this is not the biblical view. Human beings, made in the image of God, are answerable to God as stewards – even for their attitude to animals and their use of the earth.

There are several biblical passages that indicate God's care for animals. Jesus speaks of the birds being fed by our heavenly Father (Matthew 6:26). The Sabbath rest was to be enjoyed by livestock as well as by humans, and if people met an enemy's ox or donkey going astray they were to bring it back to the owner, and rescue it (and him) if they were in difficulty (Exodus 20:10; 23:4–5, 12). And they were not to muzzle an ox that was treading corn (Deuteronomy 25:4).

This last statement is cited twice in the New Testament (1 Corinthians 9:9; 1 Timothy 5:18). Paul derives from it the principle that the labourer deserves his wages. In the first Paul asks: *Is it for oxen that God is concerned?* which Singer takes to mean that Paul thought that God had no concern for animals. But this cannot be the case. As a rabbi, Paul took the law very seriously. He would not deny the original understanding of the commandment – a humane attitude to animals – but is applying it in a wider sense to humans.

Singer also cites the cursing of the fig tree (Mark 11:12–22) as an example of Jesus' indifference to plants. Was it not unreasonable to curse the tree for being fruitless when, as Mark expressly says, *it was not the season for figs*? However, a little research shows that Singer is very wide of the mark here. The problem is most satisfactorily cleared up in a discussion called *The Barren Fig Tree* published many years ago by W. M. Christie, a Church of Scotland minister in Palestine under the British mandatory regime. First he points out the time of year at which the incident is said to have occurred. (If, as is probable, Jesus was crucified on 6 April AD 30, it occurred during the first days of April). Christie continues:

> Now, the facts connected with the fig tree are these. Toward the end of March the leaves begin to appear, and in about a week the foliage coating is complete. Coincident with [this], and sometimes even before, there appears quite a crop of small knobs, not the real figs, but a kind of early forerunner. They grow to the size of green almonds in which condition they are eaten by peasants and others when hungry. When they come to their own indefinite maturity they drop off.

These precursors of the true fig are called *taqsh* in Palestinian Arabic. Their appearance is a harbinger of the fully formed appearance of the true fig, some six weeks later. So, as Mark says, the time for figs had not yet come. But if the leaves appear without any *taqsh*, that is a sign that there will be no figs whatsoever. Since Jesus found *nothing but leaves* – that is, leaves without any *taqsh* – he knew that "it was an absolutely hopeless, fruitless fig tree" and said as much. You don't criticize a gardener, much less a farmer, for cutting down a tree like that.

F. F. Bruce goes on to describe the cursing of the fig tree as a real-life parable that emphasized the spoken parable of the fig tree in Luke 13:6–9 about the need to repent and bear moral fruit. The cursing of the fig tree, much like the parable of the vineyard, is a parable of Israel running the risk of judgment. It is also reasonable to infer that Jesus, knowing in advance that his disciples would be surprised by the quick effect his curse had, used this fig tree to provoke their reaction and thus make the lesson about faith more memorable.

Singer's view, that the way to get a more humane treatment of animals is to jettison the biblical teaching on the special nature of human beings, is self-evidently flawed when we see the extreme views to which it leads (infanticide, for example). I would like to suggest that the true answer lies in the exact opposite direction. It is to recover the biblical teaching that human beings are uniquely called to be responsible stewards of creation. We are not here to exploit and destroy it but to look after it and care for it. Indeed, so seriously does God take this devolved government that part of his ultimate judgment will involve *destroying the destroyers of the earth* (Revelation 11:18).

From intellectual darkness to light

Nebuchadnezzar's punishment is clearly connected with his pride. His intellect that had proudly reared itself up to heaven became darkened, and his behaviour descended into that of an animal. It was a strange creature that prowled the fields where it was confined in Babylon for seven long years. Do we have here an echo of the Garden of Eden, where the first temptation to human pride originated in a strange animal with partly human characteristics – a serpent that talked?

Nebuchadnezzar's descent into the intellectual darkness of animal behaviour is clearly an extreme case, but nonetheless one that illustrates an important general principle. The darkening of intellect is a topic that is picked up in the New Testament, when Paul describes how rejection of God ultimately has a negative effect on the mind. He speaks of those who,

> although they knew God ... did not honour him as God or
> give thanks to him, but they became futile in their thinking,
> and their foolish hearts were darkened. Claiming to be wise,
> they became fools... (Romans 1:21–22).

The mention of "thanks" here is pivotal. Saying "thank you" to someone indicates a certain dependence upon them. Expressing gratitude to God is likewise an acknowledgment of indebtedness and dependence upon him. It is here that humans in their pride tend to go wrong. They will not acknowledge that they are dependent upon someone higher than themselves. *We have no masters*, is their cry. Nebuchadnezzar was one of them.

Paul claims that rejection of God has a detrimental effect on reason. Many atheists, who think that their position is an oasis of reason and clear-headedness, would loudly protest. It is important for me to say that I am not suggesting that atheists cannot think. Some, however, particularly those of the "New Atheist" brand, make a great fuss of what they think is the damage that belief in God does to the mind. Their descriptions of religious belief (like "virus of the mind") are not uncommon. It does not seem to occur to them that the shoe could be on the other foot.

When it comes to thinking about God, why do some otherwise rational, intelligent people seem unaware that they become irrational? For instance, some of them persist in claiming that Jesus never existed, even though the overwhelming weight of ancient historical scholarship is to the contrary. They insist on offering the public a choice between God and science, when elementary logic should tell them that theology and science are not alternatives but complementary. God is an explanation in terms of agency, and science in terms of mechanism and law. I find it easy to explain this distinction to most teenagers.

In addition, many atheists persist in maintaining that atheism is not a belief system – at the very same time as they claim to *believe* it. They have made up their minds that (Christian) faith means believing where there is no evidence, and then they refuse to consider any serious evidence offered to them.

My point is that they would not tolerate such superficiality in others, but they don't seem to be capable of seeing it in themselves. Something has happened to their minds. Their refusal to have God in their thinking has led to intellectual darkness. As a shrewd farmer in Ireland said to me many years ago, "If a man cannot see reason, then reason is not his problem."

Nebuchadnezzar was probably more of an architect and engineer than a scientist. It was his proud concept of himself as the originator and goal of the aesthetic wonders of Babylon that led to his downfall. Now he was descending so far into the dark that he was losing all discipline of himself – his hair grew like eagles' feathers and his nails like the claws of a bird.

There are gradations in that descent. When human beings reject God they die spiritually, and that death touches, spoils, distorts, twists and eventually destroys all that makes human life what it is – from the moral to the aesthetic, from family relationships to work.

We have only to think of some examples of what is accepted as art or entertainment nowadays to understand that rejection of God leads to the death of civilized culture. It leads to the inversion of values; where a pile of excrement is hailed as *avant garde* art, and blatant immorality is hailed as marvellous theatre. The darkness is such that there is little or no understanding or appreciation of what has happened – man has descended to the animal.

Putting this into reverse is what is meant by "repentance", which in the Greek is *metanoia* – "change of mind". It involves a lifting of our eyes and mind towards heaven, which is exactly what Nebuchadnezzar did at the end of the period of his discipline:

> At the end of the days I, Nebuchadnezzar, lifted my eyes to heaven, and my reason returned to me, and I blessed the Most High, and praised and honoured him who lives for ever,
> > for his dominion is an everlasting dominion,
> > and his kingdom endures from generation to generation;
> > all the inhabitants of the earth are accounted as nothing,
> > and he does according to his will among the host of heaven
> > and among the inhabitants of the earth;
> > and none can stay his hand
> > or say to him, "What have you done?"
> At the same time my reason returned to me, and for the glory of my kingdom, my majesty and splendour returned to me. My counsellors and my lords sought me, and I was established in my kingdom, and still more greatness was added to me. Now I, Nebuchadnezzar, praise and extol and honour the King of heaven, for all his works are right and his ways are just; and those who walk in pride he is able to humble. (Daniel 4:34–37.)

Twice Nebuchadnezzar states that his *reason returned* to him. For seven years, as Daniel had predicted it would happen, he had been in a mental fog. But now the madness lifted, his reasoning powers came back and, probably to his great astonishment (as this was the ancient Near East), he was even restored to his former glory.

Nebuchadnezzar had thought that he towered above his people and his empire. He discovered that, along with all other inhabitants of the world, he was as nothing in comparison with God. He was eventually brought to see how big God is, and bowed his head and heart to honour and praise him for the rightness and justice of his ways.

Nebuchadnezzar came to admit that God's severe humbling of him was right and necessary to bring him to real understanding of the nature of the kingdom of heaven and its eternal rule. It would, of course, have been more pleasant to learn this lesson without enduring seven years of intellectual darkness and bizarre behaviour; but better to learn it that way than never to learn it at all. For Nebuchadnezzar, coming to faith in God was not a forsaking of reason; in a very literal sense it was a return to reason.

One would love to know what the response was to the emperor's testimony. Was it first published as part of Daniel's book, or did it circulate independently? Alas, so far at least, that is not for us to know.

Nebuchadnezzar's journey of faith is unique to him, of course. His time may seem remote to us, and we may find it difficult to relate either to him or his circumstances. However, his experience embodies principles that have direct application to us today.

I may not have built Babylon, but there will be lesser achievements that will tempt me to pride. There is nothing wrong in enjoying the aesthetically beautiful things in life, but it is possible that our indulgence in them can take our eyes off the need to be considerate of others who are not so fortunate.

If we have been given intellectual ability, artistic or musical talent, business acumen, or aptitude in a thousand and one directions, how easy it is to think that somehow we are the source. What is more, the same thing can be true of our attitude to spiritual capacity. The apostle Paul was very aware of the danger here. In his famous "hymn" to love as the supreme virtue, he writes:

> If I speak in the tongues of men and of angels, but have not love, I am a noisy gong or a clanging cymbal. And if I have prophetic powers, and understand all mysteries and all knowledge, and if I have all faith, so as to remove mountains, but have not love, I am nothing. If I give away all I have, and if I deliver up my body to be burned, but have not love, I gain nothing. (1 Corinthians 13:1–3.)

We are used to the scenario where someone is gifted in sport or the arts but deeply flawed in their moral behaviour. Natural ability is not necessarily indicative of good character; in some sense it is independent of character. What we may find harder to understand is, as Paul says, that the same is true in the spiritual realm. We may be very gifted by God, but if we do not exhibit love in our character *those gifts are of no value to us.*

This is very sobering. Sad to say, the Christian world is not exempt from that pushy competitiveness that says in effect, "My gift is more important than yours." God gives the gifts as it pleases him and organizes the body that is the church in such a way that the prominent gifts are not necessarily the most important (1 Corinthians 12:18–26). Furthermore, though not all gifts are open to me, the development of character is. What is more, as Paul goes on to point out, one day the gifts will no longer be necessary. All that will be left is character. It is a humbling question to ask: what will be left of me when the gifts are gone?

In the early church, as today, people were lining up behind their favourite teachers and preachers. One said *I follow Paul* and another *I follow Apollos* (1 Corinthians 3:4). Paul was trenchant in his rebuke to this incipient sectarian thinking:

> *What then is Apollos? What is Paul? Servants through whom you believed, as the Lord assigned to each. I planted, Apollos watered, but God gave the growth…. So let no one boast in men. … What do you have that you did not receive? If then you received it, why do you boast as if you did not receive it? (1 Corinthians 3:5–6, 21; 4:7.)*

We are not the source of our gifts; we did not merit them. They were not given to fuel our pride, but rather to be used to the benefit of others as well as ourselves. If we do not use them in love, they may well be of service and value to others – but they will be of no value to us.

Nebuchadnezzar's system of values was flawed. Ours may be flawed too. I am sure we have noticed that when we give in to pride our behaviour may rapidly descend into the kind of raw jousting for position that is evident in the animal kingdom. It is then that we risk being cut down.

CHAPTER 13

THE WRITING ON THE WALL
Daniel 5

It was formerly assumed that Daniel 5 had little or no historical substance, for the simple reason that there was no independent verification of the existence of a monarch called Belshazzar. All of this changed, however, with the finding of the so-called Nabonidus Cylinders, which are now in the British Museum.

This was one of four cylinders found at the ziggurat of Ur (south of Babylon) in 1854. They were left, one at each corner, by Nabonidus to commemorate his rebuilding of the ziggurat between 555 and 539 BC

Translation

*I am Nabonidus, king of Babylon, patron of Esagila and
Ezida, devotee of the great gods. E-lugal-galga-sisa, the
ziggurat of E-gish-nu-gal in Ur, which Ur-Nammu, a former
king, built but did not finish it (and) his son Shulgi finished
its building. On the inscriptions of Ur-Nammu and his son
Shulgi I read that Ur-Nammu built that ziggurat but did not
finish it (and) his son Shulgi finished its building.*

*Now that ziggurat had become old, and I undertook the
construction of that ziggurat on the foundations which Ur-
Nammu and his son Shulgi built following the original plan
with bitumen and baked brick. I rebuilt it for Sin, the lord of
the gods of heaven and underworld, the god of gods, who lives
in the great heavens, the lord of E-gish-nu-gal in Ur, my lord.*

*Sin, lord of the gods, king of the gods of heaven and
underworld, god of gods, who lives in the great heavens, when
you enter with joy into this temple may the welfare of Esagila,
Ezida and Egishshirgal, the temples of your great divinity, be
always on your lips. And let the fear of your great divinity be
in the heart of your people so that they will not sin against
your great divinity.*

*Let their [the temples'] foundations be established as the
heavens. As for me, Nabonidus, king of Babylon, save me
from sin against your great divinity, and give me life until
distant days. And as for* **Belshazzar** *my firstborn son, my
own child, let the fear of your great divinity be in his heart,
and may he commit no sin; may he enjoy happiness in life.*

This is thought to be an image of Nabonidus

Nebuchadnezzar died in 562 BC and was succeeded by Amel-Marduk 562–560, the Evil-Merodach of Jeremiah 52:31 and 2 Kings 25:27. He was in turn succeeded by Mergal Shar-usar (Nergal-Sharezer) in 560–556. After him came his son Labasi-Marduk who was overthrown after six months by a group of conspirators including Nabonidus, who was to be the last actual Chaldean king.

Nabonidus made his son Belshazzar co-regent, entrusting the kingship to him during a ten-year absence in Arabia; so that Belshazzar was technically the second ruler of the kingdom. This is why Belshazzar was only able to offer the position of being the third ruler in the kingdom to anyone who could read the writing on the wall. The description of Nebuchadnezzar in Daniel 5, as the "father" of Belshazzar, is consistent with ancient Near-Eastern usage, signifying "ancestor" rather than immediate progenitor. In fact there is a suggestion that Nabonidus's mother, Adad-guppi, was a daughter of Nebuchadnezzar; so Belshazzar would have been his grandson. (See the *Archaeological Study Bible*, 2011, pages 1393–94.)

It would appear from extra-biblical evidence that Babylon fell to Persian troops without a battle in Nabonidus's absence. Herodotus records in his *Histories* (1.190–191) how the Persian troops gained access to the city by temporarily diverting the flow of the River Euphrates.

A feast fit for a king?

The story of Belshazzar's feast is one of the most famous parts of the book of Daniel. It has been notably painted by Rembrandt and set to music in the celebrated oratorio by William Walton. From it comes the memorable phrase *the writing is on the wall*, and it forms a spectacular tragic climax to the first half of Daniel's work.

We have long since noted that the vessels Nebuchadnezzar looted from the temple in Jerusalem, and installed in the museum of his treasures, form the centrepiece of the final drama of the Babylonian empire. We saw in our study of Daniel 1 that these vessels are an expression of values, and lead us into one of the main ideas dominating the first half of the book. This theme now reaches the end of its trajectory, and those golden vessels from Jerusalem are placed on the tables at the fateful, glittering banquet that has come to be known as *Belshazzar's Feast*.

Some have suggested that Belshazzar held his feast to express his confidence that Babylon was impregnable, even though he knew that, at that very moment, the armies of Cyrus were just outside the walls of the city.

Whatever the occasion, we are simply told that King Belshazzar *made a great feast for a thousand of his lords*. This is, therefore, a story about food – and as such it parallels the account in chapter 1, where Daniel and his friends refuse to eat the royal food.

Food is obviously a very important part of life, essential to physical survival. In the previous chapter of Daniel we saw how part of Nebuchadnezzar's function, as a *tree of life* in the garden of Babylon, was to provide food for his vast empire. In our enjoyment of food we share much in common with animals: dogs, for example, seem to appreciate their food as much as we do. The tragic thing, however, is that not all leaders of countries see it as their responsibility to act as "trees of life" and they heartlessly enhance themselves on the back of a starving population.

There is more to eating food than satisfying a physical appetite, vitally important though that is. In fact when trees are first mentioned in the book of Genesis, they are said to be *good to look at and good for food*. The order is interesting – first the aesthetic, and then the nutritious. Daniel 4 has brought the first to our attention. Now Daniel 5 will focus on the second, albeit in close connection with the first.

This aesthetic dimension to our eating is one of the things that distinguish us from animals. Of course, if we are in a hurry, we may refuel by unceremoniously gobbling down a tin of baked-beans in much the same way as our dog gobbles a piece of meat that is thrown to it. But we all know there is a better and more enjoyable way of eating. Indeed, therein lies the fascination of the countless television programmes on preparing food. Those of us who are non-experts are amazed by the aesthetic beauty that specialist cooks can create in a meal consisting of the most ordinary ingredients. And most of us enjoy those special occasions when a meal has been thoughtfully and artistically prepared, the various courses carefully balanced, and candles and flowers are on the table.

We can be sure that Belshazzar's banqueting hall was a magnificent spectacle, involving the very best place settings for a thousand nobles gleaming in the light of an ornate lampstand. Aesthetically, it was as perfect as the royal court could make it. As the text says, it was *a great feast*.

However, a meal can involve much more than aesthetics. Belshazzar's feast certainly did. The critical point came as King Belshazzar was drinking in front of the thousand nobles. When he tasted the wine something clearly occurred to him. He called the servants, and commanded them to bring the golden temple vessels to adorn his feast. It may sound like a whim, but clearly it was something that had been working in his mind and heart for a long time.

That Belshazzar knew about those Jerusalem vessels is obvious from what Daniel eventually says to him. He knew that Nebuchadnezzar had treated them with respect, and he knew exactly where they were to be found when he decided to have them brought to his feast. They were magnificent: the very best products of the skilled master-craftsmen of Israel. Why should they stay in a museum? Why should he not use them to increase the lavish beauty of his feast?

But that was not the only reason he called for them – in fact it may not even have been a reason. The real reason had to do with the God for whose glory those goblets had been made. Belshazzar knew of Nebuchadnezzar's supernatural experiences with the God who stood behind those vessels. He knew that Nebuchadnezzar had eventually come to worship and honour this God as the God of heaven. He knew all this and yet he rejected it: rejected it so vehemently that he made up his mind to publicly repudiate God in a gesture of deliberate blasphemy.

One cannot help wondering what his nobles thought as they watched the gleaming vessels being arranged on the tables in front of them. Surely many of them would also have known what those vessels were. It is hard to imagine that when Belshazzar invited his lords to drink out of those vessels, he did not inform them of his precise intentions. After all, what was the point of getting people to use the vessels if they did not know what they were doing? Belshazzar surely wanted them to know, so that they would be as committed as he was in their rejection of the living God.

And so his nobles joined him in lifting those sacred vessels to their lips and drinking to the Babylonian gods whose idols no doubt filled the hall around them. That would show the power brokers of Babylon what Belshazzar really thought of the God of Israel. It would show them what he expected them to do if they were to retain his favour. Whether or not they believed that there was any reality in their gods is beside the point. The vessels from which they drank were holy vessels, not to be used for anything except the worship of the one true God; so Belshazzar and his nobles were bound together in a deliberately sacrilegious act. For Belshazzar, nothing was sacred, except possibly himself – his position, wealth, and power.

The writing on the wall

Belshazzar and his guests were not prepared for what happened next – although perhaps they should have been. Some years earlier Nebuchadnezzar had mounted a ceremony where he had insisted on the worship of his golden image, only to have his fiery furnace supernaturally reduced to impotence by the God of Shadrach, Meshach, and Abednego. In light of that, it was sheer insanity now to use the vessels of God in the worship of idols.

In an instant the revelry of his lavish feast was turned into sheer terror. Every eye caught sight of what looked like a human hand, writing on the plaster of the palace wall, illuminated by a lampstand. The wine stopped flowing. Belshazzar was shaken to the core. All colour drained from his face, his body began to shudder uncontrollably, and his knees knocked together.

Years before, when Daniel and his friends had resisted an attempt to make them drink the wine in the king's court, it had led to them looking better in appearance and fitness than the other students. Now it was the emperor who was losing his colour, as a result of his uninhibited, blasphemous drinking. The God that Belshazzar didn't believe existed had broken through all his feeble defences – and finally gained the king's undivided attention. It must have been terrifying for him to discover in this way that the God he did not believe in was the God who was there.

Belshazzar hastily summoned his advisors, wildly promising them untold fortunes of wealth and position if they could read the writing on the wall. He was desperate to know what it said. But try as they did, they could not make sense of it. That was odd, for they could see the writing very clearly in the lamplight. They recognized the script, and in one sense the words were very familiar. They were words associated with weights, measures, and money – minas, shekels, and halves. But neither the light of the lampstand nor the light of their intellects was enough to enable them to see what the inscription meant.

Imagine the scene today, if at a state banquet a hand appeared and wrote in pounds and pence, or euros, or dollars and cents. The writing would be recognized, in the sense that the symbols would be familiar. The problem would be in assigning meaning to them. The thoughtful would realize, of course, that money is not quite the same thing as value – as witnessed by the expression "value for money", or by what different people do with their money. Money is really only a token of value; and the monetary value of something can have a highly subjective or relative dimension to it. The writing on the wall would undoubtedly have made the assembled throng think about

179

values. And what about the supernatural hand? Is there a realm beyond this one that is interested in values? Does that realm have a scale of value that we ought to know about?

Belshazzar, and probably many of his guests, knew the answer, because Nebuchadnezzar had taught it to them. He had even written about it, as we saw in Daniel 4. But now the nobles could actually feel that answer as they had never felt it before. Super-nature had broken into their world, and they sensed the awesome presence of the Source of ultimate values, God himself. They also knew that they had dishonoured him. Whatever his thoughts, Belshazzar's visceral response triggered consternation throughout the vast hall.

Enter the queen (or possibly queen mother), drawn to the banqueting hall by the commotion. She had not been present at the feast. She approached the emperor and told him to calm down, for she knew exactly the right person to ask about the inscription that was now dominating the room. That was Daniel, who of course had not been at the feast either. Indeed, the fact that the queen had to remind Belshazzar who Daniel was indicates that the king scarcely knew him. That ought not to surprise us, in light of Belshazzar's hatred of God. He would have had his reasons to steer clear of the man who had been instrumental in bringing Nebuchadnezzar to faith in the one God.

When Daniel was summoned he came at once, and was ushered in to face the terrified emperor, who obsequiously parroted the queen's words. He offered Daniel wealth and the third most powerful position in the empire. Belshazzar obviously still thought he could buy his way to anything.

However, it was all too plain to Daniel what was going on, and he brusquely dismissed the king's blandishments. Under the right circumstances Daniel would have been prepared to accept high office, but he was not interested in being enriched by a man who had so blatantly devalued the one true and living Creator God. It was important to him *from* whom he accepted power and authority.

The thousand nobles listened with dread fascination as Daniel now took the trembling potentate on a damning journey through the labyrinth of his mind, and showed him what the physical light of the lampstand and the feeble light of his advisors' minds had been unable to reveal. Daniel's light was spiritual. It came from God:

> O king, the Most High God gave Nebuchadnezzar your father kingship and greatness and glory and majesty. And because of the greatness that he gave him, all peoples, nations, and languages trembled and feared before him. Whom he would, he killed, and whom he would, he kept alive; whom he would, he raised up, and whom he would, he humbled. But when his heart was lifted up and his spirit was hardened so that he dealt proudly, he was brought down from his kingly throne, and his glory was taken from him. He was driven from among the children of mankind, and his mind was made like that of a beast, and his dwelling was with the wild donkeys. He was fed grass like an ox, and his body was wet with the dew of heaven, until he knew that the Most High God rules the kingdom of mankind and sets over it whom he will. And you his son, Belshazzar, have not humbled your heart, though you knew all this, but you have lifted up yourself against the Lord of heaven. And the vessels of his house have been brought in before you, and you and your lords, your wives, and your concubines have drunk wine from them. And you have praised the gods of silver and gold, of bronze, iron, wood, and stone, which do not see or hear or know, but the God in whose hand is your breath, and whose are all your ways, you have not honoured. (Daniel 5:18–23.)

Belshazzar was not only to be judged; he was also to know why God was judging him. It was a devastating indictment. Daniel reminded Belshazzar of something he knew very well: Nebuchadnezzar had come to realize that the source of his majesty, greatness, and power was God and not himself. God had humbled him when his pride had got the better of him, and brought him down to the level of a grass-eating animal that no one wanted. Perhaps Belshazzar had actually watched his hapless grandfather – if that was what Nebuchadnezzar was – with wonder. Perhaps he had also seen how God had mercy on the man; and how, when Nebuchadnezzar understood – really understood – that all he possessed was a divine gift, he was given back his sanity and restored to his former glory.

Whether he had seen it or not, Belshazzar knew all about it. And that was of prime importance. Belshazzar knew about the transformation of Nebuchadnezzar's life; and yet he had chosen to publicly insult and dishonour the God who had been responsible for it. In an act of suicidal defiance Belshazzar had decided to use God's sacred vessels in the service of the very idolatry that he knew God hated. He had used them to toast the *gods of silver and gold, of bronze, iron, wood, and stone, which do not see or hear or know.* The sacred symbolic vessels were also of gold, but Daniel's God was not a god of gold. He was not a material God at all. He was the living and true Creator God, who *did* see and hear and know. And Belshazzar now knew that God knew.

The trembling king also knew he had gone too far. It would be hard to imagine a more spectacular breach of the first commandment: *You shall have no other gods before me.* Centuries earlier the hand of God had written the Ten Commandments on two tablets of stone and given them to Moses, the great lawgiver. That hand had now written once more: this time on the wall of Belshazzar's palace. At that very moment the king's life was held in that very same hand. The searchlight of revelation pinned the king in its unwavering beam, and it was more than he could bear.

By now he must have sensed that the handwriting spelled his doom. And, sure enough, Daniel moved swiftly to explain to him God's verdict:

> *Then from his presence the hand was sent, and this writing was inscribed. And this is the writing that was inscribed:* MENE, MENE, TEKEL, *and* PARSIN. *This is the interpretation of the matter:* MENE, *God has numbered the days of your kingdom and brought it to an end;* TEKEL, *you have been weighed in the balances and found wanting;* PERES, *your kingdom is divided and given to the Medes and Persians.* (Daniel 5:24–28.)

The verdict was unequivocal and final. But why had they not understood it? In the English alphabet there are two kinds of letters – consonants and vowels. The writing on the wall was in a language whose written form only involved consonants. The vowels had to be supplied by the reader. This is not necessarily as difficult as it seems. For instance, in English it is not hard to work out what THNKS FR YR LTTR means. On the other hand, supplying different vowels could alter the meaning, and Daniel used this flexibility to interpret the words in terms of the verbal roots that lay behind the nouns. The writing on the wall had indeed to do with values, as the noun forms suggested. Daniel used the verbal forms to interpret the writing as an evaluation of Belshazzar's moral worth.

The equation was devastatingly simple: Belshazzar's value system was the polar opposite of what it should have been. By using the holy vessels for his banquet, he showed what a consummate hedonist he was. His own pleasures and desires were his supreme values. By the same token he had evaluated God at zero. Now God had responded by doing the same with him. There was nothing more to be said.

It was an extraordinarily solemn moment. The Bible makes it clear that judgment normally comes *after* death: *it is appointed for man to die once, and after that comes judgement* (Hebrews 9:27). It is very unusual that a person receives the verdict in such a spectacularly supernatural way *before* death (as well as having to face judgment after his death).

Belshazzar's alcohol-inflamed brain went into an irrational spin. In spite of the fact that he had just been tried and sentenced by God, his Creator and Judge, he still went madly on as if nothing was going to change. He insisted on performing the charade of investing Daniel with high office, and proclaimed him the third ruler in a kingdom that, unknown to Belshazzar, had only a few hours longer to exist.

Then Belshazzar gave the command, and Daniel was clothed with purple, a chain of gold was put around his neck, and a proclamation was made about him, that he should be the third ruler in the kingdom. (Daniel 5:29.)

It was a dramatic moment. Now there were two rulers of Babylon in the banqueting hall – the second and the third. One was called Belshazzar, and the other Belteshazzar. It was almost surreal. The names of the men were virtually the same, and their meanings very similar ("May Bel [Marduk] protect the king" and perhaps "May our Lady [the consort of Marduk] protect the King". Perhaps this is why Belshazzar chose to address Daniel by his Hebrew name, when the queen informed him that it was Daniel, named Belteshazzar, who should be called. The king might have been reluctant to address the man in front of him using something that sounded very like his own royal name!

Marduk (Bel), who may well have been the main object of worship that night, had signally failed to protect Belshazzar. On the other hand, by using Daniel's Hebrew name, Belshazzar was uttering the words *God is my judge* – for that is what *Daniel* means. On that fateful evening, Daniel was the interpreter of God's written, measured evaluation of Belshazzar. Daniel's very name could be seen to be part of the judicial process. Years before, Belshazzar's predecessor, Nebuchadnezzar, had tried to suppress Daniel's identity by renaming him. He had failed. Daniel's identity, as a man loyal to God, had emerged not only unscathed but enhanced.

Thus, in the palace that night, there were two men with very similar names yet totally different identities. One had decided to reject God, the other to follow him. Daniel would also have recalled from those early days how he and his three friends had determined not to compromise with idolatry, and mounted their protest against the food and wine served at the king's table. They were prepared to risk everything rather than compromise their belief that God was absolutely sacred – he was their supreme value. Perhaps even then Daniel could foresee that the logical outcome of compromise was the kind of scene that now lay before him at the king's table. He knew that God had once more vindicated his stand.

It would not be long before the banqueting hall would be deserted. The dynasty of Nebuchadnezzar, once the mighty head of gold, would be toppled to the ground and the Persians would take over, as God had said. Yet on the tables those vessels of gold, which had borne their silent witness to true and absolute values, still glittered. If only Belshazzar had listened; if only he had opened his mind to understand. But he and his nobles had ignored the message of the vessels of God and suffered the inevitable consequence. God had intervened and written his fate on the palace wall. Within a few hours Belshazzar would become a corpse – of no "value" whatsoever.

As he took a final look at the writing on the wall, Daniel may also have pondered the irony that as a young captive he had begun his language study in that very city, and now he had just interpreted an inscription for the king. And as he thought about the message of the writing, he may well have reflected that, although there had been a cost, his resistance to idolatry had resulted in immeasurable gain. What he saw in the banqueting hall proved that the cost of rejecting God was incalculably disastrous.

The finger of God

The lampstand in the banqueting hall eventually ran out of oil, and the writing was swallowed up in darkness. Yet the hand that wrote on a wall in Babylon that night would write again – next time on the ground in the city of Jerusalem. The apostle John describes the occasion as a preliminary to a famous claim that Jesus made:

> *I am the light of the world. Whoever follows me will not walk in darkness, but will have the light of life. (John 8:12.)*

Immediately before that statement, John's Gospel details an attempt by the religious leaders to entrap Jesus. As we have already noted, they had caught a woman in the act of adultery and callously brought her to Jesus: *placing her in the midst they said to him, "Teacher, this woman has been caught in the act of adultery. Now in the Law Moses commanded us to stone such women. So what do you say?"* (John 8:3–5).

The religious leaders had read a "writing", the writing of the law by the finger of God. It condemned adultery: that much they could see. So they exposed the woman to the light of the law, thinking they might force Jesus to contradict it by his refusal to apply the required penalty of stoning.

Jesus responded by bending down and writing with his finger on the ground. John does not tell us what Jesus wrote. He does tell us that they continued to press for a response. Eventually Jesus *stood up and said to them: "Let him who is without sin among you be the first to throw a stone at her." And once more he bent down and wrote on the ground* (verses 7–8).

The effect was dramatic: *But when they heard it, they went away one by one, beginning with the older ones, and Jesus was left alone with the woman standing before him* (verse 9). They had shone the light of the law into the woman's life, and were ready to stone her. They thought that they had nothing to fear from the law themselves. However, they had just come unknowingly into the presence of a much stronger light than the law: a light that penetrated even their insensitive consciences – the Light of the world. Could it have been Jesus' writing that convicted them of their sin, like the writing on Belshazzar's wall? The woman's accusers felt exposed, condemned, and ashamed. They could not bear light like that, so they walked away from it into the darkness.

The woman still remained in Jesus' presence. That was the odd thing. She felt no less guilty than the religious leaders who had left. Yet she could see that Jesus had protected her, not only from their callous attitude but also from death by stoning. He had done it in a very gracious and sensitive manner, so what would he say to her now? She clearly felt that she could safely wait in the Light and see.

He eventually straightened up and said, *"Woman, where are they? Has no one condemned you?"* *"No one, Lord,"* was her steady response. Jesus' short reply is a magnificent statement of forgiveness: *"Neither do I condemn you; go, and from now on sin no more"* (John 8:10–11). He did not condone her sin. From then on her life was to be different, but its energy would be derived from the fact that the Lord had forgiven her. The light that had driven the hypocritical and guilty religious men away had also brilliantly illuminated the path to her forgiveness.

It still has that effect.

We do not today simply have the silent witness of some symbolic golden vessels. Jesus Christ, God himself, has come into the world. He entered people's homes and ate and drank with them, in order that they could see at close quarters the pure gold of a life unsullied by sin and unmarked by the shadow of a sinful thought. Yet just as Daniel in his day was rejected by the powerful, so was the Lord Jesus. They took that life in all its beauty, and nailed it to a cross. They forced a crown of long thorns into his brow, and sneered at his claim to be Messiah the King. They covered his face with their vile spittle. They shook their fists and said: "We don't want you." They valued him at zero.

But that was their evaluation, not God's. The Lord Jesus was none other than the eternal Son of God. God the eternal Father raised him from the dead through the power of God the eternal Spirit, and gave him the name that is above every name (Philippians 2:9). In that name forgiveness is freely available to all who repent and trust him as Lord. What magnificent good news it is!

The same hand that wrote the law on the stone tablets for Moses wrote on the wall in Babylon and on the dusty ground in Jerusalem. And it writes still – on repentant and believing hearts. Paul describes the way Christian believers commend the Christian faith:

> And you show that you are a letter from Christ delivered by us, written not with ink but with the Spirit of the living God, not on tablets of stone but on tablets of human hearts. (2 Corinthians 3:3.)

It is the quality of that writing that turns many people to trust in Jesus Christ as Lord.

God's judgment and our responsibility

We have now reached the end of the first half of the book of Daniel, and with it the end of the Babylonian empire. One of its central themes has been the witness of Daniel and his friends to the emperor Nebuchadnezzar, culminating in his acknowledgment of God as Lord of lords and King of kings. It was a remarkable transformation of a pagan potentate; but, tragically, it had no effect on the man who was to be the last king of the empire: Belshazzar. Nebuchadnezzar was disciplined and eventually restored by God, whereas Belshazzar perished in the Medo-Persian invasion. This raises questions in some people's minds as to the fairness of the procedure involved. Why the differing treatment?

Similarly, in the New Testament, Paul describes how, in spite of his vehement antagonism to Jesus and his persecution of Christians, he was shown mercy because, as he himself puts it, *I had acted ignorantly in unbelief* (1 Timothy 1:13). By contrast, when King Herod, shortly after he had ordered the murder of the apostle James, gave a great oration to the people, and they responded by hailing him as a god, he was summarily judged by God (Acts 12:2, 21–23).

God revealed himself to Nebuchadnezzar through a succession of supernatural events – Daniel's interpretation of the dream image, the intervention in the fiery furnace, the dream of the tree and its consequences. Nebuchadnezzar had direct personal revelation. By contrast, Belshazzar had been presented with the evidence of what had happened to Nebuchadnezzar and presumably what Nebuchadnezzar had taught him.

These considerations show us that God's judgments are not arbitrary. Belshazzar did not act ignorantly. As Daniel forcefully pointed out to him, he was responsible for his attitude and behaviour. He acted against the evidence he had. This needs to be emphasized, since an oddly deterministic way of thinking can creep into some people's understanding of God's providences in history, whereby God's judgment and mercy are seen as entirely arbitrary decisions that do not depend on the attitude of the individual involved. That cannot be the case, since it would contradict the morality of the character of God himself.

Nor may we argue that Belshazzar was a mere puppet in God's hand as Daniel had already predicted the demise of the Babylonian empire. Such thinking assumes that God's relationship to time is the same as ours, and that his prior knowledge implies causation. This also cannot be the case, since God's judgments are based on treating Belshazzar and everyone else as responsible moral beings.

Of course, in the very nature of things, there will be differences between the kinds of evidence given to different people at different times. For instance, the earliest disciples of Jesus were eyewitnesses of his life, death, and resurrection. Those millions of others, like myself, who come later rely on their testimony – as well as on our personal experience, of course, which inevitably will differ significantly from theirs. Jesus himself commented on this situation. Here is the account as recorded by John:

> Now Thomas, one of the Twelve, called the Twin, was not with them when Jesus came. So the other disciples told him, "We have seen the Lord." But he said to them, "Unless I see in his hands the mark of the nails, and place my finger into the mark of the nails, and place my hand into his side, I will never believe."
>
> Eight days later, his disciples were inside again, and Thomas was with them. Although the doors were locked, Jesus came and stood among them and said, "Peace be with you." Then he said to Thomas, "Put your finger here, and see my hands; and put out your hand, and place it in my side. Do not disbelieve, but believe." Thomas answered him, "My Lord and my God!" Jesus said to him, "Have you believed because you have seen me? Blessed are those who have not seen and yet have believed." (John 20:24–29.)

It is clear therefore that not everyone can have the same kind of eyewitness evidence. We should note in passing that some contemporary atheists like A. C. Grayling have used the story of Thomas to buttress their idiosyncratic contention that faith means believing without evidence. He takes Jesus to be saying: "Blessed are those who have had no evidence and yet have believed." This is an astonishing conclusion for a philosopher, whose stock-in-trade is the analysis of the logic of argument. The point Jesus is making is that not everyone has the evidence of *physical sight*. But physical sight is not the only kind of admissible evidence. The very next statement in John's Gospel (how did Grayling fail to see this?) points out what that other evidence is:

> *Now Jesus did many other signs in the presence of the disciples, which are not written in this book; but these are written so that you may believe that Jesus is the Christ, the Son of God, and that by believing you may have life in his name. (John 20:30–31.)*

The apostle John's record of the signs that Jesus did constitutes evidence on which faith in him can be based. Of course, the *life in his name* that Jesus promises to those who believe in him is also powerful, confirmatory evidence that his claims are true.

A further important aspect of evidence is its moral dimension, which can be seen in the story of Belshazzar. We shall approach this issue via Jesus' account of a rich man and his neighbour, a poor man (see Luke 16:19–31). The rich man turned his life into a perpetual banquet (perhaps not unlike Belshazzar?). He appeared to regard the commandment to *love his neighbour as himself* as unimportant and ignored the impoverished Lazarus at his gate. After death he found himself excluded from the presence of God; whereas Lazarus was enjoying the fellowship of no less a person than Abraham, the father of the faithful.

Jesus describes how the rich man called upon Abraham to send Lazarus back from the dead to try to warn his brothers. Abraham's response was: *They have Moses and the Prophets; let them hear them.* To this the once rich man replied: *No, father Abraham, but if someone goes to them from the dead, they will repent.* To this Jesus replied: *If they do not hear Moses and the Prophets, neither will they be convinced if someone should rise from the dead* (Luke 16:29–31).

David Gooding points out the importance of seeing exactly why Abraham refused the rich man's request. It was not that God was determined to give the brothers no more evidence in order to bring them to repentance. It was that they needed to see that their neglect of God's law was neglect of the evidence they had already been given – a neglect so serious that it would exclude them from God's presence for ever (1987, page 277):

> And that was a moral issue, and ultimately a question
> of God's moral character. The highest possible evidence
> in the matter therefore was the plain statement of his
> Word directed to the brothers' moral conscience and
> judgment. And so it is with us. If our moral judgment is so
> irresponsible that it can make light of the Bible's warnings of
> our guilt before God … no amount of seeing of apparitions
> would convince us that we personally were in danger of
> perdition unless we repented.

The seriousness of neglecting God's law was a major part of the lesson brought home to Nebuchadnezzar in Daniel 4, in particular the very same commandment referred to above (see Exodus 20:4). Belshazzar knew all about it too, yet he deliberately rejected it. He had made up his mind, and no further evidence would have helped him.

In the current debate about the existence of God, the so-called New Atheists are constantly citing Bertrand Russell's famous quip, that if God were to ask him why he did not believe in him, Russell would say, "Not enough evidence; not enough evidence." Yet the very same New Atheists do not seem prepared to engage with serious evidence when it is offered to them; and when asked what sort of evidence they would find convincing, they are remarkably unforthcoming. One can only conclude that no amount of evidence would convince them, since they have made up their minds that there *is* no evidence. In an interview for *New Statesman*, Richard Dawkins seems to say just that:

> I don't believe in leprechauns, pixies, werewolves, jujus,
> Thor, Poseidon, Yahweh, Allah or the Trinity. For the
> same reason in every case: there is not the tiniest shred of
> evidence for any of them, and the burden of proof rests with
> those who wish to believe.[28]

Furthermore, far from blasphemy being a thing of the past, we might note that it is actively encouraged in some atheist circles. Here is an excerpt from the so-called "blasphemy challenge" taken from no less than The Richard Dawkins Foundation website.[29]

> "The Blasphemy Challenge" Rewards Participants for Demonstrating Non-Belief on YouTube Philadelphia. The Rational Response Squad has launched a $25,000 campaign to entice young people to publicly renounce any belief in the sky God of Christianity. Called "The Blasphemy Challenge," this campaign encourages participants to commit what Christian doctrine calls the only unforgivable sin – blasphemy against the Holy Spirit. (The "Holy Spirit" is an invisible ghost who Christians believe dwells on Earth as God's representative.) Participants who videotape their blasphemy and upload it to YouTube will receive a free DVD of the hit documentary "The God who wasn't there" which normally sells for $24.98. Beyond Belief Media, the distributor ... has donated 1001 DVDs to the Rational Response Squad for The Blasphemy Challenge. More than 160 participants have already blasphemed the Holy Spirit and earned free DVDs during the pre-launch phase of The Blasphemy Challenge ... While anyone can participate in The Blasphemy Challenge, the Rational Response Squad is focused on reaching a young demographic. To publicize The Blasphemy Challenge to young people, today the Rational Response Squad begins an online advertising campaign focused on 25 sites popular with teens such as Xanga, Friendster, Boy Scout Trail, Tiger Beat, Teen Magazine, YM, CosmoGirl! and Seventeen.

Is this not a strange thing to find on the website of the first Oxford Professor of the Public Understanding of Science? I wonder what would happen if the hand from Belshazzar's feast were to write again on the wall at a public gathering of atheists where such blasphemous activity was being featured. Many of these young people who are being persuaded to participate do not understand what blasphemy against the Holy Spirit is. This is not surprising, since the so-called "Rational Response Squad" do not appear to understand it either. In addition, the fact that inducements are offered does rather undermine the message.

However, let us not end on a negative note. Belshazzar's blasphemous drinking to the idols of the Babylonian pantheon stands in stark contrast to the privilege that Christians have in expressing their loyalty and worship to God as their King through a different ceremonial act of drinking. They are called upon by no less than the Lord Jesus himself to meet regularly with other believers to celebrate the New Covenant that binds them to him eternally.

CHAPTER 14

THE LAW OF THE MEDES AND PERSIANS
Daniel 6

Daniel in the Lions' Den by Peter Paul Rubens

Daniel 6 introduces us to a new world – the world of Medo-Persian rule. In terms of Nebuchadnezzar's dream, this marks a transition from the kingdom of gold to that of silver (Daniel 2:32, 39); from Babylonian rule over Babylon to Medo-Persian rule over Babylon:

> *That very night Belshazzar the Chaldean king was killed. And Darius the Mede received the kingdom, being about sixty-two years old. (Daniel 5:30–31.)*

Alec Motyer (1993) writes about that event:

> In October 539 BC, Cyrus advanced into lower
> Mesopotamia and, leaving Babylon till last, conquered
> and occupied the surrounding territory. Seeing which way
> the wind was blowing, Nabonidus of Babylon deserted his
> city, leaving it in the charge of his son Belshazzar ... the
> taking of Babylon was as bloodless and effortless as Daniel
> 5 implies.

We are faced at once with a historical puzzle. Who was Darius the Mede? After all, as Motyer says – and it is well documented on tablets like the cylinder pictured below – it was Cyrus who took over the kingdom.

The Cyrus Cylinder (British Museum)
(For a translation see Appendix B.)

The problem is that, historically, the only Darius we know of reigned from 522 to 486 BC; whereas there is historical and archaeological evidence that Cyrus took over the empire in the year 539, and Darius succeeded him. Daniel himself refers to both Darius and Cyrus in 6:28, and to Cyrus in 10:1, so he was certainly aware of both names.

Some scholars think that Darius is simply another name for Cyrus. So they read 6:28 as, "Daniel prospered in the reign of Darius, that is, in the reign of Cyrus the Persian", although this reading is deemed by other experts not to be a natural one. An alternative suggestion is that Darius was a subordinate king, appointed by Cyrus to govern Babylon. This idea is supported linguistically: (a) by the fact that Daniel 9:1 says that Darius was "made king", using a passive verb rather than an active "became king"; and (b) by the fact that Daniel 6:1 says that Darius "received the kingdom" – an unusual way of describing a conqueror. It is also argued that Daniel never refers to Darius as king of Medo-Persia, only as ruler of Babylon.

Perhaps a satisfactory resolution of this problem awaits the kind of archaeological discovery that was made in connection with Belshazzar. In light of that, it would surely be unwise to accuse Daniel of ignorance of the historical facts.

In any event, we now find Daniel serving a new master in Babylon. The city and landscape have not changed. But the culture has changed in certain ways, one of which is now highlighted – the law.

The purpose of law

As we have seen, the theme of values pervades the first half of Daniel's work. In the second half, on which we now embark, one of the major ideas is that of law. The order in which these two major themes appear is logical: laws are based on values, but they are not the same as values. Laws are enactments (by the state) for the purpose of upholding values. For them to be effective, and to ensure compliance, they are normally backed up by a system of courts and police. Chapter 5 told us about a written evaluation of a man by God. Chapter 6 will tell us about a written human law, enacted by men of power in order to discredit a man of integrity.

But first let us briefly survey the wider context.

In our introduction we drew attention to the parallel structure of the two halves of the book, and noted in particular the shape of these two halves. Each consists of an introductory section, followed by two pairs of sections that belong together:

PART A	PART B
Chapter 1	Chapter 6
Babylonian Court.	**Medo-Persian Court.**
Daniel refuses to eat the king's food.	Daniel refuses to obey the king's command and refrain from praying to God.
He and his friends are vindicated.	He is vindicated.
TWO IMAGES	**TWO VISIONS OF BEASTS**
Chapter 2	Chapter 7
Nebuchadnezzar's dream image.	Four beasts.
Chapter 3	Chapter 8
Nebuchadnezzar's golden image.	Two beasts.
TWO KINGS DISCIPLINED	**TWO WRITINGS EXPLAINED**
Chapter 4	Chapter 9
The discipline and restoration of Nebuchadnezzar.	The prophecy in the book of Jeremiah about the destruction and restoration of Jerusalem.
Chapter 5	Chapters 10–13
The "writing on the wall" and the destruction of Belshazzar.	The "Writing of Truth" and the eventual destruction of "the king".
The end of Babylonian supremacy.	The end of world history.

In this scheme, the first chapter of the first half of Daniel parallels the first chapter of the second half. They both describe court scenes in the city of Babylon, involving different regimes: chapter 1, the Babylonian; chapter 6, the Medo-Persian. They both involve protest: chapter 1 tells us how Daniel and his friends refused to partake of the food and wine in the palace, presumably because of their association with idolatry (as witnessed in Daniel 5); in chapter 6, Daniel refuses to obey the emperor's edict banning prayer to all but himself. The protests are not quite the same, for if I understand it correctly chapter 1 involves refusal to compromise with idolatry by getting involved with any pagan ceremony. The same issue also dominates Daniel 3: refusal to bow down to Nebuchadnezzar's idolatrous image. However, at no stage do we read that Nebuchadnezzar tries to stop Daniel and his friends practising their own religion according to their conscience. That step is taken by Darius in chapter 6. Here we have the first (but not the last) occasion recorded by Daniel where a pagan monarch bans the worship of God.

We can compare the two chapters, as suggested by David Gooding (see Appendix C for the complete chart):

Chapter 1	Chapter 6
Nebuchadnezzar reverently places God's vessels in his idol's temple.	Darius bans prayer to God for thirty days.
Daniel and others refuse to indulge in pagan impurities.	Daniel refuses to cease practising the Jewish religion.
Court officials sympathetic.	Court officials intrigue against him.
Daniel and his colleagues' physical and mental powers vindicated.	Daniel's political loyalty to the king vindicated.
They are promoted to high office.	He is restored to high office.

The instrument that the jealous civil servants used to attack Daniel was *the law of the Medes and Persians*. This phrase occurs three times here, indicating that the central topic of this chapter is the imposition of law to deny Daniel the right to practise his own faith and worship God according to the law of Moses. This matter of law is taken up again in the sections that follow. In chapter 7 there is a description of a powerful king who *shall think to change the times and the law* (Daniel 7:25). This king is judged by a heavenly court, at which *books are opened* (7:10). Chapter 8 tells of another powerful king (*the little horn*) who stops the regular burnt offering that was required of Israel by the law of Moses (8:9–12). Chapter 9 finds Daniel confessing that the disaster that has overtaken Jerusalem is the result of his nation's failure to keep the law of Moses. Finally, in the last section of Daniel (chapters 10–12), we read once more of a king who stops the regular burnt offering, a king whose *heart shall be set against the holy covenant* (11:28).

Law, then – both the law of the state and the law of God – forms a thread running through the second half of the book. This is how Daniel introduces it:

> It pleased Darius to set over the kingdom 120 satraps, to be throughout the whole kingdom; and over them three presidents, of whom Daniel was one, to whom these satraps should give account, so that the king might suffer no loss. Then this Daniel became distinguished above all the other presidents and satraps, because an excellent spirit was in him. And the king planned to set him over the whole kingdom. Then the presidents and the satraps sought to find a ground for complaint against Daniel with regard to the kingdom, but they could find no ground for complaint or any fault, because he was faithful, and no error or fault was found in him. Then these men said, "We shall not find any ground for complaint against this Daniel unless we find it in connection with the law of his God." (Daniel 6:1–5.)

The law of God and the laws of the state

Daniel appears to have come to Darius's attention very rapidly. No doubt the king was wise and shrewd enough to find out, as soon as possible after the conquest of Babylon, who the really able people had been in the preceding administration. The result was that Daniel soon found himself in one of the top three positions in the new kingdom, the triumvirate, to whom the 120 satraps were responsible. It was not long before Daniel distinguished himself to such an extent that Darius thought of promoting him even higher, and giving him day-to-day control of the entire kingdom.

Darius must have let his intention become known, either deliberately or inadvertently. This triggered a wave of jealousy among the administrative elite that culminated in their attempt to discredit Daniel in the eyes of the emperor. It was one of those all-too-familiar nasty intrigues that fester in the corridors of power.

However, the combined efforts of the jealous civil servants could not come up with anything substantial enough to form the basis of a complaint to the emperor. That is remarkable, since it is so easy to destroy a man by character assassination. The satraps were men of power, and in an ancient Near Eastern empire such men had ways and means of gathering information. It was as if MI6 and the CIA were put to spy on Daniel and failed to come up with anything. It makes one think. What if the same thing were attempted on me – would I come out like Daniel did? This level of personal integrity is very impressive indeed, and sadly extremely rare.

The particular thing that is singled out is Daniel's faithfulness in his job. He had been faithful to the Babylonian administration, and he was now equally faithful to the Medo-Persian. The New Testament regards faithfulness as the essential hallmark of a true servant: *it is required of stewards that they be found trustworthy* (1 Corinthians 4:2).

When they failed to find any weakness or flaw in Daniel's work they came to the conclusion that they would have to proceed against him in a different way: by somehow using his personal religious convictions against him. They focused on the law of his God; so it is clear that they were well aware of his allegiance to God. Again, this is impressive. As a student Daniel had decided that he would not keep his head beneath the parapet, reluctant to witness to his faith in case it would disadvantage him. He would witness and leave the result to God. The satraps knew what he believed and could see that it had no negative effect on the quality of his work.

This is a challenge to all of us. There is great pressure in the contemporary (Western) world for the privatization of the expression of religious belief – if not for its outright abolition. It is a widespread conviction that naturalism is the default belief system; and, ironically, Christian theism has no place in the very academies that it founded in the first place! Daniel was prepared to swim against the flow. Are we?

A plan formed in conniving minds. They sharpened their claws, pushed them deep into the velvet glove of obsequious flattery, and feigned concern to the king about the state of the nation. It was a brilliant performance.

> *Then these presidents and satraps came by agreement to the king and said to him, "O King Darius, live for ever! All the presidents of the kingdom, the prefects and the satraps, the counsellors and the governors are agreed that the king should establish an ordinance and enforce an injunction, that whoever makes petition to any god or man for thirty days, except to you, O king, shall be cast into the den of lions. Now, O king, establish the injunction and sign the document, so that it cannot be changed, according to the law of the Medes and the Persians, which cannot be revoked." Therefore King Darius signed the document and injunction. (Daniel 6:6–9.)*

Their approach to Darius was the combination of a half-truth and flattery. The half-truth was the claim that *all* the high officials were agreed on the plan. But Daniel, who was the most impressive of them in Darius's eyes, had not been consulted. The plan itself was calculated to appeal to Darius's self-esteem, as a way of consolidating his power. After all, he was the king and the official representative of the gods. Surely it was but a small step to focus the worship of the people on himself as a god? If it were only for a month, it would not lead to a religious backlash from the priests or the people. It was all for the good of the state and the unity of the nation. And so on and so forth....

We should not fail to notice a progression here. Belshazzar, in his blasphemous act, had worshipped his gods of metal and wood. He had not quite set himself up as a god to be worshipped. Darius did. Although he did not insult God in the way Belshazzar had done, it represents a deterioration. It was part of a trend that has continued through history, and will be sustained in the future – the move towards the deification of man (see 2 Thessalonians 2:4).

We should also notice that the idea of a time limit to a ban on religious practice, or even of persecution, is a recurring feature of the second half of Daniel. In chapter 7 the king, who wishes to change the law (of Moses), is granted control for *a time, times, and half a time* (7:25). In chapter 8 the regular burnt offering is stopped for 2,300 evenings and mornings (8:14). In chapter 9 Daniel understands from Jeremiah's prophecy that the term of the exile in Babylon is seventy years. He receives a vision concerning a period of seventy times seven years, decreed for his people until the restoration of Jerusalem. In the last section of the book we read of a twenty-one-day resistance to getting the message to Daniel; and finally, in discussing *the time of the end*, Daniel hears a voice asking *How long shall it be to the end of these wonders?* The answer is *a time, times, and half a time* (12:4, 6–7).

Undoubtedly there are many intriguing questions connected with these periods of time, and various answers have been given to them. Whatever those answers are, it is surely fair to say that when there is discrimination, oppression, and persecution, the uppermost question in the minds of those immediately affected is, "How long will this last?" The very fact that the conspirators suggested a time limit of thirty days may indicate that they suspected it would not be long before Daniel disobeyed the edict, and then they would have got him. The lions would make a meal of Daniel long before the thirty days had run out. Darius fell for their flattery and signed the document, *according to the law of the Medes and Persians, which cannot be revoked* (6:8, 12, 15).

Daniel rapidly got wind of what was afoot. As soon as he knew that the documents had been signed he went home to pray. He was facing exactly the same issues as his three friends had done earlier. Daniel's position, power, family (if he had one), possessions, and life were on the line. There is no record of any discussions he may have had with family or friends before he took decisive action.

As a student in the university he had nailed his colours to the mast. He would not renege and haul the flag down now. He went into his upper room that had its windows open towards Jerusalem. Staking everything on his God, he *got down on his knees three times a day and prayed and gave thanks before his God, as he had done previously* (Daniel 6:10). Regular prayer to God (and, notice, not just once but three times a day) was a non-negotiable part of the expression of his faith. He would continue to pray – law or no law. What a powerful and courageous act that kneeling was.

By facing Jerusalem Daniel was acting in the spirit of what Israel's King Solomon had said at the dedication of God's temple in Jerusalem (the one from which the vessels in chapters 1 and 5 were taken). Solomon publicly prayed to God for those who would be exiled from Israel:

> ... yet if they turn their heart in the land to which they have been carried captive, and repent and plead with you in the land of their captors ... and pray to you towards their land, which you gave to their fathers, the city that you have chosen, and the house that I have built for your name, then hear in heaven your dwelling place their prayer and their plea ... and grant them compassion in the sight of those who carried them captive, that they may have compassion on them. (1 Kings 8:47–50.)

Daniel did as King Solomon suggested and prayed towards Jerusalem – a city we have not heard named since the beginning of the book. Daniel lived *in* Babylon, and was faithful in the service of its rulers; but the secret of his integrity and faithfulness was that he did not live *for* Babylon. He lived for another city, in the spirit of Abraham and the patriarchs who were *looking forward to the city that has foundations, whose designer and builder is God* (Hebrews 11:10). Daniel lived for all that Jerusalem stood for. He knew that the future lay there and not in Babylon. Even though Nebuchadnezzar had captured it, God was not finished with Jerusalem. His promises would be fulfilled. Indeed, as Daniel himself will later tell us in chapter 9, it would be through the land of Jerusalem and not Babylon that God would one day bring King Messiah, the Saviour, into the world.

If we are city dwellers, we know what city we live *in*. But whether we are city dwellers or not, it would be good to pause and ask ourselves: what city do I live *for*?

With confidence, then, Daniel went to his open window, knelt down, and prayed towards Jerusalem. The secret of Daniel's life and witness is that he always had a window open towards Jerusalem. He knew that there was a God in heaven who would hear him. There were, however, others who might hear him too. Anticipating what would happen, the conspirators had agreed to meet under Daniel's window – which indicates that they had long known of the regularity of his prayers.

Having listened to Daniel's prayers, petitions, and pleas to God, the men of power triumphantly made haste to report to King Darius. They carefully first reminded him of the injunction; and he agreed that it had been signed and was immutable. They then put in the knife: *Daniel, who is one of the exiles from Judah, pays no attention to you, O King, or the injunction you have signed, but makes his petition three times a day* (Daniel 6:13).

Once again, this was a misleading half-truth. The first part was false, and both they and Darius knew it. Daniel was loyal to Darius to the hilt – their research had shown that Daniel was meticulous in paying attention to the king. They then played the ethnicity card, probably insinuating that Daniel was possibly more loyal to his ethnic origins than to Darius. On the second issue they were correct: Daniel paid no attention to the new law against religious freedom.

The king was devastated. He realized instantly that he had been tricked into passing the law. He could now see what he should have seen at the beginning – that the satraps had no interest in promoting his majesty's deity. They just wanted rid of Daniel. But Darius did not. He spent the rest of the day exploring every avenue to have Daniel spared, only to constantly run up against the same thing – the irrevocable nature of Medo-Persian law. After many frustrating hours getting nowhere, he was once more confronted by the insistence of the conspirators that he should put the law into effect.

Government and the rule of law

With this we have got to the heart of the difference between the Medo-Persian and the Babylonian concepts of the rule of law. The

Babylonian empire, under Nebuchadnezzar and his successors, had been an absolute monarchy. This comes out in chapter 5, where Daniel describes Nebuchadnezzar's rule to Belshazzar in the following terms: *Whom he would, he killed, and whom he would, he kept alive; whom he would he raised up, and whom he would, he humbled* (Daniel 5:19). Nebuchadnezzar regarded himself as above the law. He essentially did what he liked. Darius could not. His was a constitutional monarchy. He was also subject to the law. In his attempt to get Daniel off the hook, a law that Nebuchadnezzar would not have bothered with for an instant paralysed him.

This does not mean there had been no law in Babylon. Monarchs or dictators who do what they like often have the most repressive laws for others. Babylon was not the worst. At the legal level, its culture was very much influenced by the work of a much earlier king, Hammurabi (1792–1750 BC), who raised Babylon to the status of a world ranking capital city. It was also he who made Marduk one of its chief deities – in order to legalize his dynasty (see Roux, 1992, page 202).

Hammurabi was passionate about justice and the rule of law, and is most celebrated for his promulgation of a famous code of law:

To cause justice to prevail in the country
To destroy the wicked and the evil
That the strong may not oppress the weak.

Towards the end of his reign, he had his law code written on stone steles to be placed in temples. One of these (seen on the following page), containing 282 laws, has survived in good condition and is to be found in the Louvre in Paris.

One of the oldest functions of law is to set limits on the powers
of government; and at first sight the Medo-Persian constitutional
monarchy would seem to be an advance on an absolute monarchy,
though it was still far from the democracy later developed in Greece.
There was no separation of powers. Essentially it was the same people
who legislated, governed, and judged. But it was surely a step in the

right direction. In theory at least, it offered some protection from the excesses of a despot.

In many parts of the world, particularly in the West, equality before the law is something that is now taken for granted as one of the basic human rights for citizens of a democracy. The origins of this important tradition are not so much to be found in Medo-Persia but much earlier, in Daniel's homeland of Israel. It was a fundamental tenet of the people of Israel that everyone was subject to the law regardless of status. Through Moses God gave laws governing the behaviour of all, including the king:

> And when he sits on the throne of his kingdom, he shall write
> for himself in a book a copy of this law.... And it shall be with
> him, and he shall read in it all the days of his life, that he may
> learn to fear the Lord his God by keeping all the words of this
> law and these statutes, and doing them, that his heart may
> not be lifted up above his brothers, and that he may not turn
> aside from the commandment, either to the right hand or to
> the left, so that he may continue long in his kingdom, he and
> his children, in Israel. (Deuteronomy 17:18–20.)

It was equality under a law given by God. It reflected the deeper and all-important principle of equality itself, which goes back to the biblical teaching that human beings are made in the image of God.

Far from it being a law given by God, the particular law of the Medes and Persians that was concocted by the jealous civil servants contradicted basic morality. A legal system that had been designed for the protection of the citizens (and the emperor) was being misused to discriminate against Daniel and deprive him of what is usually regarded as a universal human right.

The empire that followed the Medo-Persian was the Greek. It was the Greek philosopher Aristotle who divided law into two kinds: the natural law, which is determined by our understanding of who we are, our human nature; and the positive law, which is determined simply by the will of the lawmaker. On this understanding, the law contrived by the Medo-Persian conspirators was a positive law. It conflicted with what most civilized nations would regard as Daniel's right to practise his faith according to his conscience. It was not only contrary to natural law, it was contrary to the law of Daniel's God; which, of course, was the motivation for passing it in the first place.

We must be thankful that in many if not most cases there is no conflict between God's law, natural law, and the law of the state. In fact the last often draws deeply on the first two. The issue at the heart of this chapter is the legal engineering of a clash of two laws in order to compromise an individual.

Darius soon discovered what many others, with less power than he had, have discovered: once a law is on the statute books it is well nigh impossible to get it repealed. Indeed, that is the whole point of having law: it should not be easy to ignore or get round. The Medo-Persians insisted on this to such an extent that even the chief signatory to a law could not get it reversed. On this occasion it was used to trap Daniel. On a later occasion it was used by the Medo-Persian king Ahasuerus to protect the Jews in the time of Queen Esther (Esther 8:8).

A contemporary example of the irreversibility of a law once it has been passed is given by the landmark Roe v. Wade 1973 ruling, legalizing abortion in the United States. The name Jane Roe is a pseudonym given for her protection, but it is now well known that she is Norma McCorvey. She became a Christian twenty years later and changed her mind about abortion. But she could not get the law reversed, even though she had been the one in whose name it was decided.

What happened to Daniel shows us that, in the hands of unscrupulous men, what should be a strength of the law can become a weakness. It alerts us once more to the core message of the dream – no human system of governance is perfect.

A higher law

When Daniel was put into the execution chamber – a den of hungry lions – the distraught and impotent Darius had at least the courage to say to Daniel: *May your God, whom you serve continually, deliver you* (Daniel 6:16). This statement shows that the king was aware of Daniel's consistent and frequent expression of his faith. How could it have slipped his mind, then, when the conspirators had first suggested their law? How could he have been such a fool as not to see that they had Daniel in their sights? Had their appeal to his vanity really deadened his judgment that badly?

Troubled by such questions, the king spent a sleepless night without food or entertainment. He got up at dawn the next day and personally went to the lions' den. Anxiously yet with a remarkable degree of hope he called out: *O Daniel, servant of the living God, has your God, whom you serve continually, been able to deliver you from the lions?* (6:20). His heart must have leapt with joy when he heard Daniel's strong reply: *O king, live for ever! My God sent his angel and shut the lions' mouths, and they have not harmed me, because I was found blameless before him; and also before you, O king, I have done no harm* (6:21–22).

Darius was delighted, and then he took swift action against the conspirators. He put them and their families into the den they had intended for Daniel, and the lions tore them to pieces.

What now of the law of the Medes and Persians that could not be revoked? How was Darius able to ignore it completely and act in this way? What happens next implies that Darius saw in Daniel's amazing survival an indication that there was a law higher even than the law of the Medes and Persians, the law of God, and that when they clashed, the latter was to be obeyed. Darius issued a decree and sent it throughout his empire:

Peace be multiplied to you. I make a decree, that in all my royal dominion people are to tremble and fear before the God of Daniel, for he is the living God, enduring for ever; his kingdom shall never be destroyed, and his dominion shall be to the end. He delivers and rescues; he works signs and wonders in heaven and on earth, he who has saved Daniel from the power of the lions. (Daniel 6:25–27.)

Interestingly, there is no mention here of any sanction to be taken against those who did not comply. Sadly, there have been times in history where the ruling power has tried to impose religion by force, resulting in the same kind of tyranny as the enforced imposition of paganism or atheism. (For a discussion of Christianity and the use of violence, see my book *Gunning for God*, chapter 2.)

The story of Daniel in the lions' den has captivated children over the centuries, and rightly so. It is a thrilling story with a strong moral dimension – courage in the face of extreme danger, a remarkable deliverance from wild animals, and the ultimate vindication of a principled stand. Yet it is no fantasy. And as we have seen, it is far from being only a story for children. It is an analysis of the nature of law – its use and abuse.

In fact, it relates the first attempt to ban the practice of the Jewish religion. The way it was done has immediate relevance for the contemporary world. In many countries we can observe the increasing use of (positive) law to discriminate against believers in God.

Take, for instance, this statement of Judge Samuel B. Kent of the US District Court for the Southern District of Texas on his 1995 ruling that any student mentioning the name of Jesus in a graduation prayer would be given a jail sentence:

> And make no mistake, the court is going to have a United States Marshal in attendance at the graduation. If any student offends this court, that student will be summarily arrested and will face up to six months incarceration in the Galveston County jail for contempt of court ... Anyone who violates these orders ... is going to wish that he or she had died as a child when this court gets through with it.[30]

In June 2011 Chief US District Judge Fred Biery handed down the following ruling, banning prayer:[31]

> Accordingly, it is hereby ORDERED that the Medina Valley Independent School District and its officials, agents,

servants, and employees, as well as all persons acting in concert with them, are prohibited from allowing a prayer (as defined in paragraph (b) below) to be included in the June 4, 2011 graduation ceremony for Medina Valley High School. More specifically:

(a) The District shall remove the terms "invocation" and "benediction" from the program of ceremonies for the graduation exercises. These terms shall be replaced with "opening remarks" and "closing remarks".

(b) The District, through its officials, shall instruct the students previously selected to deliver the "invocation" and "benediction" to modify their remarks to be statements of their own beliefs as opposed to leading the audience in prayer. These students, and all other persons scheduled to speak during the graduation ceremony, shall be instructed not to present a prayer, to wit, they shall be instructed that they may not ask audience members to "stand," "join in prayer," or "bow their heads," they may not end their remarks with "amen" or "in [a deity's name] we pray," and they shall not otherwise deliver a message that would commonly be understood to be a prayer, nor use the word "prayer" unless it is used in the student's expression of the student's personal belief, as opposed to encouraging others who may not believe in the concept of prayer to join in and believe the same concept. The students may in stating their own personal beliefs speak through conduct such as kneeling to face Mecca, the wearing of a yarmulke or hijab or making the sign of the cross.

(c) The District, through its officials, shall review, and make any necessary changes to, the students' revised remarks to ensure that those remarks comply with this Order, and shall instruct the students that they must not deviate from the approved remarks in making their presentations.

Because this suit seeks to enforce fundamental constitutional norms, it is further ORDERED that the security requirement of Federal Rule of Civil Procedure 65(c) is waived, and that this injunctive order shall be effective immediately and shall be enforced by incarceration or other sanctions for contempt of Court if not obeyed by District officials and their agents.

Shades of Darius.

CHAPTER 15

THE LAW OF THE JUNGLE
Daniel 6

Mesopotamian emperors thought that lion hunting was the proper sport of kings. Depictions of lions, for instance on ceramic glazed tiles, were much in evidence in buildings in Babylon. The lion was a potent symbol of imperial power.

Stone panel from the north-west palace of Ashurnasirpal II at Nimrud, northern Iraq, neo-Assyrian, 883–859 BC (copyright of the Trustees of the British Museum)

This alabaster relief shows that royal lion hunts were an ancient tradition in Mesopotamia. There are examples of similar scenes going back as far as 3000 BC. Ashurnasirpal, who reigned 883–859 BC, seems to have been an especially enthusiastic hunter. Inscriptions claim that he killed a total of 450 lions.

Palace relief depicting Ashurbanipal killing a lion

It is suggested that Ashurnasirpal sought to emulate the Mesopotamian mythological hero Gilgamesh, who proved his prowess by killing a pride of lions by himself. Creating an association like this reinforced the king's right to rule, by connecting him to the illustrious past and symbolically demonstrating his bravery and strength.

Using a lions' den as an execution chamber solved two problems at once: getting rid of tiresome opponents and keeping the palace lions well fed. However, there just might have been more to it than that. The book of Daniel shows considerable interest in animals and their behaviour. In chapter 4 Nebuchadnezzar spends seven years behaving as an animal; and chapters 7 and 8 contain visions concerning strange animals. The present chapter does not simply tell us that lions were the preferred method of execution at that time; it tells us that God delivered Daniel from the power of the lions. Darius expressed the hope that God would deliver Daniel, and when he returned to the den in the morning Daniel told him that God had sent his angel to shut the lions' mouths.

Power politics

People who reject the supernatural realm out of hand will regard talk of angels restraining lions as sheer legend. However, as I have argued elsewhere (*Gunning for God*, chapter 7), the rejection of the supernatural in principle is unscientific – and, indeed, irrational. The account deserves to be taken seriously as an analysis of power, for the situation Daniel describes is one of power politics. It starts with a group of conspirators using the law to have power over Daniel, and simultaneously to deprive their king of the power to protect him. On the other hand, the power of God restrains the power of the lions to harm Daniel, but it does not do so in the case of the conspirators.

Law has no power in itself, of course. That is why we need the police. If there is no enforcement, the law is disregarded. History shows this only too clearly. The satraps were the enforcers, but their power was less than that of the emperor. The cleverness of their plot lay in their construction of a law calculated to destroy Daniel and simultaneously to disempower the king from doing anything to hinder them.

It would be impossible to do the same with lions. Lions, in common with other animals, act by instinct. You cannot prevent them from eating humans by passing a corresponding law! Furthermore, if a lion bites the head off a zookeeper, we do not take the lion to court, put it on trial and pass sentence. Lions are not moral beings. Humans are.

Nor by passing laws can you prevent lions from fighting and killing each other. Of course, lions have observable patterns of behaviour, but they do not sit down and make laws to govern themselves as we do. They operate on the principle of the survival of the fittest. Making and enforcing written laws is a peculiarly human phenomenon.

That raises a very interesting and important question. Where did the very concept of law, as we know it, come from? Hardly through the same principle, of the survival of the fittest, that it transcends!

The satraps professed to believe in doing things according to the law. But now their law was the law of jungle lions – the survival of the fittest. According to these jealous administrators, Daniel did not deserve to survive, so they conspired to have him killed. They had no interest in genuine law or morality. Although these men were moral beings, they behaved like amoral animals. Daniel threatened their territory, so they decided to eliminate him.

They came unstuck when they were themselves thrown into the lions' den as a result of Darius's rough justice. The law of the jungle operated there with a vengeance and, unfortunately for the satraps, the stronger and bigger animals survived.

This understanding of the principle of the survival of the fittest can be seen to operate in many areas of life. We have come to expect it in politics and business, but it is not only there that the "dog eat dog" philosophy holds sway. In the first half of the twentieth century this principle was at the heart of the wave of Social Darwinism that spawned eugenics programmes on both sides of the Atlantic. And the danger is with us still. Postmodern relativism has made deep inroads into many people's minds, resulting in an erosion of the concepts of truth, morality, and the value of human life. Put that together with the cult of the *self*, and you are well on the way to engineering an egocentric society, where truth and morality can be defined in such a way as to make sure it is "I" who survive.

Even though his loyalty to the emperor was established beyond question, Daniel was clearly prepared to swim against the tide of polytheism and assert his conviction that there was only one true God – the God of heaven, whom he worshipped. He was not prepared to compromise that position, even if the emperor commanded it. That left him open to accusations of being arrogant, narrow-minded, bigoted, and anti-social. How could he possibly believe that he was right and the rest were wrong? Who did he think he was? It is all too familiar.

All down history it has been the same. In the Roman empire, for instance, there was widespread tolerance of religion. You could worship whatever god you wished, provided you were also prepared to join in the worship of the emperor, or state deities, whenever public ceremony demanded it. The Christians were not prepared to do so, and consequently many of them were thrown for public entertainment into that huge lions' den, the Coliseum.

What is it about Christianity that continues to stir up opposition? It is its claim to be unique. Jesus said *I am … the truth* (John 14:6); and that claim enrages those who claim that there is no (absolute) truth. For them, it represents the height of unacceptable intolerance.

True tolerance

What does *tolerance* mean? I ask the question, because it seems to me that one of the things that pose a real threat to human freedom is the contemporary understanding of tolerance. I say contemporary, because the old and good meaning of tolerance has been abandoned for something insidious and dangerous. The original meaning of the statement "I tolerate you" was famously (and perhaps rather extremely) expressed by Voltaire: "I disapprove of what you say, but I will defend to the death your right to say it."

Tolerance asserts the right to have convictions, to make judgments about right and wrong, which differ from those of others. It also asserts the right to express those views without fear. The word comes from the Latin *tolerare,* meaning "to bear, endure, sustain hardship". Tolerance does not demand that we accept the opinions, beliefs, and lifestyles of others, but only that we learn to live without forcing them to line up with us. The seventeenth-century philosopher John Locke advocated tolerance in order to protect religious adherents from state coercion. Such coercion, we should remember, was one of the reasons the Pilgrim Fathers sailed for America.

True tolerance is principled; yet it involves knowing how to put up with things and people, as well as knowing when to offer criticism. True tolerance makes judgments without being judgmental. It is, therefore, capable of being intolerant of the fanaticism (both religious and secular) that inhibits true freedom. A classic example of the view that toleration is wrong was expressed by the French theologian

Jacques Bénigne Bossuet, who wrote in 1691, "I have the right to persecute you because I am right and you are wrong." Such a view is, of course, offensive, and principled tolerance is always careful to avoid offence wherever possible. However, offence may not always be avoidable, especially where truth is concerned.

The new tolerance, however, is completely different. It seizes on the idea of offence and holds that I must not ever offend anyone else by expressing disapproval of any aspect of his or her behaviour or ideas. The new tolerance disapproves of all absolutes except this one: you will be tolerant of everyone else's view. You must, however, be intolerant of intolerance. This means that criticism is forbidden, and must be replaced by unrestrained affirmation and praise, or silence. The new tolerance is intolerant of the old, and indeed negates it. To put it another way: the old tolerance accepted the existence of other views while disagreeing with them; the new tolerance insists on accepting the views themselves and not merely their existence.

Such tolerance acts as an acid that not only dissolves human freedom and flourishing but also dissolves truth and morality – other views are to be accepted to be as true as your own. If we are not allowed to make judgments or have convictions any more, then all that is left is for us to descend to a kind of ethical neutrality. In the end, tolerance simply becomes a synonym for unconditional approval. We have lost our human dimensions of virtue and truth. In that sense, we have become merely animal. (For a much more detailed study of tolerance see D.A. Carson, 2012.)

At first glance, this seems light years removed from the court of Medo-Persia. The satraps were prepared to tolerate neither Daniel nor Darius's tolerance of him. The relevance of Daniel's story, however, lies in the fact that there is a powerful drive to embed the new tolerance in enforceable legislation. The new tolerance wishes to invoke the state to impose its view. It does not heed the warning of nineteenth-century philosopher John Stuart Mill about the tyranny of public opinion that stigmatizes and silences minority and dissident beliefs.

The influence of this type of thinking is to be seen in the UNESCO Declaration on the Principles of Tolerance:

Tolerance is respect, acceptance and appreciation of the rich diversity of our world's cultures, our forms of expression and our ways of being human.

British sociologist Frank Furedi points out:

For UNESCO toleration becomes an expansive and diffuse sensibility that automatically accepts and offers unconditional appreciation of different views and cultures.

As Furedi shows (2011, pages 8–9), this detaches tolerance from any specific object, and encourages "children to 'tolerate diversity' or 'tolerate difference'". He continues:

Such pedagogy self-consciously avoids encouraging children to develop their capacity for moral reasoning or the making of moral judgments.

The result is that we increase the sense of moral uncertainty, rather than diminish it.

None of us likes to be exposed to talk that is offensive to us; and it is true that some people have difficulty in differentiating between attacking people personally and criticizing the ideas they hold. The danger is now, however, that the desire to be completely insulated from any kind of offence leads to the paralysing of robust discussion through which all participants could learn.

Taming the tongue

Finally, we should earth this discussion in something that affects all of us. When we think of humans behaving like animals, there is a danger that we think it is other people who do so and not ourselves. However, the Bible realistically points out that we need to direct it very practically at ourselves.

The apostle James discusses the problem that we all have with our tongues:

For every kind of beast and bird, of reptile and sea creature,
can be tamed and has been tamed by mankind, but no
human being can tame the tongue. It is a restless evil, full of
deadly poison. With it we bless our Lord and Father, and with
it we curse people who are made in the likeness of God. From
the same mouth come blessing and cursing. My brothers, these
things ought not to be so. (James 3:7–10.)

The comparison is sobering. We can successfully tame wild animals; yet we fail with our tongues. James is writing to challenge those of us who are believers to face the embarrassing fact that we can appear to be ever so pious – *we bless God* – and yet, in complete inconsistency, we can use the very same tongue to destroy a fellow human being who is made in God's image.

Moved by animal passion to stop Daniel becoming "top dog", the satraps connived at having a law passed that would allow them to get Daniel to transgress with his tongue (by praying). Then they would destroy him with their tongues in their report to Darius. What about the converse situation, where we have a law that is designed to stop what people do with their tongues? In some countries today there are laws against so-called "hate speech". That topic raises all sorts of questions: whether such laws achieve their objective, or if they have the effect of closing down rational moral debate.

At the more humble level of our daily lives, we humans find it difficult to control the little wild animal in our mouths. We may (rightly) criticize the Machiavellian behaviour of the satraps; but do we not know of situations in churches where feuds have broken out over trivialities but have been represented as matters of principle or doctrine? Have we not watched Christian families tear themselves apart over legacies? As James says, *these things ought not to be so*.

The apostle Peter, who is known the world over as the disciple who used his tongue to deny the Lord, tells us that there is a supernatural resource for dealing with our tongues: ... *you have been born again, not of perishable seed but of imperishable, through the living and abiding word of God* (1 Peter 1:23). Simply passing our own personal law to try to control our tongues is not enough. We need the resource of God's Spirit, who is implanted in us when we repent and trust Jesus Christ as Lord and Saviour. We need God's power to enable us to obey Peter's teaching: *Do not repay evil for evil or reviling for reviling, but on the contrary, bless, for to this you were called, that you may obtain a blessing* (1 Peter 3:9).

Taming the tongue does not mean taking a vow of silence. The idea that we can witness without words is highly misleading. God's method of communication is his Word. It will only be credible if it is backed up by a consistent lifestyle. But lifestyle is not enough. To explain the Word, you must use words.

Christians have no option here – we are called to be Christ's witnesses. And for most people witnessing involves getting through the barrier of fear. Peter can be a great help and encouragement to us. It was fear that paralysed him and led to his denial of Christ. But that was not the end of his witness. Christ not only forgave him; soon afterwards he gave him the strength to overcome his fear and stand up in Jerusalem on the day of Pentecost, powerfully preach the gospel, and so launch the witness of the Christian church. Daniel too, whatever trepidation he may have had, received strength from God to maintain his witness in spite of the machinations of the satraps.

Fear can cause us to hold our tongues when we ought to be using them to witness. Peter has something to say to those of us (all of us) who feel fear and even shame at times – especially if, like Daniel, we are facing a very tight situation.

> Now who is there to harm you if you are zealous for what is good? But even if you should suffer for righteousness' sake, you will be blessed. Have no fear of them, nor be troubled, but in your hearts honour Christ the Lord as holy, always being prepared to make a defence to anyone who asks you for a reason for the hope that is in you; yet do it with gentleness and respect, having a good conscience, so that, when you are slandered, those who revile your good behaviour in Christ may be put to shame. For it is better to suffer for doing good, if that should be God's will, than for doing evil. (1 Peter 3:13–17.)

We are called upon to be always ready to defend the Christian message. In order to do so, of course, we need to know what are the grounds for our hope. That will involve thought and discussion about what our reasons are for believing that Jesus is the Lord, the Son of God. It will also involve answering misunderstanding and misrepresentation, and that can lead to some scary situations.

For instance, one tactic used against Christians in the first century was to accuse them of fomenting anti-state activity. The book of Acts records an occasion when Paul was preaching in Thessalonica. Some Jews became jealous of his success, gathered a mob, and hauled some of the local believers before the authorities, saying:

> These men who have turned the world upside down have come here also ... and they are all acting against the decrees of Caesar, saying there is another king, Jesus. (Acts 17:6–7.)

The Romans did not approve of political subversives who *turned the world upside down*. But the charges were false, and it was important for Luke to explain why.

We may be afraid of what people will think of us. However much we know, we shall always encounter people who ask questions that we have never thought of, and to which we can't immediately think of an answer. That can be scary, but the worst way of combating it is to pretend to know what we don't know! We should never be afraid to be honest and confess our ignorance, saying that we would need to think about it.

We may also be afraid of what some people may do to us. Daniel was threatened with the lions because of his praying. Peter and John were arrested for preaching in Jerusalem, and hauled before the highest court of Jewish law, the Sanhedrin. They did not hesitate, however, to tell the court what the religious rulers did not want to hear:

> This Jesus is the stone that was rejected by you, the builders, which has become the cornerstone. And there is salvation in no one else, for there is no other name under heaven given among men by which we must be saved. (Acts 4:11–12.)

Such exclusivity infuriated the council, and many are offended by it today. The apostles were ordered not to preach in the name of Jesus. They refused and were imprisoned. On that occasion God supernaturally delivered them to preach again. But he doesn't always do so. We understand that Peter was eventually crucified for his faith, and John was banished to the island of Patmos.

The thing that delivered them (and will deliver us) from fear was not knowledge so much, but what Peter says at the beginning of his exhortation: *in your hearts honour Christ the Lord as holy*. It is our conscious dependence on Christ, and deliberately giving him the most sacred place as the chief value in our lives, that is the key to overcoming fear.

That was the open secret of Daniel's witness when he faced the threatening of wild animals, both leonine and human. His specific knowledge of Christ was, of course, far less than ours. It was confidence in the risen Lord that enabled Paul to "fight with beasts" (the human variety) at Ephesus (see 1 Corinthians 15:32).

Finally, Peter tells us all that we face a particularly dangerous "lion":

> *Be sober-minded; be watchful. Your adversary the devil*
> *prowls around like a roaring lion, seeking someone to devour.*
> *Resist him, firm in your faith, knowing that the same kinds*
> *of suffering are being experienced by your brotherhood*
> *throughout the world. (1 Peter 5:8–9.)*

We must turn now from the very real flesh and blood animals of the lions' den to the fantastical and surreal animals of Daniel's earlier dreams.

CHAPTER 16

THE FOUR BEASTS AND THE SON OF MAN
Daniel 7

The remainder of the book of Daniel consists of four visions that he himself saw: two in the Babylonian period, and two in the Medo-Persian. The first two visions occurred during the reign of Belshazzar and so predate the events of chapter 6. The second two visions were given to Daniel after those events. Hence the first two visions break the chronological sequence of the narrative. This shows us that Daniel's primary concern at this point is not chronology. The visions are related here for logical reasons that become apparent when we view them in the context of the wider structure of the book. We have already seen that the visions fall into two natural pairs: chapter 7 pairing with chapter 8, and chapter 9 pairing with the final section of the book, chapters 10–12.

Daniel dates his first vision in the first year of the reign of Belshazzar, so it occurred about ten years before the fateful feast recorded in chapter 5. As we read chapter 7, we are fully aware of the end of Belshazzar's empire and his life; and it could well be that one of the reasons for Daniel including the details of chapter 7 at this point is that he wishes us to bear in mind the full story of Belshazzar. For if at the start of his reign Belshazzar began to show the kind of character he exhibited at the end, it is not surprising then that Daniel's first vision reflects the evil that lurks under so much power politics. The fact that Daniel had to be summoned to the feast by Belshazzar who then did not seem to recognize him, shows that Daniel may well have been gradually sidelined by this new administration that was not as sympathetic to his God-talk – and God-walk – as Nebuchadnezzar had been.

Such a marked decline would have raised new questions in Daniel's able and godly mind as to what the future held. Up to this point he had enjoyed a spectacular career. It is true that it had had its moments of peril, but he had generally enjoyed great esteem and the patronage of the emperor himself. But that esteem was evaporating, and we can easily imagine Daniel beginning to realize that the instability of earthly powers was due in part to their extreme vulnerability to the pride and evil that could rise up in human nature.

Certainly, Daniel had learned this and much more from the vision given to Nebuchadnezzar of the colossal man. But that was just one side of the story. There was another, more sinister, aspect to the corridors of power, that he had experienced in real time through his work. In this vision and the next, God stepped in to reveal it to him.

These visions concern a zoo of strange and frightening animals. The first of them, in chapter 7, is of four wild beasts, depicting four empires. As such, it forms a striking parallel to the four-part statue seen in Nebuchadnezzar's vision in chapter 2. Both visions concentrate in particular on the fourth empire and its eventual destruction. It is surely not unreasonable, therefore, to take it that these visions represent two distinct ways of looking at the same four empires.

In chapter 2, two of the empires are specifically identified. *You are the head of gold*, Nebuchadnezzar is told (2:38). The words *after you* (2:39) clearly refer to Medo-Persia and the rest. In chapter 7 no identification is made. That would not be surprising if we are correct in assuming the beasts represent the same empires as in chapter 2. The imagery of beasts is used not as a code simply to identify the empires (since we already know what they are) but rather to tell us more about the nature of the empires – that in various ways they behave like beasts.

In chapter 2 the metals that represent the empires differ in value and strength. In chapter 7 the beasts that represent the empires differ in their animal fierceness. What is immediately striking is that whereas the fourth kingdom in chapter 2 is characterized by its weakness, in chapter 7 that kingdom is marked out by its strength – its hideous strength. The second vision, therefore, is not simply a repetition of the first.

David Gooding (1981) summarizes the main similarities and contrasts as follows:

Chapter 2	Chapter 7
A survey of the whole course of Gentile imperial power.	A survey of the whole course of Gentile imperial power.
Four empires in the form of a man.	Four empires in the form of wild beasts.
The fatal weakness: an incoherent mixture of iron and clay in the feet.	The hideous strength: a frightening mixture of animal destructiveness with human intelligence.
The whole man destroyed by the stone cut out by divine power. The universal messianic kingdom set up.	The final beast destroyed and universal domination given to the Son of Man.

Chapter 7 falls naturally into four parts, each introduced by a similar phrase:

1. *I saw in my vision by night* … (verse 2)
Three beasts introduced.

2. *I saw in the night visions* … (verse 7)
The fearsome fourth beast and its judgment and destruction.

3. *I saw in the night visions* … (verse 13)
The coming of the Son of Man, and the saints receiving the kingdom.

4. *The visions of my head alarmed me* (verse 15)
The explanation of the vision. The fourth beast and its judgment and destruction.

The four beasts

Daniel saw a great sea, lashed by powerful winds, out of which emerged four strange, surreal beasts, one after the other. The image of a troubled sea sometimes occurs in the Bible as representing the restless nations of the earth (see Isaiah 17:12; Revelation 17:15), and Daniel is subsequently told that they represent empires that come out of the earth (Daniel 7:17). The beginning of the vision echoes the creation narrative of Genesis, where we read that *the Spirit of God was hovering over the face of the waters* (Genesis 1:2). The Hebrew word for *Spirit* can be used of breath or wind. But in Daniel's vision the wind and the sea are a prelude not to making earth into a home fit for human beings but to the rise of a sequence of animals representing world empires bent increasingly on destruction.

The animal imagery here is clearly designed to convey a message very different from that projected by the metallic sections of the colossal man. There are, however, important elements in common. For instance, we saw that the impression conveyed by the colossal man was not all darkly apocalyptic and doom-laden. The same is true here to a certain extent, although the picture is generally much grimmer.

Just as the variety of metals in Nebuchadnezzar's dream indicates the differing values of the successive empires, the various animals in Daniel's dream denote what is probably best described as the relative "animal ferocity" of those empires. The first animal, for instance, is given a human heart. The subsequent animals become increasingly brutal, the fourth being rapacious in the extreme. It has the eyes of human intelligence but shows no trace of human compassion.

The perspective is clear: from one point of view, empires resemble wild animals. But, unlike humans, animals are not inhibited by moral considerations, since animals are not moral beings. Empires tend to behave like that – as amoral power blocs. The overall impression of the vision is of the dark underbelly of politics: the jockeying for power, with less and less moral qualm, until a sense of humanity and compassion disappears under the ruthless lust for domination.

Of course, not all wild animals behave in the same way. They are not equally dangerous; and those that are, are not necessarily dangerous all of the time. For instance, a lion-keeper can walk among the lions after they have had a good meal, but not when they are hungry. Nor are wild animals usually dangerous to their own kind, with the exception of power struggles to obtain mates or to become top dog (or cat!).

The first beast in Daniel's "zoo" is a strange hybrid of a lion and an eagle. As we saw earlier, there is archaeological evidence for the aptness of a lion to represent Babylon – to say nothing of Daniel's experience in the lions' den (which at this point has yet to occur). The same imagery is found also in the writings of the prophet Jeremiah (4:7; 50:17). He describes Babylon (Nebuchadnezzar in particular) as an eagle (48:40; 49:22), as does Ezekiel (17:3). The reference to the lion having its wings plucked off, made to stand like a human and given a human heart may refer to Nebuchadnezzar's progress – albeit erratic – to a more human attitude (at least by ancient standards).

The second animal is a bear, representing Medo-Persia. Some scholars suggest that, being raised up on one side, it refers to the supremacy within the empire of the Persians over the Medes; and that the three ribs possibly refer to Babylon, Lydia, and Egypt.

The leopard with wings conveys the impression of great speed, which fits well as a symbol for the Greek empire led by Alexander the Great, who conquered country after country with legendary rapidity. The leopard's four heads could well allude to the fact that, on his death, Alexander's empire split into four parts. They were governed by four of his generals respectively: Cassander took control of Macedon and Greece, Seleucus took command in Syria and Upper Asia, Lysimachus ruled Asia Minor and Thrace, and Ptolemy took over Egypt and Arabia.

Then there is a pause. *After this I saw in the night visions ...* Daniel's undivided attention is now focused on a terrifying fourth beast (Daniel 7:7): *It had great iron teeth; it devoured and broke in pieces and stamped what was left with its feet.*

Unlike the others, the fourth kingdom is not likened to any named animal, but simply described as different from all the others. It had ten horns. Daniel watched as another little horn grew up among them, displacing three of them. Looking more closely, Daniel could see that this strange little horn had human eyes, and a mouth *speaking great things* (7:8). It was utterly surreal.

A glimpse of heaven

As he watched, the scene changed. He found himself looking into another world – the very throne room of the universe, into heaven itself. It was an awe-inspiring, vertiginous sight, as he watched the august figure of the Ancient of Days taking his place on a throne that looked like a blazing fire. The throne had wheels that were on fire, and a river of fire flowed out of it. God's holiness is absolute – he *is a consuming fire* (Hebrews 12:29). No attempt is made to describe the One on the throne. We are simply told that *the Ancient of Days took his seat; his clothing was white as snow, and the hair of his head like pure wool* (Daniel 7:9).

The image conveys a sense of the unsullied purity and wisdom of the Judge who sits resplendent on his throne before an unimaginably large crowd: *ten thousand times ten thousand* is a hundred million! It was an overwhelming sight – a vision of the supreme court of the universe. Books were opened, indicating that the session was about to begin, when Daniel's attention was drawn once more by the sound of the great words of the horn, the fearsome fourth beast. Incredibly, in the very presence of God, the final Judge himself, it was still insisting on being heard. No details of the subsequent trial are given. The sentence is carried out, the beast killed, and its body destroyed by fire. The other beasts do not suffer quite the same fate. Their power was removed, *but their lives were prolonged for a season and a time* (7:12).

There is a pause before Daniel resumes his description by repeating the phrase *I saw in the night visions....* There now follows a passage of seminal importance for the whole of biblical revelation:

> *I saw in the night visions, and behold, with the clouds of heaven there came one like a son of man, and he came to the Ancient of Days and was presented before him. And to him was given dominion and glory and a kingdom, that all peoples, nations, and languages should serve him; his dominion is an everlasting dominion, which shall not pass away, and his kingdom one that shall not be destroyed. (Daniel 7:13–14.)*

Daniel was deeply disturbed by what he saw, and wanted to know what it meant. He approached one of those who stood there – presumably a member of the heavenly court – and asked him the truth about the vision. He was told: *These four great beasts are four kings who shall arise out of the earth. But the saints of the Most High shall receive the kingdom and possess the kingdom for ever, for ever and ever* (7:17–18).

God will not always deliver

Not surprisingly, Daniel was especially interested in the fourth beast, with its frightening little horn, and with good reason. As he continued to watch, something unprecedented and ghastly happened: *this horn made war with the saints and prevailed over them* (7:21).

It was a most frightening prospect. This fourth beast, with all its horrific power, would not only fight with but overcome the saints. So far in the book of Daniel, when the state threatened Daniel or his friends with death, God supernaturally intervened and delivered them. It is true that Daniel's three friends told Nebuchadnezzar that their God might not deliver them from the fiery furnace; yet on that occasion he did. Daniel and his friends not only survived; they were able to play a leading role in the nation, without compromising the principles of their faith.

Now God reveals to Daniel that his three friends had been right when they said that God might not always deliver his people from suffering and oppression. Powerful and ruthless enemies would arise one day, wage outright war against God's people, savage and kill them. The horn on the fourth beast represents one of those enemies. (The symbol of a horn is used in the Bible to denote power – see, for example, Deuteronomy 33:17; Zechariah 1:18–19.) As we pointed out above, the fourth beast's horn has eyes, symbolizing human insight and intelligence, coupled with brutal animal strength. Notably, it lacks a human heart: it is dreadful, evil, ruthless genius.

Many of the worst atrocities that the world has known were (and are still) committed by highly intelligent people in whose hands are the levers of political power – witness Nazi Germany. It should not escape our attention that one of their main targets was the nation that gave birth to Daniel. Nor should we ignore the fact that the twentieth century was the bloodiest in history, with millions perishing to satisfy the animal lust for power in dictatorships of both right and left. The crimes of Hitler, Stalin, Mao, and Pol Pot are beyond comprehension. In the hands of such beasts many millions perished: Christians, and those of other faiths and none.

What shall we think, then, when we consider the many faithful believers who have been and are being subjected to every kind of hideous torture and method of killing that powerful, heartless human beasts can devise – and yet God appears to do nothing?

Daniel certainly does not hesitate to raise this issue several times. Chapter 8 tells us of an insolent king who *shall cause fearful destruction and shall succeed in what he does, and destroy mighty men and the people who are the saints* (8:24). It disturbed Daniel, and it continues to disturb us. How can we make any sense of it? If God can deliver his people, why doesn't he? If God can prevent suffering, why doesn't he? The problem of moral evil is inescapable. What is the answer to it?

The vision gives three responses:

1. There is to be a judgment.

2. The Son of Man will come.

3. The saints will receive the kingdom.

There is to be a judgment

Whatever the detail may mean, the key message is crystal clear: this world is not going to be trampled and smashed by brutal, amoral regimes for ever. A day will come when God will bring to an end the state war-machines, the terrorist bombs, the consummate evil of totalitarian oppression, the gas chambers, death camps, killing fields, and countless other infamous instruments of death. There will be a judgment.

The fact that there is to be a judgment is of paramount importance; and I emphasize this point, since there are some who say that the less said about such things, the better. After all, they argue, God is a God of love; and talk about judgment is grim and medieval. They could not be more wrong, as a little thought will show.

Long before Daniel was exiled to Babylon, Hebrew poets wrote many psalms that in later years would be sung with great feeling by the displaced people of Israel. Here is an example:

> Say among the nations, "The Lord reigns! Yes, the world is
> established; it shall never be moved; he will judge the peoples
> with equity." Let the heavens be glad, and let the earth rejoice;
> let the sea roar, and all that fills it; let the field exult, and
> everything in it! Then shall all the trees of the forest sing
> for joy before the Lord, for he comes, for he comes to judge
> the earth. He will judge the world in righteousness, and the
> peoples in his faithfulness. (Psalm 96:10–13.)

The poet imagines all of creation celebrating the fact that God is coming to judge the earth. Far from future judgment being a dark and negative concept, it is the exact opposite. It is a cause for joy, and the reason is obvious. When you are suffering unfairness, discrimination, harassment, or outright persecution, the uppermost thought on your mind is: how long is this going to last? And will anything ever be done about it?

Human beings long for justice, yet many of them never experience it in this life. What Daniel tells us is that this is not the end of the matter. No, one day ultimate justice will be meted out. Records have been kept of all the horrors and evil to which human beings have been subjected by the beasts that have stalked the jungles of power. When the awesome heavenly court sits and God, the Ancient of Days, presides, the books will be opened, and rational, measured, and righteous justice will be done.

The Son of Man will come

In Nebuchadnezzar's vision in chapter 2 the unstable colossus was destroyed by a supernatural stone that eventually filled the whole earth: the unstable and temporary was ousted by the utterly stable and permanent. Now, in chapter 7, an incredibly powerful and ferocious beast is destroyed and *one like a son of man* – a human being – takes over the kingdom for ever (7:13–14).

The imagery conveys a powerful message. The beasts of power politics, however invincible they may sometimes think they are, will not reign for ever. A perfect human, the Son of Man, will come with all authority finally to take over from the beasts and rule in perfect justice. The law of the jungle will cease for good. This is really good news. It holds out real and glorious hope to a despairing society.

Furthermore, we live in a privileged time in history in the sense that we know who the Son of Man is. Long after the time of Daniel he visited earth and massively carried forward God's programme for history. He is, of course, none other than the Lord Jesus Christ. He used the title *Son of Man* as a unique description of himself.

Daniel tells us about the Son of Man in the context of judgment. He does not tell us explicitly that the Son of Man himself is to be the final Judge, although that is the reasonable implication. The Lord Jesus himself makes this role explicit:

> *The Father judges no one, but has given all judgement to the*
> *Son, that all may honour the Son, just as they honour the*
> *Father. Whoever does not honour the Son does not honour*
> *the Father who sent him. Truly, truly, I say to you, whoever*
> *hears my word and believes him who sent me has eternal*
> *life. He does not come into judgement, but has passed from*
> *death to life … For as the Father has life in himself, so he has*
> *granted the Son also to have life in himself. And he has given*
> *him authority to execute judgement, because he is the Son of*
> *Man. (John 5:22–27.)*

God's judgment will be judgment by peer. It is humans that have done the sinning; it will be a perfect human who does the judging.

Not long after saying these words Jesus was arrested in Jerusalem and tried for blasphemy before the supreme religious court, the Sanhedrin. The crux of the cross-examination came when the high priest, acting as judge, put him on oath to force him to answer a question – indeed, the question of all questions:

> *"I adjure you by the living God, tell us if you are the Christ,*
> *the Son of God." Jesus said to him: "You have said so. But I*
> *tell you, from now on you will see the Son of Man seated at*
> *the right hand of Power and coming on the clouds of heaven."*
> *(Matthew 26:63–64.)*

The members of the Sanhedrin all knew that Jesus was claiming to be the one that Daniel, their own prophet, had seen: the one into whose hands the government would be given; the one who would be served and worshipped by all nations and people, whose reign would be universal and eternal. Jesus was claiming to be the promised Jewish Messiah (Christ), the King. They were apoplectic with rage at what they imagined was the ultimate in blasphemy. They were judging him: the idea that he would judge them seemed preposterous. But it was the truth. For though he was human, Jesus was never *merely* human. He is *one like a son of man,* the Son of Man who is the Son of God. The title *Son of Man* appearing in this context in Daniel implies the deity of Jesus, and not just his humanity.

Those judges did not realize (then) that they had arrested and tried *the* Judge of the whole world. Had they only listened to him they could have known, but they refused to listen. Instead, like a pack of maddened wild animals, they vilified him, flogged him, spat at him, mocked him, crowned him with thorns, and spiked him on a cross. But, as Jesus said to them, they would not for ever remain in ignorance of who he was.

God shut the lions' mouths for Daniel. He did not do the same for his Son. Jesus Christ, the perfect Son of Man in whom there was no personal sin, so loved us that he gave his life for our many sins. He, therefore, is alone worthy to take over all government and power – to the eternal and immense relief and joy of the whole of groaning creation (see Romans 8:22). This is the big story that alone makes sense of history. Twenty-six centuries ago Daniel in a vision saw the Son of Man coming on the clouds of heaven. Six centuries later Jesus told the Sanhedrin that they would see the Son of Man at the right hand of God and coming on the clouds of heaven. He was not speaking of a vision, but the reality. He did not say when it would happen… yet happen it will.

Stephen, the first Christian martyr, also saw the glorified Son of Man not long after the crucifixion. As Stephen came to the end of his powerful and courageous defence of the gospel before the Sanhedrin, he looked skywards and said, *I see the heavens opened, and the Son of Man standing at the right hand of God* (Acts 7:56). The very same Sanhedrin that had heard Jesus' personal claim to be the Son of Man were now forced to listen to that claim again. It produced the same effect. Once more they flew into a murderous rage, and they stoned Stephen to death.

The fact that Jesus *is* the Son of Man has enabled Daniel, Stephen, and countless others through the ages to face that kind of pent-up hostility. The only thing that can steady the mind and steel the heart of believers to face all the forces that anti-God brutality can muster, is a steady vision of the One to whom is given all power on earth and in heaven and who will one day return to the planet that rejected him.

The saints will receive the kingdom

The word *saint* means one who is "set apart" and therefore "sacred", "holy". It refers to those people who, like Daniel, are set apart because they in turn have set God apart as their Lord, honouring him above all others. Such people will eventually share in his kingdom. (See Appendix A for a detailed discussion of the biblical concept of "kingdom".)

True to this vision, the Son of Man himself told his disciples that they would eventually participate in his kingdom in a very special way:

> *Truly I say to you, in the new world [literally, the regeneration], when the Son of Man will sit on his glorious throne, you who have followed me will also sit on twelve thrones, judging the twelve tribes of Israel. (Matthew 19:28.)*

Some scholars take the term *saints* to apply exclusively to the Jewish nation, of which Daniel was part. However, Paul makes it very plain that the term is more widely applicable. In the first instance the term *saint* applies to Jewish believers, but through the cross of Christ both Jews and non-Jews have the same standing:

> *For through him we both have access in one Spirit to the Father. So then you are no longer strangers and aliens, but you are fellow citizens with the saints and members of the household of God, built on the foundation of the apostles and prophets, Christ Jesus himself being the cornerstone, in whom the whole structure, being joined together, grows into a holy temple in the Lord. (Ephesians 2:18–21.)*

This means that all believers of whatever ethnic background will share in that kingdom, as Paul reminded the multi-racial church in Corinth: *do you not know that the saints will judge the world?* (1 Corinthians 6:2).

But how is this possible? If they have been murdered by a bestial enemy, how can the saints possibly receive the kingdom, as Daniel claims? With that question we reach the heart of this matter. If death is the end, if there is no life to come, then one thing is sure: the saints will never receive the kingdom. It is essential to grasp the implications of this. We are naturally concerned at the difficulty we have sometimes in knowing what to say to people who have become agnostics or atheists because of failure to resolve the problem of evil. However, it is important to see that atheism itself has no answer to this question. Most people do not get justice in this life; and if, according to atheism, there is no life after death, they will never get justice.

However, atheism is wrong. Death is not the end. Towards the end of the book, God reveals to Daniel that there is to be a resurrection of the dead (Daniel 12:2, 13). In chapter 7 there is no explicit mention of resurrection, though the sight of a hundred million people standing before the throne of God prompts the obvious question: how did they get there? The biblical answer is given not by Daniel but by the apostle John, who sees

> *a great multitude that no one could number, from every nation, from all tribes and peoples and languages, standing before the throne and before the Lamb. (Revelation 7:9.)*

John is told who they are:

> *These are the ones coming out of the great tribulation. They have washed their robes and made them white in the blood of the Lamb. Therefore they are before the throne of God … and God will wipe away every tear from their eyes. (Revelation 7:14–17.)*

The scene in Revelation matches that depicted in Daniel. Vast crowds will watch the judgment of a beast that has eliminated millions. Justice will not only be done: justice will be seen to be done, by the men and women who were victims of injustice on earth. They shall suffer no more. They have been resurrected to stand before the throne of God. And it is God himself who wipes away their final tears.

This is powerful imagery: wiping away tears has to be done very carefully because of the extreme sensitivity of the human eye – which is why we normally wipe away our own tears. This says to us that God is sensitive to the cry of our heart and the accumulated hurt of our experience. God will eventually wipe away hurt and pain and replace it with something unimaginably glorious.

The apostle Paul confirms this hope. He experienced supernatural deliverance on multiple occasions, but he was not spared suffering or execution under the "beast" that was Nero – the iron teeth (Daniel 7:19) finally took Paul's head off. Before that happened, aware that he was facing the end, he wrote a letter to the capital of the iron empire to encourage his fellow believers:

> For I consider that the sufferings of this present time are not worth comparing with the glory that is to be revealed to us. ... Who shall separate us from the love of Christ? Shall tribulation, or distress, or persecution, or famine, or nakedness, or danger, or sword? As it is written, "For your sake we are being killed all the day long; we are regarded as sheep to be slaughtered." No, in all these things we are more than conquerors through him who loved us. For I am sure that neither death nor life, nor angels nor rulers, nor things present nor things to come, nor powers, nor height nor depth, nor anything else in all creation, will be able to separate us from the love of God in Christ Jesus our Lord. (Romans 8:18, 35–39.)

Paul tells us to hang on. God loves us, and he will bring us to our destination – even if we have to leave this world with many unresolved questions and uncertainties.

A vision of the future

Daniel still wished to know more about the fourth kingdom. What, in particular, was meant by the ten horns, and the little horn with eyes and a mouth that spoke great things and made war with the saints and prevailed over them?

We come now to matters on which there are differing opinions, even among those who, like myself, are convinced of the inspiration and authority of Scripture. Some take the view that we should not concern ourselves with the details in such prophecies, but rather rest content with the general principles. After all, they point out – and not without justification – the interpretation of the details of prophecy is fraught with difficulty and often leads to unseemly dogmatism and unchristian squabbling.

Certainly the general principles are important. We have already seen that there is a sense in which horrific persecution of believers by heartless regimes, like that depicted by the fourth beast described by Daniel, has been going on for centuries. At that level, then, the prophecy holds out great hope that one day God will judge and destroy such evil powers. That principle is of great value, and it would be rather foolish to allow disagreements over details to stop us believing and preaching such general principles.

However, none of this means that there cannot *also* be several levels of fulfilment of a biblical prophecy; some of which are much more detailed and specific than others. A clear example of this is given by the prophecy of "the seed". In Genesis God predicted that the seed of the woman would destroy the serpent's head: *I will put enmity between you and the woman, and between your offspring* [literally *seed*] *and her offspring* [*seed*]; *he shall bruise your head, and you shall bruise his heel* (Genesis 3:15).

Eve gave birth to a son, but he was not the promised seed in the fullest sense. Subsequently, Abraham and Sarah were told that all the nations of the world would be blessed through their seed. They had a son, but he was not the seed in the fullest sense either. Later, King David was told that God would establish his seed and give it a kingdom that would endure for ever. David had a son, who turned out not to be the promised seed in the fullest sense. Finally, we read that Christ is the promised seed (Galatians 3:16).

All through history we get partial fulfilments of this prophecy, which has the effect of keeping faith alive. However, this does not alter the fact that there is a final and complete fulfilment that is distinct from all partial ones. We might notice also that the predictions tend to become more and more specific the nearer we get to their fulfilment.

Similarly, here in Daniel, we have the general principle that believers will be persecuted by intelligent yet inhuman regimes. That does not mean that there is nothing more specific in the detail of the prophecy. We must take the detail seriously at the same time as trying to avoid being over-dogmatic.

If we are right in thinking that the fourth beast corresponds to the iron kingdom of the dream image, the Roman empire, then Daniel was, by definition, being given insight into events future to his time. What events?

One way that I find helpful to proceed is to stand back for a moment and collect the leading concepts. They would appear to be the following:

1. An immensely powerful beast with ten horns and a little horn speaks great words.

2. The beast makes war with the saints and prevails.

3. The Son of Man comes on the clouds of heaven.

4. The heavenly court passes judgment on the beast and destroys it.

5. The saints receive the kingdom.

We might reasonably ask then: is there anywhere else in the Bible that we read anything like this? There is! In the book of Revelation we find the following description of an immensely powerful beast:

And I saw a beast rising out of the sea, with ten horns and seven heads, with ten diadems on its horns and blasphemous names on its heads. And the beast that I saw was like a leopard; its feet were like a bear's, and its mouth was like a lion's mouth. And to it the dragon gave his power and his throne and great authority. One of its heads seemed to have a mortal wound, but its mortal wound was healed, and the whole earth marvelled as they followed the beast. And they worshipped the dragon, for he had given his authority to the beast, and they worshipped the beast, saying, "Who is like the beast, and who can fight against it?"

And the beast was given a mouth uttering haughty and blasphemous words, and it was allowed to exercise authority for forty-two months. It opened its mouth to utter blasphemies against God, blaspheming his name and his dwelling, that is, those who dwell in heaven. Also it was allowed to make war on the saints and to conquer them. And authority was given it over every tribe and people and language and nation, and all who dwell on earth will worship it, everyone whose name has not been written before the foundation of the world in the book of life of the Lamb that was slain. (Revelation 13:1–8.)

We note the many features that this beast has in common with Daniel's beast:

1. It has ten horns that are said to be ten kings (Daniel 7:24; compare Revelation 17:12).

2. It utters haughty words.

3. It makes war with the saints and prevails.

4. Its authority is limited. Daniel: time, times, and half a time, probably three-and-a-half times. Revelation: forty-two months, three-and-a-half years.

5. The beast in Revelation combines features of the first
three beasts in Daniel's vision: it was like a leopard, its feet
like a bear's, and its mouth like a lion's.

These similarities are remarkable. Furthermore, the beast in Daniel
is judged in the context of the coming of the Son of Man on the
clouds of heaven. The beast in Revelation is destroyed by the coming
from heaven to earth of the Rider on the White Horse, who is said to
be the Word of God, the King of kings and Lord of lords.[32]

Daniel and Revelation are surely describing the same thing, in
very similar, highly symbolic language. The question arises: what is
the reality of which the beast is a symbol? In order to answer this
we might ask if Scripture talks elsewhere about anything like this,
in non-symbolic language. The passage that immediately springs to
mind is 2 Thessalonians 2,where Paul is writing about the coming of
Christ:

> Now concerning the coming of our Lord Jesus Christ and our
> being gathered together to him, we ask you, brothers, not to
> be quickly shaken in mind or alarmed, either by a spirit or a
> spoken word, or a letter seeming to be from us, to the effect
> that the day of the Lord has come. Let no one deceive you
> in any way. For that day will not come, unless the rebellion
> comes first, and the man of lawlessness is revealed, the son
> of destruction, who opposes and exalts himself against every
> so-called god or object of worship, so that he takes his seat
> in the temple of God, proclaiming himself to be God. Do you
> not remember that when I was still with you I told you these
> things? And you know what is restraining him now so that he
> may be revealed in his time. For the mystery of lawlessness is
> already at work. Only he who now restrains it will do so until
> he is out of the way. And then the lawless one will be revealed,
> whom the Lord Jesus will kill with the breath of his mouth
> and bring to nothing by the appearance of his coming. The
> coming of the lawless one is by the activity of Satan with
> all power and false signs and wonders, and with all wicked

deception for those who are perishing, because they refused to love the truth and so be saved. (2 Thessalonians 2:1–10.)

It would seem that Paul is here describing in plain language what Daniel and Revelation describe in symbolic form – the final form of world power that will be destroyed by the coming of Christ. Not surprisingly, there has been much speculation about precisely what this means. In each generation there have been those who claim to be able to identify the details, only to have their theories shown false by events or superseded by those that come after them.

In 2 Thessalonians Paul does not use the metaphorical description *beast* but speaks of a *man of lawlessness*. However, Revelation assigns a number to the beast – the famous number 666 – and we are told that it is *the number of a man* (Revelation 13:18). Here again, there has been endless guessing as to who this powerful leader will be. Such speculation seems to me to be self-evidently fruitless. If we have to guess who it is, we are by definition likely to be wrong, since Scripture teaches that the *man of lawlessness* will be revealed by satanic power. When the time comes there will be no need to guess who it is. The code number 666, presumably a gematria, will be a simple check, not a profound puzzle.

A gematria is a number that is formed by adding together the numbers representing the letters of the name according to some agreed scheme. So, for example, $A = 1$, $B = 2$, and so on. So a boy in the ancient world might have carved on a tree: "I love the girl whose number is 53," and would have left others to work out, by a trial-and-error process of substituting letters for numbers, that her name was Julia.

As with many of the symbols in Revelation, the important issue is not *who* the symbol represents, but *what* it is in itself – the number of a man. That is, this beast does not represent some abstract idea of power, but is an actual human being. And this is, perhaps, the most hideous thing about it. According to 2 Thessalonians, the power of the state will be vested in a man who sets himself up against God.

Playing God has always been a temptation for powerful leaders. Paul pointed out in his day that *the mystery of lawlessness* was *already at work* (2 Thessalonians 2:7). He was not referring to the law of the state. The Romans were proud of their law, which reigned from one end of the empire to the other – and which still forms the basis of some of our European law. Paul was referring to *spiritual* lawlessness: that defiance of God that characterized the Roman emperors (and many before them), who thought of themselves as gods and demanded that they should be worshipped.

This resonates with a further detail in the description of the fourth beast: he *shall think to change the times and the law; and they shall be given into his hand for a time, times, and half a time* (Daniel 7:25). Daniel has already experienced a clash between the law of his God and the law of the state, engineered by evil power brokers. This vision says that his experience will not be the last of its kind. Indeed, worse is to come. Darius forbade worship of God for a month. Under the fourth beast, the ban will last for much longer – three-and-a-half *times*, usually understood to mean three-and-a-half years.

What is more, this beast will think to *change the times*; that is, the set times of the feasts and ceremonies that Israel celebrated as part of their worship of God – a matter that is picked up in Daniel's next vision.

Thus the fourth beast can be seen as the final manifestation of human rebellion against God. Both 2 Thessalonians and Revelation point out that the man-beast is energized by the dark power of Satan and is a master of deception. This information is not contained in Daniel's description. In fact, the account in Revelation is more detailed than Daniel's in several other respects. It tells us additionally that the beast has seven heads, and introduces a second beast that *exercises all the authority of the first beast in its presence, and makes the earth and its inhabitants worship the first beast ... it deceives those who dwell on earth...* (Revelation 13:12–14).

We are also told:

> And the ten horns that you saw are ten kings who have not yet received royal power, but they are to receive authority as kings for one hour, together with the beast. These are of one mind and hand over their power and authority to the beast.

> *They will make war on the Lamb, and the Lamb will conquer them... (Revelation 17:12–14.)*

So, just as we found with the prophecy of *the seed*, the nearer we get to the time of fulfilment, the more detail is given to us. If we put it all together, a picture emerges of an extraordinary political arrangement, where ten kings or leaders cede their authority to a leader of immense power and authority. The implication is that, whoever these ten leaders are, they exist simultaneously; and, either voluntarily or forcibly, they hand over the reins of their power to a single dictator – the man of lawlessness. Since he appears to hold power over the entire planet, what is envisaged here is nothing less than a world government. (This is why, incidentally, the identification in earlier years with ten European countries was wide of the mark.)

A future world government?

We have never yet seen anything like this in history, but it is far from being a wild idea. In recent times nations have felt the need to form international organizations, like the United Nations, in order to help the balance of power, police the world, and keep the peace. However, the UN has had a mixed record; and some very influential leaders have suggested, and still do, that the only real solution to the world's political and social problems is an international government.

In 1946, in the aftermath of the Second World War, Albert Einstein wrote (1956, page 138):

> A world government must be created which is able to
> solve conflicts between nations by judicial decision. This
> government must be based on a clear-cut constitution
> which is approved by the governments and nations and
> which gives it the sole disposition of offensive weapons.

The idea of world government has actually been around for a long time:

"World government" refers to the idea of all humankind united under one common political authority. Arguably, it has not existed so far in human history, yet proposals for a unified global political authority have existed since ancient times – in the ambition of kings, popes and emperors, and the dreams of poets and philosophers.[33]

For instance, in the middle ages the Italian poet, philosopher, and statesman Dante Alighieri (1265–1321) argued it was possible to eliminate war if

> the whole earth and all that humans can possess be a monarchy, that is, one government under one ruler. Because he possesses everything, the ruler would not desire to possess anything further, and thus, he would hold kings contentedly within the borders of their kingdoms, and keep peace among them. (Convivio [The Banquet] 169.)

The German philosopher Immanuel Kant held that reason suggested the formation of "an *international state (civitas gentium)*, which would necessarily continue to grow until it embraced all the peoples of the earth" (*Perpetual Peace*, 1795, page 105). Yet Kant had strong reservations about a world monarchy. He thought that a federal union of free and independent states "is still to be preferred to an amalgamation of the separate nations under a single power which has overruled the rest and created a universal monarchy".

His reason for hesitation was: "For the laws progressively lose their impact as the government increases its range, and a soulless despotism, after crushing the germs of goodness, will finally lapse into anarchy" (page 113). Kant thought that a "universal despotism" would end "in the graveyard of freedom" (page 114).

In the light of Daniel's vision these words strike a chilling note. The oppression of the fierce fourth beast sounds very much like a "graveyard of freedom". It is for this reason that the message of Daniel 7 is of great importance. It would appear that Daniel is saying that the final form of government will be a world government of hideous strength, overtly and maximally hostile towards God.

I would reiterate that I am not attempting to identify the final world-state, let alone who will be its leader. I do not know. In any case, as I mentioned above, when the time comes there will be no need to speculate – it will be all too obvious. Why, then, should we even bother thinking about such details? For all we know, these events may well be in the far distant future, so how can they be relevant to us?

There are at least two answers to that. Firstly, twenty centuries ago these events were, by definition, even more distant than they are now. Yet Paul thought it was important even then to tell the Christians in Thessalonica about the man of lawlessness. He gives the reason: *For the mystery of lawlessness is already at work* (2 Thessalonians 2:7). That is, the kind of power that would eventually come was already foreshadowed in what was happening at the time in Roman society. There was increasing hostility towards those who, because of their faith in the one true Creator God, refused to offer their pinch of incense on Caesar's altar and worship him.

Paul warns that we should pay close attention to such trends in history. They are not innocent. They will lead inexorably to the greatest state-orchestrated hostility to God that the world has ever seen. Genesis tells us, of course, that the war against God started a long time ago, at the dawn of human history; but in the Western world we have lived to see a ramping up of open hostility not only to God but also to public expression of belief in God. One major negative effect of the Enlightenment was the propagation of the idea that all true knowledge was factual, value free, and objective. By contrast with facts, values were held to be subjective, essentially a matter of taste. The conviction then grew that religious belief belonged to the realm of private values rather than public truth. Link that with the increasing notion that human beings are autonomous and emancipated, and you have a potent recipe for banishing God. Nowadays, the scathing New Atheist demagogues announce that science, with its reliance on reason and evidence, leaves no room for belief in God, since, as they falsely assume, faith in him has no evidential basis.

With what I can only describe as culpable shortsightedness, the New Atheists stir up hostility by accusing Christianity of a great deal of cruelty and violence. In making such accusations they fail to take into account what they surely must know: that Jesus himself forbade violence in his name; and that the worst violence in history is to be seen in the mass murders perpetrated by atheist regimes in the twentieth century. (For more details see my book *Gunning for God*.) Thinking of that always reminds me of what a Russian intellectual said to me in the 1990s: "We thought we could get rid of God and retain a value for human beings, but we found that was impossible."

These are big issues; and the very fact that they are in the public domain means that we can use them as a bridge to get people thinking about God and human freedom. Daniel shows us what the attempt to eliminate God will eventually lead to – not freedom, but incalculable oppression. Atheists like Nietzsche saw this clearly – the "death of God" would not lead to human freedom but to nihilism and the loss of everything, including meaning. These issues need to be brought again into public discourse.

Not only that, those of us who follow Christ need to know that this will happen, if we are to keep our nerve and maintain the public profession of our faith. As we have seen with Daniel, if we are on a journey in unfamiliar territory, and the trail gets so narrow, steep, and difficult that we begin to think we have lost the way, and we wonder about turning back, it is very useful to possess a map that shows we must expect the going to be difficult at this very point, and that we should therefore press on. The Bible is just such a map for the times, and we need to follow its directions in order to navigate the rough bits of history as well as the smooth.

In our study of Daniel 2 we pointed out the danger of thinking that the kingdom of God on earth would eventually be brought about by Christian teaching permeating society, such that the world and its governmental structures would become Christian. The biblical "map" says the very opposite – both in chapter 2 and here in chapter 7. The kingdom of God in its outward sense will arrive with the supernatural return of Christ to oppose the beast and his kingdom.

Preparing for the future

Surely, someone will say, we can prepare ourselves for this kind of thing without all the bizarre details about horns and heads! That leads me to the second reason for such predictions in Scripture. The apostle John describes how Jesus drove the moneychangers out of the temple at Passover time in Jerusalem:

> So the Jews said to him: "What sign do you show us for doing these things?" Jesus answered them, "Destroy this temple, and in three days I will raise it up." The Jews then said, "It has taken forty-six years to build this temple, and will you raise it up in three days?" But he was speaking about the temple of his body. When therefore he was raised from the dead, his disciples remembered that he had said this, and they believed the Scripture and the word that Jesus had spoken. (John 2:18–22.)

Jesus' disciples made no sense of this prediction until the actual event occurred; then they remembered it and it stimulated their faith in him.

Just before the crucifixion, in order to comfort his disciples, Jesus told them that he was going away, and then explained why: *And now I have told you before it takes place, so that when it does take place you may believe* (John 14:29).

These two examples from John's Gospel refer to highly specific events. The value of the predictions was only realized at the time of the events themselves – not before. Therefore, one would expect that some of the details in Daniel – and Revelation – would only be understood at the time of their fulfilment. Daniel expressly states that some of his prophecy will be sealed (that is, will not be understood) until the time of the end (Daniel 12:4). So we cannot, indeed must not, expect to understand all the detail – a consideration that should help us to keep a balance between taking the prophecies and their details seriously and grasping their general outline without indulging in wild speculation.

Over the centuries this chapter of Daniel has been a source of real hope to millions of people who have experienced persecution and suffering for their faith in God. However powerful the beasts may be, when they have done their worst they can only kill the body. They cannot destroy the person who is you:

> And do not fear those who kill the body but cannot kill the soul. Rather fear him who can destroy both soul and body in hell. Are not two sparrows sold for a penny? And not one of them will fall to the ground apart from your Father. But even the hairs of your head are all numbered. Fear not, therefore; you are of more value than many sparrows. So everyone who acknowledges me before men, I also will acknowledge before my Father who is in heaven, but whoever denies me before men, I also will deny before my Father who is in heaven. (Matthew 10:28–33.)

Daniel tells us that there is a heaven from which the Son of Man will one day come. As a perfect human, he will take the reins of government from the beasts of earth. There will be a judgment, when justice will be done. The final ferocious expression of hostility towards God and his people will be destroyed, and the saints – those who have clung on to God in spite of overwhelming odds, even martyrdom – will receive the kingdom.

At the end of this most powerful of visions Daniel records his honest reaction: *my thoughts greatly alarmed me, and my colour changed, but I kept the matter in my heart* (Daniel 7:28). However strong and deep our faith, however real our experience of God, we are still human beings beset with frailty, and we simply cannot think about the kind of thing that is in this vision without being shaken, any more than Daniel could.

Daniel kept it in his heart. He thought about it all and pondered the questions that it raised. And so should we, for we too have our questions. And we will be challenged: how can we be so sure of the future? It is all very well singing rousing Christian hymns in church, but what about when we are a minority – maybe only consisting of one – facing brutal antagonism because of our faith in God? Let us listen to the advice given by one man who was facing just that. To steel him for the battle, Paul wrote a letter to his young friend Timothy:

> *Remember Jesus Christ, risen from the dead, the offspring of David, as preached in my gospel, for which I am suffering, bound with chains as a criminal. But the word of God is not bound! Therefore I endure everything for the sake of the elect, that they also may obtain the salvation that is in Christ Jesus with eternal glory. The saying is trustworthy, for: If we have died with him, we will also live with him; if we endure, we will also reign with him; if we deny him, he also will deny us; if we are faithless, he remains faithful – for he cannot deny himself. (2 Timothy 2:8–13.)*

Remember Jesus Christ, risen from the dead... This is the key to hope. Death is not the end: it is a fact of history that Jesus has risen, and is alive for evermore. Years earlier Paul had told the thinkers at Athens that the resurrection of Jesus was the supreme evidence that he would be the Judge in that coming day:

> *The times of ignorance God overlooked, but now he commands all people everywhere to repent, because he has fixed a day on which he will judge the world in righteousness by a man whom he has appointed; and of this he has given assurance to all by raising him from the dead. (Acts 17:30–31.)*

The day of judgment has been fixed. The evidence is there for all to consider. (The resurrection of Christ, with its consequences, is the historical event that is the basis for faith. Faith, in the Christian sense, is thoroughly evidence-based; it is not blind belief.) The Lord Jesus has risen. In that certainty Paul's confidence was unbounded to the last, as he prepared for his final battle with the *iron empire* of his day:

251

For I am already being poured out as a drink offering, and the time of my departure has come. I have fought the good fight, I have finished the race, I have kept the faith. Henceforth there is laid up for me the crown of righteousness, which the Lord, the righteous judge, will award to me on that Day, and not only to me but also to all who have loved his appearing. (2 Timothy 4:6–8.)

The vision of chapter 7 brought Daniel, as it brings us, face to face with some stern realities. How should we react to them? This is an important question. There have been believers throughout history who have felt that the only way to respond to the evil that is embedded in the governmental structures of this world is to withdraw into a private ghetto or monastery.

Even though he was deeply distressed by the vision, Daniel did not react by withdrawing. He continued to serve the emperor of Babylon, and survived to serve at the top level in the Medo-Persian empire. Perhaps one reason for this is that the visions of chapters 2 and 7 balance each other. Chapter 2 is more positive and affirming (while recognizing flaws and weaknesses); chapter 7 is more negative and disaffirming (while recognizing a few positive characteristics). The New Testament presents us with the same balance. Writing at the time of Nero, Paul says that, on the one hand, the authorities are instituted by God: rulers are not a terror to good conduct but to bad, and we should respect them (see Romans 13:1–7). On the other hand, as we saw above, Paul does not hesitate to say that the "mystery" that will lead to the man of lawlessness is already operating in the very same Roman society (2 Thessalonians 2:7). Paul is utterly realistic when it comes to the evil endemic in government, yet he does not urge believers to withdraw but encourages them to live productive lives in society as model citizens and Christians.

There are times, of course, when this balance is hard to hold. Indeed, Daniel and the apostles were prepared to disobey authorities that usurped the place that only God should fill. We shall need all the wisdom that God can give us in order to fulfil the directive of our Lord that we should be salt and light in our society (Matthew 5:13–14). Some of that wisdom is to be found in the book of Daniel.

CHAPTER 17

THE VISION OF THE RAM AND THE GOAT
Daniel 8

A couple of years after he had the vision of the four wild animals Daniel had yet another vision. This time it was of two animals, a ram and a male goat. It is clear from the common animal theme that this vision forms a pair with the vision that precedes it, but there are obvious differences between the two – for instance, the number of animals involved. In chapter 7 none of the animals is specifically identified. In chapter 8 the ram is said to be the Medo-Persian empire, and the male goat the Macedonian (or Greek) empire that followed it. If we are correct in identifying the four animals in chapter 7 with the empires of chapter 2 – Babylon, Medo-Persia, Greece and Rome – this means that chapter 8 concerns itself with the middle pair of these empires.

Daniel saw the vision when he was in the important eastern city of Susa (now in modern Iran) about 250km east of Babylon in the province of Elam. He was standing by the Ulai river (or canal) when he saw a two-horned ram on the bank of the river charging around in every direction. The ram was incredibly powerful – no other animal could stand in its way and no one could rescue anything from its grip. It did exactly as it pleased – that is, until a male goat came scurrying from the west with such rapidity that its feet scarcely touched the ground. The goat had a prominent horn between its eyes and gored the ram, breaking its horns and trampling on it. Now it was the turn of the goat to have unparalleled power. It became immensely strong but, at the peak of its power, its horn broke and was then replaced by four other horns.

As Daniel watched these horns he saw yet another horn growing out of one of them. It was small at first but rapidly increased to an enormous size, so that it challenged heaven and cast some of the host of heaven and the stars to the ground. It proceeded to put an end to the regular burnt offering, desecrating the sanctuary. Daniel then overheard holy beings speaking to each other about how long this violent desecration would last, until the sanctuary was restored again. He was told that it would be 2,300 evenings and mornings. Although it was fearful, the persecution would not last for ever.

Before we go into any of the details, we should pause to take in the overall impression of this vision. There is frequent repetition of the idea of power – it is said of both the ram and the goat that *there was no one who could rescue from his power* (8:4, 7). This echoes the statement by Nebuchadnezzar to Daniel's three friends: *who is the god who will deliver you out of my hands?* (3:15).

In the structure of the book, chapters 3 and 8 are parallel.

Chapter 3	Chapter 8
Nebuchadnezzar thinks that no god can deliver the Jews out of his hand.	The ram and the male goat: no one can rescue from their power.
He commands them to worship his god.	The power of the little horn who stops the Jews' worship of their God, and who defies God himself.
The Jews defy him.	God's sanctuary and truth are finally vindicated.
They are preserved in the furnace.	
God's ability to deliver is demonstrated.	

The explanation of the vision is then given to Daniel by *one having the appearance of a man* (8:15) who is called Gabriel. In one sense it is relatively simple to follow, since it gives a very clear outline of what subsequently happens. The two animals are identified: the ram is Medo-Persia, and the male goat Greece. The large horn of the goat is Alexander the Great (356–323 BC), a military genius tutored by Aristotle, who masterminded a series of lightning conquests that made him ruler of a vast empire extending from Greece to India. The defeat of the ram by the male goat anticipates the Battle of Issus in 333 BC, in which Alexander defeated the armies of Darius III. Ten years later, aged thirty-two and at the height of his powers, Alexander died in Babylon in the palace of Nebuchadnezzar – probably entirely unaware that a man in that very same city had written a prophecy about him nearly 300 years earlier.

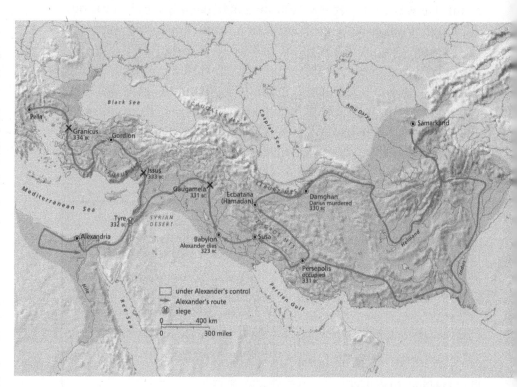

The empire of Alexander

Alexander the Great

When Alexander died he had no clear natural successor, and forty years of struggle ensued between his generals whom he had appointed as satraps. The empire was eventually divided into four parts, each ruled by one of the generals. Cassander ruled Macedonia and Greece; and Lysimachus ruled Thrace and Asia Minor; of particular importance for our study, Seleucus was in charge of northern Syria, Mesopotamia, and regions to the east; and Ptolemy took southern Syria, Palestine, and Egypt.[34] Geographically, Judea was sandwiched between these two kingdoms, and inevitably suffered in the constant battles between them. (There is more about this in Daniel 11.)

The four kingdoms are aptly symbolized by the four horns of the goat that replaced the broken single horn. From the description given by Daniel, the little horn that sprang out of one of the four horns and desecrated the sanctuary can be none other than the Seleucid king, Antiochus IV, who reigned from 223–187 BC. The description *little horn* fits what we know of his personality very well, since he seems to have been a man of a mean and servile disposition, who used deceit and cunning to establish and enlarge his power base (Daniel 8:25). In particular, he gained control in *the glorious land* whose capital was Jerusalem, Daniel's home city. The atrocities he committed there against the Jewish people were utterly horrific, and led to his being referred to in rabbinical sources as *harasha*, "the wicked".

We should remember that we look back at these events, whereas they were still future in Daniel's day. Daniel was not, as we argued earlier, simply a historian, reporting his experiences in the second century BC. He was a prophet in the sixth century BC, who received a special supernatural revelation from God as to what the future held. He was shown enough of the contours of that future to understand that what would happen to his people in the course of history would be terrible in the extreme. From his first vision he had learned that the fierce fourth beast would *think to change the times and the law* and overcome the people of God. Now he is told that this *little horn* would similarly trample on Daniel's people and some of its leaders and *cause fearful destruction and ... succeed in what he does, and destroy mighty men and the people who are the saints* (8:24).

Not only that but he would also defile the very sanctuary of God in Jerusalem by banning the regular burnt offering which was a public expression of Israel's devotion to God – and which God himself had commanded. That is, the *little horn* would defy both God and his law – just like the fourth beast of chapter 7.

A pattern begins to emerge in these first three sections of the second half of the book. First, Daniel records his own experience of the Medo-Persian law that was enacted in an attempt to force him into disobeying the law of his God. Next, he records an earlier vision which he had, of a fierce king in the fourth empire that *thinks to change the times and the law*. Then he sees a further vision: another powerful king from the third empire stops the people of God obeying the law by banning their public ceremony of burnt offering. It is a pattern of deteriorating attitudes to God and his law on the part of pagan kings.

It was an appalling vision that so overwhelmed Daniel that he was ill for several days. When we see from the later historical records what actually happened under Antiochus IV, it is not at all surprising that Daniel was so affected by what he saw. In fact, the brazen defiance of God that Antiochus displayed was so serious and so significant that it is also a major focus of Daniel's final vision.

There is a further reason for this emphasis on Antiochus that we might easily overlook on a first reading. Not only does the vision point forward to the time of Antiochus, but Daniel is explicitly told that it is *for the time of the end* (8:17).

The future - and beyond

That immediately raises the question: how can the description of a Seleucid king in the second century BC possibly relate to the time of the end? The answer is, surely, that the figure of Antiochus and the horrors he perpetrated throw long shadows into the future. At the time of the end another leader like Antiochus will arise, who will do similar things. In Antiochus there were the seeds of an evil that will gestate and come to its fearful fruition in a time yet to come. Antiochus and the events of his time, therefore, form a prototype or thought model of the future, which will help Daniel and us imagine what is to come – and to be aware of similar tendencies in our own day.

Indeed, as we read the explanation given to Daniel by Gabriel, it is hard to resist the impression that something much more distant and much more sinister than Antiochus is in view.

Speaking of the four kingdoms, Gabriel says:

> And at the latter end of their kingdom, when the transgressors
> have reached their limit, a king of bold countenance, one who
> understands riddles, shall arise. His power shall be great – but
> not by his own power; and he shall cause fearful destruction
> and shall succeed in what he does, and destroy mighty men
> and the people who are the saints. By his cunning he shall
> make deceit prosper under his hand, and in his own mind he
> shall become great. Without warning he shall destroy many.
> And he shall even rise up against the Prince of princes, and he
> shall be broken – but by no human hand. (Daniel 8:23–25.)

As we read this passage it is almost as if we are looking *through* the contours of Antiochus and his time to a much bigger and, sadly, more terrible scenario in the future, when a bold and fierce king who is like Antiochus in his deceit, cunning, and power rises up against the Prince of princes and is destroyed by supernatural power.

This description links conceptually with another passage that we have already considered, 2 Thessalonians 1–10 (see the previous chapter). The parallels are striking. Both the bold king in Daniel's vision and the man of lawlessness get their power from a dark source. They exalt themselves against God; they fight against Christ who is the Prince of princes; and they are killed by the supernatural power of God.

Therefore the prophecies of Daniel 2, 7, and 8 (and also, as we shall see, 9 and 11) all home in on this final manifestation of evil government that shall be destroyed by the coming of Christ. This means that we have several perspectives on that time – much as we have four Gospels in the New Testament that give us four perspectives on the historical events that underlie the Christian faith.

Or we could think of the way in which astrophotographers take three separate monotone pictures of a galaxy through red, green, and blue filters, and then combine them to form a stunning colour photograph. In Daniel's visions we are presented with separate images, and by collecting them together we can get a composite idea of the whole. Antiochus is but one prototype of what shall happen in the future.

The spread of Greek culture

Since Antiochus IV plays a central role as a thought model of the future, it is important for us now to get a flavour of the times in which he lived. They hold much to interest us, but we shall have to be content with a thumbnail sketch.

One of the legacies of Alexander's conquests was the spread of Greek culture over a vast area, and this led to "a new type of civilisation of multiple nations united culturally by the Greek language".[35] Alexander ushered in what is known as the Hellenistic Age (from 323 to 30 BC). It was a time of high and heady culture. In particular, the period from about 280 to 160 BC produced a long list of intellectual luminaries who laid the foundations of those disciplines that would eventually become science as we now know it.

For instance, one of my heroes is the mathematician Euclid (around 300 BC). His fascinating insights into the axioms of geometry instilled in me a love for the axiomatic method.

There was the astronomer Aristarchus of Samos (310–230 BC). He presented the first known heliocentric model of the solar system in which he got the order of the planets correct in relation to the sun – 1,800 years before Copernicus did his work. Brilliant!

Archimedes (287–212 BC) developed mathematics further. He calculated the number *pi* to a good approximation. His friend Eratosthenes of Cyrene (276–195 BC), the third chief librarian of the great library at Alexandria, was a polymath (mathematician, geographer, astronomer, music theorist, poet, and athlete). And he was not simply a geographer – he was the founder of geography as a discipline! He was the first to construct trigonometric tables and calculate the circumference and tilt of the earth with remarkable precision.

Then there was Hipparchus (190–120 BC), who ranks as the greatest observational astronomer of ancient times. He built on the wisdom of Babylonia and developed a method of predicting solar eclipses.

Lest my predilection for science should get out of hand, I must mention the historian Polybius (200–118 BC), who was noted for his *Histories* that covered the period 264–146 BC. He developed ideas on the separation of powers in government that ultimately influenced the drafting of the Constitution of the United States of America.

Dionysius Thrax (170–90 BC) is credited with the first extant grammar of the Greek language. It was a time when the Epicurean and Stoic philosophers thrived; and the artistic period when such famous works as the *Venus de Milo* were created.

The museum at Alexandria, with its large library, was a leading research centre, and a meeting place for scholars and writers.

Callimachus, the leading Greek poet of the third century BC, was responsible for cataloguing its estimated 500,000 scrolls. Other cities besides Alexandria had substantial libraries. On the island of Rhodes, for example, there were famous schools of rhetoric and philosophy.

Many Greeks went abroad as traders and mercenaries, and settled in Alexandria and other cities Alexander had founded. They built gymnasiums, theatres, wrestling schools, and all kinds of clubs. Greek law formed the basis of the economy and political activity. Inevitably, the locals came to see that the more they adopted of the Hellenistic culture the more advantageous it was to them, since that culture marked the ruling class. Many took Greek names and got involved in grammar school education.

Where Greek culture went, so also did Greek religion. Greek temples were built everywhere – even as far east as Iran. The travelling Greeks met Eastern religions, including the Babylonian worship of Marduk and Ishtar, with the result that beliefs got combined. Many felt that there was only one god, no matter how many names were used to describe him. Mystery religions that offered some kind of personal salvation flourished all over the empire, as did magic and the occult. Interestingly, in the East, the Seleucid rulers encouraged the revival of Babylonia, which led to a renaissance of interest in their ancient religion and cuneiform writing – the culture of Nebuchadnezzar reborn.

It all begins to sound very familiar – and that is important for us to appreciate, as we need to realize that the Hellenistic time has many things in common with our own. That should not really surprise us, for the simple reason that our contemporary civilization owes much to the Greeks.

We narrow our focus now to the Seleucid kingdom from which Antiochus IV came. Its capital was at Antioch, and it covered a vast geographic area comprising Asia Minor, Mesopotamia, and Iran. This was an unwieldy melting pot, its size and diversity making it hard to control, its many factions producing weak government.

It was a time of ceaseless strife and tension, under the increasingly large shadow of the encroaching Romans, who would finally annex the Greek empire for themselves. Antiochus's father, Antiochus III, was driven out of Greece after being defeated by the Romans at the Battle of Thermopylae in 191 BC. The Romans imposed a crippling treaty on him, in terms of both a war indemnity and the giving up of territory in Asia Minor, thus frustrating his ambitions to emulate Alexander the Great. He turned his military attention to the south, and in 198 BC defeated the Egyptians at the Battle of Panium, near the source of the River Jordan, and so brought Ptolemaic rule in Judea to an end.

Initially Antiochus III gave the Jews a degree of autonomy. Josephus records that he let them live "according to the laws of their forefathers". Nevertheless, he began a programme of Hellenization that involved, for instance, placing pagan idols in the Jewish temple. Not surprisingly the Jews protested; Antiochus backed down.

Tetradrachm of Antiochus IV

The inscription reads: King Antiochus, God Manifest, Bearer of Victory

His son, Antiochus IV, who took the throne in 175 BC and ruled over the Jews until 164 BC, turned out to be a very different man from his father. He was the first Seleucid king to record his claim to divinity on the coins of his kingdom, choosing the title *Epiphanes* to express his belief that he was "God manifest". However, as a result of his eccentric and bizarre behaviour, this was often parodied as *Epimenes* – "madman".

Antiochus Epiphanes

In order to consolidate his power in his vast multi-cultural empire Antiochus drove forward the process of Hellenization. Part of that process was to try to create one religion for all – by force if necessary. He could not tolerate what to him was the narrow-minded exclusivism of Judaism's devotion to one God, to the rejection of all others. In doing so, he was unconsciously following the path of many emperors before him, including Nebuchadnezzar when he constructed his golden image, and Darius when he proclaimed his edict. As we soon shall see, Antiochus was to go much further.

He shocked the Jews when he encouraged the peoples of the Mediterranean region to worship him as the Canaanite god, Baal – a nature god that had been decisively rejected by Israel as the idolatrous epitome of all that they stood against. Antiochus was trying to force them back to a compromise that centuries before had cost them the "locust years" of exile.

There were some Jews who accepted the compromise – indeed, welcomed it. The apocryphal books of the Maccabees are a very important source for the history of this period. They tell us what happened from the traditional Jewish perspective:

> In those days certain renegades came out from Israel and
> misled many, saying, "Let us go and make a covenant with the
> Gentiles around us, for since we separated from them many
> disasters have come upon us." This proposal pleased them, and
> some of the people eagerly went to the king, who authorized
> them to observe the ordinances of the Gentiles. So they built
> a gymnasium in Jerusalem, according to Gentile custom,
> and removed the marks of circumcision, and abandoned the
> holy covenant. They joined with the Gentiles' rule and sold
> themselves to do evil. (1 Maccabees 1:11–15 NRSV.)

Clearly these "renegades" felt that they were missing out, even attributing their misfortunes to their original separation from the

Gentiles (under Abraham, presumably). They found Greek culture and lifestyle very attractive. It made far fewer moral demands than the law of Moses, for instance, and allowed them to give free rein to their impulses and desires. It also opened up a whole new world of entertainment and sport that had been foreign to them, to say nothing of the intellectual stimulation of the free exchange of ideas, without having to be committed to any particular world-view. It was not only some of the ordinary people that welcomed the wave of Hellenization, but a group of the leaders led by no less than Jason the high priest, who had abandoned any sense that their Bible (our Old Testament) was a definitive revelation from God.

It was a heady taste of freedom. And Antiochus was giving it to them.

That concept of freedom is shared by many people today, and given as their reason for abandoning God. They say that God is out to stifle them – their self-expression, their creativity, and their flourishing. They want freedom from any authority above that of man, and they think that secular society can deliver it to them.

As it is for many today, the Greek ideal in life was the pursuit of the good (happiness); and they laid great emphasis on human reason as the vehicle for achieving it. For them, man was the measure of all things. And, just as there were many Jews who bought into it, today we have a Christianized version:

> A conscience soothing Jesus, with an unscandalous cross,
> an otherworldly kingdom, a private, inwardly limited
> spirit, a pocket God, a spiritualized Bible, and an escapist
> church. Its goal is a happy, comfortable, and successful life,
> obtainable through the forgiveness of an abstract sinfulness
> by faith in an unhistorical Christ. (Costas, 1982, page 80.)

In traditional Jewish eyes Greek religion was a complete inversion of all they stood for. Its gods were only mythological (Freudian, we might say) projections of human desire, fear, greed, envy, and anger. Orthodox Jews believed in revelation – a notion beyond the comprehension of the Greeks – as it is of many moderns.

Like many other rulers, Antiochus had difficulty in unifying a large and diffuse collection of peoples and religions. He was also well aware that religious loyalties run very deep. He could see that the centre of gravity for the Jews was their God, not him. Their loyalty to God and his revelation clearly transcended any loyalty they could give to a human king and his dictates. Their very first commandment, *You shall have no other gods apart from me*, was a direct provocation to a king who called himself "God made manifest". Antiochus hated and determined to destroy this pestilential religion. If only he could harness that religious loyalty for himself. And so, like Nebuchadnezzar and the unwitting Darius, he tried to do so – with horrific consequences for the tiny province of Judea.

On the way back from one of his campaigns against Egypt he invaded Jerusalem and deliberately desecrated the Jewish temple by entering the holy place, and removing the golden altar where the high priest prayed, and the golden lampstand, together with many of the precious vessels of gold and silver.

These things are not enumerated in the vision that talks about the desecration of the sanctuary, but one cannot help thinking back to the very beginning of Daniel's story, when Nebuchadnezzar removed some of those vessels and carried them to Babylon. How significant they became, as they sat on Belshazzar's dining table. Now Antiochus was meddling with them once more. Yet far worse was to come.

A couple of years later, Antiochus sent a large expeditionary force to Jerusalem and attacked it, shedding a great deal of blood. He then issued an edict, which is described in the book of Maccabees:

> *Then the king wrote to his whole kingdom that all should be one people, and that all should give up their particular customs. All the Gentiles accepted the command of the king. Many even from Israel gladly adopted his religion; they sacrificed to idols and profaned the sabbath. And the king sent letters by messengers to Jerusalem and the towns of Judah; he directed them to follow customs strange to the land, to forbid burnt-offerings and sacrifices and drink-offerings in the sanctuary, to profane sabbaths and festivals, to defile the*

sanctuary and the priests, to build altars and sacred precincts and shrines for idols, to sacrifice swine and other unclean animals, and to leave their sons uncircumcised. They were to make themselves abominable by everything unclean and profane, so that they would forget the law and change all the ordinances. He added, "And whoever does not obey the command of the king shall die."

In such words he wrote to his whole kingdom. He appointed inspectors over all the people and commanded the towns of Judah to offer sacrifice, town by town. (1 Maccabees 1:41–51 NRSV.)

Antiochus banned Jewish religious practices on a scale that even Darius's scheming civil servants could never have imagined. He forbade Sabbath observance and the holding of the annual cycle of Jewish festivals. And, as Daniel had predicted – *he stopped the daily sacrifice.* This was a daily ceremony in which a whole animal was burnt as a symbol of Israel's single-minded devotion to God: *You shall love the Lord your God with all your heart, mind, soul and strength.* Antiochus could not tolerate that, so he banned it. He then had pagan sacrifices made on the altar, which was an utter abomination to the Jews. (This will come up again in Daniel 9.)

Like Nebuchadnezzar and many others before and after him, Antiochus could not tolerate people who would not bow down to him. He was determined to break their spirit. So, not content with banning the sacrifices, he proceeded to ban the reading of the law of Moses, and ordered that all copies of it should be collected and burned. He went further, and banned even the observance of the law, on penalty of death. In particular, he outlawed the Jewish practice of circumcision, even going to the extent of murdering Jewish babies who had been circumcised, hanging them round the necks of their mothers, and hurling them down from the walls of Jerusalem.

This frenzied anti-God madness reached its height on the twenty-fifth day of the month Chislev (corresponding to our December) in the year 167 BC. In a final act of supreme and studied blasphemy, Antiochus had the Jerusalem temple rededicated to the

Greek Olympian God, Zeus. Nothing like it had ever happened to the Jews before. Nebuchadnezzar, Belshazzar, and Darius had defied God, but they had never done anything like this. Antiochus's act was in an entirely new category. For the Jews it was abomination upon abomination, and came to be known as the *abomination of desolation* (see Daniel 9:27; Matthew 24:15).

Daniel says that something very like it will happen at the time of the end. And, in the plain non-symbolic language of Paul, we read:

> ... *and the man of lawlessness is revealed, the son of destruction, who opposes and exalts himself against every so-called god or object of worship, so that he takes his seat in the temple of God, proclaiming himself to be God. (2 Thessalonians 2:3–4.)*

Antiochus got very near to this as, in his megalomaniac rage, he strode into the temple and desecrated it.

And God did nothing. How could a pagan polytheist boldly stride onto the holiest ground on earth, defy the living God who had placed his name there, abolish God's commandments, reverse his ordinances, and get away with it?

It seemed as if every trace of God had been drained out of the universe. Antiochus must have gloated in triumph at the thought of having banished God from the world. How could anyone in his right mind hold on to such a religion any more, when there was clearly nothing in it? It was a devastating moment for the faithful Jews.

But Antiochus had failed to reckon with the depth of anger he had provoked. That anger erupted in what we now call the Maccabean Revolt, after its leader Judas Maccabeus ("Judas the Hammer"). Judas was one of five sons of a priest, Mattathias, who lived in Modi'im, a village about seventeen miles from Jerusalem. It was Mattathias himself who lit the flame of resistance by killing a Jew who was about to offer a sacrifice to pagan gods, as well as a king's officer who was present. Mattathias and his family took flight to the hills and built up a band of warriors who were determined to reverse the evils that Antiochus had imposed upon them.

The campaign that followed is historically very complex. The resistance group fought not only against the Seleucid occupation but also against all collaborators from the Jewish side, so that at times the conflict resembled a civil war. In 164 BC, three years after Antiochus's desecration of the temple, Judas and his warriors recaptured all of Jerusalem except for Antiochus's citadel, the Acra, which was built on a hill overlooking the temple area. In order to cleanse the sanctuary and build the new altar of unhewn stones, Judas chose priests with a reputation for integrity. They performed a ceremony of rededicating the temple that is celebrated by Jews to this day. It is the festival of *Hanukkah* (Dedication) that lasts for eight days, and begins on 25 Kislev in the Jewish calendar year.

God made manifest

Nearly two centuries later the Prince of princes was himself in Jerusalem at the time of *Hanukkah*, walking in the temple precincts in the colonnade of Solomon. John tells us what happened:

> So the Jews gathered around him and said to him, "How long will you keep us in suspense? If you are the Christ, tell us plainly." Jesus answered them, "I told you, and you do not believe. The works that I do in my Father's name bear witness about me, but you do not believe because you are not part of my flock. My sheep hear my voice, and I know them, and they follow me. I give them eternal life, and they will never perish, and no one will snatch them out of my hand. My Father, who has given them to me, is greater than all, and no one is able to snatch them out of the Father's hand. I and the Father are one."
> The Jews picked up stones again to stone him. Jesus answered them, "I have shown you many good works from the Father; for which of them are you going to stone me?" The Jews answered him, "It is not for a good work that we are going to stone you but for blasphemy, because you, being a man, make yourself God." (John 10:24–33.)

In the very place where Antiochus had stood – a man who named himself *Epiphanes*, "God made manifest" – Jesus now stood. He said, *I and the Father are one*, and the Jews were appalled. Could this be *Hanukkah* history repeating itself? There were only two possible answers: either it was utter blasphemy, or it was true. They decided it was blasphemy, and took up stones to kill him. It was not long before their religious court had him executed by the Romans.

But this time they got it wrong. Jesus proceeded to tell them that the consequences of their rejection of him as their lawful King would mean another period of exile and a further destruction of their city. But he would return one day, and as a sign of that return he referred them to Daniel's prophecy:

> *So when you see the abomination of desolation spoken of by the prophet Daniel, standing in the holy place (let the reader understand), then let those who are in Judea flee to the mountains. … For then there will be great tribulation, such as has not been from the beginning of the world until now, no, and never will be. … Immediately after the tribulation of those days … will appear in heaven the sign of the Son of Man, and then all the tribes of the earth will mourn, and they will see the Son of Man coming on the clouds of heaven with power and great glory. (Matthew 24:15–30.)*

We note the obvious. For Jesus, the fulfilment of Daniel's prophecy was yet future, and he connected it with his return as the glorious Son of Man on the clouds of heaven. In this way, he shows us that Daniel 7 and 8 are speaking about the same thing.

So, in a future day another man will stand in the place where Antiochus blasphemed God, and where Jesus made the valid claim to be God. To rapturous global adulation, this future potentate will claim to be the Supreme Being in the universe. At this point, human defiance of God will reach its evil harvest of supreme spiritual anarchy. The original lie of the snake will appear to be the truth – *when you eat of it your eyes will be opened, and you will be like God, knowing good and evil* (Genesis 3:5). It will appear to be the ultimate triumph of man over God.

When this man claims to be God, he will not be speaking as a theist. These, surely, are the words of an anti-theist. This man will not believe that there is a supernatural God who is Creator of heaven and earth and Lord of history. He will have rejected all that. His faith will be solely in himself, no doubt as the pinnacle of the evolutionary process – the omega point of history, the biological superman. And he will deliberately harness that most powerful of human emotions, religious devotion, to enhance his own position and power. He will be supremely intelligent (the *eyes of a man* as in Daniel 7:8) and possess unparalleled power far beyond that of Nebuchadnezzar, Darius, Alexander, or the caesars, who seemed invincible in their day. This man of consummate evil will reject the supernatural God of heaven. In a tragic irony, the power he will possess to deceive and enthral the world will come from the dark supernatural realm of the very devil himself – whether the man believes in such a being or not.

But his dominion will not last. As with all other earthly dominions, it will be temporary. Just as Judas Maccabeus cleansed the sanctuary in Antiochus's time, Daniel 8 predicts that after 2,300 days (some six-and-a-half years) the sanctuary will be restored. Jesus confirmed this by saying that after a horrific period of extreme tribulation he would return in power and glory, destroy the man of lawlessness, and usher in his kingdom.

All of this still lies before us, of course. There is not much more that we wish to say about Antiochus's time. He died in the same year that the temple was rededicated, and for a while Judas Maccabeus was able to maintain a peace of sorts. When he died five years later, his brother Jonathan succeeded him. Jonathan became a friend of the new king, Alexander Balas, who elected him as high priest in Jerusalem, around 153 BC, thus starting what is known as the Hasmonean dynasty. However, Jonathan was not descended from Aaron, as the law of Moses stipulated the high priest should be, and this alienated the traditional party, who formed themselves into a powerful opposition, later to be known as Pharisees.

Jonathan died as a result of treachery, and was replaced by his brother Simon, who was assassinated in 135 or 134 BC. The next in

271

succession was Simon's son John, known as John Hyrcanus I. He possessed none of the zeal of his grandfather who had instigated the uprising. At heart he was a Sadducee. As such he denied the supernatural and accepted the very world-view his grandfather, father, and uncles had fought so hard against.

Anti-God ideologies will continue

What are we to make of it all: the forced imposition of a pagan religion, the defiling of holy places, and the consequent blood-letting as resistance manifests itself? In a way it seems very remote to us, particularly in the Western world.

But history is not over yet. Daniel insists that we need to pay heed, for something very like it will happen again – on a greater scale. For some years we in the West have enjoyed an unusually calm period of history, living in a more or less Christian culture conducive to the development of many institutions that enable life to flourish in relative peace. Yet, in the last century, there was more bloodshed in the world as a whole than in all the intervening centuries put together. We need to wake up to the fact that a great proportion of that bloodshed has been as a direct consequence of anti-God ideologies, forced upon people by dictators who held enormous power. Stalin, Mao, and Pol Pot tower over Antiochus Epiphanes in terms of the millions they put to death. Hitler's rage against the Jewish people, and his murder of millions of them, has been unparalleled. If we replace the state-enforced pagan culture of Seleucid times by the state atheism of more recent times, the motives that drove Antiochus are still very much alive.

Indeed, Enver Hoxha, the leader of the Socialist People's Republic of Albania, who banned every form of religion, evokes strong memories of Antiochus. Article 37 of the Albanian Constitution of 1976 stipulated: "The State recognizes no religion, and supports atheistic propaganda in order to implant a scientific materialistic world outlook in people." The penal code of 1977 imposed prison sentences of three to ten years for "religious propaganda and the production, distribution, or storage of religious literature".

We might also think of *Juche*, the official state ideology of North Korea. According to the New World Encyclopedia:

> Kim Jong-il has explained that the doctrine is a component part of Kimilsungism, after its founder and his father, Kim Il-sung. The core principle of the Juche ideology since the 1970s, has been that "man is the master of everything and decides everything". … Juche literally means "main body" or "subject"; it has also been translated in North Korean sources as "independent stand" and the "spirit of self-reliance".
>
> Juche theory is a type of political ideology, but it is built upon the deification and mystification of Kim Il-sung (1912–1994). Its religious or pseudo-religious characteristics distinguish Juche ideology from all other forms of Marxism, including Marx-Leninism of the former Soviet Union, European Neo-Marxism, Maoism, and even Stalinism. Juche ideology characterizes Kim as the "eternal head of state", a Messianic liberator of humankind, and describes North Korea as a chosen nation, and North Koreans as a chosen people who have a mission to liberate the world. While fear and terror are used to externally dominate the masses in a totalitarian state, Juche Ideology is a tool for the internal domination of their minds....[36]

In the twenty-first century this is the ideology of a country that has at its heart the deification of a leader – Kim Il-sung. It is just like what we found in the ancient world. To cite the Encyclopedia once more:

> His birthplace and sites where he conducted his activities are holy grounds that are destinations for North Koreans to make their pilgrimages. His portrait is hung on the wall of every household and people begin each day by reading his words. Reflection meetings are held on a regular basis, where people can repent their wrong doings and unfaithful thoughts and behaviors based upon Kim's words as the sacred text. Based upon the deification of Kim, North Korea is characterized as

the chosen nation, and North Koreans are educated as chosen people who have a mission to "liberate mankind".

As a pseudo-religion, Juche ideology defines people's value-system, gives meaning to their life and activities, and establishes norms for everyday life. It is immersed into every aspect of social and cultural life of North Koreans, and access to information outside of the country is strictly controlled. The glorification of Kim is also reflected in the constitution. Every paragraph of the preface of the constitution begins with phrases of admiration for Kim, and builds the worship of Kim into the legal system. In other words, casting doubt on Kim Il-sung or having a critical view or a faithless attitude towards this ideology is subject to legal punishment.

Juche ideology creates a belief system where people can, at least on the surface, voluntarily choose to support its totalitarian rule. Those who are unwilling to accept the belief system are considered as "traitors", and any attempt at deviating from this norm is legally punishable. Juche ideology is, in reality, forced upon its subjects with terror and fear. In this sense, North Korea's political ideology is a prime example of totalitarianism.

One of the frightening things about totalitarianism is the level of deceit and manipulation that is employed to keep people from perceiving the truth. In this connection, we should note something that is said about *the little horn* in Daniel 8. When it gets power, *it will throw truth to the ground* (Daniel 8:12). In the subsequent explanation of the vision, we are told that the *king of bold countenance* prospers by cunning and deceit.

We notice also that Paul speaks of the coming of the man of lawlessness in the following terms:

The coming of the lawless one is by the activity of Satan with all power and false signs and wonders, and with all wicked deception for those who are perishing, because they refused to love the truth.... (2 Thessalonians 2:9.)

The relation of power to truth is very important, particularly in the contemporary world where there is a strong current of postmodern relativism – an attitude that has its roots in ancient Greek scepticism. Many people are far more interested in their own feelings, or what "works for them", than in the question of what is actually true. But there is a price to be paid for rejecting the truth.

After ceasing to be a Marxist, Arthur Koestler wrote (1950, page 68):

> My party education had equipped my mind with such
> elaborate shock-absorbing buffers and elastic defences
> that everything seen and heard became automatically
> transformed to fit a preconceived pattern.

Relativism weakens intellectual and moral resistance to totalitarianism, and opens us up to manipulation and deceit; so that in the end the "truth" we believe is dictated by those who hold the power. This is a hideous situation, of course, that demeans human beings. I am well aware that many will respond to the examples I have given above by saying: "Well, yes, but this extreme kind of thing is dying out and will vanish because it is unsustainable. Why should we think that there is any danger of it happening again? We are surely too civilized now to get involved in such violence. Why should I take Daniel seriously when he suggests that not only will it happen again, but on an intensified and global scale?"

I can understand this reaction, since I recognize some of it in myself. It is a comforting idea to think that we are past all this kind of stuff. However, realism tells me that there is another side to the story. Certain things are not dying out. Violence is not dying out – in spite of Stephen Pinker's claim to the contrary (see Chapter 10 above). As I write, there are wars raging in many parts of the world, and Western nations are engaged in some of them. Whether we like it or not, much of international terrorism is linked to extreme religious fundamentalism.

Then there is an increase in aggressive atheism at the intellectual and propagandist level. In secularized Western societies there is massive pressure to marginalize, if not exterminate, religious belief. The laws of nations are increasingly being used to discriminate against believers, just as they did in Darius's day.

In many of our countries force has not been used yet in any obvious way. But we would surely be very naive to suppose that it will never be used. How easily we forget what the whole communist experiment was about. Was it not Comrade Khrushchev who claimed that he would soon show the world the last remaining Russian Christian? I wonder why I thought of this when I read Steven Weinberg's words, encouraging scientists to contribute "*anything* we can do to weaken the hold of religion". This hint of totalitarianism may only be a straw in the wind. But straws show which way the wind is blowing, and not so long ago it blew in the direction of the Gulag.

I wish to stress that many of us who are not atheists share the New Atheists' antipathy to the patent evil that has been perpetrated in the name of religion.[37] Potentially, however, their atheistic programme is equally, if not more, dangerous, though superficially attractive to many; and for exactly the same reasons that the New Atheists advance against religion (with less justification). For instance, Dawkins warns (against the evidence, in the case of Christianity at least) that "the teachings of moderate religion are an open invitation to extremism" (2006, page 342). By the same token, might it not be wise for him to heed his own advice and give us a similar warning about the teachings of moderate atheism? After all, there is a noticeable straight line from the Enlightenment to the violence of the nineteenth and twentieth centuries.

The biblical diagnosis (reflected in Nebuchadnezzar's dream image) is that the human race is flawed by evil. In light of our common experience, that contention is hardly surprising; though it is resisted by those people whose minds are full of over-optimistic notions of "progress". John Gray, an expert on the history of European thought, insists (2007, page 198):

> The cardinal need is to change the prevailing view of human
> beings, which sees them as inherently good creatures
> unaccountably burdened with a history of violence and

oppression. Here we reach the nub of realism and its chief stumbling-point for prevailing opinion: its assertion of the innate defects of human beings. Nearly all pre-modern thinkers took it as given that human nature is fixed and flawed, and in this as in some other ways they were close to the truth of the matter. No theory of politics can be credible that assumes that human impulses are naturally benign, peaceable or reasonable.

The source of that evil flaw is given in the following key statement by St Paul:

> *Therefore, just as sin came into the world through one man, and death through sin… so death spread to all men because all sinned. (Romans 5:12.)*[38]

This says, firstly, that we have all inherited a nature that is fallen, sinful, and mortal. Secondly, we have all individually sinned. Sin is universal. We note that Paul says "sin" entered the world and not "sins", for he is not thinking of particular sins but of sin as a principle. It is an attitude consisting of a deep-seated egotism, where the human creature asserts its own will against that of the Creator.

John Gray points out (2007, page 36):

> The totalitarian regimes of the last century embodied some of the Enlightenment's boldest dreams. Some of their worst crimes were done in the service of progressive ideals, while even regimes that viewed themselves as enemies of Enlightenment values attempted a project of transforming humanity by using the power of science, whose origins are in Enlightenment thinking. The role of the Enlightenment in twentieth-century terror remains a blind spot in western perception.

It is certainly a blind spot in New Atheist perception, and it is not hard to see why. Dawkins' argument for banning the teaching of religion would lead to banning the teaching of atheism because of the horrors it has provoked, even within the living memory of many people.

It is no small irony that a filmed discussion between the four leaders, Dawkins, Dennett, Harris, and Hitchens, is entitled *The Four Horsemen*. Undoubtedly this is an allusion to the "four horsemen of the apocalypse", described in the book of Revelation as conquest, war, famine, and death (Revelation 6:1–8). One just wonders whether their choice of this epithet is yet more evidence of their ignorance of the book they attempt to rubbish. I hope so, for I find some of the statements of these "horsemen" rather chilling. For example, the following reprehensible statement by Sam Harris sounds just like a harbinger of death (2005, pages 52–53):

> Some propositions are so dangerous that it may even be ethical to kill people for believing them.

We might well ask if the New Atheists will have authority to decide in the end what those deadly propositions are, and who will execute the sentence. In that case, woe betide the world if they also gain political power. Shades of the beast?

Daniel's visions become more credible every day.

CHAPTER 18

JERUSALEM AND THE FUTURE
Daniel 9

There now lies before us the final pair of visions given to Daniel. They both concern writings. First, the book of the prophet Jeremiah that Daniel has been reading; and the second, a *book of truth* whose contents are given to Daniel by an angelic messenger. By contrast with the preceding pair of visions that featured symbolic animals, this pair is much more prosaic: narrating events to come in a down-to-earth, historical style.

Both visions are dated at the time of the Medo-Persian empire. In the first, we jump forward from the time of Belshazzar to the first year of Darius the Mede, and so rejoin the chronological sequence in the book that stopped with chapter 6. As we know, Darius was tricked into passing a law designed to stop Daniel praying to his God. Daniel refused, and carried on with his daily practice of praying at a window that opened towards Jerusalem in the west. It is clear that the beloved city, from which Nebuchadnezzar had taken him captive, was daily on Daniel's heart.

What would happen to Jerusalem? That is where God's promises were centred; and yet God does not seem to have told him much about the future of the city, so his visions must have been very disturbing. The first tells of an evil king who wishes to change the times and the law, and who overcomes the saints. The second tells of a little horn that stops the regular burnt offering in the Jerusalem temple and tramples the sanctuary. Why was Jerusalem not explicitly mentioned in either of these visions? It sounded very grim for the city, and yet the visions said that the evil king would be destroyed and the saints receive the kingdom. How was this going to work out?

Thoughts like these must have been daily on Daniel's mind; and it is perhaps for this reason that he placed one vision after chapter 6 and the other vision before chapter 9, so that we should read Daniel 9 against the correct background. He has only explicitly mentioned the name of *Jerusalem* twice up to this point, although his previous vision – about the desecration of the holy place – is a direct reference to *the city*. The desecration will feature again in this present chapter, this time in the context of the broader history of the city. In the first part of chapter 9 we find Daniel praying about the desolated city of Jerusalem and its future. In the second part, in the famous prophecy of the "seventy sevens", God reveals to him what is in store for the city in the future.

Chapter 9 is the fourth section of the second half of the book. It stands in stark contrast to the fourth section of the first half, chapter 4. Each of these chapters concerns a city. Chapter 9 is about Babylon, and chapter 4 is about Jerusalem. Babylon was magnificent – one of the wonders of the ancient world. By contrast Jerusalem lay desolate, her glory gone.

Nebuchadnezzar was the architect of Babylon but, as we have seen, he was so full of pride at his achievements that God disciplined him. He was driven out from human society to behave like an animal for a period of seven "times", or years, and then restored to his former glory.

In answer to Daniel's humble prayer about the desolations that Jerusalem had experienced for her rebellion, God told him that there would eventually be restoration. However, since increased privilege brings increased responsibility, the restoration would take a period, not of seven times, but seventy times seven times. The contrast looks like this:

Chapter 4	Chapter 9
The glory of Babylon Nebuchadnezzar is warned that he deserves discipline.	The desolations of Jerusalem. Israel's sins have brought on them the discipline warned of by Moses and the prophets.
He persists in pride, is chastised for a period of seven times.	Israel's continued sin will bring on further desolations lasting to the end of seventy times seven times.
He is then restored.	Jerusalem will then be restored.

We pointed out in Chapter 4 that the Bible's storyline is, in a sense, a tale of two cities – Jerusalem and Babylon. The issue is not so much what city we live *in* but what city we live *for*. Daniel lived in Babylon; but, in an ultimate sense, he lived for Jerusalem and all that it stood for. Like Abraham before him, he was *looking forward to the city that has foundations, whose designer and builder is God* (Hebrews 11:10). While he served Babylon faithfully, the centre of gravity in his life was his faith in God, and all that he did was an expression of that trust and commitment.

One of the evidences of this was Daniel's interest in *the books*. The exiles had brought with them precious scrolls of Scripture that were a vital life support for Daniel. As we have already seen, he was a man of regular prayer. He was also a man of *the books*. Indeed, Daniel's prayer in this chapter shows that he had immersed himself in what we call the Old Testament – as much as was so far written and available to him. On this occasion Daniel had been reading what Jeremiah the Hebrew prophet had quite recently predicted about the exile – in particular about its duration:

Therefore, thus says the Lord of hosts: Because you have not obeyed my words, behold, I will send for all the tribes of the north, declares the Lord, and for Nebuchadnezzar the king of Babylon, my servant, and I will bring them against this land

*and its inhabitants ... This whole land shall become a ruin
and a waste, and these nations shall serve the king of Babylon
seventy years. Then after seventy years are completed, I will
punish the king of Babylon and that nation, the land of the
Chaldeans for their iniquity... (Jeremiah 25:8–12.)*

Daniel's response is very instructive:

*... I, Daniel, perceived in the books the number of years that,
according to the word of the Lord to Jeremiah the prophet,
must pass before the end of the desolations of Jerusalem,
namely, seventy years. Then I turned my face to the Lord God,
seeking him by prayer and pleas for mercy with fasting and
sackcloth and ashes. (Daniel 9:2–3.)*

Praying with the Scriptures

From this, we see at once that Daniel was convinced that what
Jeremiah had written was the Word of the Lord. This is one of the open
secrets of Daniel's life and witness. He believed that the Scriptures
were the Word of the living God. This conviction is still the secret
of how to live in "Babylon" without "Babylon" living in you. Just as
God had revealed Nebuchadnezzar's dream and its significance for
the future to Daniel in chapter 2, so Daniel believed that God had
similarly revealed the future to Jeremiah.

Realizing that the seventy years specified by Jeremiah had almost
run their course, Daniel had many questions. What did the prophecy
really mean? Was Jerusalem, his beloved city, about to be restored? If
so, there was not much sign of it. In any case, by what means would it
be done? He may even have wondered if he could use his high office
to help in some way. We can only speculate. What he does tell us is
that he turned his face to seek God in prayer. That is, he is not just
saying that he set himself to seek God's wisdom and guidance on the
matter. He is telling us more than that: he set himself to seek God.

The importance of this cannot be exaggerated. Daniel not only believed that God had spoken to Jeremiah; he believed that it was possible for God to speak to him. For him, there was an intimate relationship between the scrolls (the Bible) and living contact with God himself. Not only had God spoken through his Word; his voice could still be heard through what he had spoken. Wonderfully, this remains the case.

We have seen that Daniel challenged the material gods of Babylon in the name of the supernatural God of creation – the God who is there. In chapter 2 he discusses the question of revelation and shows that he is perfectly aware of the issues connected (ironically) with the provenance of his own work. Is it real prophecy, written in the sixth century BC; or just recorded history, written in the second century? He also gives us several dramatic examples of supernatural deliverance. Daniel is very interested in the ways in which God authenticates his existence. In chapter 9 he prompts us to consider the most important of them – God's self-authentication through his Word.

All Scripture is breathed out by God, claims the New Testament (2 Timothy 3:16). We should therefore expect corroborative external evidence from history, archaeology, and related disciplines, but in the end the Word of God will authenticate itself by being perceived to be the Word of God by what it says, by its inner coherence and ring of truth. Without indulging in sentimentality or over-imagination, when we engage with the Word of God we can sense in our spirit and heart at times the very presence of God, and know that he is speaking to us.

In my early days as a student in Cambridge I can recall my own questions concerning biblical inspiration. It was not that I did not believe that God had inspired the Scriptures. I did believe it – and that was the source of my problem. If the Bible really was the Word of God, why did I not find it more interesting? Surely, if God was behind it, I should be getting more out of it? I noticed too that many of my Christian friends also paid lip service to the doctrine of inspiration, but spent very little time reading and thinking about the book they claimed to be inspired. There seemed to be a deep inconsistency here that affected them as well as me.

This began to concern me, and I sought advice from a much older friend and mentor whose grasp of Scripture was profound. He invited me to an evening's Bible study that was sufficient to transform my entire attitude. For what I saw modelled in him was the attitude of Daniel – a willingness to seek God in his Word and spend time doing so.

The Lord Jesus warned some religious people in his day: *You search the Scriptures because you think that in them you have eternal life; and it is they that bear witness about me, yet you refuse to come to me that you may have life* (John 5:39–40). My friend did not make that mistake. He sought God *through* his Word, and showed me how to do the same.

I realized that I had been far too superficial in my approach. After all, I was prepared to spend hours trying to understand a few lines of mathematics, and yet only a few minutes on a passage from the Bible. What I learned was the need to be patient, to spend time motivated by the desire to hear from God through his Word. God is a person, not a mere set of propositions; and there is therefore a difference between seeking knowledge about God and seeking God himself.

In more recent years, I found myself having to speak at the funeral of a lifelong friend from my Cambridge days. He was younger than me, and I had certainly not expected him to die before me. Some weeks before he died, I asked him what he would like me to say at his funeral. Without hesitation he replied: "Encourage them to do what we did when we were students. Tell them to read the Word of God together, discuss it, think about it, pray about it, and wait on God until his face appears." He paused, and then added: "And then they will have something to say."

That encapsulates Daniel's attitude precisely. Daniel waited on God until he saw his face and heard his voice, and so he had something to say that still speaks to us twenty-five centuries after he wrote it.

Daniel's prayer, recorded in chapter 9, forms a telling contrast with the attitude of Nebuchadnezzar in chapter 4. Nebuchadnezzar is admiring Babylon – his Babylon, the city he built – and bursts with pride as he contemplates his own genius. His mind soars out of control and God brings him down to the level of an animal. By contrast Daniel has not an ounce of pride in him as he humbly contemplates the ruins of his beloved city, Jerusalem, which Nebuchadnezzar has devastated.

His prayer is one of the great confessions in Scripture, and we notice that it is in three parts. He first addresses God directly in the second person: *To you, O Lord ...* (verses 4–7). Then he speaks indirectly of the Lord in the third person: *To the Lord God belongs mercy ...* (verses 8–14). Finally, he addresses God directly once more (verses 15–19):

> *O Lord, the great and awesome God, who keeps covenant*
> *and steadfast love with those who love him and keep his*
> *commandments, we have sinned and done wrong and*
> *acted wickedly and rebelled, turning aside from your*
> *commandments and rules. We have not listened to your*
> *servants the prophets, who spoke in your name to our kings,*
> *our princes, and our fathers, and to all the people of the land.*
> *To you, O Lord, belongs righteousness....* (Daniel 9:4–7.)

Daniel stands with his people as he confesses their sin. He uses every word he knows to emphasize the depths to which the nation has sunk. They have *sinned, done wrong, acted wickedly, rebelled, turned aside, not listened, not obeyed, committed treachery, not walked in God's laws ...* Twice he describes their situation as one of *open shame* (9:7–8). He makes no excuse for their behaviour, acknowledging that God had spoken to them through the prophets time and again – to all of them, leaders and common people – and they had simply refused to listen.

As a result, a devastating and unprecedented calamity had overtaken the people and their city. They should have known it would occur, since Moses himself, their great lawgiver, had long ago predicted it. Moses had given them great promises of blessing – if they obeyed God's commands. God was a God who kept his covenant, and showed steadfast love to those who obeyed him. But if they did not obey him, catastrophe would follow:

But if you will not listen to me and will not do all these
commandments, if you spurn my statutes, and if your
soul abhors my rules, so that you will not do all my
commandments, but break my covenant... I will set my
face against you, and you shall be struck down before your
enemies. Those who hate you shall rule over you... And if in
spite of this you will not listen to me, then I will discipline you
again sevenfold for your sins, and I will break the pride of
your power, and I will make your heavens like iron and your
earth like bronze...

Then if you walk contrary to me and will not listen to
me, I will continue striking you, sevenfold for your sins. And
I will let loose the wild beasts against you... I will lay your
cities waste and will make your sanctuaries desolate... and
I will scatter you among the nations... and you shall perish
among the nations, and the land of your enemies shall eat you
up. (Leviticus 26:14–38.)

Having studied the books, Daniel knew all of this; we have already
seen that his own book contains many echoes of these words. One
cannot help comparing this warning of the compounded sevenfold
punishments for transgression in Leviticus with the *seven times* of
Daniel 4, and the *seventy years* and the *seventy times seven* of Daniel
9. The threatened calamity had now happened and the future looked
very bleak, if there was any future at all.

Yet there was a ray of hope. God was a God of mercy. He was
prepared to respond positively to his people, if only they would
repent:

But if they confess their iniquity and the iniquity of their
fathers in their treachery that they committed against me...
if then their uncircumcised heart is humbled and they
make amends for their iniquity, then I will remember my
covenant with Jacob... I will not spurn them, neither will
I abhor them so as to destroy them utterly and break my
covenant with them, for I am the Lord their God. But I will

for their sake remember the covenant with their forefathers,
whom I brought out of the land of Egypt in the sight of the
nations, that I might be their God: I am the Lord. (Leviticus
26:40–45.)

Daniel seizes on that promise, and we cannot fail to be moved by the deep passion with which he continues:

And now, O Lord our God, who brought your people out of
the land of Egypt with a mighty hand, and have made a name
for yourself, as at this day, we have sinned, we have done
wickedly. O Lord, according to all your righteous acts, let your
anger and your wrath turn away from your city Jerusalem,
your holy hill, because for our sins, and for the iniquities of
our fathers, Jerusalem and your people have become a byword
among all who are around us. (Daniel 9:15–16.)

Daniel is now pleading with all the sincerity and concern-driven energy he possesses. He drops the first person plural, *we*, and now becomes as one man speaking for himself. No one is standing with him, as alone he magnificently throws himself without reserve on the sheer mercy of God:

Now therefore, O our God, listen to the prayer of your servant
and to his pleas for mercy, and for your own sake, O Lord,
make your face to shine on your sanctuary, which is desolate.
O my God, incline your ear and hear. Open your eyes and
see our desolations, and the city that is called by your name.
For we do not present our pleas before you because of our
righteousness, but because of your great mercy. (Daniel
9:17–18.)

Daniel knows in his heart that if anything is going to happen it will be due solely to God's mercy and grace. But Daniel is going to hold nothing back of how he feels, so he reaches a crescendo with his final heart-rending and desperate staccato appeal:

O Lord, hear; O Lord, forgive. O Lord, pay attention and act.
Delay not, for your own sake, O my God, because your city
and your people are called by your name. (Daniel 9:19.)

The emotional tension is palpable. Not only does Daniel care about Jerusalem; he cares about God's reputation in the world. Yes, there are profound moral reasons why God has allowed the desolation of Jerusalem and the desecration of the holy place. Yet there is more to it than that. Daniel would have known of another tragic episode in the earlier history of his people. Having lost a sense of the glory of God and their commitment to him, the people of Israel thought that the ark of the covenant, a physical symbol of God's presence, could save them from the Philistines. It did not. The ark was captured by the Philistines, and God permitted the *glory* to *depart* (see 1 Samuel 4). However, the story did not end there. The God who stood behind the ark was real, and he proceeded to demonstrate this fact to the Philistines. When they placed the ark in the temple of their god, the next morning they found his toppled statue in pieces on the ground before the ark.

Therefore Daniel pins his faith to the fact that God is real, despite Judah's rebellion and sin. God must surely in the end vindicate himself in connection with Jerusalem – the world must get to know that God is real.

Daniel would never forget this prayer. Later he vividly recalls when it ended, and how it ended (Daniel 9:21). It was at the time the evening sacrifice would normally have been offered, back when the temple still functioned in Jerusalem. That sacrifice consisted of a whole burnt offering, symbolizing Israel's wholehearted devotion to God – *loving him with all their heart, mind and strength* – an attitude that had just been shown by Daniel in his prayer.

God answers Daniel's prayer

What happened next was dramatic. As Daniel finished his prayer, what looked like a flying man landed at his side. He is identified as

Gabriel. Daniel had seen him earlier in the vision recorded in chapter 8: *there stood before me one having the appearance of a man* (Daniel 8:15). Daniel was so frightened that he fell on his face and went into a deep sleep. He then sensed Gabriel touching him and making him stand up. (A similar thing will happen again in the vision described in chapter 10.)

Gabriel addresses Daniel by name, and informs him that at the very beginning of his prayer he, Gabriel, had been summoned to convey a message to Daniel – a message of insight and understanding, because Daniel is *greatly loved* (9:23).

Daniel had started his prayer by addressing God as the God *who keeps covenant and steadfast love with those who love him and keep his commandments* (9:4). Now Gabriel tells Daniel that God greatly loves him. It is difficult for us to imagine what those words must have meant to him. To receive such a personal message, carried by a special messenger from the world beyond this one, must have been overwhelmingly reassuring.

We read of Gabriel in connection with only three people in Scripture: Daniel, to whom he appears twice; Zechariah, the father of John the Baptist; and Mary, the mother of Jesus. Luke describes him as *an angel of the Lord*, and Gabriel himself says to Zechariah: *I am Gabriel. I stand in the presence of God, and I was sent to speak to you and to bring you this good news* (Luke 1:11, 19).

The context in Luke is that Zechariah, a priest, is in the temple at Jerusalem, standing at the altar of incense leading the nation's prayer, when Gabriel comes to announce to him that he is to be the father of the forerunner to the Messiah: *your prayer has been heard, and your wife Elizabeth will bear you a son, and you shall call his name John* (Luke 1:13). Zechariah cannot bring himself to believe the message because, as he says, both he and his wife are old. For his unbelief, Gabriel strikes him temporarily *silent and unable to speak* (Luke 1:20).

The contrast with Daniel could not be greater. Daniel is in exile in Babylon, the city and temple at Jerusalem are in ruins; and yet he believes that God can respond to his prayer. Zechariah is not in exile, the city and temple are thriving. He is praying, but unbelief nestles in his heart. He does not believe in the ability of God to restore nature's processes and allow him and his wife to have a child – an attitude that changed dramatically when Elizabeth became pregnant!

Finally, Gabriel comes to Nazareth, *to a virgin betrothed to a man whose name was Joseph, of the house of David* (Luke 1:27). Daniel was told that he was greatly loved, and now Gabriel tells Mary that she is highly favoured. She receives the most staggering message of all. Gabriel announces to her the coming into the world, not of some angel or prophet, but of God himself:

> *And behold, you will conceive in your womb and bear a son,*
> *and you shall call his name Jesus. He will be great and be*
> *called the Son of the Most High. And the Lord God will give*
> *to him the throne of his father David, and he will reign over*
> *the house of Jacob for ever, and of his kingdom there will be*
> *no end. (Luke 1:31–33.)*

On each occasion, therefore, Gabriel's visits involve prophecies about major supernatural interventions in history. In Daniel 8 he tells of the time of the end, when *the little horn* will stop the regular burnt offering and even rise up against the Prince of princes, only to be *broken – but by no human hand* (Daniel 8:25) – that is, supernaturally. In chapter 9 Gabriel announces the lengthy period of seventy weeks that will have to run, *to finish the transgression, to put an end to sin, and to atone for iniquity, to bring in everlasting righteousness, to seal both vision and prophet, and to anoint a most holy place* (9:24).

So Gabriel is chosen by God to announce to Zechariah the birth of the last and greatest prophet, John the Baptist, who will prepare the way for the coming of the Lord Messiah himself. And, as Gabriel finally tells Mary, the Lord will be the one who will bear the name Jesus, and fulfil Gabriel's message in Daniel 9. He will atone for iniquity, and ultimately bring in everlasting righteousness, as indicated in Daniel 7 and 8.

This is a big story – the Big Story – and, in response to Daniel's prayer at a time in history where it looked as if it had all petered out, Gabriel's message takes it a quantum leap forward.

Daniel's concern about Jerusalem is rewarded. We may be moved by his passion, but in the back of some readers' minds there could lurk the thought that this, after all, is the Old Testament, and now that Jesus the King has come, concern for the people of Israel, Jerusalem, and its future is a thing of the past. But this would be a false deduction. We shall look at this matter in detail in Appendix A. For the moment, it is enough to notice that the Lord Jesus himself showed immense concern for Jerusalem and its people. He wept as he announced to the city the devastating consequences of its rejection of him as the Messiah. In his Olivet discourse he predicted its downfall and the destruction of Herod's temple by the Romans, which eventually occurred in AD 70. He warned of desolations and exile for the nation, leading far into the future up to his coming:

> For there will be great distress upon the earth and wrath
> against this people. They will fall by the edge of the sword
> and be led captive among all nations, and Jerusalem will
> be trampled underfoot by the Gentiles, until the time of the
> Gentiles are fulfilled ... And then they will see the Son of
> Man coming in a cloud with power and great glory. (Luke
> 21:23–27.)

Here we have many allusions to Daniel. Chapters 7 and 8 mention the trampling; chapter 7, the coming of the Son of Man; and the series of beasts in chapter 7 are Gentile world powers spanning the times of the Gentiles until the time of the end.

Just as Daniel viewed the time of the end through the lens of the abominable deeds of Antiochus Epiphanes (the Greek empire, 168 BC), we find that our Lord viewed the time of the end through the lens of the destruction of the temple (by the Roman empire, AD 70). Indeed, in the Olivet discourse, it is sometimes difficult to know whether you are reading about AD 70 or the end time, or both at once – particularly the version in Matthew 24.

In a private conversation, Jesus tells his disciples that the temple will be destroyed, and they ask him:

Tell us, when will these things be, and what will be the sign of
your coming and of the close of the age? (Matthew 24:3.)

The disciples associated the destruction of the temple with Christ's
return. It is because there are aspects of the first event that recur at
the time of the second that the Lord's answer to their questions was
given in those terms.

Jesus cites the fulfilment of one of Daniel's predictions as a key
event in the future:

So when you see the abomination of desolation spoken of by
the prophet Daniel, standing in the holy place ... then there
will be great tribulation... Immediately after the tribulation
of those days ... Then will appear in heaven the sign of the
Son of Man ... and they will see the Son of Man coming on
the clouds of heaven with power and great glory. (Matthew
24:15–30.)

In Daniel there are three references to an abomination of desolation.
Of this future evil power he writes:

1. *And ... he shall put an end to sacrifice and offering. And on*
the wing of abominations shall come one who makes desolate,
until the decreed end is poured out on the desolator (9:27).

2. *Forces from him shall appear and profane the temple and*
fortress, and shall take away the regular burnt offering. And
they shall set up the abomination that makes desolate (11:31).

3. *And from the time that the regular burnt offering is taken*
away and the abomination that makes desolate is set up, there
shall be 1,290 days (12:11).

We are not told in detail what this abomination is but, as we mentioned
earlier, the root idea presumably comes from the desecration of the
temple by Antiochus, when he dedicated it to Zeus and offered a pig

on the altar. As we saw in Chapter 16, that incident is a foreshadowing of the time of the end. Thus, Daniel 9 has the same ultimate focus as the visions of Daniel 7 and 8.

CHAPTER 19

THE SEVENTY WEEKS
Daniel 9

If we ask what Daniel 9 adds to what we can learn from chapters 2, 7, and 8, then the obvious answer is: the famous prophecy of *the seventy weeks* contained in 9:24–27:

> *Seventy weeks are decreed about your people and your holy city, to finish the transgression, to put an end to sin, and to atone for iniquity, to bring in everlasting righteousness, to seal both vision and prophet, and to anoint a most holy place. Know therefore and understand that from the going out of the word to restore and build Jerusalem to the coming of an anointed one, a prince, there shall be seven weeks. Then for sixty-two weeks it shall be built again with squares and moat, but in a troubled time. And after the sixty-two weeks, an anointed one shall be cut off and shall have nothing. And the people of the prince who is to come shall destroy the city and the sanctuary. Its end shall come with a flood, and to the end there shall be war. Desolations are decreed. And he shall make a strong covenant with many for one week, and for half of the week he shall put an end to sacrifice and offering. And on the wing of abominations shall come one who makes desolate, until the decreed end is poured out on the desolator. (Daniel 9:24–27.)*

There is much controversy and disagreement concerning the interpretation of this prophecy, even among the experts I have read; it would be a foolhardy person who thought he had arrived at the definitive view on the topic. I shall content myself, therefore, with reviewing some of the considerations that I have found useful in trying to get to grips with this text that has intrigued people for generations, and give my own conclusions – not too dogmatically, I trust. I shall have to leave most of the alternative views for the interested reader to investigate, since a fair treatment of all of them (even if I were competent to give it) would double the size of this book.

The first thing I notice is that the seventy weeks, whatever they are, are represented as the sum of seven weeks, sixty-two weeks, and finally one week. The ESV (quoted above) puts a full stop after *there shall be seven weeks*, whereas the NIV translates the text (verses 25–26):

> *From the time the word goes out to restore and rebuild*
> *Jerusalem until the Anointed One, the ruler, comes, there will*
> *be seven "sevens", and sixty-two "sevens". It will be rebuilt*
> *with streets and a trench, but in times of trouble. After the*
> *sixty-two "sevens", the Anointed One will be put to death and*
> *will have nothing.*

The word "week" is a translation of the Hebrew word for "seven", as shown here, and so the first question is: to what units does it refer? Some hold that we are to see these periods as symbolic, not tied to any particular chronology. However, many others think that the week refers to a period of seven years, so the total period is 490 years. This means that, apart from any other considerations, the ESV rendering is scarcely likely to be correct. For if the anointed one appears after forty-nine years (seven sevens), but is not cut off for another 434 years (sixty-two sevens), it would imply that he had lived for over four centuries![39] The NIV is surely the more natural reading here – the anointed one appears after sixty-nine sevens, 483 years (if these are years).

The next question to ask is: when does the period of seventy sevens begin? Daniel writes of a period *from the going out of the word to restore and build Jerusalem* (9:25). The return from Babylonian exile to restore Jerusalem city figures prominently in the Bible, and several decrees are mentioned concerning its various stages.

Ezra starts his prophecy by referring to a decree by Cyrus, authorizing the return of the exiles to their own territory and permitting the rebuilding of their temple (see Ezra 1). A long list is given of the returnees who initially went back to their own towns and then gathered in Jerusalem to rebuild the temple. They immediately recommenced the daily burnt offering (Ezra 3:2) – showing just how important this ceremony was to the identity of the nation. They then started to rebuild the temple, but soon ran into trouble from local adversaries who were powerful enough to bring the work temporarily to a halt.

Eventually Artaxerxes came to power in Medo-Persia, and the adversaries of the Jews wrote to him complaining:

> *And now be it known to the king that the Jews who came up from you to us have gone to Jerusalem. They are rebuilding that rebellious and wicked city ... Now be it known to the king that if this city is rebuilt and the walls finished, they will not pay tribute, custom, or toll, and the royal revenue will be impaired. (Ezra 4:11–13.)*

Their letter was misleading, since the exiles had been engaged in rebuilding the temple and not the city, as Ezra carefully notes. Artaxerxes' response was swift: *Therefore make a decree that these men be made to cease, and that this city be not rebuilt, until a decree is made by me* (Ezra 4:21). They were made to stop their work, and there was no more activity until the second year of Darius.

Rebuilding began again, and was once more the subject of criticism by the governor: *Who gave you a decree to build this house and to finish this structure?* (Ezra 5:3). This makes it clear that the temple was the problem. To clear things up, the governor wrote to King Darius, who found the original authorization in the archives and upheld it in his response, telling the governor not only not to meddle in the work on the temple but also to help with the cost of the reconstruction from the royal revenue. With this royal edict, the temple building got under way in earnest, and was eventually completed (see Ezra 6).

Ezra gained the confidence of the emperor Artaxerxes, and some time later he and others were sent to Jerusalem with considerable state aid for the maintenance of the temple. However, the city of Jerusalem was still ruined, and when Nehemiah, a Jew who was in Artaxerxes' court, heard of this, it weighed heavily on him. Like Daniel, he set himself to pray about the situation.

Though shorter than Daniel's, his prayer is based on the same deep sense of God's love, and his willingness to bring his people back to their land, provided they repent (Nehemiah 1:4–11). At the end of his prayer he specifically prays about a crucial conversation with Artaxerxes. Nehemiah was the king's cupbearer, which was a high position of trust. He was essentially responsible for the king's security, and poison was a favoured method of getting rid of people in those days. His job therefore brought him into regular contact with the king. Having committed the outcome to God, he approached Artaxerxes and didn't attempt to hide his sadness. The emperor noticed this and asked what it was all about. Showing such emotion in the presence of an emperor was a risky thing. Nehemiah was terrified, yet he summoned up courage to mention Jerusalem. The shrewd king came straight to the point: *What are you requesting?* (Nehemiah 2:4). With a lovely touch of humanity Nehemiah writes: *So I prayed to the God of heaven. And I said to the king: "If it pleases the king ... send me to Judah, to the city of my fathers' graves, that I may rebuild it"* (2:4–5).

It was an enormous and daring request. Yet such was the character and demeanour of Nehemiah that the emperor (with his queen present) granted it.

One wonders whether the king recalled his letter, written years before, regarding that very possibility: *that this city be not rebuilt, until a decree is made by me* (Ezra 4:21). His new decree, permitting the rebuilding of Jerusalem, was issued in the month of Nisan in the twentieth year of Artaxerxes (i.e. March 444 BC). It was a historic moment. God's plans for Jerusalem took a major leap forward: the city would be rebuilt, and the seventy weeks began to run. (I shall refer to another view of the starting point of the seventy weeks in the next chapter.)

Hence, on a first approximation (whatever the fine detail of Daniel's prophecy means), 490–7 = 483 years from that decree would bring us to what we call the first half of the first century AD. In fact, it brings us to the 30s AD, which is remarkable since Daniel says that at that time an anointed one shall be cut off (Daniel 9:26). Surely this was fulfilled when Jesus of Nazareth, who claimed to be the anointed one (Messiah) of God, was "cut off" by being crucified in Jerusalem – in or around AD 30.

All we have done is to make a rough calculation based on the Gregorian calendar which is now in use; and even that shows that we are in the presence of something intriguing. However, the situation becomes even more interesting when we realize that the Gregorian calendar may not be appropriate for the calculation. One way of seeing this is to notice that Daniel says that the sacrifices and offerings are to be banned for half of the final week – that is, for three-and-a-half years. In Chapter 17 we saw that a limit was set for the power of the fierce beast to trample the holy place, to a *time, times, and half a time*; and we noted that the book of Revelation says that the holy city is to be trampled on for a period of *forty-two months* (Revelation 11:2). The very next verse in Revelation speaks of two witnesses who, against all attempts to destroy them, are given power to prophesy for *1,260 days*. In the next chapter of Revelation we read of a woman who is protected from the serpent's power for *1,260 days* (Revelation 12:6). Subsequently this period of time is said to be forty-two months (13:5). If, as seems reasonable, these periods are identical in length, then *a time* would be a year of 360 days: i.e. a lunar year.

This accords with both Babylonian and Jewish reckoning. For example, as early as the book of Genesis we find it stated that from the seventeenth day of the second month to the seventeenth day of the seventh month it was 150 days (Genesis 7:11; 8:3–4). Interestingly, Sir Isaac Newton refers to this matter (1728, page 71):

All nations, before the just length of the solar year was known, reckoned months by the course of the moon and years by the return of winter and summer, spring and autumn; and in making calendars for their festivals they reckoned thirty days to a lunar month and twelve lunar months to a year, taken to the nearest round numbers, whence came the division of the ecliptic into 360 degrees.

We note that Newton says "taken to the nearest round numbers". That is because twelve lunar cycles take 354 days. This means that the lunar year is just over eleven days shorter than the solar year, and it would appear that around the time of the Babylonian captivity an extra intercalary thirty-day month (*Ve'adar*) was added to make the necessary correction (just as we have a leap year of 366 days every four years, since the solar year is actually a little over 365 days long). We should also note in passing that the English word "month" is related to the word "moon". Its Hebrew equivalent, *hodesh*, means "new moon".

On this basis then:

- the 69 sevens – or 483 – years of 360 days, each amount to 173,880 days;
- 1 solar year = 365.24219879 days;
- so 173,880 days = 476.067663 solar years = 476 years + 24.7 days.

Using the familiar Gregorian calendar, if we start from the beginning of the month Nisan in 444 BC and add 476 years plus 25 days, then we get to the month Nisan in AD 33.

The two dates for the crucifixion of Jesus that appear most often in scholarly writings are AD 30 and 33. One reason for this is that in those two years 14 Nisan, on which the Passover lamb was killed, fell on a Friday. Recently Cambridge scientist Sir Colin Humphreys, working with astrophysicist Graeme Waddington of Oxford, calculated that Jesus died on 3 April 33 AD (Humphreys, 2011). Humphreys' work involves the idea that Jesus would have used the lunar calendar, invented in the time of the captivity as mentioned above. These findings have been widely accepted[40] and they show that Daniel's sixth-century BC prophecy turns out to be a phenomenally accurate prediction of the time when "Messiah the Prince" would be *cut off* (Daniel 9:26).

And of course even if "Daniel" were a second-century writer – which I do not accept – and knew the historical date of the edict to rebuild Jerusalem, Daniel 9 still represents a real and extremely accurate prediction. That being so, one might be forgiven for thinking that our calculation makes the second-century view even less tenable, since it is often associated with a naturalistic rejection of the possibility of predictive prophecy.

Unfortunately, disagreement about the interpretation of the seventieth week sometimes has the effect of obscuring the validity, accuracy, and importance of the messianic prophecy of the first sixty-nine weeks, even though the two issues are logically separate. The important thing to grasp is that however we interpret the final week of the prophecy, the amazingly accurate prediction of the death of the Messiah contained in Daniel 9 is powerful evidence for the supernatural character of Scripture – as well, of course, as adding to the evidence for the truth of Jesus' claim to be the Messiah.

CHAPTER 20

THE SEVENTIETH WEEK
Daniel 9

There are two main interpretations of the final week of Daniel's prophecy regarding the seventy weeks. The first, often called "the traditional view", is that the seventieth week immediately follows the first sixty-nine. The second holds that the seventieth week is still in the future, so that there is an unspecified gap between it and the first sixty-nine weeks.

The obvious merit of the first view is that it treats the seventy weeks as a continuous period of time, without the introduction of an "unnatural" gap. However, when we try to make sense of it in historical terms, we run at once into serious difficulties. For instance, Daniel is told:

> *Seventy weeks are decreed about your people and your holy city, to finish the transgression, to put an end to sin, and to atone for iniquity, to bring in everlasting righteousness, to seal both vision and prophet, and to anoint a most holy place. (Daniel 9:24.)*

Certainly we can say that Christ's death atoned for iniquity; but it is very hard to see how the other things mentioned were fulfilled in the seven-year period following his death. Indeed, far from solving Israel's and Jerusalem's problems, the situation there rapidly got worse, leading up to the destruction of the temple by the armies of Titus in AD 70, and the dispersion that followed lasted for centuries.

Moreover, if the seventieth week follows at once on the first sixty-nine, we must ask what Daniel is referring to when he writes:

> *And the people of the prince who is to come shall destroy the*
> *city and the sanctuary. Its end shall come with a flood, and*
> *to the end there shall be war. Desolations are decreed. And he*
> *shall make a strong covenant with many for one week, and for*
> *half of the week he shall put an end to sacrifice and offering.*
> *And on the wing of abominations shall come one who makes*
> *desolate, until the decreed end is poured out on the desolator.*
> *(Daniel 9:26–27.)*

There seems to be nothing in the history of the time that could fit this description. For instance, sacrifice and offering continued in Jerusalem for years after the death of Christ, until the destruction of the city in AD 70 – much longer than seven years after the crucifixion. The difficulties rapidly become insuperable.

It will be noticed that the foregoing argument is based on starting the course of the seventy weeks with the decree of Artaxerxes in 444 BC. Some scholars date the seventy weeks from the earlier decree that Artaxerxes gave to Ezra, even though it refers to the reconstruction of the temple and not the city. They calculate that the sixty-nine weeks run up to the time of the Lord's anointing at his baptism. They take the seventieth week as following immediately, with Christ dying in the middle of the week (around three-and-a-half years after his baptism) – and so, of course, after the sixty-nine weeks. The end of the seventieth week is then dated to the martyrdom of Stephen and the call of the apostle Paul. The covenant in Daniel 9:27 is held to be the *new testament* that Christ made with his disciples at the Last Supper.

This view certainly takes seriously the predictive value of the first sixty-nine weeks. However, its interpretation of the seventieth week seems (to me, at least) to be very strained. For instance, the week would have been complete long before the destruction of the city, whereas the covenant that Christ made was not limited to seven years.

Let us think then of another suggested interpretation that arises from a parallel with Daniel 8, where the vision takes events from the time of Antiochus Epiphanes, and uses them as a lens to study the end time when similar things will happen. Could this also be the case in Daniel 9?

Let us look once more at this crucial passage:

> And after the sixty-two weeks, an anointed one shall be cut
> off and shall have nothing. And the people of the prince who
> is to come shall destroy the city and the sanctuary. Its end
> shall come with a flood, and to the end there shall be war.
> Desolations are decreed. And he shall make a strong covenant
> with many for one week, and for half of the week he shall
> put an end to sacrifice and offering. And on the wing of
> abominations shall come one who makes desolate, until the
> decreed end is poured out on the desolator. (Daniel 9:26–27.)

Suppose we take the anointed one being cut off to refer to the death of Jesus the Messiah, and we were then asked what the next statement seemed to suggest: *And the people of the prince who is to come shall destroy the city and the sanctuary.* We might well reply that this could very naturally be taken as a description of the destruction of Jerusalem and its temple by Titus in AD 70.

The question then arises: what does the rest of the passage refer to? The mention of abominations and desolations reminds us of Daniel 8, and also 11:31, as we shall see later. These two passages both have a double reference – to Antiochus Epiphanes and to the time of the end. Could it be that Daniel 9 is doing a similar thing – but this time looking at the time of the end through the lens of AD 70? That is, *the prince who is to come* is Titus, who shall destroy Jerusalem, and there will follow an indefinite period of war *to the end.* Then the "he" who is referred to next in the phrase *he shall make a strong covenant with many for one week* is not Titus but someone who, like Titus, desecrates the sanctuary in Jerusalem; the final embodiment of Gentile power: the man of lawlessness referred to in 2 Thessalonians.

It is arguable that there is internal evidence in Daniel 9 that the final week does not run immediately after the first sixty-nine. There is an implied gap, involving the kind of prophetic telescoping we have seen in other parts of Daniel. Support for this view is given by the fact that the Lord himself taught his disciples about

- the destruction of Jerusalem, followed by an indefinite period of *wars and rumours of wars* (Matthew 24:6) – compare with Daniel 9:26, *to the end there shall be war*;
- how *Jerusalem will be trampled underfoot by the Gentiles* (Luke 21:24);
- Daniel's *abomination of desolation* (Matthew 24:15) in connection with his second coming.

The book of Revelation also refers to a period of time during which the holy city is trampled underfoot (11:2), and this period of time is connected with the return of Christ. Since there is desecration of the sanctuary, trampling down of the people and the city, and violent persecution leading up to the time of Christ's return, it is obvious that *the finishing of transgression* and *bringing in of everlasting righteousness,* promised in Daniel 9:24, did not occur in AD 33, 70, or any subsequent time up to the present.

As the vision of Daniel 7 reveals, justice is not done, the saints do not receive the kingdom, nor is everlasting righteousness brought in, until *the Son of Man comes on the clouds of heaven* (Matthew 24:30). This fits in with what the apostle Paul told the philosophers at Athens – the Lord Jesus would return to *judge the world in righteousness* (Acts 17:31). Similarly, the apostle Peter taught that the promise of righteousness would be fulfilled at the return of Christ in the new heavens and the new earth (see 2 Peter 3:11–13).

I can well imagine that someone reading what I have just written may say: "Even supposing you are right, what is the point of thinking about a period of seven years, in what might be the distant future? Such a tiny bit of time can have no relevance to us; thinking about it only detracts from the actual business of Christian living in the real world of today! Is it not this kind of speculation that gives Christianity a bad name? Why don't we just avoid it completely, and concentrate on what really matters?"

I take the point. If thinking about the book of Daniel leads us to endless speculation, and fails to produce a life like Daniel's, we have understood neither his message nor his call to live for God as salt and light in the world. However, I believe Daniel was a prophet who spoke the Word of God. Daniel 9 is part of that Word, so I must treat it as such. Of course I must not lose a sense of proportion and spend all my time thinking about one short part of God's Word and ignore the rest. It means, however, that I should give Daniel 9 its due weight, and not dismiss it as irrelevant.

Several things weigh with me in this connection. The first is that the prophecy of the seventy weeks was God's response to Daniel's concern for the city of Jerusalem, which bore God's name and was connected with God's reputation in the world. On the one hand, God was preparing Daniel for the fact that it would take a long time to deal with the problem of Israel's sin (and, indeed, with the sin of the world). On the other hand, God was encouraging Daniel that Jerusalem's fortunes would be reversed one day. This message was amplified by the Lord Jesus himself to his disciples, who became very concerned when they heard him describe the devastating future that awaited Jerusalem because of its rejection of him as Messiah. He gave them hope too; the times of Gentile domination and desecration of the city would end one day, and redemption would come.

The apostle Paul was similarly concerned for his people and his nation. He wrote to the Christians in Rome:

> ... I have great sorrow and unceasing anguish in my heart. For I could wish that I myself were accursed and cut off from Christ for the sake of my brothers, my kinsmen according to the flesh. (Romans 9:2–3.)

Notice that Paul is not here expressing his concern for the church, although the burden of its problems was always on his mind. He was heartbroken because his own nation, Israel, with all of its God-given privileges, such as the patriarchs, the giving of the law, the covenants, the promises – the very nation into which the Messiah had been born – had rejected their Messiah. Like Daniel, he wondered what the future held. Like Daniel also, he saw that there would be a day in which the fortunes of his nation would be reversed.

Paul seizes on a prophecy that was made even before the time of Daniel, and looks forward to its fulfilment:

> *a partial hardening has come upon Israel, until the fullness*
> *of the Gentiles has come in. And in this way all Israel will be*
> *saved, as it is written, "The Deliverer will come from Zion,*
> *he will banish ungodliness from Jacob"; "and this will be my*
> *covenant with them when I take away their sins." (Romans*
> *11:26–27; see Isaiah 59:20–21.)*

Throughout the whole of the biblical revelation we get the sense of an arrow of time, flying towards the future return of the Messiah in his power and glory. This is the central hope that Jesus gave to his disciples in private conversation:

> *And if I go and prepare a place for you, I will come again*
> *and will take you to myself, that where I am you may be also.*
> *(John 14:3.)*

That hope for the future was designed to shape the disciples' character (as it had shaped Daniel's): *And everyone who thus hopes in him purifies himself as he is pure* (1 John 3:3).

Someone may well react and say: "Yes, I can see the point of this general hope of Christ's coming. The principle is clearly very important. My problem is in the detail. I cannot see the necessity of concerning myself with this period of seven years."

Perhaps an analogy can help. There is a certain period of three days in past history that is of central importance to millions of people, including me and many of my readers. It is, of course, the time of the death and resurrection of Christ. Now you can understand this immediately because the most significant events in the history of the planet took place during those three days. It is not the length of time that is important but what happened in it. Even so, historical events must occupy a specific period of time.

The same reasoning applies to the future, as we well understand. Suppose, for example, you are speaking to a young woman who says to you: "There is a day next year, 14 September in fact, that is very important . . ." Suppose you break in without waiting for her to finish, and say: "How can one period of twenty-four hours nearly a year ahead have any special importance?" She replies: "I am getting married on that day!" I think you might feel embarrassed, for you would see that the importance lies not in the length of the time but in what is going to happen in it.

I would like to suggest that the same is true of Daniel's seventieth week – and the period of *time, times, and half a time* mentioned by Daniel (12:7) and again in the book of Revelation (12:14). The important thing about it is not the length of time involved but what happens during that time. Of course the length of time is not unimportant. Indeed if, as it would seem, that period involves fierce persecution, its duration will be of great concern for those directly involved; just as the length of the Babylonian captivity was of concern to Daniel.

Daniel's prophecies of the end times would appear to focus on what Paul describes as the rule of the *man of lawlessness*. He will be an incredibly brutal leader, energized by devilish power, and will have the unbridled arrogance eventually to attempt to take the place of God. The length of time his cruel dominion lasts, therefore, will be of great concern to those who are caught up in it. We do not know when it will all occur; but even if we are not involved, it is still important for us to know about it. Indeed, if Paul insisted on telling new converts about it in the first century (see 2 Thessalonians 2:5), how much more seriously should we take it in the twenty-first?

Those future events are but the harvest of seeds sown by the ideas, attitudes, movements of thought and ideologies that have permeated society throughout history, even from ancient times. In our own time secularist naturalism in particular, with its marginalization of God and devaluation of human life and dignity, is no innocent thing. We need to recognize it for what it is, and spell out its implications for everyone who is prepared to listen.

Much more could be said – but not here. The book of Revelation gives us more insight into the movements of thought and culture that will come to their harvest in the end times. Further comment belongs to a study of that book and not Daniel. However, we need to realize that we cannot expect to have a full understanding of everything that is written in these books. There are many things that will remain hidden. Daniel himself will tell us about that in the final section of his book.

Implications for the dating of the book

David Gooding points out (1981) that the deliberate placing of Daniel 9 parallel to Daniel 4 in the main structure of the book makes it very unlikely that the book was written at the time of Antiochus IV in the second century BC. Gooding's observations are of such importance that I quote them at considerable length:

> For several reasons it is difficult to think that these chapters were first written and this symmetry first constructed during Antiochus' persecution of the Jews. First, no criticism is made of the culture of which the building of Babylon was such a superb expression. Rather the builder of Babylon is represented as a majestic tree set up by God himself for the preservation and delight of his subjects. His sin lies solely in his pride. It is, then, unlikely that Chapter 4 was first written at a time when Gentile culture, in the form of Hellenism, which hitherto had penetrated Palestine peacefully, had now become one of the chief evils against which the Maccabees fought, and compromise with which was regarded as apostasy (1 Macc. 1:11–15; 2 Macc. 4:9–17).
>
> Secondly, Nebuchadnezzar had been the one who had laid Jerusalem desolate, destroyed the sanctuary and taken the gold and silver vessels to Babylon. Yet in Chapter 9 no blame is laid on him for Jerusalem's original or continuing desolations; all the blame is laid on Israel's persistence in

sin. It is difficult to think that Chapter 4 was first written
and placed over against Chapter 9 at the very time when
Antiochus IV had come to Jerusalem and arrogantly
entered the sanctuary and taken "the silver and gold and
the costly vessels" and "departed to his own land", or
when two years later his officer after "deceitfully speaking
peaceable words" to the Jews of Jerusalem "suddenly fell on
the city, dealt it a severe blow ... plundered the city, burned
it with fire ... stationed there a sinful people, lawless men
..." (1 Macc. 1:20–24, 29–34). Actually, if Chapter 4 had
alleged that Nebuchadnezzar prospered uninterruptedly
while Jerusalem lay desolate, and only later came to some
monstrous fate, one might suppose that it may have been
times when Antiochus was still flourishing, and Jerusalem
desolate. For 2 Maccabees 6:12–16 urges Jewish readers not
to be depressed by the desolations suffered by Jerusalem but
"to recognize that these punishments were designed not to
destroy but to discipline our people. In fact, not to let the
impious alone for long, but to punish them immediately, is
a sign of great kindness. For in the case of the other nations
the Lord waits patiently to punish them until they have
reached the full measure of their sins; but he does not deal
in this way with us, in order that he may not take vengeance
on us afterward when our sins have reached their height
... Though he disciplines us with calamities, he does not
forsake his own people." (RSV)

Now Daniel, in deliberately placing Chapters 4 and
9 one against the other in a symmetry, is likewise inviting
the reader to compare God's discipline of Nebuchadnezzar
with God's discipline of Jerusalem. But in Daniel
Nebuchadnezzar is not allowed to go on in his sin until it
is too late and until he meets some terrible death as 1 and 2
Maccabees say Antiochus did (1 Macc. 6:8–13; 2 Macc. 9:5–
28). Instead Nebuchadnezzar is given the treatment which
2 Maccabees says is reserved for Israel and which it says
is a mark of God's great kindness to Israel. God with great

care disciplines him so as not to destroy him, but to bring him to repentance, and thus to restore him to his original political majesty and cultural glory. And what is more, Nebuchadnezzar responds to this discipline and is restored; whereas Israel is confessed by Daniel to be so intransigent in her sin that Jerusalem, though presently restored, will be laid desolate again, and suffer desolations right up until the end.

It is, therefore, difficult to believe that Chapters 4 and 9 of Daniel were written and made to stand over against each other in the symmetry of the book in Maccabean times. And it is even more difficult to believe that the story of Nebuchadnezzar's discipline was incorporated in the book in Maccabean times to encourage the faithful in the hope that just as God had treated Nebuchadnezzar so he would treat Antiochus.

CHAPTER 21

THE MAN ABOVE THE RIVER
Daniel 10

The last section of the book, chapters 10–12, contains the fourth vision that God gave to Daniel. He dates it to the third year of Cyrus, locates it as happening on the bank of the River Tigris, and describes it as the revelation of a great conflict. Once more he makes it clear that what he writes is not produced by his own brilliant intellect – it was given as a revelation. What is more, Daniel claims that what was revealed to him is true: *And the word was true, and it was* [or, *it was about*] *a great conflict* (Daniel 10:1).

Since this is the longest of the visions, we shall introduce it by giving a brief sketch of its contents. First of all Daniel sees the glorious figure of a man above the great River Tigris, and he is so overwhelmed that he falls asleep. He is awakened by a heavenly messenger, who tells him that he has come to make him understand what is to happen to his people in the future. The messenger says that his journey to Daniel has been resisted by certain powers in the unseen world, but now he has finally arrived to reveal to Daniel *what is inscribed in the book of truth* (Daniel 10:21).

There follows a lengthy historical survey, which we can now interpret as beginning in Daniel's time in Medo-Persia, tracing the rise of the Greek empire under Alexander the Great, and detailing the subsequent division of that empire into four parts under his generals. There follows the constant conflict between the various parts, particularly between the Seleucids (the "kings of the north") and the Ptolemies (the "kings of the south"), culminating in the desecration of the temple in Jerusalem by the Seleucid king Antiochus IV "Epiphanes" in the second century BC.

Next, in a way that should now be familiar to us, the narrative uses the time of Antiochus as a prototype of *the time of the end*, when a fierce king will arise that *shall exalt himself and magnify himself above every god* (Daniel 11:36). There will be a time of unparalleled trouble for Daniel's people, Israel, followed by deliverance and the resurrection of both the just and the unjust.

At that point Daniel is told to seal the book *until the time of the end* (12:4).

He then observes two figures standing, one on each bank of the river, and he hears a voice asking the man above the river, *How long shall it be till the end of these wonders?* (12:6). The answer comes: *a time, times, and half a time*. Daniel does not understand it, so he asks what it means. He is again told that the words are sealed *until the time of the end* (12:7). The book concludes with a wonderful promise to Daniel: *you shall rest and shall stand in your allotted place at the end of the days* (12:12).

A message from heaven

Let us now proceed to have a closer look at some of the detail of this vision. Daniel is told that its content is *inscribed in the book of truth* (10:21). In his previous vision Daniel was studying another book of truth – the prophecy of Jeremiah. That book was accessible to him. However, in this final vision, the book of truth is not the kind of book that is available in a library, so its content will be revealed to him directly. This makes explicit what we already know: Daniel was a prophet in his own right, in the sense that God revealed information directly to him.

Daniel is told that the book of truth contains detailed information about historical events after his time. The fact that it had already been written is very striking. Some people will then say that we cannot take it seriously. If it were true, they argue, it would lead to a deterministic – or, at least, a semi-deistic – view of God that would be totally unacceptable, whereby God has wound everything up and just let it run like clockwork, with no room for human responsibility or interaction with the divine. We note at once that this would also apply to Jeremiah's prophecy about the captivity in Babylon, which Daniel was reading before he had the vision of the seventy weeks. Indeed, it would apply to all prophecy, including that of Daniel himself.

Some people think that if it is the case that certain events have been predicted in writing then whoever is behind the prediction causes those events to occur, and thus eliminates any freedom of decision or action on the part of those involved. However, that would only be arguably the case if we were naively to assume that God's relationship to time is the same as ours. In fact, we do not even know what time is, let alone the complexities of God's relationship to it.

Nor is this the place for detailed biblical teaching on the relationship between God's sovereignty and human responsibility. Suffice to say that even if certain events have been predicted by God's revelation, that does not in any way remove moral agency – and therefore responsibility and accountability. This is as much an issue in the New Testament as it is in the Old. Think, for instance, of Peter's statement at Pentecost to the crowds in Jerusalem: *this Jesus, delivered up according to the definite plan and foreknowledge of God, you crucified and killed by the hands of lawless men* (Acts 2:23).

Daniel dates his vision to the third year of Cyrus, so it was over seventy years after his deportation from Jerusalem. He was an old man, therefore, at least eighty-five years of age. It is interesting how he identifies himself here. He tells us the name that he was given all those years before in the Babylonian period. It's as if he is saying: "Yes, I am the very same Daniel, whom Nebuchadnezzar named Belteshazzar."

The date is important, since it enables us to deduce something that Daniel does not explicitly mention: this vision occurred two years after some of the Jews were allowed by an edict of Cyrus to return to Jerusalem and begin the task of rebuilding the temple (Ezra 1:1). Daniel had not gone back with the pilgrims – possibly due to age or infirmity, or because he was still an important figure in the administration of Babylon. As Edward Young points out (1949, page 223), if the Daniel of the sixth century BC were a fictitious person, created by the imagination of a writer in the second century BC, it would have been a plausible fiction to have Daniel returning to Jerusalem as soon as possible: "The fact that Daniel does not return to Palestine is a strong argument against the view that the book is a product of the Maccabean age."

Judging from the tone of the book of Ezra, we can imagine that reports had reached Daniel that things were not going very well in Jerusalem. Daniel was still deeply troubled about his people and their future. It must have been very depressing, then, to learn from the vision of the seventy weeks that the ultimate restoration of Jerusalem and of his people would take a very much longer period than Daniel might have hoped.

> *In those days I, Daniel, was mourning for three weeks. I ate*
> *no delicacies, no meat or wine entered my mouth, nor did*
> *I anoint myself at all, for the full three weeks. (Daniel 10:2–3.)*

His use here of the Hebrew expression, literally "three weeks of days", may be a subtle but deliberate hint at the contrast between that short time and the seventy interminable weeks of years in Daniel 9.

It was the first month of the Jewish year, the month Nisan, just past the time of Passover, when he and his nation ought to have been joyfully celebrating their marvellous deliverance by God from slavery. Passover celebrations started on the fourteenth day of the month, and normally took one week. Presumably Daniel had celebrated the Passover, yet such was the depth of his sorrow that he extended the period of his mourning for three times that length. It was as if his people were dead. Daniel could not know that centuries later Paul, who shared the same heartbreak, would express the hope that "dead" Israel would rise again:

> *For if their rejection means the reconciliation of the world,*
> *what will their acceptance mean but life from the dead?*
> *(Romans 11:15.)*

The matter of his people's predicament weighed so heavily on Daniel's mind that he ate very little, no fine food, meat, or wine. This mention of food is like an echo from the introduction to the book, where Daniel refused the king's food in order not to defile himself with the surrounding pagan culture.

Incidentally, from what Daniel now says, his initial stance did not mean that he felt it necessary in other circumstances to refrain from good food and wine. He voluntarily gave up such things for this period of three weeks, not now to avoid compromise with paganism; he was fasting out of concern for his nation.

We cannot read Daniel's mind, of course, but there is something very human about what is written here. Daniel has had a lifetime's experience of God's providential care and supernatural intervention. He has seen God working at the highest levels of state – even in the heart of an emperor. He has received three direct revelations from God about the future: each of them involving predictions of terrible things that will happen to his people. And yet here he is, one of those people: resolute still in the faith he developed as a student in Babylon, but deeply puzzled at the twists and turns in the fate of his nation. It was almost too much for a sensitive, brilliant, and caring man like Daniel to bear. So he fasted and mourned, not even bothering to soothe and refresh his skin and protect it from the heat by the usual means of rubbing in oil.

Perhaps he hoped that God had something more to say to him – truth not sentiment that could comfort him in his old age, so that he could die in peace knowing that the future was safe. He longed for his mourning to end in joy.

He was standing one day by the River Tigris, contemplating its flow. Where he stood the river was about a mile wide – it was one of the mightiest rivers on earth. The massive expanse of water was constantly on the move, surging past him on its irresistible journey. The flow of great rivers had already been used by Jewish writers as a poetic metaphor to express the flow of history in the nations of the world, as they surged against each other in conflict, calmed down for a time, surged again, broke their banks, and flooded across each other in what seemed to be a ceaseless maelstrom of war, conflict, and suffering. For instance, Isaiah wrote of the Assyrian war machine:

> The Lord spoke to me again: "Because this people has refused
> the waters of Shiloah that flow gently, and rejoice over
> Rezin and the son of Remaliah, therefore, behold, the Lord
> is bringing up against them the waters of the River, mighty
> and many, the king of Assyria and all his glory. And it will
> rise over all its channels and go over all its banks, and it will
> sweep on into Judah, it will overflow and pass on, reaching
> even to the neck, and its outspread wings will fill the breadth
> of your land, O Immanuel." (Isaiah 8:5–8.)

Vivid imagery – picturing Jerusalem, perched as a head on the neck of a mountain, about to be engulfed by the rising flood of the mighty armies of Assyria pouring into the land around.

The flow of history

Daniel had already heard such imagery used of Jerusalem in the previous vision: *Its end shall come with a flood, and to the end there shall be war* (Daniel 9:26). Now, as he watches the restless flow of the Tigris, his mind is drawn once more to the inexorable flow of history. Where is it all going? What does it all mean? He will speak of forces that come, *overflow and pass through*, as they wreak their destructive path (11:10, 40). He started his book by drawing attention to God's sovereignty over history, even as he allowed Nebuchadnezzar to defeat the king of Judah (1:2). Now, at the end of the book, he is returning to the same theme. How is he to navigate the complexities of what he has already been told? After all, Judah's defeat was relatively easy to understand. The moral and spiritual reasons for it lie at the heart of Daniel's prayer in chapter 9. He has been deeply shaken by this knowledge that only he possessed, of all his people: their future is going to be long and dark, and they have yet to experience waves of fierce persecution by the nations of the world. The vision of chapter 9 had left too much unclear. Daniel longed to know more.

Where was the Tigris going? Where was history going? Where was Daniel's nation going? Where was Daniel going? Could anything impede the flow? Could one swim against it? What was the meaning of it all anyway? His mind is crammed with questions as he stands gazing across the vast expanse of the river. Then he becomes aware of the glowing figure of a majestic man *above* the river. The man is dressed in linen, with a belt of fine gold, his body incandescent with light like a jewel, his face like lightning, his eyes fiercely flaming like a torch, and his legs gleaming like bronze. The man is speaking, and his voice is like the roaring sound of a vast multitude. This is no mere human, or even an angel; here is overwhelmingly transcendent glory.

Six centuries later the apostle John saw him: the same glorious man, his face like the sun, eyes like flame, feet like glowing bronze, and a voice like the ocean's roar. He was Jesus Christ, the risen and ascended Son of God. How could Daniel have seen him? We are now on the edge of something unfathomably profound. It was the same apostle John who wrote: *No one has ever seen God; the only God, who is at the Father's side, he has made him known* (John 1:18). He is the Word, who was with God, was God, and uniquely reveals God. This is the one Daniel saw.

Daniel was not alone that day. Perhaps he had brought some close friends who shared his burdens. We do not know, but whoever these companions were, they, like Paul's companions on the road to Damascus (Acts 9:7), did not see the vision. Sensing that something awesome was happening, they began to tremble and ran to seek a place to hide. Daniel was left alone to gaze at this overpowering sight of the dazzling glory of the man who was above the river.

The vision had such an effect on his emotions that his strength ebbed away, and he was aware that his normally radiant facial expression had fearfully changed. The volume of the cataract of words coming from above the river caused his senses to go into overload. He collapsed on the ground and fell into a deep sleep. The apostle John reacted the same way. He fell as dead at the feet of the glorious man, until he felt a hand on his shoulder and heard the voice of Jesus telling him not to fear.

The next thing Daniel knew was that a hand was touching him, which set him on his hands and knees trembling with weakness and fear. And then a voice spoke to him. It is not said to be the voice of Gabriel, but the language of address is very similar:

> *O Daniel, man greatly loved, understand the words that I speak to you, and stand upright, for now I have been sent to you. (Daniel 10:11.)*

Once more, a supernatural messenger tells Daniel personally that he is greatly loved. Far from being rejected because he has been asking questions, he is much loved in that world that is the source of all love. By far the most wonderful thing any human can hear is that he or she is loved by God. It brings stability and hope into the worst of situations.

Daniel was told this twenty-six centuries ago, and any one of us can know it today. A heavenly Messenger, greater than the one sent to Daniel, has come to our world – God himself, incarnate in his Son, Jesus Christ the Lord. He came to tell us the good news:

> *For God so loved the world, that he gave his only Son, that whoever believes in him should not perish but have eternal life. (John 3:16.)*

Those people who respond and trust him shall enjoy the friendship and love of God eternally. They can hear the voice of God himself saying to them, "O man, O woman, greatly loved."

There are times when those of us who are believers may find the way difficult; we are faced with apparently unanswerable questions and insoluble difficulties – many of them to do with the flow of life. It is at those times that we most need reassurance that there is a world beyond this one; there is a God who is real, and he loves me.

Daniel stood up, still shaking, as the voice continued:

*Fear not, Daniel, for from the first day that you set your
heart to understand and humbled yourself before your God,
your words have been heard, and I have come because of
your words. The prince of the kingdom of Persia withstood
me twenty-one days, but Michael, one of the chief princes,
came to help me, for I was left there with the kings of Persia,
and came to make you understand what is to happen to your
people in the latter days. For the vision is for days yet to come.
(Daniel 10:12–14.)*

These words give us insight into Daniel's state of mind as he began
his three-week fast. He wanted to understand, and so he humbled
himself before God. That is the way the heavenly world evaluated his
attitude. Daniel's life had been spent with proud men whom God had
humbled. God did not need to bring Daniel down to humble reality;
he had humbled himself.

We all detest false humility – a cloak of assumed lack of pride that
is not genuine. It is possible for us, however, to humble ourselves in
a genuine way that does not involve hypocrisy. Indeed, it is expected
of Christians. The apostle Peter writes:

*Clothe yourselves, all of you, with humility towards one another,
for God opposes the proud but gives grace to the humble.
Humble yourselves, therefore, under the mighty hand of God
so that at the proper time he may exalt you, casting all your
anxieties upon him, because he cares for you. (1 Peter 5:5–7.)*

It all has to do with our mindset and our attitude towards others.
Instead of regarding ourselves as more important than others, we are
to consider others better than ourselves.

Daniel had walked his whole life with kings and emperors. It
had not gone to his head. In God's eyes – and that is what counts –
he was still a humble man. And the heavenly world was watching
him. The moment Daniel started his three-week fast to wait on God,
the other world responded, and a messenger was detailed to take a
message to him.

A messenger from heaven

But the messenger was hindered. This is an extraordinary statement. It opens a window into an unseen realm about which we know very little. The messenger tells Daniel of a strange conflict in that realm: *The prince of the kingdom of Persia withstood me twenty-one days, but Michael, one of the chief princes, came to help me* (Daniel 10:13). Prince Michael is mentioned later in the vision as *the great prince who has charge of your people* (12:1).

The sceptic will hoot with derision if we add to our confession of faith in God the belief that another realm exists where there are supernatural beings – angels and demons. Such laughter strikes me as decidedly out of place, especially nowadays. If any scientist announces with confidence that there is life elsewhere in the universe – or, as is very likely these days, that there is a multiverse: a plurality of universes, many of which are teeming with life – there is no derision, but rather fascinated and respectful attention. Yet when the Bible suggests that this may not be the only world (or universe), and there are other beings "out there", it gets laughed to scorn. This is intellectually inconsistent, and simply shows the depth of prejudice that the naturalistic world-view has generated.

So far Daniel has given us very good reason to take him seriously. He is an exceptionally brilliant and wise man who has governed two empires, and has been used by God to demonstrate to his emperors that God and the supernatural are real. He has not taken leave of his senses here. As we have already seen as we considered Gabriel's role, both the Old and New Testament testify to the reality of angels. Christ himself said to those who came to arrest him:

> *Do you think that I cannot appeal to my Father, and he will at once send me more than twelve legions of angels? But how then should the Scriptures be fulfilled, that it must be so? (Matthew 26:53–54.)*

Our Lord was not speaking metaphorically; he was explaining to Peter why he should not try to protect him by force. Jesus could have summoned all the protection he needed from supernatural angelic forces, but he chose not to.

Who or what are angels? The Bible tells us that they are *ministering spirits sent out to serve for the sake of those who are to inherit salvation* (Hebrews 1:14). By contrast we are told that humans are, from one point of view, *a little lower than the angels* (Hebrews 2:7) since they are spirit plus flesh. The term "spirit" does not mean that angels have no substantive being. Unfortunately, the influence of materialism is so deep that many people unconsciously assume that matter is the only reality. The truth is, matter is not even the primary reality. Jesus taught that *God is spirit* (John 4:24), so spirit is the primary reality. Matter is derivative: *All things were made through him* (John 1:3).

There should therefore be no problem in principle in accepting that God has made other beings that are spirit. Certainly, that is the claim of the Bible, and the book of Daniel in particular.

The angelic messenger reveals to Daniel that a battle is raging in another world that in some sense reflects, and may also be reflected by, the conflicts in this one. This idea recurs in the book of Revelation:

> *Now war arose in heaven, Michael and his angels fighting*
> *against the dragon. And the dragon and his angels fought*
> *back, but he was defeated and there was no longer any place*
> *for them in heaven. And the great dragon was thrown down,*
> *that ancient serpent, who is called the devil and Satan,*
> *the deceiver of the whole world – he was thrown down*
> *to the earth, and his angels were thrown down with him.*
> *(Revelation 12:7–9.)*

It needs to be emphasized that the idea of a cosmic conflict is not some peripheral notion, generated by the overheated imagination of Christian extremists. Paul tells all Christians that there are spiritual forces arrayed against them and that in order to stand firm they need to put on the armour of God:

Finally, be strong in the Lord and in the strength of his might.
Put on the whole armour of God, that you may be able to
stand against the schemes of the devil. For we do not wrestle
against flesh and blood, but against the rulers, against the
authorities, against the cosmic powers over this present
darkness, against the spiritual forces of evil in the heavenly
places. (Ephesians 6:10–12.)

Atheistic rejection of the supernatural dimension can lead even Christians to underestimate the forces of evil. This part of the book of Daniel would have served us well if it alerted us to take the level of the conflict seriously.

When Daniel heard that the angel had come to tell him what would happen to the Jewish nation in the latter days, he turned his face towards the ground and found himself unable to speak. Someone who looked like a man (but presumably wasn't) touched his lips, which enabled Daniel to speak and describe the debilitating effects of the vision. He wondered how he would have the strength to speak to such a superior being. Daniel sensed that he was in the presence of a greatness that far exceeded his own.

Again the supernatural being touched and strengthened him, and told him once more that he was greatly loved. Then he asked Daniel if he knew why he had come to him. Without waiting for a response, the angel said that he must soon return to fight in the ongoing spiritual war against the prince of Persia and a new foe, the prince of Greece, who was yet to come. But first he would reveal to Daniel what was in *the book of truth*.

Before he did, however, there was another important piece of background information that Daniel needed to know:

… there is none who contends by my side against these except
Michael, your prince. And as for me, in the first year of
Darius the Mede, I stood up to confirm and strengthen him
[that is, Michael]. (Daniel 10:21 – 11:1.)

322

In the supernatural battle with the mighty princes of Medo-Persia and Greece, Daniel's angelic messenger (whom we may presume to be Gabriel) was aided by another prince. His name was Michael, and Daniel is told that he is *your prince ... the great prince who has charge of your people* (10:21; 12:1). It was Gabriel who had strengthened Michael at the beginning of Darius's reign, though Daniel had not realized it. Indeed he had probably not known of his existence.

This takes Daniel's mind back to the very beginning of the Medo-Persian kingdom (and so to the first section of the second half of the book). Was the messenger informing Daniel that Gabriel, or Michael, or both of them, were involved in rescuing Daniel from the lions' den? Daniel was being assured that there was a mighty prince in a higher realm, guarding his people. That knowledge would enable Daniel to face the contents of *the book of truth* that would now be opened to him.

CHAPTER 22

THE BOOK OF TRUTH
Daniel 11

And now I will show you the truth (Daniel 11:2). With these words the angel embarks on a remarkable survey of what will happen in the time after Daniel. We should note the emphatic truth claim. What is written here does not purport to be the forecast of a group of clever wise men, using the unaided light of their reason. It claims to be a supernatural revelation of truth.

As we mentioned earlier, this claim was rejected by Porphyry in the third century AD. He argued that Daniel 11 is not genuine prophecy but a history, written in the second century BC at the time of Antiochus IV Epiphanes, masquerading as prophecy. The same argument has also been popular since the eighteenth century, especially among those who, as a matter of principle, reject the possibility of real prophecy – usually as part of their more general denial of the supernatural.

We should notice that the basis of this rejection is the acknowledged historical accuracy of a great deal of Daniel 11 – particularly that major part of it which is concerned with the time of Antiochus IV. The key question, therefore, is not whether Daniel 11 is a good fit with history. That much is agreed. It is precisely that fit with history which creates the problem. So the key question is: when was the book written? We have already given some reasons for the traditional view that the book was written in the sixth century BC, and in due course we shall offer additional evidence from this final section of Daniel.

The angelic messenger tells Daniel that the vision *is for days yet to come* (10:14). The phrase *at the time of the end* occurs at 11:40; and in 12:2 we have one of the few Old Testament references to the resurrection of the dead. This final section of Daniel, then, brings us to the time of the end. However, in 11:21–25 Daniel is, by common consent, describing the time of Antiochus IV. It would seem therefore that chapter 11, like chapter 8, uses the time of Antiochus as a thought model or prototype of what will happen in the end times. This at once leads to the question: what does this second, more detailed, description add to what has already been said in chapter 8?

A prototype of the end time

If an event in history is a thought model or prototype of the end time, there will inevitably be a danger of confusing the prototype with the event that it foreshadows. The former Chief Rabbi of the UK, Lord Sacks, in his analysis of why religion goes wrong, writes (2011, page 5): "Sometimes it is because religious people attempt to bring about the end of time in the midst of time."

In order to avoid that danger, it was important for Daniel to make it very clear that the time of Antiochus was not the end time. But the people living then might have thought it was. According to David Gooding (1981), that is one of the major reasons for Daniel writing chapter 11.

An exact parallel occurs in the New Testament. Christ used the fall of Jerusalem as a thought model of the end time, but explicitly warned his disciples against being taken in by many who would confuse it and other events with the end time:

> See that you are not led astray. For many will come in my name, saying, "I am he!" and, "The time is at hand!" Do not go after them. And when you hear of wars and tumults, do not be terrified, for these things must first take place, but the end will not be at once. (Luke 21:8–9.)

As examples of attempting to bring the end of time within time, Lord Sacks cites the two major rebellions against Rome – AD 66 and AD 132 – that led to the destruction of the temple, the razing of Jerusalem, and 58,000 deaths. He comments (2011, page 258): "Prior to the Holocaust, it was the greatest catastrophe in Jewish history."

Throughout the centuries of Christian history there has been a constant danger of people failing to heed Christ's warning. They thought that their time was the end time: a mistake that often led to behaviour which discredited the Christian message. During the Second World War, for instance, there were those who thought the activity of Hitler and Mussolini was evidence that the end times had come. But they were wrong.

In this final section of his book it should not surprise us, therefore, that Daniel issues a similar warning to those who would live four centuries after him. The angelic messenger told Daniel that some of his people would misread not only the time of Antiochus but other historical situations also, and think the end had come. That would sometimes lead them to disaster. For instance, some would even make a futile attempt to bring in God's kingdom by force of arms:

> In those times many shall rise against the king of the south,
> and the violent among your own people shall lift themselves
> up in order to fulfil the vision, but they shall fail. (Daniel
> 11:14.)

Therefore, chapter 11 should not be read simply as a list of predictions to be checked against subsequent historical events in order to confirm faith, even though it does perform that role. It was also written to warn people in the future (from Daniel's perspective) of the danger of misreading the signs of the times, and thinking that the end time had come when it hadn't.

So far in this book we have made use of information from history and archaeology, and I trust this has helped us to gain a deeper understanding of the events described by Daniel. When it comes to chapter 11, however, we face a problem in this respect. It is not that there is too little information, but the exact opposite. In a sense, there is too much! So many of these details have been illuminated by historians like Polybius, Livy, Herodotus, Josephus, and the books of Maccabees (and that is not a complete list) that a book could be written on this section of Daniel alone. I have decided, therefore, to devote Appendix D to historical comments on how Daniel 11 fits into Hellenistic history. That means we can concentrate here on the significance of the chapter within the book of Daniel as a whole.

Bust of Antiochus IV at the Altes Museum in Berlin

The general structure of Daniel 11

After an introductory paragraph that brings us to the death of Alexander the Great and the division of his kingdom among his four generals, the future is divided up into four movements: 11:5–19; 11:20–28; 11:29–35; 11:36 – 12:3.

David Gooding (1981) makes this analysis:

> By a very precise and consistent use of terms the author indicates that only the last of these movements is "the time of the end"; it alone introduces the End itself. Before 11:40 the only reference in the chapter to "the time of the end" (11:35) indicates that it is still future; only with the event of 11:40 is it announced as having begun.
>
> But then by a deliberate repetition of vocabulary, this preview of history calls attention to the fact that while only the last movement is the time of the end and finally the End itself, all four movements show features in common, and witness the repetition of almost identical situations: a king will stage an enormous attack upon Egypt, and either on his outward or return journey, or both, will station armies in "the glorious land" [Israel], threatening or actually perpetrating destruction and outrage of one kind or another. In other words, each of the first three movements, though lacking the distinctive features, and the distinctive combination of events, of the time of the end, will to some extent look like the time of the end, and yet will not be the time of the end.

Daniel's concern, therefore, was that there would be people in the first three periods who would make the mistake of thinking that the time of the end had come.

Period 1 (11:5–19). The angelic messenger warned Daniel that in the first period, when the Seleucid king (Antiochus III) occupied Israel, some violent Jews would rebel in fulfilment of the vision (11:14), but they would fail. Presumably they would be under the misapprehension that the end was near.

Period 2 (11:20–28). In the second period, there would come a time when the cruel king of the north (Antiochus IV) would sit at the negotiating table with the king of the south (Ptolemy V of Egypt), with their scheming hearts *bent on doing evil*. The angel pointed out to Daniel that their plans would come to nothing, *for the end is yet to be at the time appointed* (11:27). Again, we may infer that there is a warning here against mistakenly thinking that the wars and intrigues of these kings, with Israel caught in the middle and suffering constant harassment and violence, meant that the end time had arrived.

Period 3 (11:29–35). Daniel was also told that, in the third period, the king of the north (Antiochus IV once more), enraged by the Roman-imposed limitation of his power in Egypt, would vent his wrath against those Jews who refused to join their compatriots in welcoming Antiochus's imposition of Greek culture on their land:

> At the time appointed he shall return and come into the south, but it shall not be this time as it was before. For ships of Kittim shall come against him, and he shall be afraid and withdraw, and shall turn back and be enraged and take action against the holy covenant. He shall turn back and pay attention to those who forsake the holy covenant. Forces from him shall appear and profane the temple and fortress, and shall take away the regular burnt offering. And they shall set up the abomination that makes desolate. He shall seduce with flattery those who violate the covenant…. (Daniel 11:29–32.)

We have already described the horrors of Antiochus's persecution and wholesale slaughter as he vented his rage against the Jewish people – bringing to an end the daily sacrifice, sacrificing a pig on the altar, and rededicating the Jewish temple to the Greek god Zeus (see Chapter 17). His outrages were utter abominations to godly Jews, and led to the Maccabean uprising that eventually succeeded in winning back the temple and having it rededicated to God.

Yet, horrific as that time was, the third period was not to be the time of the end.

... but the people who know their God shall stand firm and take action. And the wise among the people shall make many understand, though for some days they shall stumble by sword and flame, by captivity and plunder. When they stumble, they shall receive a little help. And many shall join themselves to them with flattery, and some of the wise shall stumble, so that they may be refined, purified, and made white, until the time of the end, for it still awaits the appointed time. (Daniel 11:32–35.)

Even though Antiochus's oppression of the Jews would not usher in the time of the end, Daniel predicted that the people of Israel would experience persecution, war, captivity, and death over an unspecified period, until the time of the end. (The nightmare of the Holocaust was yet to come.) There is no expectation here of the kind of deliverance that Daniel and his friends experienced in the earlier part of his book. His prediction is analogous to the warning issued by Jesus to his disciples regarding his return and the time of the end:

And Jesus answered them, "See that no one leads you astray. For many will come in my name, saying, 'I am the Christ', and they will lead many astray. And you will hear of wars and rumours of wars. See that you are not alarmed, for this must take place, but the end is not yet. For nation will rise against nation, and kingdom against kingdom, and there will be famines and earthquakes in various places. All these are but the beginning of the birth pains.

"Then they will deliver you up to tribulation and put you to death, and you will be hated by all nations for my name's sake. And then many will fall away and betray one another and hate one another. And many false prophets will arise and lead many astray. And because lawlessness will be increased, the love of many will grow cold. But the one who endures to the end will be saved. And this gospel of the kingdom will be proclaimed throughout the whole world as a testimony to all nations, and **then the end will come.** *(Matthew 24:4–14, emphasis mine.)*

Christ warns that, in the course of world history, the occurrence of events like wars and rumours of wars, persecutions, famines, and earthquakes will mislead some into thinking that the end has come. However, such events will not signify the end.

Our analysis of Daniel 11 seems to show that Daniel is warning that the three periods of Hellenistic history culminating with Antiochus Epiphanes are *not* the time of the end, just as Christ in his time warned of events that preceded but were not themselves the time of the end.

If we take it that the warnings were written in advance – which is not unreasonable when the end point is the time of the very end – then it is surely reasonable to conclude that the book was not written at the time of Antiochus IV, but much earlier.

Period 4 (11:36 – 12:3). In spite of this, there are many who think that all of Daniel 11 and 12 concerns only the time of Antiochus. It is worth pausing, therefore, to spell out what that would mean.

Antiochus would make another major attack on Egypt (11:40), which would meet with great success and increase his wealth and power (11:43). However, on his return from that campaign, he would meet *his end* somewhere between the Mediterranean and Jerusalem (11:45). After that there would be a *time of trouble* in Israel, unprecedented ferocity, but the nation would eventually be delivered (12:1). This would lead to the resurrection from the dead (12:2).

Clearly, this is the end!

Not only that, but a time scale is given. Daniel was understandably concerned as to how long all this would last, and he was told *that it would be for a time, times, and half a time* (12:7). He was also told that roughly three-and-a-half years would elapse after the regular burnt offering was taken away and the abomination of desolation was set up in the temple area of Jerusalem (12:11).

David Gooding (1981) addresses the implications of taking 12:11 and 11:31 to be referring to the same outrage:

But this last event, according to the majority view, must have already taken place before the book was written and

331

published (for had the book been published before that event, the prediction of it would have been a genuine predictive prophecy). How long after the setting up of the abomination of desolation it took our author to compile this book with its remarkably complex structure the majority view does not tell us; nor how long it took to get it published and into circulation. Practical sense suggests that by the time it was written and published, a considerable part of the three and a half years must have gone by. The book would now be promising that the End would occur within an even shorter time than three and a half years.

Fortunately, when the book was published, Daniel's reading public, close-knit though they must have been, never realized who the author was, the publisher never spilt the beans, and took the book for an ancient book without wondering why they had never heard of it before. They believed its *vaticinium ex eventu* ["prophecy after the event", i.e. history disguised as prophecy] to have been a genuine prophecy, and put their faith in the author's prediction, were very encouraged by it, and prepared to meet the End. Unfortunately, of course, nothing happened. Antiochus did not invade Egypt again. He did not encamp between Jerusalem and the sea. He died, but not there: he died in fact far away out east. There was trouble for Israel as always, but nothing unprecedented. And the resurrection of the dead did not take place. The other things which other chapters in Daniel had promised would happen at the End, did not take place either: all Gentile imperial power was not everywhere removed, and universal dominion was not given to Israel.

The only thing that took place within the time was the deliverance and cleansing of the sanctuary. Nevertheless the faithful having discovered the predictions to be false were not discouraged. They still accepted the predictions as genuine predictions and the whole book as authoritative and they carefully preserved it and quoted it (e.g. 1 Maccabees 2.60) and canonized it.

At this point the majority view, based as it is on the alleged incredibility of predictive prophecy, becomes itself … incredible.

The majority view is incredible for another, independent reason. Since Daniel himself predicted the rise of a fourth empire (Rome) after that of the Greeks, he could not have thought or taught that the time of Antiochus IV was actually the end. Daniel seems to have been clearer on the distinction between prototype and fulfilment than his critics are.

Predictive prophecy

We have now reached a crucial stage in our consideration of this section of Daniel, where again we face the critical question: is there such a thing as predictive prophecy? It may seem to my readers that I have unduly laboured this point. But I do not think so, since it lies at the heart of an even bigger issue: which world-view is true? Is it biblical theism, with its supernatural dimension; or naturalism, which denies the possibility of miracles? Since one of the main objectives of the book of Daniel is to establish the biblical world-view, it must not surprise us that this issue confronts us regularly. There is a great deal at stake.

If, under the influence of Scottish Enlightenment philosopher David Hume's well-advertised rejection of miracles,[41] there should be a lingering suspicion in our minds that naturalism may be true, we will be incapable of seeing how significant the book of Daniel is as prophecy. Hence, the proper thing to do at this juncture would be to demonstrate that an *a priori* rejection of the supernatural is not only unscientific, but the existence of reason and our resultant ability to do science points in the other direction.

It is impossible to undertake that task within the confines of this book, but I have written about it extensively elsewhere, from the scientific perspective.[42] If, as I believe, there is no *a priori* scientific difficulty with the possibility of predictive prophecy, then we are free to take Daniel seriously on his own terms, and may now get back to the text to see what it actually says.

Looking beyond Antiochus

Up to this point (11:35), by using extra-biblical sources, it has been possible to identify the main historical events. But it now becomes more difficult:

> *And the king shall do as he wills. He shall exalt himself and magnify himself above every god, and shall speak astonishing things against the God of gods. He shall prosper till the indignation is accomplished; for what is decreed shall be done. He shall pay no attention to the gods of his fathers, or to the one beloved by women. He shall not pay attention to any other god, for he shall magnify himself above all. He shall honour the god of fortresses instead of these. A god whom his fathers did not know he shall honour with gold and silver, with precious stones and costly gifts. He shall deal with the strongest fortresses with the help of a foreign god. Those who acknowledge him he shall load with honour. He shall make them rulers over many and shall divide the land for a price. (Daniel 11:36–39.)*

At first it looks as if Daniel is still talking about Antiochus IV Epiphanes. He was certainly a wilful and proud king, as were many before him – Daniel refers to some of them (8:4; 11:3; 11:16). Antiochus exalted himself and was the first of the Seleucid dynasty to assume divine honours for himself. As we saw earlier, even his coinage bore the inscription "God manifest". His most violent aggression was directed against the *God of gods*, the God of Israel. He was anti-God. He reminds us of a new breed of atheist, the so-called "New Atheists", who are not content simply to disbelieve in the existence of God themselves but actively campaign against God and all manifestations of belief in him on the part of others.

However, Antiochus IV did not go as far as to exalt himself above every god. For instance, he sought to get the Jews to worship the familiar gods of the Greek pantheon, rather than force them to worship him.

The statement *he shall prosper till the indignation is accomplished* (11:36) is puzzling. For, once Antiochus stepped outside the line drawn by the Roman legate, he was doomed as far as his political ambitions were concerned. It is hard to see how he could have prospered after that.

Also problematic are the statements regarding the king of the north's views of the Greek gods at this stage. According to Daniel, he would show no regard for the gods of his ancestors. Yet Mark Mercer cites Livy and Polybius to argue that the contrary was true of Antiochus:

> Nevertheless in two great and important respects his soul was truly royal – in his benefactions to cities and in the honours paid to the gods (Livy 41.20.5).

> But in the sacrifices he furnished to cities and in the honours he paid to the gods he far surpassed all his predecessors . . . (Polybius 26.1.10).

Mercer concludes:

> From what Livy and Polybius have to say about Antiochus IV Epiphanes, to view him as the King of the North in Dan. 11:36–45 is difficult.[43]

And who is "the god of fortresses" that he honours – a god unknown not only to his fathers, but to contemporary history? Joyce Baldwin writes (2009, page 219):

> ... while it is true that Antiochus IV fulfills in a general way the description given in these verses, there are discrepancies when it comes to detail regarding his religious practices.

The next paragraph of Daniel 11 now strains identification of its king of the north with Antiochus to breaking point:

> *At the time of the end, the king of the south shall attack*
> *him, but the king of the north shall rush upon him like a*
> *whirlwind, with chariots and horsemen, and with many ships.*
> *And he shall come into countries and shall overflow and pass*
> *through. He shall come into the glorious land. And tens of*
> *thousands shall fall, but these shall be delivered out of his*
> *hand: Edom and Moab and the main part of the Ammonites.*
> *He shall stretch out his hand against the countries, and the*
> *land of Egypt shall not escape. He shall become ruler of the*
> *treasures of gold and of silver, and all the precious things of*
> *Egypt, and the Libyans and the Cushites shall follow in his*
> *train. But news from the east and the north shall alarm him,*
> *and he shall go out with great fury to destroy and devote*
> *many to destruction. And he shall pitch his palatial tents*
> *between the sea and the glorious holy mountain. Yet he shall*
> *come to his end, with none to help him. (Daniel 11:40–45.)*

Ernest Lucas writes (2002, page 290):

> These verses have been a source of perplexity to
> commentators down the centuries. On the one hand, they
> seem to continue the story of Antiochus IV, providing
> the expected account of his downfall and death. On the
> other, they do not correspond in any way with the events
> following his second withdrawal from Egypt and the
> beginning of the persecution of the Jews.

Regarding ancient accounts of Antiochus's death, Lucas continues (page 291):

> Despite their disagreements and legendary elements, these
> accounts all agree that Antiochus embarked on a campaign
> in Persia, failed in an attempt to rob a temple, and met an

untimely death, which three of them attribute to a sudden illness ... None of this bears any relation to what is said in Dan. 11:40–45.

James A. Montgomery (1927, page 423), who thought that in some general sense the passage concerned Antiochus's death, nevertheless held that the passage

> cannot ... be taken in any way as an exact prophecy of the actual events of his ruin. The alleged final victorious war with Egypt, including the conquest of Cyrenaica and Ethiopia, in the face of Rome and the silence of secular history is absolutely imaginary.

These verdicts are striking, since there is agreement that up to verse 36, if not to verse 40, the history is impressively accurate. Where does this leave us? It leaves us with the fact that the events of Daniel 11:40–45 cannot be identified in ancient history because *they have not happened yet*. The fourth period of Daniel 11 is still future. As Daniel himself insists, it is *the time of the end* (11:40).

This distinction between the first three periods and the fourth is the central point Daniel is making – only the final period is *the time of the end*.

As in Daniel 8, so it is here. Daniel uses the life and times of Antiochus IV as a thought model of the end time (see Chapter 17 above), when an altogether more sinister leader will appear, who will exalt himself as God. The transition between periods three and four in 11:35–39 involves a blending of Antiochus IV, as king of the north, into the end-time king of the north.

Theodotion, who translated the Hebrew Bible into Greek in 150 AD and Hippolytus of Rome (third century AD) thought that the transition to the time of the end occurred at 11:36; whereas Jerome (fourth century AD) put the transition at 11:21 – with some historical allusions occurring later.

Daniel 11, then, adds to chapters 7, 8, and 9 by giving us a fourth preview of the time of the end; and of its domination by the final human enemy of God, the last king of the north, the man of lawlessness, the beast from the sea who exalts himself above all that is called God or that is worshipped.

CHAPTER 23

THE TIME OF THE END
Daniel 12

Since we are now in the realm of things future, it would be well to remind ourselves that the fulfilment of biblical prophecy usually turns out to be much more complex than we might at first imagine.

Think of the well-known prophecies regarding the Messiah. Daniel spoke of him coming on the clouds of heaven, whereas Zechariah said he would come riding on a donkey. The apparent contradiction is solved by the fact that the "coming" of Messiah turned out not to be simply a point in time, but two distinct comings separated by a very lengthy period during which the Messiah would be absent. His first coming, during which he fulfilled Zechariah's prophecy (among many others), was not a point in time but lasted just over thirty years, and his second coming has not happened yet. If we were asked to set all this out in a time-line, based only on our knowledge of the Old Testament prophecies, would any of us even have realized that the "coming" was to be in two stages, let alone place the details in their correct sequence? Scarcely.

Having uttered this caution, however, it is worth reflecting on what we might have deduced if we had been able to read chapter 11 just after Daniel had written it, bearing in mind that we would not have had the evidence of Hellenistic history that is now available. There are many things we could not have known – for instance the names of the kings of the north and the south. Nor might we have concluded that Daniel had left out a number of the kings of Medo-Persia. But we might surely have observed that there were to be the three periods leading up to the time of the end, which were not *the* time of the end. We could also have confirmed from other parts of the book (chapters 2 and 7) that the end time would occur not during the time of the Greek empire but much later. If we had done that much, we would surely have grasped the main thrust of what Daniel intended.

Approaching Armageddon

It is in such a spirit that we now turn to the part of Daniel's prophecy that concerns the future, not only for Daniel but also for us. Even though the end time is likely to be more complex than we could ever guess, some of its broad contours are discernible. According to Daniel it will be a future end-time leader, not Antiochus, who will invade Egypt and the land of Israel (*the beautiful land*), resulting in great loss of life. He will sequester the wealth of Egypt and gain control of a wider region of North Africa. He will eventually leave that region in fury, alarmed by threats from the east and north. On his way to neutralize those threats he will meet his end, between the mountains and the sea.

This appears to parallel the statement of John in Revelation regarding the summoning of kings (including those from the east):

> ... *to assemble them for battle on the great day of God the Almighty. ... And they assembled them at the place that in Hebrew is called Armageddon. (Revelation 16:14, 16.)*

John later refers to that final battle in the following terms:

> *And I saw the beast and the kings of the earth with their armies gathered together to make war against him who was sitting on the horse and against his army. (Revelation 19:19.)*

Revelation tells us that, in the last battle, it is the rider on the white horse descending from heaven who conquers the despotic ruler of the end time. Using less symbolic[44] language, the apostle Paul says: *And then the lawless one will be revealed, whom the Lord Jesus will kill with the breath of his mouth and bring to nothing by the appearance of his coming* (2 Thessalonians 2:8). The Judge of Daniel 7 will appear *with the clouds of heaven*, and the end will come.

Sometimes the articulation of such an end-time scenario, with its implied immense conflagration in the Middle East, is met with ridicule – and not only because the supernatural is involved. In my experience, that ridicule (at least in part) is based on the unjustified optimism that human beings will make such moral progress that aggression and wars will become unthinkable. But, in the twenty-six centuries since Daniel, it is the last century – not the early or middle ones – that has seen by far and away the most bloodshed. The Battle of the Somme occurred in the twentieth century, not the second.

According to Daniel, the worst of times will come. Just as there was a horrific attack on the Jews in the third period (11:29–35), there will be another great time of suffering for the nation in the end time:

> *At that time shall arise Michael, the great prince who has*
> *charge of your people. And there shall be a time of trouble,*
> *such as never has been since there was a nation till that time.*
> *(Daniel 12:1.)*

Michael has already been introduced to us. He is the mighty angelic prince who stands up to protect Israel in a realm beyond this world. Just as Michael was involved in bringing the vision to Daniel long ago, he will arise in the future to defend Israel in her final trial. It is described as *a time of trouble, such as never has been since there was a nation till that time.*

It is hard to get one's mind around this grim statement. The time of Antiochus was horrendous, as was the period around the later fall of Jerusalem. The Holocaust beggars description. But Daniel indicates that there is even worse to come at the time of the end. Christ said the same – two centuries after Antiochus he reiterated Daniel's prediction to his disciples:

*So when you see the abomination of desolation spoken of
by the prophet Daniel, standing in the holy place ... then
there will be great tribulation, such as has not been from the
beginning of the world until now, no, and never will be. And if
those days had not been cut short, no human being would be
saved. But for the sake of the elect those days will be cut short
... Immediately after the tribulation of those days ... Then
will appear in heaven the sign of the Son of Man ... and they
will see the Son of Man coming on the clouds of heaven with
power and great glory. And he will send out his angels with
a loud trumpet call, and they will gather his elect from the
four winds, from one end of heaven to the other. (Matthew
24:15–31.)*

Christ places the final time of tribulation in the context of his return
and the *gathering of his elect*. Daniel places it in the context not only
of a great deliverance for his people but of the very resurrection. In
one of the few passages in the Old Testament to explicitly mention
that topic, he writes:

*But at that time your people shall be delivered, everyone
whose name shall be found written in the book. And many of
those who sleep in the dust of the earth shall awake, some to
everlasting life, and some to shame and everlasting contempt.
(Daniel 12:1–2.)*

This explicitly teaches bodily resurrection. We have already had
several occasions to point out that the book of Daniel challenges
the "closed-world" naturalistic world-view. Daniel was a man
who, though he lived in this world, lived for another world that
would outlast this one, a supernatural realm that from time to
time had unmistakably manifested itself to him and his friends.
God had intervened to protect their witness, save their lives, and
reveal to them things to come, with such power and precision that
even pagan kings could not fail to recognize the invasion of the
supernatural.

This passage on the resurrection near the end of Daniel's account is consistent with that supernatural dimension. The God that spans history in his knowledge, and can reveal things to come, is the God who will raise the dead. Daniel did not, of course, know what we know: that the molecules in our bodies are in constant flux, so that they undergo total replacement every seven years or so, while each one of us remains the same person. There is a pattern somewhere that defines and holds each individual human in existence. And if we grant the reality of God and the supernatural, it is surely not hard to think that God himself holds those patterns in memory. He can re-use each pattern to fashion a resurrection body in the future.

I am well aware that it is fashionable in the name of research in neuroscience to deny any separate meaning to "mind" and "body" these days, and to hold that there is only the material brain. However, I would suggest that such a conclusion is increasingly unwarranted – for two reasons.

First, information is coming to play a central role in the understanding of nature, and information is not material, even though it is usually carried on a material substrate. Information is not therefore reducible to matter, and some physicists even suggest that information is primary and matter secondary. (See my book *God's Undertaker* for more on this.) This notion converges with the biblical claim that God the Word is primary and matter is secondary (John 1:1–3).

Secondly, although neuroscience has given us fascinating and important insights into the correlations between thoughts and different areas of the brain, the mind story and the brain story are not the same. The neuroscientist can tell me what is in my brain (at least, some of it). She cannot tell me what is in my mind. (See my essay in Varghese, 2013, for more on this.)

Indeed, according to the biblical world-view, not only is mind not the same as brain, mind actually is the primary "stuff" of the universe. For the eternal Word who is God is spirit and not material at all (John 4:24).

Commenting on this part of Daniel, John of Damascus wrote in the eighth century AD:

> *"Many shall awake" means the resurrection of their bodies, for I do not suppose that anyone would speak of souls sleeping in the dust of the earth ... the Lord, too, has clearly shown in the holy Gospels that there is a resurrection of the body, for "they that are in the graves", he says, "shall hear the voice of the Son of God ..." Now no person in his right mind would ever say that it was the souls that were in the graves. (Orthodox Faith, 4.27.)*

After all the misery and darkness of suffering and persecution that has dominated the story up to now, this is magnificent news. Daniel has been deeply concerned about the fate of his nation. He now learns from the angelic messenger that ultimate deliverance will come, but not until the time of the end. The deliverance will be permanent and final. Ultimately, for those who have been faithful to God, it will involve resurrection from the dead to everlasting life.

We have now reached the climax of the message of the book of Daniel. There has been so much suffering, horror, bloodshed, and death. There have also been many disappointments, dashed hopes, vanished dreams, and utter despair. There will yet be more, but can it really be true that one day it will all come to an end, for ever?

Names written in the book

Yes – for those *whose names shall be found written in the book*. In two brief sentences Daniel describes the worst of times and the best of times. Resurrection of the body, from the dead *to everlasting life*, will be the ultimate great reversal. It is the only answer to all the longings and hopes of which humans are capable. It alone can remove the shadow of death that has dogged humanity since the entry of sin into the world.

However, there is another side. The angel also informs Daniel that some shall awake *to shame and everlasting contempt*. This is a moral universe, and it matters therefore how human beings behave. History is not controlled by inexorable fate. Human beings have been given the immense dignity of freedom of choice; and that moral capacity inevitably carries with it ultimate accountability. We have already learned from Daniel 7 that God will judge the world in righteousness when the Son of Man returns (see Chapter 16).

Furthermore, Daniel is told that the criterion for being raised to everlasting life is that one's name *shall be found written in the book*. Notice the emphasis: it is not simply that the name should be written, but that it shall be *found written*, implying the meticulous search characteristic of a judicial process.

We read about a similar procedure in the description of the final judgment in the book of Revelation:

> *And I saw the dead, great and small, standing before the throne, and books were opened. Then another book was opened, which is the book of life. And the dead were judged by what was written in the books, according to what they had done. … And if anyone's name was not found written in the book of life, he was thrown into the lake of fire. (Revelation 20:12, 15.)*

There are several parallels between this passage and Daniel's. First of all, books are opened; then another book is mentioned, the book of life, and the criterion of judgment has to do with names being written in that book. In Daniel's vision, fire destroys the hideous beast.

We are not to think literalistically here, of the sort of books that would be familiar to us. These are records held by God in ways that would presumably be unintelligible to us. However, although they may not be literal books, they are real records.

The final reference to the book of life in Revelation helps us to see what is involved. Concerning entry to the heavenly city, John writes:

> *But nothing unclean will ever enter it, nor anyone who does what is detestable or false, but only those who are written in the Lamb's book of life. (Revelation 21:27.)*

Having one's name written in this book is essential, therefore, for entry into God's heavenly kingdom. As John explains in his Gospel, entry into God's kingdom depends on receiving new life – being born again (John 3:3). That life is obtained through trusting Jesus Christ. Indeed, John explicitly states that his objective in writing is *that you may believe that Jesus is the Christ, the Son of God, and that by believing you may have life in his name* (20:31). According to John, then, the way to receive life is to trust in Jesus, believe that he is the Christ, the Son of God: the one who became *the Lamb of God, who takes away the sin of the world* (1:29).

It is whether or not one has trusted Christ for salvation that will determine the verdict at the final judgment. It is a fundamental of the Christian gospel. Indeed, the gospel message *is* that salvation comes by faith and not through "works" – the things we do. Abraham, the great father of the Hebrew nation, is the primary example of a person who trusts God:

> *For if Abraham was justified by works, he has something to boast about, but not before God. For what does the Scripture say? "Abraham believed God, and it was counted to him as righteousness." Now to the one who works, his wages are not counted as a gift but as his due. And to the one who does not work but trusts him who justifies the ungodly, his faith is counted as righteousness....* (Romans 4:2–5.)

The principle of faith is crystal clear, and it is the ground of real hope. Why, then, it will be asked, do we read, *the dead were judged by what was written in the books, according to what they had done*? Does this not contradict the claim that salvation is by faith alone? No, it does not. When the books are opened, they do not include the book of life. In all courts of law a distinction is made between the *verdict* (guilty, or not guilty) and the *sentence*. Two people may be declared guilty of murder, but the sentences may vary greatly according to whether or not there are mitigating circumstances. We all understand this as the outworking of a basic moral principle.

The same holds true at the higher level. On one occasion Christ solemnly comments on the fact that people have rejected him, in spite of having seen many of his mighty works. He indicates that the sentence will vary according to opportunity and privilege:

> *Then he began to denounce the cities where most of his mighty works had been done, because they did not repent. "Woe to you, Chorazin! Woe to you, Bethsaida! For if the mighty works done in you had been done in Tyre and Sidon, they would have repented long ago in sackcloth and ashes. But I tell you, it will be more bearable on the day of judgment for Tyre and Sidon than for you. And you, Capernaum, will you be exalted to heaven? You will be brought down to Hades. For if the mighty works done in you had been done in Sodom, it would have remained until this day. But I tell you that it will be more tolerable on the day of judgment for the land of Sodom than for you." (Matthew 11:20–24.)*

Similarly, Paul reminds Christians that their behaviour matters:

> *According to the grace of God given to me, like a skilled master builder I laid a foundation, and someone else is building upon it. Let each one take care how he builds upon it. For no one can lay a foundation other than that which is laid, which is Jesus Christ. Now if anyone builds on the foundation with gold, silver, precious stones, wood, hay, straw – each one's work will become manifest, for the Day will disclose it, because it will be revealed by fire, and the fire will test what sort of work each one has done. If the work that anyone has built on the foundation survives, he will receive a reward. If anyone's work is burned up, he will suffer loss, though he himself will be saved, but only as through fire.*
> *(1 Corinthians 3:10–15.)*

Paul is speaking to people who have "the foundation"; that is, they have trusted Christ for salvation. However, they should concern themselves not to build rubbish into their lives, because one day

347

they will be assessed and what is deemed unacceptable shall be destroyed. It matters, therefore, what we build on the foundation. However, it is important to notice that if a person's work is burned up, he or she is still saved, even though they suffer loss. The condition for salvation is not merit, but faith in Christ. Paul is making precisely the same distinction implied in both Daniel and Revelation. The books that are opened determine the sentence; the book of life pronounces the verdict.

Since it is Christ as Judge who will have the final word, let us listen to him once more:

> *For God so loved the world, that he gave his only Son, that whoever believes in him should not perish but have eternal life. For God did not send his Son into the world to condemn the world, but in order that the world might be saved through him. Whoever believes in him is not condemned, but whoever does not believe is condemned already, because he has not believed in the name of the only Son of God. (John 3:16–18.)*

This passage contains one of the best-known and most powerful statements of the love of God, yet it is striking how it also contains a warning. It is possible to perish! The alternative to believing in Christ and receiving eternal life is to perish. The criterion on which judgment will turn is explained in the final sentence: *whoever does not believe is condemned already.* The reason is, *because he has not believed in the name of the only Son of God.* Men and women will be condemned, not on the grounds of their merit but because they do not believe in Christ. It is that information which is contained in the Lamb's book of life.

We should note also that, since the verdict will turn on whether a person has trusted Christ or not, it follows both logically and morally that he or she must have been capable of doing so. Indeed, in the verse immediately following those quoted above, Christ is emphatic about us taking responsibility for our personal choices:

And this is the judgement: the light has come into the world,
and people loved the darkness rather than the light because
their deeds were evil. (John 3:19.)

The reason they did not believe is that they loved "darkness". It was their own choice, their own preference, and therefore their own responsibility. It would be morally absurd to judge people for failing to do something they were incapable of doing. And yet there are some people who think that this is exactly the case. Among other statements of Scripture they cite one about the book of life:

... and all who dwell on earth will worship it [the beast],
everyone whose name has not been written before the
foundation of the world in the book of life of the Lamb that
was slain. (Revelation 13:8.)

Some deduce from this that long before humanity or even the earth existed God put the names of those and only those he had chosen for salvation into the book of life. That list is definitive: those whose names are in it will be saved; those whose names are not in it will never be put into it, no matter what they do.

It is obvious that this deterministic interpretation stands in complete contradiction to what we have suggested above, so we need to look more carefully at what the Bible says elsewhere about the book of life. First of all we should note that the exact wording of the verse just cited is "written from [not 'before'] the foundation of the world". Secondly, the idea of names being written in a book originates in Exodus, again in the context of judgment. After the people of Israel had set up the golden calf and worshipped it, Moses said to them:

"You have sinned a great sin. And now I will go up to the
Lord; perhaps I can make atonement for your sin." So Moses
returned to the Lord and said, "Alas, this people has sinned
a great sin. They have made for themselves gods of gold. But
now, if you will forgive their sin – but if not, please blot me

out of your book that you have written." But the Lord said to Moses, "Whoever has sinned against me, I will blot out of my book." (Exodus 32:30–33.)

Moses, therefore, understood that his name was already in the book and so concerned was he that Israel should be forgiven, he was prepared to have his name removed from the book if it would help achieve that result. It seems reasonable to deduce from this statement that the names are already in the book, but may be removed from it because of sin against God. This deduction is supported by the promise given to the church at Sardis in the book of Revelation:

The one who conquers will be clothed thus in white garments, and I will never blot his name out of the book of life. I will confess his name before my Father and before his angels. (Revelation 3:5.)

It is important to note that the word "conquers" used in this verse has a clear technical meaning when used by the apostle John. In 1 John it is translated "overcome". We are told: *Who is it that overcomes the world except the one who believes that Jesus is the Son of God?* (1 John 5:5).

Putting these two statements together it means that it is the believer in Jesus as Son of God whose name is never blotted out of the book of life. It is those who refuse to believe whose names are blotted out and they are responsible for the consequences. This is not determinism and there is no contradiction here with our Lord's explicit statements regarding both our capacity to believe, as moral beings created in the image of God, and our consequent personal responsibility to do so.

Coming on to the positive side, the wonderful thing about the Christian message is that because salvation is a gift of God it is possible for us to know that our name is written in the book. On one occasion Jesus spoke to a group of his disciples on their return from a mission:

*The seventy-two returned with joy, saying, "Lord, even the
demons are subject to us in your name!" And he said to
them, "I saw Satan fall like lightning from heaven. Behold, I
have given you authority to tread on serpents and scorpions,
and over all the power of the enemy, and nothing shall hurt
you. Nevertheless, do not rejoice in this, that the spirits are
subject to you, but rejoice that your names are written in
heaven." (Luke 10:17–20.)*

Jesus saw the danger of them placing their confidence (*rejoicing*) in
the abilities he had given them, so he told them that their confidence
should not be in what they could do, but rather in the knowledge that
their names were written in heaven.

And how could they know that? Only by trusting in Jesus' word.
Here, once more, is the crucial issue. We humans have a tendency
to put our trust in anything other than God: our deeds, our merits,
or even our spiritual gifts, as in this case. Like Abraham, we have to
learn to trust what God says. Everything will ultimately depend on it
– including the quality of our life and works. God is deeply interested
in our works, but the secret of being able to do them does not lie in
those works themselves but in placing our trust in God. I repeat:
salvation is from God – it is his gift apart from any merit we have.
And God has given us the wonderful capacity and freedom to receive
the gift of salvation by faith. As Paul has written:

*For by grace you have been saved through faith. And this is
not your own doing; it is the gift of God, not a result of works,
so that no one may boast. For we are his workmanship,
created in Christ Jesus for good works, which God prepared
beforehand, that we should walk in them. (Ephesians 2:8–10.)*

Rising from the sleep of death

The hope of resurrection expressed in Daniel 12 is not the product
of myth, fantasy, or utopian wish-fulfilment. According to Paul,

resurrection is like a great harvest, guaranteed by the all-important appearance of the firstfruits:

> *But in fact Christ has been raised from the dead, the firstfruits of those who have fallen asleep. For as by a man came death, by a man has come also the resurrection of the dead. For as in Adam all die, so also in Christ shall all be made alive. But each in his own order: Christ the firstfruits, then at his coming those who belong to Christ. Then comes the end.... (1 Corinthians 15:20–24.)*

Paul here uses the term "sleep" as a synonym for death; but it was Daniel who was the first to do so. The English word "cemetery" means "a place where people sleep", and bears its own witness to the biblical teaching. Just as sleep is temporary, there will also be an awakening from death. For Paul and Daniel, at the time of the end there will be a vindication of their hope in the resurrection of the body. That hope is guaranteed by the resurrection of Christ, an event that is already part of world history. It lies at the heart of the Christian message, and it is a message that I hold to be true – on the basis of very substantial evidence.

The New Atheists are constantly telling us that they are scientifically literate people who are prepared to follow evidence where it leads. However, I do not get that impression from their books. I find that they have not begun to take seriously the historical evidence for the existence of Jesus, let alone his resurrection. For anyone who is open to consideration of the evidence, I have attempted to give an account of it in my book *Gunning for God*, and therefore will not repeat it here.

For those who trust Christ, one of the practical implications of his resurrection is that it gives their life and work for him a wonderful, ultimate validation. It also guarantees them a glorious resurrection in the future. At the end of his lengthy defence of the resurrection, Paul adds:

*Therefore, my beloved brothers, be steadfast, immovable,
always abounding in the work of the Lord, knowing that in
the Lord your labour is not in vain. (1 Corinthians 15:58.)*

Centuries earlier, Daniel expressed it this way:

*And those who are wise shall shine like the brightness of the
sky above; and those who turn many to righteousness, like the
stars for ever and ever. (Daniel 12:3.)*

At no stage in history should the grim elements in the prophecy
be taken as a fatalistic argument to detract us from working for the
good of our fellow-citizens, and sowing peace and truth where we
can. Even in the worst of times it is possible for men and women to
turn many to righteousness, and shine like the stars for ever and ever.
The heavenly messenger then gives Daniel a final instruction:

*But you, Daniel, shut up the words and seal the book, until
the time of the end. Many shall run to and fro, and knowledge
shall increase. (Daniel 12:4.)*

We have tried to understand as much as we can of the book of Daniel,
but we must realize that there are aspects of it, and information in it,
that will not find their full relevance and application until the time of
the end. This ought not to surprise us. A similar thing happened with
the prophecies concerning the death, resurrection, and ascension
of the Messiah, particularly on the day of Pentecost. Peter was able
then to explain from Scripture exactly what point had been reached
in God's great scheme for redemption and restoration. We who live
between that time and the time of the end must remain humble
and open to the fact that we don't understand everything. In all our
running to and fro, and increase of knowledge, we might even be
wrong about some of our attempts to understand prophecy!

How long?

The vision was over. Indeed, the whole series of visions was over. But there was something still to be learned. Daniel describes in the first person how he saw three figures – one on each bank of the river, and one (the glorious one, dressed in linen) above the stream that still flowed beneath him:

> And someone said to the man clothed in linen, who was above the waters of the stream, "How long shall it be till the end of these wonders?" And I heard the man clothed in linen, who was above the waters of the stream; he raised his right hand and his left hand towards heaven and swore by him who lives for ever that it would be for a time, times, and half a time, and that when the shattering of the power of the holy people comes to an end all these things would be finished. I heard, but I did not understand. (Daniel 12:6–8.)

The question asked by the unidentified *someone* (might it have been Daniel himself?) was the question that had been uppermost in Daniel's mind for years – as we have seen in chapters 7, 8, and 9. Note that the question was not about whether these things would happen or when they would happen, but *how long shall it be till the end of these wonders?* That is, how long would the final period of horror for Daniel's nation last? The answer is given in a dramatic and solemn fashion. The man above the river raises both hands to heaven and swears a solemn oath that it would be limited to *a time, times, and half a time.* Our Lord similarly promised his disciples that, at the future time of tribulation, *those days will be cut short* (Matthew 24:22).

Daniel heard what was said, but confessed that he didn't understand. He simply asked the figure above the river: *O my lord, what shall be the outcome of these things?* On receiving the answer, Daniel finishes his book:

*He said, "Go your way, Daniel, for the words are shut up
and sealed until the time of the end. Many shall purify
themselves and make themselves white and be refined, but
the wicked shall act wickedly. And none of the wicked shall
understand, but those who are wise shall understand. And
from the time that the regular burnt offering is taken away
and the abomination that makes desolate is set up, there
shall be 1,290 days. Blessed is he who waits and arrives at the
1,335 days. But go your way till the end. And you shall rest
and shall stand in your allotted place at the end of the days."
(Daniel 12:9–13.)*

There remained much that Daniel did not understand, as there
remains much that we do not understand. It is sealed until the time
comes when it will be needed. In the meantime, Daniel went on his
way until this life for him came to an end. But that would not be his
ultimate destiny. He would rest in the sleep of death, but he will stand
up again in resurrection. (The Greek word for resurrection, *anastasis*,
that is used in the New Testament, literally means "a standing up
again".) Daniel survived Babylon, he survived Medo-Persia, and he
will eventually survive death itself.

And if we have placed our trust in Jesus, the Son of Man, the Son
of God, we too have our own allotted eternal place. The Lord Jesus
has left us these remarkable words:

*"Let not your hearts be troubled. Believe in God; believe
also in me. In my Father's house are many rooms. If it were
not so, would I have told you that I go to prepare a place
for you? And if I go and prepare a place for you, I will come
again and will take you to myself, that where I am you may
be also. And you know the way to where I am going." Thomas
said to him, "Lord, we do not know where you are going. How
can we know the way?" Jesus said to him, "I am the way, and
the truth, and the life. No one comes to the Father except
through me." (John 14:1–6.)*

THE NATURE OF THE KINGDOM OF GOD

The word "kingdom" in biblical usage has several different meanings, depending on its context.

First of all, it may refer to *the authority to rule*. For instance, when King David organized the materials for the building of the temple at Jerusalem he prayed in front of his nation:

> *Yours is the kingdom, O Lord, and you are exalted as head above all. Both riches and honour come from you, and you rule over all. (1 Chronicles 29:11–12.)*

Clearly David was referring to the fact that God is the ruler of the universe. Similarly in the New Testament Jesus encouraged his disciples to *seek first the kingdom of God and his righteousness, and all these things will be added to you* (Matthew 6:33). He meant that they were to seek God's rule in their lives and the lives of others.

Thus, in the first instance, the kingdom of God is the rule of God; as such it has always existed, exists still, and will always exist. Therefore, the kingdom of God *is*. This was one of the important things that Nebuchadnezzar had to learn about God: *His kingdom is an everlasting kingdom, and his dominion endures from generation to generation* (Daniel 4:3).

In light of this, when Daniel speaks of God setting up a kingdom in the days of certain kings, he cannot be referring to God's eternal rule as going on in eternity, but rather to how that rule touches history at specific times. This reminds us that one of the central expectations of the Old Testament is the coming of Messiah, the King.

This messianic hope can be traced back to the origins of the nation of Israel. When God called Abraham from the very region where Daniel was exiled, he promised that kings would come from Abraham's descendants. That promise was realized in part in the illustrious King David, who united the nation and ruled over Israel from his capital in Jerusalem. However, David was aware that he was not the final fulfilment of the prophecy; nor indeed was his son Solomon, although Solomon started his reign with great promise. God was speaking of a future son of David who would reign on David's throne for ever (2 Samuel 7:13).

Sadly first Israel and then Judah compromised with the idolatrous practices that emanated from the tribes and nations around them. The prophets warned the nation again and again that judgment was inevitable if they failed to repent and abandon their idolatry. Israel refused to do so, and was overrun by Assyria. Later, as Daniel among others records, Judah was subsequently overrun by Babylon for the very same reason.

When in that sense Israel and Judah lost their kingdoms, it must have seemed to many that the promise of a future King Messiah had finally been extinguished. Yet the very prophets who had announced the deportations to Assyria and Babylon also spoke of the hope of a future restoration for Israel.

Daniel clearly shared that hope, as his message to Nebuchadnezzar shows. With historical hindsight, we know that after centuries of silence another prophet finally arose, John the Baptist, who announced the arrival of Messiah the King. As the earliest records show, John pointed to Jesus who began his teaching by announcing, *the time is fulfilled, and the kingdom of God is at hand; repent and believe in the gospel* (Mark 1:15).

The precise nature of the kingdom announced by Jesus was of great concern to the religious and political authorities of the time, led by the high priest and Pontius Pilate, respectively. They did not approve of Jesus' increasing popularity with the crowds. They felt threatened when the air began to buzz with the notion that Jesus might even be the long awaited Messiah who would lead a popular revolt against the Roman occupying power and set their nation and capital city free.

The ancient historian Luke records two very significant events that occurred when Jesus was brought as a child to be presented to God in the temple at Jerusalem.

> *Now there was a man in Jerusalem, whose name was Simeon, and this man was righteous and devout, waiting for the consolation of Israel, and the Holy Spirit was upon him. And it had been revealed to him by the Holy Spirit that he would not see death before he had seen the Lord's Christ. And he came in the Spirit into the temple, and when the parents brought in the child Jesus, to do for him according to the custom of the Law, he took him up in his arms and blessed God and said, "Lord, now you are letting your servant depart in peace, according to your word; for my eyes have seen your salvation that you have prepared in the presence of all peoples, a light for revelation to the Gentiles, and for glory to your people Israel."*
>
> *And his father and his mother marvelled at what was said about him. And Simeon blessed them and said to Mary his mother, "Behold, this child is appointed for the fall and rising of many in Israel, and for a sign that is opposed (and a sword will pierce through your own soul also), so that thoughts from many hearts may be revealed."*
>
> *And there was a prophetess, Anna, the daughter of Phanuel, of the tribe of Asher. She was advanced in years, having lived with her husband seven years from when she was a virgin, and then as a widow until she was eighty-four. She did not depart from the temple, worshipping with fasting and prayer night and day. And coming up at that very hour she began to give thanks to God and to speak of him to all who were waiting for the redemption of Jerusalem. (Luke 2:25–38.)*

Simeon had been told that *he would not see death before he had seen the Lord's Christ* – the Messiah. One day in the temple at Jerusalem Simeon recognized Jesus as the Messiah. Also, around the same time, there was a prophetess, Anna, who spoke of the Messiah *to all who were waiting for the redemption of Jerusalem*. These two ideas – the coming of the Messiah, and the liberation of Jerusalem – were inextricably connected in Jewish expectation. When Jesus started teaching, it was not surprising, therefore, that the crowds and the authorities paid close attention to what he had to say about his kingdom.

And there was much more to it than some of them initially thought, as was evident on an occasion that Luke records, when Jesus spoke first to some Pharisees and then to his disciples about the nature of that kingdom:

> *Being asked by the Pharisees when the kingdom of God would come, he answered them, "The kingdom of God is not coming with signs to be observed, nor will they say, 'Look, here it is!' or 'There!' for behold, the kingdom of God is in the midst of you." (Luke 17:20–21.)*

The Pharisees, a strictly conservative group within Judaism, were interested in an outward visible kingdom. It is clear from what Jesus said to his disciples on this occasion that such an outward and visible kingdom was certainly part of God's programme. That kingdom would one day come. However, by concentrating on the outward and visible aspect of it, the Pharisees were in danger of missing something of prior and vital importance. The King himself was standing in front of them, and they couldn't see it! The reason was not for lack of evidence – Jesus had given a great deal of that. Their problem was that they lacked the discernment necessary to perceive that Jesus' kingdom had a spiritual dimension.

Jesus explained this in detail to one of the Pharisees, a leading Jewish scholar in Jerusalem named Nicodemus, who came to Jesus by night for a discussion about the kingdom of God (or kingdom of heaven, as it is also called). *Jesus answered him, "Truly, truly, I say to you, unless one is born again he cannot see the kingdom of God"* (John 3:3). Jesus went on to explain to this astonished professor of theology that the way to be born again – to receive the eternal life of which Jesus was speaking, and thus to enter his kingdom – was to trust in him: *For God so loved the world, that he gave his only Son, that whoever believes in him should not perish but have eternal life* (John 3:16).

It had never occurred to Nicodemus that the kingdom of God had an intensely spiritual dimension. In common with the experts of his day, and with many of the common people, Nicodemus would have been looking for an outward political kingdom that would rid the nation of the hated Roman occupation army once and for all, and set them free. They wanted the dominion of the "iron empire" in Daniel's vision to cease.

However, when you consider who King Messiah is and what he stands for, a spiritual dimension to his kingdom is inevitable. The existence and survival of any kingdom depends on the loyalty of its citizens to the king; but when the king is none other than God incarnate, it is clear that more than politics and physical freedom from oppression will be involved. There must be trust, and loyalty of the human heart. It was, after all, lack of trust that caused the problem in the first place, when the deadly poison of sin entered the world. The way back must involve learning to trust God. It is when a person learns to trust Jesus Christ, the Son of God, as Saviour and Lord that a spiritual miracle occurs: he or she is born again into the kingdom of God.

The question now arises of the relationship between the inner spiritual kingdom and the outer visible kingdom. This brings us back to Luke's record of what Jesus said to his disciples on the occasion recorded above.

"The days are coming when you will desire to see one of the days of the Son of Man, and you will not see it. And they will say to you, 'Look, there!' or 'Look, here!' Do not go out or follow them. For as the lightning flashes and lights up the sky from one side to the other, so will the Son of Man be in his day. But first he must suffer many things and be rejected by this generation. Just as it was in the days of Noah, so will it be in the days of the Son of Man. They were eating and drinking

and marrying and being given in marriage, until the day
when Noah entered the ark, and the flood came and destroyed
them all. Likewise, just as it was in the days of Lot – they
were eating and drinking, buying and selling, planting and
building, but on the day when Lot went out from Sodom, fire
and sulphur rained from heaven and destroyed them all – so
will it be on the day when the Son of Man is revealed. On that
day, let the one who is on the housetop, with his goods in the
house, not come down to take them away, and likewise let the
one who is in the field not turn back. Remember Lot's wife.
Whoever seeks to preserve his life will lose it, but whoever
loses his life will keep it. I tell you, in that night there will be
two in one bed. One will be taken and the other left. There
will be two women grinding together. One will be taken and
the other left." And they said to him, "Where, Lord?" He said
to them, "Where the corpse is, there the vultures will gather."
(Luke 17:22–37.)

Just as the Pharisees made the mistake of concentrating on the visible aspect of the kingdom of God, to the extent that they missed its spiritual nature, it is possible to make the opposite mistake and to so emphasize the spiritual dimension of God's kingdom that we miss its visible aspect. Therefore Jesus also explained to his disciples that the kingdom of God would come in such a way that not only would it be visible, it would be universally visible.

Jesus said this in order to protect his followers from false claims that the kingdom of God had already come without their having noticed it. He pointed out that people would come and claim that they knew where the kingdom of God was. They would say, *Look, there! Look, here!* Such claims were to be ignored, for the simple reason that when the Son of Man is finally revealed, it will be immediately and universally unmistakable.

However, as a further protection from false anticipation, Jesus told the disciples that certain events would happen first. He would have to suffer many things. His claims would be examined and eventually rejected by his contemporaries. But they should not be surprised at this, bearing in mind the reaction in earlier times to the preaching of Noah and Lot.

We can see, then, that the kingdom of God involves at least two phases: an initial spiritual phase, and a later outward manifestation that will await Jesus' return.

The nature and circumstances of the rejection of Jesus give us further insight into the nature of his kingdom. Luke records how Jesus rode into Jerusalem on a donkey, on what we now call Palm Sunday. The meaning of this act was unmistakable – Jesus was coming to the nation as its rightful Messiah King.

> As he was drawing near – already on the way down the
> Mount of Olives – the whole multitude of his disciples began
> to rejoice and praise God with a loud voice for all the mighty
> works that they had seen, saying, "Blessed is the King who
> comes in the name of the Lord! Peace in heaven and glory
> in the highest!" And some of the Pharisees in the crowd said
> to him, "Teacher, rebuke your disciples." He answered, "I tell
> you, if these were silent, the very stones would cry out." (Luke
> 19:37–40.)

The ruling chief priests took a stronger line. They conspired to have Jesus arrested by a squad of Roman soldiers, and arraigned him before their court:

> When day came, the assembly of the elders of the people
> gathered together, both chief priests and scribes. And they
> led him away to their council, and they said, "If you are the
> Christ, tell us." But he said to them, "If I tell you, you will
> not believe, and if I ask you, you will not answer. But from
> now on the Son of Man shall be seated at the right hand of
> the power of God." So they all said, "Are you the Son of God,
> then?" And he said to them, "You say that I am." Then they
> said, "What further testimony do we need? We have heard it
> ourselves from his own lips." (Luke 22:66–71.)

As Jesus had predicted to his disciples, the religious authorities examined his claims (in an unbelievably superficial manner) and rejected them. Such rejection would mean that Jesus would ascend to the right hand of the power of God. Indeed, Matthew adds that Jesus said to the Sanhedrin: *I tell you, from now on you will see the Son of Man seated at the right hand of Power and coming on the clouds of heaven* (Matthew 26:64).

This last phrase, as we know, is taken straight from Daniel (7:13). Jesus was therefore claiming to be the divine Son of Man that Daniel saw in his vision, who would come on the clouds of heaven to establish the kingdom of God. Such a claim was blasphemous in the eyes of the high priests, and they condemned Jesus to death.

However, they did not possess the authority to execute anybody. The Romans had withheld it from them. In order to secure Jesus' death, therefore, they needed the corresponding verdict from the Roman authorities; so they now sent Jesus to them:

> *Then the whole company of them arose and brought him*
> *before Pilate. And they began to accuse him, saying, "We*
> *found this man misleading our nation and forbidding us to*
> *give tribute to Caesar, and saying that he himself is Christ, a*
> *king." And Pilate asked him, "Are you the King of the Jews?"*
> *And he answered him, "You have said so." Then Pilate said to*
> *the chief priests and the crowds, "I find no guilt in this man."*
> *But they were urgent, saying, "He stirs up the people, teaching*
> *throughout all Judea, from Galilee even to this place." (Luke*
> *23:1–5.)*

Armed with this geographical detail, Pilate sent Jesus to King Herod in whose jurisdiction Galilee fell, but Herod sent him back to Pilate for judgment. A verdict was then pronounced:

> *Pilate then called together the chief priests and the rulers*
> *and the people, and said to them, "You brought me this man*
> *as one who was misleading the people. And after examining*
> *him before you, behold, I did not find this man guilty of any*

of your charges against him. Neither did Herod, for he sent him back to us. Look, nothing deserving death has been done by him. I will therefore punish and release him." (Luke 23:13–16.)

For our understanding of the various phases of God's kingdom, this "not guilty" verdict is very important. The apostle John gives us more insight into why it was made, by recording the details of Pilate's cross-examination of Jesus:

So Pilate entered his headquarters again and called Jesus and said to him, "Are you the King of the Jews?" Jesus answered, "Do you say this of your own accord, or did others say it to you about me?" Pilate answered, "Am I a Jew? Your own nation and the chief priests have delivered you over to me. What have you done?" Jesus answered, "My kingdom is not of this world. If my kingdom were of this world, my servants would have been fighting, that I might not be delivered over to the Jews. But my kingdom is not from the world." Then Pilate said to him, "So you are a king?" Jesus answered, "You say that I am a king. For this purpose I was born and for this purpose I have come into the world – to bear witness to the truth. Everyone who is of the truth listens to my voice." Pilate said to him, "What is truth?" After he had said this, he went back outside to the Jews and told them, "I find no guilt in him." (John 18:33–38.)

Jesus made it completely clear to Pilate that his kingdom posed no political threat to Pilate at that time, for the simple reason that his kingdom was *not of this world*. (Nor would it be "of this world" until Jesus' return, as he had made clear to the high priests.) Pilate had incontrovertible evidence to back this up: when he had sent the soldiers to arrest Jesus, he had not resisted arrest. In fact, Jesus had commanded his disciples to put away the two swords they had between them (Luke 22:38). His kingdom was evidently not a worldly kingdom with armies that would defend their king by force. Pilate, who was a shrewd political and military operator, could see that Jesus was harmless in that sense, and gave his verdict accordingly. But his ruling was not allowed to stand – not because it was false, but because the religious authorities and the crowds eventually forced him to back down and deliver Jesus up to be crucified.

The importance of grasping this is obvious in a world scarred by religious military conflict. As Jesus told his disciples, because the current phase of his kingdom is *not of this world*, it would be inappropriate to attempt to defend him or his message by the use of violence. One of the scandals in the history of Christendom is that misunderstanding of the Scriptures on this score has led to many deaths. However, since I have written on this topic in detail elsewhere (in *Gunning for God*), I content myself here by saying that those who take weapons in the cause of Christ are not following him but actually disobeying him.

Jesus had said repeatedly that he would be rejected and killed, but the disciples had not taken it in. It contradicted their deeply ingrained expectations of what the Messiah would be like and what he would do when he came. In his account of the events surrounding the death and resurrection of Jesus, Luke records the dejection and puzzlement of some of those disciples, and in so doing shows us what the problem was. After the crucifixion, Luke mentions two disciples who were walking to the village of Emmaus about seven miles outside Jerusalem. They were unaware that Jesus had risen. Luke records how Jesus joined them on their walk, but they did not recognize him. The conversation turned to the events that had just occurred in Jerusalem, and the two disciples were feeling very dejected. Jesus asked them what they were talking about and they said:

> *Concerning Jesus of Nazareth, a man who was a prophet*
> *mighty in deed and word before God and all the people,*
> *and how our chief priests and rulers delivered him up to be*
> *condemned to death, and crucified him. (Luke 24:19–20.)*

And then they made explicit the ground of their disappointment:

But we had hoped that he was the one to redeem Israel. (Luke 24:21.)

They had expected liberation and it had not come. Their leader had been executed. It appeared to be all over. When they still failed to recognize him Jesus said to them:

"O foolish ones, and slow of heart to believe all that the prophets have spoken! Was it not necessary that the Christ should suffer these things and enter into his glory?" And beginning with Moses and all the Prophets, he interpreted to them in all the Scriptures the things concerning himself. (Luke 24:25–27.)

To their utter astonishment and joy they were soon to discover that it was not all over. Luke records how Jesus was made known to them as he broke bread with them that evening. The stranger conversing with them had been none other than the risen Lord.

During a period of forty days after the resurrection Jesus appeared to his disciples on several occasions, and it is not surprising that such appearances revived in them the hope of freedom for their nation. After all, they now knew that he had power over death. Surely the time was ripe for him to take political action, overthrow the government, and set the nation free? Eventually, they decided to put the matter to him. At the start of the book of Acts, which chronicles the beginnings of the Christian church, Luke tells us about it:

So when they had come together, they asked him, "Lord, will you at this time restore the kingdom to Israel?" (Acts 1:6.)

Their question was precise. They did not say, "Lord, do you intend to restore the kingdom to Israel?" They would not have asked that question, for the simple reason that they already fully expected such a restoration. That is, their question was not about the *fact* of the restoration but its *timing*. It was not, "Are you going to do it?" but, "Are you going to do it *now*?" Jesus replied accordingly:

> *It is not for you to know times or seasons that the Father*
> *has fixed by his own authority. But you will receive power*
> *when the Holy Spirit has come upon you, and you will be my*
> *witnesses in Jerusalem and in all Judea and Samaria, and to*
> *the end of the earth. (Acts 1:7–8.)*

There are three main thrusts to Jesus' reply:

1.   The disciples were not to concern themselves regarding the timing of the restoration.

2.   That timing had already been fixed by the Father, and the restoration would happen at a time of his choosing.

3.   In the meantime their task was to witness to the world in the power of the soon-coming Holy Spirit.[45]

The next event that Luke records is the ascension of Jesus – further clear evidence that he was not going to restore the kingdom to Israel, with himself as King, at that time. On the other hand, the ascension had a positive message to convey. It was relayed to the disciples by two men in white robes, who suddenly appeared beside them:

> *Men of Galilee, why do you stand looking into heaven? This*
> *Jesus, who was taken up from you into heaven, will come in*
> *the same way as you saw him go into heaven. (Acts 1:11.)*

At the ascension they saw Jesus move vertically away from the earth's surface and disappear into a cloud. God intended this event to be a thought model to help the disciples grasp the fact that, just as Jesus left the earth physically and visibly, he should so return.

The importance of understanding the ascension is seen in Peter's sermon on the day of Pentecost. He explained to the crowd that the events that had happened in the preceding eight weeks had been predicted in the Old Testament. The prophet Joel had foretold that there would be a great outpouring of the Holy Spirit before the final day of the Lord (the day of judgment). That happened on the day of

Pentecost. It was very significant, because it showed that the words of a much more recent prophet had been fulfilled.

It was only about three years earlier that John the Baptist had announced that Jesus was the one who would baptize in the Holy Spirit (Acts 1:5). Joel and John were both talking about the same event. Because the Spirit had come, said Peter, it demonstrated that something else had been fulfilled. It had been predicted by the prophet, and also centuries earlier by King David: *For you will not abandon my soul to Hades, or let your Holy One see corruption* (Acts 2:27, quoting from Psalm 16:10).

Peter argued that David had obviously not been talking about himself. Everyone listening to Peter knew that David's body still lay in a tomb not far from where Peter was speaking. David had been prophesying about the resurrection of the Messiah. That event had just recently taken place: Peter and the others were witnesses.

Not only had Jesus been raised from the dead, he had been exalted to supremacy at the right hand of God. Peter quoted more of what David had said: *The Lord said to my Lord, Sit at my right hand, until I make your enemies your footstool* (Acts 2:34–35).

David did not ascend to the heavens, so he was referring to God (the Lord) speaking to someone greater than David (David's Lord, the Messiah) and inviting him to sit at the position of supreme power. Thus the prophecies of Scripture combine with the events in Jerusalem to make it certain that *God has made him both Lord and Christ* (Messiah), *this Jesus whom you crucified* (Acts 2:36).

It was important for both Peter and his audience to understand exactly what point in history had been reached. Recent events constituted a major step forward in God's programme for redemption. Jesus had died, risen, and ascended to God's right hand. But that was not the end of the story – the Lord Jesus would be at God's right hand *until* God's enemies were dealt with. Restoration would clearly not be complete until that occurred.

Though not stated explicitly in Peter's first sermon, the connection between that final restoration and the return of Jesus is made in Peter's second major address in Jerusalem, as recorded by Luke. On that occasion, through Peter and John, God healed a lame man at the Beautiful Gate of the temple. Peter at once used this demonstration of the power of God to explain to the people that the miracle had been done in the name of Jesus – whom they had killed but whom God had raised from the dead.

Peter then pointed out that, since it had been foretold, the people should have understood what had happened:

> And now, brothers, I know that you acted in ignorance, as did also your rulers. But what God foretold by the mouth of all the prophets, that his Christ would suffer, he thus fulfilled. Repent therefore, and turn again, that your sins may be blotted out, that times of refreshing may come from the presence of the Lord, and that he may send the Christ appointed for you, Jesus, whom heaven must receive until the time for restoring all the things about which God spoke by the mouth of his holy prophets long ago. (Acts 3:17–21.)

We notice that Peter once more uses the temporal conjunction, *until*. This time it is not referring to the task of dealing with God's enemies as much as to the positive restoration of all things. It includes the restoration of the kingdom to Israel, mentioned in Acts 1:6, but it is a much greater programme than that. Peter says this restoration will occur at the return of Jesus.

This is also the implication of one of the phrases in the prayer that Jesus taught his disciples: *Your kingdom come, your will be done, on earth as it is in heaven* (Matthew 6:10). God's will is not yet being done on earth as it is in heaven, but one day it will be.

Summary

During his public teaching, and notably around the time of his death, Jesus made it increasingly clear to his disciples that his kingdom would be in two phases.

The first and primary phase would be a spiritual kingdom, entered into by repenting and trusting Jesus as Saviour and Lord, thereby receiving eternal life – being *born again* into the kingdom of God.

Following the ascension of Jesus and his sending of the Holy Spirit, this message of the kingdom, the gospel of Jesus Christ, is to be preached by Christians until Jesus returns.

At that return, the second phase of the kingdom will be set in operation. Christ will come as earth's rightful king. It is for these reasons that we refer to both a first and a second coming of Christ.

APPENDIX B

TRANSLATION OF THE TEXT ON THE CYRUS CYLINDER⁴⁶

Translation by Irving Finkel Assistant Keeper, Department of the Middle East

[When ... Mar]duk, king of the whole of heaven and earth, the .... who, in his ..., lays waste his ....

[...]broad ? in intelligence, ... who inspects} (?) the wor]ld quarters (regions)

[...…....] his [first]born (=Belshazzar), a low person was put in charge of his country,

but [...] he set [a (...) counter]feit over them.

He ma[de] a counterfeit of Esagil, [and ......…........]... for Ur and the rest of the cult-cities.

Rites inappropriate to them, [impure] fo[od-offerings ….....
....] disrespectful [...] were daily gabbled, and, as an insult,

371

he brought the daily offerings to a halt; he inter[fered with the rites and] instituted [.......] within the sanctuaries. In his mind, reverential fear of Marduk, king of the gods, came to an end.

He did yet more evil to his city every day; ... his [people ....], he brought ruin on them all by a yoke without relief.

Enlil-of-the-gods became extremely angry at their complaints, and [...] their territory. The gods who lived within them left their shrines,

angry that he had made (them) enter into Shuanna (Babylon). Ex[alted Marduk, Enlil-of-the-Go]ds, relented. He changed his mind about all the settlements whose sanctuaries were in ruins,

and the population of the land of Sumer and Akkad who had become like corpses, and took pity on them. He inspected and checked all the countries,

seeking for the upright king of his choice. He took the hand of Cyrus, king of the city of Anshan, and called him by his name, proclaiming him aloud for the kingship over all of everything.

He made the land of Guti and all the Median troops prostrate themselves at his feet, while he shepherded in justice and righteousness the black-headed people

whom he had put under his care. Marduk, the great lord, who nurtures his people, saw with pleasure his fine deeds and true heart,

and ordered that he should go to Babylon. He had him take the road to Tintir (Babylon), and, like a friend and companion, he walked at his side.

372

His vast troops whose number, like the water in a river, could not be counted, were marching fully-armed at his side.

He had him enter without fighting or battle right into Shuanna; he saved his city Babylon from hardship. He handed over to him Nabonidus, the king who did not fear him.

All the people of Tintir, of all Sumer and Akkad, nobles and governors, bowed down before him and kissed his feet, rejoicing over his kingship and their faces shone.

The lord through whose help all were rescued from death and who saved them all from distress and hardship, they blessed him sweetly and praised his name. ....

I am Cyrus, king of the universe, the great king, the powerful king, king of Babylon, king of Sumer and Akkad, king of the four quarters of the world,

son of Cambyses, the great king, king of the city of Anshan, grandson of Cyrus, the great king, ki[ng of the ci]ty of Anshan, descendant of Teispes, the great king, king of the city of Anshan,

the perpetual seed of kingship, whose reign Bel (Marduk)and Nabu love, and with whose kingship, to their joy, they concern themselves. When I went as harbinger of peace i[nt]o Babylon

I founded my sovereign residence within the palace amid celebration and rejoicing. Marduk, the great lord, bestowed on me as my destiny the great magnanimity of one who loves Babylon, and I every day sought him out in awe.

My vast troops were marching peaceably in Babylon, and the whole of [Sumer] and Akkad had nothing to fear.

I sought the safety of the city of Babylon and all its sanctuaries. As for the population of Babylon [..., w]ho as if without div[ine intention] had endured a yoke not decreed for them,

I soothed their weariness; I freed them from their bonds(?). Marduk, the great lord, rejoiced at [my good] deeds,

and he pronounced a sweet blessing over me, Cyrus, the king who fears him, and over Cambyses, the son [my] issue, [and over] all my troops,

that we might live happily in his presence, in well-being. At his exalted command, all kings who sit on thrones,

from every quarter, from the Upper Sea to the Lower Sea, those who inhabit [remote distric]ts (and) the kings of the land of Amurru who live in tents, all of them,

brought their weighty tribute into Shuanna, and kissed my feet. From [Shuanna] I sent back to their places to the city of Ashur and Susa,

Akkad, the land of Eshnunna, the city of Zamban, the city of Meturnu, Der, as far as the border of the land of Guti – the sanctuaries across the river Tigris – whose shrines had earlier become dilapidated,

the gods who lived therein, and made permanent sanctuaries for them. I collected together all of their people and returned them to their settlements,

and the gods of the land of Sumer and Akkad which Nabonidus – to the fury of the lord of the gods – had brought into Shuanna, at the command of Marduk, the great lord,

I returned them unharmed to their cells, in the sanctuaries that make them happy. May all the gods that I returned to their sanctuaries, every day before Bel and Nabu, ask for a long life for me, and mention my good deeds, and say to Marduk, my lord, this: "Cyrus, the king who fears you, and Cambyses his son,

may they be the provisioners of our shrines until distant (?) days, and the population of Babylon call blessings on my kingship. I have enabled all the lands to live in peace.

Every day I increased by [… ge]ese, two ducks and ten pigeons the [former offerings] of geese, ducks and pigeons.

I strove to strengthen the defences of the wall Imgur-Enlil, the great wall of Babylon,

and [I completed] the quay of baked brick on the bank of the moat which an earlier king had bu[ilt but not com]pleted its work.

[I …… which did not surround the city] outside, which no earlier king had built, his workforce, the levee [from his land, in/int]o Shuanna.

[…..with bitum]en and baked brick I built anew, and [completed] its [work].

[…..] great [doors of cedarwood] with bronze cladding,

[and I installed] all their doors, threshold slabs and door fittings with copper parts. […........................] I saw within it an inscription of Ashurbanipal, a king who preceded me;

[…...] his … Marduk, the great lord, creator (?) of […]

[…...] my [… I presented] as a gift....................] your pleasure forever."

THE STRUCTURE OF THE BOOK OF DANIEL

Group 1	Group 2
Chapter 1	Chapter 6
Nebuchadnezzar reverently places God's vessels in his idol's temple.	Darius bans prayer to God for thirty days.
Daniel and others refuse to indulge in pagan impurities.	Daniel refuses to cease practising the Jewish religion.
Court officials sympathetic.	Court officials intrigue against him.
Daniel and his colleagues' physical and mental powers vindicated.	Daniel's policital loyalty to the king vindicated.
They are promoted to high office.	He is restored to high office.
Chapter 2	Chapter 7
A survey of the whole course of Gentile imperial power.	A survey of the whole course of Gentile imperial power.
Four empires in the form of a man.	Four empires in the form of wild beasts.
The fatal weakness: an incoherent mixture of iron and clay in the feet.	The hideous strength: a frightening mixture of animal destructiveness with human intelligence.
The whole man destroyed by the stone cut out by divine power. The universal messianic kingdom set up.	The final beast destroyed and universal domination given to the Son of Man.

Group 1	Group 2
Chapter 3	Chapter 8
Nebuchadnezzar thinks that "no god can deliver [the Jews] out of his hand".	The little horn: "none can deliver out of his hand".
He commands them to worship his god.	He stops the Jews' worship of their God, and defies the God himself.
The Jews defy him.	God's sanctuary and truth are finally vindicated.
They are preserved in the furnace.	
God's ability to deliver is thereby demonstrated.	
Chapter 4	Chapter 9
The glory of Babylon.	The desolations of Jerusalem.
Nebuchadnezzar is warned that he deserves discipline.	Israel's sins have brought on them the curse warned of in the Old Testament.
He persists in pride, is chastised, and his chastisement lasts for seven years.	Jerusalem will be restored, but Israel's persistence in sin will bring on further desolations lasting to the end of seventy times seven years.
He is then restored.	Jerusalem will be finally restored.
Chapter 5	Chapters 10–12
Belshazzar makes a god of his pleasures, but still recognizes the gods of stone, etc.	The king exalts himself above every god, and regards no god.
The writing on the wall.	The "writing of truth".
The end of Belshazzar and the end of the Babylonian empire.	The series of apparent "ends" leading up to "the time of the end", and eventually to the end itself.

DANIEL 11 AND HISTORY

Chapter 11 of the book of Daniel forms a fascinating commentary on historical events from a unique perspective. It describes events of considerable complexity, and the purpose of this appendix is to try to show how the text of Daniel fits in with information obtained from other historical sources.

> *And now I will show you the truth. Behold, three more kings shall arise in Persia, and a fourth shall be far richer than all of them. (Daniel 11:2.)*

Daniel is told that there will be four more kings in the Medo-Persian empire, with the fourth being the richest of all. Since Daniel was writing in the reign of Cyrus, the kings are Cambyses (530–522), Smerdis (522), Darius I (522–486), and finally Xerxes I (486–465), who was indeed fabulously wealthy. Xerxes used his wealth, exactly as Daniel predicted, to build up his power base and mount an attack on Greece:

> *And when he has become strong through his riches, he shall stir up all against the kingdom of Greece. (11:2.)*

In 500 BC an enclave of Ionian Greeks who had settled on the western coast of Asia Minor mounted an insurrection against Darius I, the father of Xerxes. They appealed to Athens for help, and made a raid on the Persian city of Sardis, which they burned. It took six years to quell the Greeks, and Darius vowed to punish the Athenians for getting involved. Darius's first attempt in 491 BC had to be abandoned because of a violent storm that wrecked much of his fleet.

A year later, in full view of the enemy, a Persian force landed on the plain of Marathon, and there followed one of the most famous battles of history. The Athenians, instead of remaining to defend their city, decided to come out and fight the invaders at Marathon. The odds were overwhelmingly against them, but their speed in closing with the enemy rendered the Persian bowmen ineffective and they were defeated. The Greek historian Herodotus records: "There fell in this battle of Marathon, on the side of the barbarians, about six thousand and four hundred men; on that of the Athenians, one hundred and ninety-two. Such was the number of the slain on the one side and the other." The remainder of the Persian fleet sailed for Athens, but the Athenian army reached the capital before them. (The famous marathon race owes its origin to the way the information was carried to Athens by a runner.) The Persians gave up and went home.

Darius was furious and determined even more to punish the Greeks. However, he died before the preparations for war were complete and left the campaign to his son Xerxes. Eventually, after some hesitation, Xerxes assembled a vast army and over a thousand ships. He gained a victory over the Greeks at Thermopylae, but was then defeated by them in the famous sea battle of Salamis.

The Medo-Persian empire limped on for a century and a half after that, and no further mention of that later history is made in Daniel's prophecy. We are next informed:

> *Then a mighty king shall arise, who shall rule with great dominion and do as he wills. And as soon as he has arisen, his kingdom shall be broken and divided towards the four winds of heaven, but not to his posterity, nor according to the authority with which he ruled, for his kingdom shall be plucked up and go to others beside these.* (11:3–4.)

If, as we think, this is a genuine prediction, it is very remarkable indeed, since it refers unmistakably to Alexander the Great, who rapidly rose to immense power and died very young. Because he had no direct heir his kingdom was split into four parts, each headed up by one of Alexander's erstwhile generals.

He is said to be a king who does *as he wills*, showing that the prophecies relayed to Daniel are not meant to indicate an arbitrary, deterministic rule of God over history that leaves human rulers (and everyone else) as helpless puppets. God's relationship to the historical process leaves Alexander, and others mentioned subsequently, free to act as responsible moral beings. Their authority and decisions are real, and have moral consequences for themselves and others.

After this introduction, from 11:5 the focus of Daniel's attention now narrows to the rivalries and tensions among two of the parts into which Alexander's vast empire disintegrated: the Seleucid kingdom (the kings of the north) and the Ptolemies (the kings of the south). "North" and "south" are relative to Palestine. The terms "king of the north" and "king of the south" are generic and apply to a number of different people in the course of the chapter – thirteen kings in all.

> *Then the king of the south shall be strong, but one of his princes shall be stronger than he and shall rule, and his authority shall be a great authority. (11:5.)*

And so it happened. In 316 BC another of Alexander's generals attacked Babylonia, and Seleucus fled to Egypt, where he assisted Ptolemy in winning the battle of Gaza against Antigonus. In a re-allocation of territory after the battle of Ipsus, in which Antigonus was killed, Seleucus – to whom the victory was attributed – received the lion's share of Antigonus's kingdom, and thus became the founder of the Seleucid dynasty.

The years passed, and the succeeding kings of the respective dynasties became weary of incessant strife. Around 250 BC the king of the south, Ptolemy II Philadelphus, and the king of the north, Antiochus II Theos, made an attempt to forge an alliance by marriage, in the manner indicated in the prophecy:

After some years they shall make an alliance, and the
daughter of the king of the south shall come to the king of the
north to make an agreement. (11:6.)

This arrangement was a disaster from the start. Ptolemy had a daughter, Berenice; and Antiochus (a weak man) agreed to divorce his wife, Laodice (who had given him two sons, Seleucus Callinicus and Antiochus), and marry Berenice. A grand wedding ensued, Antiochus received a huge dowry, and the respective kings thought that the future was assured.

However, Ptolemy died not long afterwards. Antiochus at once rejected Berenice, sending her back to Egypt, and took back his former wife, Laodice. Her gratitude (if it existed) was fleeting, since she proceeded to poison him and organize a contract murder on Berenice and her child. As the prophecy said of Berenice:

But she shall not retain the strength of her arm, and he and
his arm shall not endure, but she shall be given up, and her
attendants, he who fathered her, and he who supported her in
those times. And from a branch from her roots one shall arise
in his place. He shall come against the army and enter the
fortress of the king of the north, and he shall deal with them
and shall prevail. (11:6–7.)

Berenice's brother, Ptolemy III Euergetes, was determined to avenge his sister. He attacked Seleucia, the fortified port of the capital city of Antioch, captured it, and had Laodice executed. He annexed most of the Seleucid territory in Asia, and returned to Egypt with a great haul of booty, again as predicted.

He shall also carry off to Egypt their gods with their metal
images and their precious vessels of silver and gold... (11:8.)

This action is reminiscent of what Nebuchadnezzar did to Jerusalem, recorded in Daniel 1 – with one striking difference: Ptolemy carried off Seleucus's gods, whereas Nebuchadnezzar only carried back the vessels – for the simple reason that the Hebrews had no idols to their God. What Ptolemy did constituted a devastating blow for the northern kingdom, since removing a nation's gods was a sign of total conquest.

> ... and for some years he shall refrain from attacking the king of the north. Then the latter shall come into the realm of the king of the south but shall return to his own land. (11:8–9.)

For two years there was peace, until Seleucus II attempted an invasion of Egypt. His fleet foundered in a storm, and he had to return empty-handed. He died in a fall from a horse and was succeeded by his sons.

> His sons shall wage war and assemble a multitude of great forces, which shall keep coming and overflow and pass through, and again shall carry the war as far as his fortress. (11:10.)

These sons were Seleucus III, Ceraunus (226–223 – he was murdered in Turkey), followed by Antiochus III, "the Great" (223–187). Antiochus III managed to recover some of his dynastic pride by assembling a great force and recapturing the aforementioned fortress of Seleucia that was situated only sixteen miles away from his capital, Antioch. Its occupation by Egypt had been a great embarrassment. At that time the ruler of Egypt, Ptolemy IV Philopater (221–203), was a feeble and indecisive man whose forces were no match for those from the north, which swept through like an irresistible torrent. On the way through, Antiochus invaded Palestine and conquered a considerable part of it. Once again we note the imagery of a mighty river – as though Daniel, as he stood by the mighty Tigris, saw it as the carrier of history, bearing it inexorably into the future.

Ptolemy IV reacted with fury and sent his army to fight Antiochus III at Raphia, an Egyptian town on the border with Palestine.

> Then the king of the south, moved with rage, shall come out and fight with the king of the north. And he shall raise a great

multitude, but it shall be given into his hand. And when the multitude is taken away, his heart shall be exalted, and he shall cast down tens of thousands, but he shall not prevail. (11:11–12.)

The historian Polybius gives a fascinating account of the famous battle of Raphia that ensued. This passage gives a flavour of it:

By the beginning of spring Antiochus and Ptolemy had completed their preparations and were determined on deciding the fate of the Syrian expedition by a battle. Now Ptolemy started from Alexandria with an army of seventy thousand foot, five thousand horse, and seventy-three elephants, and Antiochus, on learning of his advance, concentrated his forces. These consisted first of Daae, Carmanians, and Cilicians, light-armed troops about five thousand in number organized and commanded by Byttacus the Macedonian. Under Theodotus the Aetolian, who had played the traitor to Ptolemy, was a force of ten thousand selected from every part of the kingdom and armed in the Macedonian manner, most of them with silver shields. The phalanx was about twenty thousand strong and was under the command of Nicarchus and Theodotus surnamed Hemiolius. There were Agrianian and Persian bowmen and slingers to the number of two thousand, and with them two thousand Thracians, all under the command of Menedemus of Alabanda. Aspasianus the Mede had under him a force of about five thousand Medes, Cissians, Cadusians, and Carmanians. The Arabs and neighbouring tribes numbered about ten thousand and were commanded by Zabdibelus. Hippolochus the Thessalian commanded the mercenaries from Greece, five thousand in number. Antiochus had also fifteen hundred Cretans under Eurylochus and a thousand Neocretans under Zelys of Gortyna. With these were five hundred Lydian javelineers and a thousand Cardaces under Lysimachus the Gaul. The cavalry numbered six thousand in

383

*all, four thousand of them being commanded by Antipater
the king's nephew and the rest by Themison. The whole
army of Antiochus consisted of sixty-two thousand foot,
six thousand horse, and a hundred and two elephants.
(Histories, 5.79.)*

Antiochus III was defeated and, according to Polybius, lost more than ten thousand of his troops. However, the indolent Egyptian monarch, Ptolemy IV, did not capitalize on his resounding victory. He made peace with Antiochus and, according to Polybius, abandoned himself to a life of dissolution that eventually helped fan the flames of unrest in Egypt (*Histories*, 14.12.3–4). His infant son Ptolemy V under a regent, Agathocles, succeeded Ptolemy IV.

After spending around fourteen years greatly enlarging the borders of his realm as far as central Asia, Antiochus III saw a new opportunity to avenge himself against the Egyptians. Forming a league with the king of Macedonia, Philip V, he recaptured the southern part of Syria and invaded Judea. After an initial setback in 200 BC he finally defeated the Egyptians under their general, Scopas, at Paneas, near the headwaters of the Jordan. The Egyptians retreated to the coastal fortress of Sidon, which Antiochus besieged. Scopas and his troops were eventually starved into surrendering the city. Thus Antiochus III occupied the territory once held by Israel.

Daniel describes these events as follows:

*For the king of the north shall again raise a multitude, greater
than the first. And after some years he shall come on with a
great army and abundant supplies. In those times many shall
rise against the king of the south, and the violent among your
own people shall lift themselves up in order to fulfil the vision,
but they shall fail. Then the king of the north shall come and
throw up siege-works and take a well-fortified city. And the
forces of the south shall not stand, or even his best troops, for
there shall be no strength to stand. (11:13–15.)*

We should recall that the heavenly messenger is relating all of this to Daniel; so the reference to *the violent among your own people* is to the Jews whose land was constantly being invaded. Daniel is then told that *they shall lift themselves up in order to fulfil the vision*. Since the vision is not additionally specified, it is surely reasonable to take it as being the major vision that is in Daniel's mind and heart throughout the book – the vision of the messianic kingdom that is to be fulfilled in the end time.

Certainly, there were Jews who joined Antiochus III. We have already seen that many Jews welcomed the imposition of Hellenistic culture on Palestine: a circumstance that would play a central role in the critical days of Antiochus IV "Epiphanes". We are just beginning to get a hint here of something that was extremely important for what was to follow.

Josephus describes the situation as follows:

> But afterward, when Antiochus subdued those cities of
> Celesyria [Coelesyria] which Scopas had gotten into his
> possession, and Samaria with them, the Jews, of their own
> accord, went over to him and received him into the city
> [Jerusalem], and gave plentiful provision to his army...
> whereupon Antiochus thought it but just to requite the Jews'
> diligence and zeal in his service: so he wrote to the generals of
> his armies, and to his friends, and gave testimony of the good
> behaviour of the Jews towards him, and informed them what
> rewards he had resolved to bestow on them for their behaviour.

Josephus then cites a letter from Antiochus, which mentions that the Jews had helped Antiochus to evict an Egyptian garrison from a fortress within Jerusalem.

According to Josephus, Antiochus also issued instructions that the Jews were to be helped with necessary works to be done on the temple and given tax exemption on some of the materials needed:

> ... and let all of that nation live according to the laws
> of their own country; and let the senate and the priests,

and the scribes of the temple, and the sacred singers be
discharged from poll-money and the crown tax and other
taxes also.

Antiochus also upheld the right of the Jews to keep non-Jews out of
the temple precincts. (See Josephus, *Antiquities*, 12, 3.3.)

In this way Antiochus III upheld the rights granted to the Jews
by the decree of Artaxerxes, referred to in Daniel 9:25.

> *But he who comes against him shall do as he wills, and none*
> *shall stand before him. And he shall stand in the glorious*
> *land, with destruction in his hand. He shall set his face to*
> *come with the strength of his whole kingdom, and he shall*
> *bring terms of an agreement and perform them. He shall give*
> *him the daughter of women to destroy the kingdom, but it*
> *shall not stand nor be to his advantage. (11:16–17.)*

Antiochus III (by this time called "The Great" because of his triumphs
in the east) was powerful enough to do what he willed. (Note once
more the non-deterministic implications of this comment.) However,
aware of the growing threat from Rome in the west, Antiochus
forged an alliance with the young Ptolemy V, by means of giving
him his daughter Cleopatra, still a child, to be his wife. The marriage
was celebrated at Raphia, the scene of Antiochus's earlier victory.
However, Cleopatra turned out to be deeply loyal to Ptolemy, to the
extent that she even supported a treaty between Egypt and Rome
against her father. Thus, as Daniel was told, the marriage turned out
to be of no help to Antiochus in furthering his political and territorial
aims in Egypt.

> *Afterwards he shall turn his face to the coastlands and shall*
> *capture many of them, but a commander shall put an end to*
> *his insolence. Indeed, he shall turn his insolence back upon*
> *him. Then he shall turn his face back towards the fortresses of*
> *his own land, but he shall stumble and fall, and shall not be*
> *found. (11:18–19.)*

Thwarted from advancing his control in Egypt, in spite of his alliance, Antiochus III annexed Egyptian-held territory situated along the coast of Asia Minor. He also took advantage of the weakness of the Macedonian king Philip to win some of the territory of Macedonia. He was then unwise enough to attack Greece, even though he had been warned not to do so by the Romans. The Romans defeated him in Greece, first at Thermopylae in 191 BC and then further east at Magnesium in 190 BC. These victories paved the way for the expansion of the Roman empire.

It was the Roman commander Lucius Scipio who *put an end to his insolence*, with the result that Antiochus III was forced to become a vassal to Rome, even having to send his son (the future Antiochus IV) to Rome as a hostage. He returned ingloriously to his fortresses in Syria and was eventually assassinated during an attempt to loot the temple of Bel at Elam (Elymais) in order to pay off his dues to the Romans. It was in this way that he *stumbled and fell, and could not be found* – as the prophet had succinctly predicted.

> *Then shall arise in his place one who shall send an exactor of tribute for the glory of the kingdom. But within a few days he shall be broken....* (11:20.)

Antiochus's son, Seleucus IV Philopator, succeeded him. We recall that his other son, the future Antiochus IV, was still held hostage at Rome. Philopator was at once faced with the mountain of tax debt to the Romans incurred by his father. When he learned of the treasure in the temple at Jerusalem, he decided to requisition it in the interests of the state. He despatched *an exactor of tribute*, named Heliodorus. The story is told in grand dramatic style in the books of Maccabees, and is worth reproducing in full:

> *While the holy city was inhabited in unbroken peace and the laws were strictly observed because of the piety of the high priest Onias and his hatred of wickedness, it came about that the kings themselves honoured the place and glorified the temple with the finest presents, even to the extent that*

*King Seleucus of Asia defrayed from his own revenues all the
expenses connected with the service of the sacrifices.*

*But a man named Simon, of the tribe of Benjamin, who
had been made captain of the temple, had a disagreement
with the high priest about the administration of the city
market. Since he could not prevail over Onias, he went to
Apollonius of Tarsus, who at that time was governor of
Coelesyria and Phoenicia, and reported to him that the
treasury in Jerusalem was full of untold sums of money, so
that the amount of the funds could not be reckoned, and
that they did not belong to the account of the sacrifices,
but that it was possible for them to fall under the control of
the king. When Apollonius met the king, he told him of the
money about which he had been informed. The king chose
Heliodorus, who was in charge of his affairs, and sent him
with commands to effect the removal of the reported wealth.
Heliodorus at once set out on his journey, ostensibly to make
a tour of inspection of the cities of Coelesyria and Phoenicia,
but in fact to carry out the king's purpose.*

*When he had arrived at Jerusalem and had been kindly
welcomed by the high priest of the city, he told about the
disclosure that had been made and stated why he had come,
and he inquired whether this really was the situation. The high
priest explained that there were some deposits belonging to
widows and orphans, and also some money of Hyrcanus son of
Tobias, a man of very prominent position, and that it totalled
in all four hundred talents of silver and two hundred of gold.
To such an extent the impious Simon had misrepresented the
facts. And he said that it was utterly impossible that wrong
should be done to those people who had trusted in the holiness
of the place and in the sanctity and inviolability of the temple
that is honoured throughout the whole world.*

*But Heliodorus, because of the orders he had from the
king, said that this money must in any case be confiscated for
the king's treasury. So he set a day and went in to direct the
inspection of these funds.*

There was no little distress throughout the whole city. The priests prostrated themselves before the altar in their priestly vestments and called toward heaven upon him who had given the law about deposits, that he should keep them safe for those who had deposited them. To see the appearance of the high priest was to be wounded at heart, for his face and the change in his colour disclosed the anguish of his soul. For terror and bodily trembling had come over the man, which plainly showed to those who looked at him the pain lodged in his heart. People also hurried out of their houses in crowds to make a general supplication because the holy place was about to be brought into dishonour. Women, girded with sackcloth under their breasts, thronged the streets. Some of the young women who were kept indoors ran together to the gates, and some to the walls, while others peered out of the windows. And holding up their hands to heaven, they all made supplication. There was something pitiable in the prostration of the whole populace and the anxiety of the high priest in his great anguish.

While they were calling upon the Almighty Lord that he would keep what had been entrusted safe and secure for those who had entrusted it, Heliodorus went on with what had been decided. But when he arrived at the treasury with his bodyguard, then and there the Sovereign of spirits and of all authority caused so great a manifestation that all who had been so bold as to accompany him were astounded by the power of God, and became faint with terror. For there appeared to them a magnificently caparisoned horse, with a rider of frightening mien; it rushed furiously at Heliodorus and struck at him with its front hoofs. Its rider was seen to have armour and weapons of gold. Two young men also appeared to him, remarkably strong, gloriously beautiful and splendidly dressed, who stood on either side of him and flogged him continuously, inflicting many blows on him. When he suddenly fell to the ground and deep darkness came over him, his men took him up, put him on a stretcher, and carried him away – this man who had just entered the aforesaid treasury with a great retinue and all his bodyguard but was now unable to help himself. They recognized clearly the sovereign power of God.

While he lay prostrate, speechless because of the divine intervention and deprived of any hope of recovery, they praised the Lord who had acted marvellously for his own place. And the temple, which a little while before was full of fear and disturbance, was filled with joy and gladness, now that the Almighty Lord had appeared.

Some of Heliodorus's friends quickly begged Onias to call upon the Most High to grant life to one who was lying quite at his last breath. So the high priest, fearing that the king might get the notion that some foul play had been perpetrated by the Jews with regard to Heliodorus, offered sacrifice for the man's recovery. While the high priest was making an atonement, the same young men appeared again to Heliodorus dressed in the same clothing, and they stood and said, "Be very grateful to the high priest Onias, since for his sake the Lord has granted you your life. And see that you, who have been flogged by heaven, report to all people the majestic power of God." Having said this they vanished.

Then Heliodorus offered sacrifice to the Lord and made very great vows to the Saviour of his life, and having bidden Onias farewell, he marched off with his forces to the king. He bore testimony to all concerning the deeds of the supreme God, which he had seen with his own eyes. When the king asked Heliodorus what sort of person would be suitable to send on another mission to Jerusalem, he replied, "If you have any enemy or plotter against your government, send him there, for you will get him back thoroughly flogged, if he survives at all; for there is certainly some power of God about the place. For he who has his dwelling in heaven watches over that place himself and brings it aid, and he strikes and destroys those who come to do it injury." This was the outcome of the episode of Heliodorus and the protection of the treasury. (2 Maccabees 3:1–40 NRSV.)

The Greek historian Appian of Alexandria (AD c.95–165) describes the subsequent course of events including the death of Philopator in 175 BC by the hand of Heliodorus:

> Afterward, on the death of Antiochus the Great, his son Seleucus succeeded him. He gave his son Demetrius as a hostage in place of his brother Antiochus [3 September 175]. When the latter arrived at Athens on his way home, Seleucus was assassinated as the result of a conspiracy of a certain Heliodorus, one of the court officers. When Heliodorus sought to possess himself of the government he was driven out by Eumenes [II Soter of Pergamon] and Attalus, who installed Antiochus therein in order to secure his good-will; for, by reason of certain bickerings, they had already grown suspicious of the Romans. (Syrian Wars, 45.)

Demetrius, Philopator's son, was the natural heir to the throne. However, as Appian tells us, Seleucus sent him to Rome to take the place of Seleucus's brother, Antiochus. Demetrius had an infant brother, also called Antiochus, who was in Syria at that time. The older Antiochus was in Athens when news arrived of the murder of his brother by Heliodorus. He gained the help of Eumenes King of Pergamum, and by dint of various intrigues (historians regard the details as somewhat obscure) he seized power from Heliodorus, who had in turn seized power on the death of Philopator – possibly claiming to do so on behalf of the infant Antiochus. Heliodorus fled the scene, and Antiochus IV Epiphanes entered on his infamous reign that lasted from 175 to 164 BC. The young Antiochus was murdered in 170 BC.

Daniel's prophetic summary captures all of the main elements in the most economical of statements:

> *In his place shall arise a contemptible person to whom royal majesty has not been given. He shall come in without warning and obtain the kingdom by flatteries. (11:21.)*

He continues:

> *Armies shall be utterly swept away before him and broken,*
> *even the prince of the covenant. And from the time that an*
> *alliance is made with him he shall act deceitfully, and he*
> *shall become strong with a small people. Without warning*
> *he shall come into the richest parts of the province, and he*
> *shall do what neither his fathers nor his fathers' fathers have*
> *done, scattering among them plunder, spoil, and goods. He*
> *shall devise plans against strongholds, but only for a time.*
> *(11:22–24.)*

This passage gives us insights into the character of Antiochus that are amply confirmed by historians. He started off with the relatively limited backing of King Eumenes II of Pergamum, but made alliances that he subsequently broke without compunction if it suited his ambitions. In order to gain influence and support he distributed his growing wealth on an unprecedented scale. Polybius reports: "In the sacrifices he furnished to cities and in the honours he paid to the gods he far surpassed all his predecessors" (*Histories*, 26.10).

As we have seen, Antiochus's generally bizarre and excessive behaviour led to him being nicknamed "Epimanes" (madman) rather than "Epiphanes" (God made manifest). Polybius tells us of him:

> … escaping from his attendants at court, he would often
> be seen wandering about in all parts of the city with one or
> two companions. He was chiefly found at the silversmiths'
> and goldsmiths' workshops, holding forth at length and
> discussing technical matters with the moulders and other
> craftsmen. He used also to condescend to converse with any
> common people he met, and used to drink in the company
> of the meanest foreign visitors to Antioch.
>
> Whenever he heard that any of the young men were at
> an entertainment, he would come in quite unceremoniously
> with a fife and a procession of musicians, so that most of the
> guests got up and left in astonishment. He would frequently

put off his royal robes, and, assuming a white toga, go round the market-place like a candidate, and, taking some by the hand and embracing others, would beg them to give him their vote, sometimes for the office of aedile and sometimes for that of tribune. Upon being elected, he would sit upon the ivory curule chair, as the Roman custom is, listening to the lawsuits tried there, and pronouncing judgment with great pains and display of interest. In consequence all respectable men were entirely puzzled about him, some looking upon him as a plain simple man and others as a madman. His conduct too was very similar as regards the presents he made. To some people he used to give gazelles' knucklebones, to others dates, and to others money. Occasionally he used to address people he had never seen before when he met them, and make them the most unexpected kind of presents. (Histories, 26.1–9.)

The reference to *the prince of the covenant* is striking, since it clearly refers to an individual; yet it is included in a general statement about armies being *swept away … and broken*. The title *prince of the covenant* was borne by the Jewish high priest in Jerusalem, and introduces us to the unsavoury world of abuse of the ecclesiastical office. The high priest at the time was Onias III, a man known for his integrity and zeal for the law, who had earlier opposed Heliodorus's attempt to raid the temple in Jerusalem. Onias was opposed to the Hellenization programme that Antiochus wished to drive forward. According to Errington, in 172 BC Onias's brother Jason, who was the leader of the Hellenizing party in Jerusalem, offered Antiochus a large sum of money for the high priesthood. He informs us (2008, page 270) that Jason "planned to reorganize Jerusalem as a Greek city-state, under the dynastic name Antiocheia, with a registered citizen list (which he would himself provide!), a gymnasium for exercising…" Antiochus, always a man for a good deal, acquiesced, and had Onias deposed.

However, not long afterwards, Menelaus (who was not even a member of the high priestly family but of the rival Tobiad family) bribed Antiochus with even more money than Jason, and gained the office of high priest. Menelaus, who had bought the high priesthood from Antiochus, had problems in coming up with the promised cash without raiding the temple treasury, and this brought him into conflict with an increasing number of people – and not only the hard-line, anti-Hellenist, orthodox Jews. Public feeling began to run high, and led to military intervention by the Seleucid garrison stationed in Jerusalem.

Onias publicly accused Menelaus of stealing some golden vessels from the temple to pay his debts (shades of Nebuchadnezzar!) – but he had to flee for safety to Daphne, where Menelaus pursued him and had him assassinated. This was an indicator of worse to come. Baldwin writes (2009, page 213):

> The date marks the interference of the secular state in things spiritual. A precedent had been set which Roman emperors would not be slow to follow and which has become a commonplace in twentieth-century politics. To remove from office and subject to persecution those who are legitimately set over God's people is to attack the originator of the covenant, God himself.

> *And he shall stir up his power and his heart against the king of the south with a great army. And the king of the south shall wage war with an exceedingly great and mighty army, but he shall not stand, for plots shall be devised against him. Even those who eat his food shall break him. His army shall be swept away, and many shall fall down slain. And as for the two kings, their hearts shall be bent on doing evil. They shall speak lies at the same table, but to no avail, for the end is yet to be at the time appointed. (11:25–27.)*

In 170 BC the courtiers Eulaeus and Lenaeus, of the still youthful King Ptolemy VI of Egypt (son of Cleopatra, Antiochus's sister), advised him to seek the return of Coelo-Syria to Egypt. In 169 BC Antiochus launched a pre-emptive strike and defeated the Egyptians. He captured Ptolemy and overcame most of their country, apart from the city of Alexandria. The city leaders made Ptolemy's younger brother – the future, famously pot-bellied Ptolemy VIII and his sister-wife Cleopatra joint rulers. Antiochus responded by installing Ptolemy VI (Philometor) as a vassal king in the Egyptian city of Memphis.

Daniel's account of the two kings (Antiochus and Ptolemy VI) scheming to outwit each other, and *speaking lies at the same table*, is a wonderful description of diplomacy through the ages. It is surely not to be taken cynically, but as a realistic analysis of why the result of such round-table discussion is ultimately of *no avail, for the end is yet to be at the time appointed*. Even though certain aspects of the machinations of these kings may have looked to some like the time of the end, it was not yet.

Antiochus mounted two campaigns against Egypt (169 and 168 BC). The historical record of their relationship, and Antiochus's aggression against the Jews on his way to and from Egypt, is somewhat unclear, in the sense that it is not certain which brutal act is associated with what campaign, although the general outline of what happened is not in doubt – it was horrific.

> *And he shall return to his land with great wealth, but his heart shall be set against the holy covenant. And he shall work his will and return to his own land. (11:28.)*

The book of Maccabees tells us:

> *When news of what had happened reached the king, he took it to mean that Judea was in revolt. So, raging inwardly, he left Egypt and took the city by storm. He commanded his soldiers to cut down relentlessly everyone they met and to kill those who went into their houses. Then there was massacre of young and old, destruction of boys, women, and children, and slaughter of young girls and infants. Within the total of three days eighty thousand were destroyed, forty thousand in hand-to-hand fighting, and as many were sold into slavery as were killed.*

> *Not content with this, Antiochus dared to enter the*
> *most holy temple in all the world, guided by Menelaus, who*
> *had become a traitor both to the laws and to his country.*
> *He took the holy vessels with his polluted hands, and swept*
> *away with profane hands the votive offerings that other kings*
> *had made to enhance the glory and honour of the place.*
> *Antiochus was elated in spirit, and did not perceive that the*
> *Lord was angered for a little while because of the sins of those*
> *who lived in the city, and that this was the reason that he*
> *was disregarding the holy place. ... So Antiochus carried off*
> *eighteen hundred talents from the temple, and hurried away*
> *to Antioch, thinking in his arrogance that he could sail on*
> *the land and walk on the sea, because his mind was elated.*
> *(2 Maccabees 5:11–17, 21–22* NRSV.*)*

Earlier in Maccabees we have additional detail on what appears to be the same event:

> *After subduing Egypt, Antiochus ... went up against Israel*
> *and came to Jerusalem with a strong force. He arrogantly*
> *entered the sanctuary and took the golden altar, the*
> *lampstand for the light, and all its utensils. He took also*
> *the table for the bread of the Presence, the cups for drink-*
> *offerings, the bowls, the golden censers, the curtain, the*
> *crowns, and the gold decoration on the front of the temple;*
> *he stripped it all off. He took the silver and the gold, and the*
> *costly vessels; he took also the hidden treasures that he found.*
> *Taking them all, he went into his own land. He shed much*
> *blood, and spoke with great arrogance. (1 Maccabees 1:20–24*
> NRSV.*)*

Daniel is next concerned with a further expedition that Antiochus mounted against Egypt:

> *At the time appointed he shall return and come into the*
> *south, but it shall not be this time as it was before. For ships*

> *of Kittim shall come against him, and he shall be afraid and*
> *withdraw, and shall turn back and be enraged and take*
> *action against the holy covenant. (11:29–30.)*

"Kittim" was originally denoted as a town in Cyprus; then used of the inhabitants of Cyprus; and later of (inhabitants of) the isles and coasts of the Mediterranean. In the Septuagint *ships of Kittim* is translated as "Romans". These ships were dispatched in response to a request for help for Rome from the Ptolemy brothers; and in all probability they belonged to the fleet of Laenas, which sailed to Egypt in June 168 BC after the Roman victory of Macedon over Perseus.

Polybius takes up the story of the successful Roman intervention to stop Antiochus's aggression against Egypt: an event that marked the beginning of the end of Seleucid power – and also gave us the expression "drawing a line in the sand".

> At the time when Antiochus approached Ptolemy and
> meant to occupy Pelusium, Caius Popilius Laenas, the
> Roman commander, on Antiochus greeting him from a
> distance and then holding out his hand, handed to the king,
> as he had it by him, the copy of the senatus-consultum, and
> told him to read it first, not thinking it proper, as it seems to
> me, to make the conventional sign of friendship before he
> knew if the intentions of him who was greeting him were
> friendly or hostile.
>
> But when the king, after reading it, said he would like
> to communicate with his friends about this intelligence,
> Popilius acted in a manner which was thought to be
> offensive and exceedingly arrogant. He was carrying a
> stick cut from a vine, and with this he drew a circle round
> Antiochus and told him he must remain inside this circle
> until he gave his decision about the contents of the letter.
> The king was astonished at this authoritative proceeding,
> but, after a few moments' hesitation, said he would do all
> that the Romans demanded. Upon this Popilius and his
> suite all grasped him by the hand and greeted him warmly.

The letter ordered him to put an end at once to the war with Ptolemy. So, as a fixed number of days were allowed to him, he led his army back to Syria, deeply hurt and complaining indeed, but yielding to circumstances for the present. (Histories, 29.4, 27.)

For an account of what happened next, please go back to the main text in Chapter 22.

THE DATING OF THE BOOK OF DANIEL

According to his book, Daniel lived to see the end of the Babylonian empire and its replacement by the Medo-Persian empire. Later on, this was in turn succeeded by the Greek empire of Alexander the Great. After that, although he does not name the characters, Daniel gives a great number of accurate details and then concentrates on the activities of one emperor who is easily recognizable as Antiochus IV "Epiphanes".

Because of the general accuracy of his predictions, the dating of Daniel's book has been a matter of considerable controversy. Traditionally, the book has been seen as a work written in the time it describes, in Babylon in the sixth century BC. But this has been challenged at several points throughout the centuries by those who commonly believe it to be a work of the second century BC.

Reasons have been given for affirming the sixth-century date at various points throughout the present volume. The following summary of the arguments may be helpful.

1. The reality of supernatural revelation

The book of Daniel affirms strongly that there is a God in heaven who reveals mysteries to his chosen servants, interpreting the meaning of events past, present, *and future*, as all these are "present" to God in eternity.

That said, we might ask *why* God would have revealed these details. For the suggestion of an answer, we may think of the reasons Jesus told his disciples beforehand what was going to happen to him and to them. Jesus was concerned that when persecutions, wars, famines, and plagues came, they should be forewarned and comforted by the knowledge that these things would not last for ever but would ultimately herald the beginning of a new order of creation.

2. The implication of historical evidence

The date preferred by those who do not accept supernatural revelation is the second century BC, during the time of the Maccabean revolt. This view gained ground with the rise of higher criticism and the anti-supernaturalism of the Enlightenment. However, there is historical evidence arising from the discovery of the Dead Sea Scrolls at Qumran that makes this date difficult. The book of Daniel was clearly already seen as part of holy Scripture, yet it is almost inconceivable that it would have achieved canonical status by 100 BC if a Maccabean sect had written it just fifty years earlier.

3. The internal structure of the book itself

The placing of Daniel 9 parallel to Daniel 4 in the overall structure of the book compares God's discipline of Nebuchadnezzar with God's discipline of Jerusalem, whereas in the time of the Maccabean revolt we would have expected Nebuchadnezzar to be paralleled with Antiochus, whose judgment prefigured the eternal judgment of the wicked and not the temporary disciplining of God's people.

BIBLIOGRAPHY

Frequently consulted

Anderson, Sir Robert, *The Coming Prince*, Grand Rapids, Kregel, 1975.

Baldwin, Joyce, *Daniel*, Tyndale Old Testament Commentaries, Nottingham and Downers Grove, IVP, 2009.

Boutflower, Charles, *In and around the Book of Daniel*, Grand Rapids, Kregel, 1977.

Fyall, Bob, *Daniel: A Tale of Two Cities*, Fearn, Christian Focus, 1998.

Goldingay, John E., *Daniel*, Dallas, Word Books, 1989.

Lucas, Ernest C., *Daniel*, Apollos Old Testament Commentary, Leicester, IVP, 2002.

Tatford, Fredrick A., *The Climax of the Ages*, London, Oliphants, 1953.

Walvoord, John F., *Daniel*, Chicago, Moody, 2012.

Roux, Georges, *Ancient Iraq*, London, Penguin 1992.

Wiseman, D. J., *Nebuchadnezzar and Babylon*: The Schweich Lectures, Oxford, OUP, 1991.

Referred to in the text

Archaeological Study Bible, Grand Rapids, Zondervan, 2011.

Bosch, David J., *Transforming Mission*, Maryknoll, Orbis Books, 2011.

Butterfield, Herbert, *Christianity and History*, London, G. Bell & Sons 1949; Collins: Fontana, 1957, 1964.

Carson, D.A., *The Intolerance of Tolerance*, Nottingham, IVP, 2012.

Costas, Orlando E., *Christ Outside the Gate*, Maryknoll, New York, Orbis Books, 1982.

Davies, Paul, *The Cosmic Blueprint*, New York, Simon and Schuster, 1988.

Dawkins, Richard, *Unweaving the Rainbow*, Boston, Houghton Mifflin, 1998.

--, *A Devil's Chaplain*, London, Weidenfeld and Nicholson, 2003.

--, *The God Delusion*, London, Bantam Press, 2006.

Einstein, Albert, "Towards a World Government" (1946), *Out Of My Later Years: The Scientist, Philosopher, and Man Portrayed Through His Own Words*, New York, Wings Books, 1956.

Errington, R. Malcolm, *A History of the Hellenistic World*, Oxford, Blackwell, 2008.

Feuerbach, Ludwig, *The Essence of Christianity*, ed. and transl. George Eliot (Marion Evans), New York, Harper Torchbooks, 1957.

Frankl, Viktor, *Man's Search for Meaning*, New York, Simon and Schuster Pocket Books, 1985.

Furedi, Frank, *Tolerance*, London, Continuum, 2011.

Gooding, D. W., "The Literary Structure of Daniel and its Implications", *Tyndale Bulletin 32*, 1981.

--, *According to Luke*, Leicester, IVP, 1987.

--, *True to the Faith,* London, Hodder & Stoughton, 1990; Myrtlefield House, 2013.

Gray, John, *Straw Dogs*, London, Granta Publications, 2003.

--, *Black Mass*, London, Allen Lane, 2007.

Habermas, Jürgen, *Time of Transitions*, New York, Polity Press, 2006.

Harris, Sam, *The End of Faith: Religion, Terror, and the Future of Reason*, London, Free Press, 2005.

Harrison, Roland K., *Introduction to the Old Testament*, Grand Rapids, Eerdmans, 1969.

Hoffmeier, J. K. and Magary, D. R., ed., *Do Historical Matters Matter to Faith?: A Critical Appraisal of Modern and Postmodern Approaches to Scripture*, Wheaton, Crossway, 2012.

Humphreys, Colin J., *The Mystery of the Last Supper: Reconstructing the*

Final Days of Jesus, Cambridge, Cambridge University Press, 2011.

Jaeger, Werner, *The Theology of the Early Greek Philosophers*, Oxford, Oxford University Press, 1967.

Jerome, *Commentary on Daniel*, transl. Gleason L. Archer Jr., Grand Rapids, Baker, 1958.

Koestler, Arthur, *The God that Failed*, London, Hamish Hamilton, 1950.

Lennox, John, *Gunning for God: Why the New Atheists Are Missing the Target*, Oxford, Lion Hudson, 2011.

––, *God's Undertaker: Has Science Buried God?*, Oxford, Lion, 2007, 2009.

Lewis, C. S., *Miracles*, London and Glasgow, Collins: Fontana, 1947, rev. ed. 1960.

Marx, K., and Engels, F., *On Religion,* Moscow, 1955.

Montgomery, James A., *A Critical and Exegetical Commentary on the Book of Daniel*, International Critical Commentary, Edinburgh, T & T Clark, 1927.

Motyer, Alex, *The Prophecy of Isaiah*, Leicester, IVP, 1993.

Moule, C. F. D., *The Phenomenon of the New Testament*, London, SCM Press, 1967.

Newbigin, Lesslie, *The Gospel in a Pluralist Society*, London, SPCK, 1989.

Newton, Isaac, *The Chronology of Ancient Kingdoms Amended*, London, 1728.

Pinker, Stephen, *The Better Angels of our Nature: A History of Violence and Humanity*, London and New York, Penguin, 2012.

Sacks, Jonathan, *The Great Partnership: God, Science and the Search for Meaning*, London, Hodder and Stoughton, 2011.

Schaeffer, Francis, *He is There and He is not Silent*, Wheaton, Tyndale House, 1972.

Singer, Peter, *Practical Ethics*, Cambridge, Cambridge University Press, 1979.

––, *Rethinking Life and Death*, Oxford, Oxford University Press, 1995.

––, *The Life You Can Save*, New York, Random House, 2009.

Varghese, Roy, ed., *The Missing Link*, University Press of America, Lanham, 2013.

Ward, Keith, *Why There Almost Certainly is a God*, Oxford, Lion Hudson, 2008.

Wilson, Andrew, *If God, then What?*, Nottingham, IVP, 2012.

Wittgenstein, Ludwig, *Tractatus Logico-Philosophicus*, London, 1922.

--, *Notebooks*, 1914–16, 2nd ed., trans. G. E. M. Anscombe, Chicago, University of Chicago Press, 1979.

Young, Edward J., *The Prophecy of Daniel*, Grand Rapids, Eerdmans, 1949.

NOTES

1. We note that there are additions to Daniel in the Apocrypha that are not included in the Hebrew canon of the Old Testament and therefore are not treated here. They are to be found in: The Prayer of Azaraiah and Song of the Three Holy Children; Susanna and the Elders; and Bel and the Dragon.

2. For a scholarly discussion of questions regarding the dating of this and other events in Daniel, see A. R. Millard, "Daniel in Babylon – An Accurate Record?" in Hoffmeier and Magary, 2012, pp. 263–80.

3. Richard Dawkins, "Is Science a Religion?" in *The Humanist*, Jan/Feb 1997, pp. 26–39.

4. *Daily Telegraph Science Extra*, 11 September 1989.

5. See for example the *Jerusalem Post*, 14 October 2014.

6. Joseph Ratzinger, *Homily*, Vatican Basilica, 18 April 2005.

7. For a detailed analysis the reader is referred to the clear explanation given by D. W. Gooding, 1990, pp.172ff.

8. L. W. King, transl., in *The Seven Tablets of Creation*, London 1902.

9. Review of Carl Sagan, *The Demon Haunted World: Science as a Candle in the Dark*, New York Review of Books, 9 January 1997.

10. See the excellent article by Peter May at www.bethinking.org entitled "What is evangelism?".

11. D. W. Gooding, "The Literary Structure of Daniel and its Implications", Tyndale Bulletin 1981.

12. The question of biblical miracles and science is discussed in detail in my books *God's Undertaker, God and Stephen Hawking* and *Gunning for God*. This last book also contains a detailed investigation of the evidence for the bodily resurrection of Jesus against the background of sceptical criticism.

13. G. F. Hasel, http://www.biblearchaeology.org/post/2012/07/31/New-Light-on-the-Book-of-Daniel-from-the-Dead-Sea-Scrolls.aspx#Article

14. In "Daniel, Book of", *International Standard Bible Encyclopedia*, Vol. 1, Grand Rapids, Eerdmans, 1979, p. 862.

15. For more detail on this see Boutflower, 1977.

16. On the ABC Network at http://www.abc.net.au/religion/articles/2013/01/20/3672846.htm

17. Hymn to Enlil, in James B. Pritchard, ed., *Ancient Near Eastern Texts Relating to the Old Testament*, 3rd Edition, Princeton, Princeton University Press, 1969, p. 575.

18. Andrew Wilson (2012, pp. 104–5) suggests that Chesterton's letter is in fact apocryphal; although, as he himself points out, it is still a profound piece of writing, no matter when it was first written.

19. "The Difference between the Natural Philosophy of Democritus and the Natural Philosophy of Epicurus", transl. in Marx, 1955.

20. *The Humanist*, Spring 1945.

21. "Religion as the Integration of Human Life", *The Humanist*, Spring 1947, p. 161.

22. M. J. Inwood, "Feuerbach, Ludwig Andreas", in *The Oxford Companion to Philosophy*, ed. Ted Honderich, Oxford, New York, Oxford University Press, 1995, p. 276.

23. George Weigel, *Christian Number-Crunching*, 9 February 2011.

24. Recent research by Dr Stephanie Dalley of Oxford has cast doubt as to whether these gardens were actually in Babylon and not rather in Nineveh. However, this uncertainty does not detract from the fact that Babylon was a beautiful city that presumably contained many gardens.

25. Peter Singer, "Sanctity of Life or Quality of Life?", *Paediatrics* Vol. 72, No.1, July 1983, pp. 128–29.

26. The abolition of distinctions between human beings and animals is not the only source of attack on the traditional (theistic) view. Another is the abolition of distinctions between human beings and machines: for example, Richard Dawkins' dismal genetic reductionism that diminishes human beings to "gene-survival machines" (Dawkins, 1998, p. 286).

27. An interview with Peter Singer: "Animals join man's 'circle of ethics'", *Monash Reporter*, April 1983, p. 8.

28. Andrew Zak Williams, "Faith is no more", *New Statesman*, 25 July 2011.

29. http://old.richarddawkins.net/videos/425-the-blasphemy-challenge

30. See Brannon Howse, "The People and the Agenda of Multicultural Education", *Understanding the Times*, January 1997, 3.

31. *Civil Action* no. SA-11-CA-422-FB.

32. Some scholars understand *the coming of the Son of Man with the clouds of heaven* as a reference to the ascension of Christ, when he came to God and his throne. However, I think: (a) that our Lord's citation of this text at his trial is more naturally understood in terms of his coming to earth, and thus being visible to those who have rejected him; (b) if Daniel 7 is referring to the ascension, it is fair to ask: did God's judgment occur at the ascension? And, if so, what beast was then destroyed?

33. *Stanford Encyclopedia of Philosophy,* 4 December 2006, rev. 2 July 2012 http://plato.stanford.edu/entries/world-government

34. We note that the politics of the time was extremely complex, and the interested reader should consult major histories of the Hellenistic period for more detail. A good starting point is the article on "Graeco-Roman Civilisation" in the *Encyclopaedia Britannica.*

35. "Hellenistic Age", *Encylopaedia Britannica.*

36. http://www.newworldencyclopedia.org/entry/Juche

37. See my *Gunning for God*, chapter 3, from which this and the following paragraphs are taken (with some modification).

38. In light of the caricatures of "original sin" promoted by Dawkins, Hitchens, and others, it is important to notice that the last clause in this quotation does not say (as is sometimes suggested) that "all sinned *in him*" (i.e. in Adam). The last clause is introduced by the Greek conjunction *eph' hō* which cannot mean "in whom", or "in him", for that would have required *en hō*. *Eph' hō* means "because". In any case, if the text meant that "all sinned in Adam" then it follows that all sinned Adam's sin, and this is explicitly denied in Romans 5:14. It is also to be noted that the translation "have sinned" would give the sense better (see Romans 3:23 where the same Greek word occurs and is translated by the perfect "have sinned").

39. Unless, of course, the prophecy has two anointed ones in mind. In what is sometimes called the Antiochene Interpretation, the first anointed one is held to be one of the major participants in the return from Babylon (possibly Joshua or Zerubbabel), and the second anointed one is taken to be Onias III, the high priest in 171 BC. This interpretation holds that the starting point of the seventy weeks is from a prophecy of Jeremiah. However, apart from other difficulties, in order for this to work a simple calculation based on Daniel's prophecy shows that Onias would have to have died around 105 BC.

40. http://www.cam.ac.uk/research/news/the-penultimate-supper

41. A full treatment of Hume's views is to be found in my book *God's Undertaker.*

42. See *God's Undertaker* and *Gunning for God.*

43. Mark Mercer, "The Benefactions of Antiochus IV Epiphanes and Dan. 11.37–38, An Exegetical Note", *TMSJ* 12/1, Spring 2001, pp. 89–93.

44. It is, of course, a mistake to think that where symbol or metaphor is used, it is not describing something real. Jesus described himself as a door. He is a real door into a real experience of God. He is not a door in the literalistic sense. It is our familiarity with the latter that helps us to grasp the former.

45. For a more detailed analysis of the significance of Jesus' reply, see D. W. Gooding, 1990, 2013.

46. http://www.britishmuseum.org/explore/highlights/article_index/c/cyrus_cylinder_-_translation.aspx

INDEX

TEXT ACKNOWLEDGMENTS

pp. 150, 191, 308–310, 328, 331–33: Extracts from "The Literary Structure of Daniel and its Implications" by David Gooding copyright © 1980, David Gooding. Reprinted by permission of Tyndale House.

p. 163: Extract from "Sanctity of Life or Quality of Life?" by Peter Singer in *Pediatrics* copyright © 1983, Peter Singer. Reprinted by permission of Peter Singer.

PICTURE ACKNOWLEDGMENTS

Alamy: pp. 26, 195, 263 BibleLandPictures; p. 28 B.O'Kane; p. 148 Jan Palmer; p. 174 World History Archive; p. 175 FineArt; p. 194 B Christopher; p. 206 EmmePi Images; p. 214 VPC Travel Photo

Bridgeman: p. 27 Chinch Gryniewicz

British Museum: pp. 7, 172

Corbis: p. 257 Araldo de Luca

Getty: p. 213 Alinari Archives

Lion Hudson: p. 256

Topfoto: p. 152

Jniemenmaa/wikimedia: p. 327